W9-DIA-405

When Boys Become Parents

When Boys Become Parents

Adolescent Fatherhood in America

MARK S. KISELICA

RUTGERS UNIVERSITY PRESS

NEW BRUNSWICK, NEW JERSEY, AND LONDON

LIBRARY OF CONGRESS CATALOGING-IN-PUBLICATION DATA

Kiselica, Mark S.
When boys become parents : adolescent fatherhood in America / Mark S.
Kiselica.
   p.   cm.
Includes bibliographical references and index.
ISBN 978–0-8135–4358–1 (hardcover : alk. paper)
  1. Teenage fathers—Counseling of—United States. 2. Teenage fathers—
Services for—United States. 3. Teenage fathers—United States—Life skills guides.
4. Unmarried fathers—United States. I. Title.
  HQ756.7.K58 2008
  306.874′2—dc22   2007048279

A British Cataloging-in-Publication record for this book is available
from the British Library.

Visit our Web site: http://rutgerspress.rutgers.edu

Manufactured in the United States of America

To John, Mary, Patty, Matt, and Dennis–my
dear brothers and sisters and lifelong friends

CONTENTS

ACKNOWLEDGMENTS

Each day that I worked on this book, I said a small prayer of thanks for my beautiful family and their support of me. To Sandi, Andrew, Christian, and Sasha, I thank you for your understanding and patience regarding every moment I have had to devote to my professional duties, including my work on this book, which I consider in many ways to be an expression of my love for all of you. To my precious parents, Otto and Winnie Kiselica, please know I am always inspired by you and the admirable example you have set for me. To John, Mary, Patty, Matt, and Dennis, you are all wonderful siblings, and I thank you for supporting me my entire life.

I am fortunate to be member of a wonderful kinship network that extends far beyond the realms of my biological family and includes dozens of professionals from the American Counseling Association, the American Psychological Association, and especially the Society for the Psychological Study of Men and Masculinity, who have affirmed my desire to help troubled boys and their families. I thank all of you—especially those of you who have helped me to see the light in all living things—for your support and encouragement and for the important lessons you have taught me about boys, men, and masculinity.

I am privileged to be a faculty member of The College of New Jersey. I thank my colleagues in the Department of Counselor Education—Charleen Alderfer, Marion Cavallaro, MaryLou Ramsey, Atsuko Seto, and Mark Woodford—and Bill Behre, dean of the School of Education, as well as my students for your support of this project.

I am grateful to the many people who contributed their expertise to this project, including two esteemed colleagues, Dr. James Garbarino, professor and Maude C. Clarke Chair in Humanistic Psychology at Loyola College Chicago, and Michael Hayes, Director of Family Strengthening Initiatives of the Office of the Attorney General of Texas, who kindly provided me with invaluable feedback on the first draft of this book. For many years, I have greatly admired these two fine professionals, whose competent and compassionate work has advanced our understanding of boys and men, their strengths and struggles, and how to help them. I want to express a special thanks to Adi Hovav of Rutgers University Press, who guided this book through every stage of its development, and to her coworkers, Lyman Lyons, the copyeditor, and Alicia Nadkarni, production editor for this book, for their respective roles in launching this project and moving it toward its completion.

And to the boys and men—the hundreds of boys and men I have counseled, taught, and coached—thank you for helping me to understand your ways of relating to the world, your many splendid qualities, your hardships, your pain, and your accomplishments. It has been an honor to share in your experiences, which have informed and inspired my work as a scholar, teacher, practitioner, and advocate.

Mark Kiselica

Ewing, New Jersey

AUTHOR'S NOTE

This book contains numerous stories reported by teenage fathers about their experiences. Many of these are drawn from the professional literature on the subject, while others are based on the clinical experiences of the author. In compliance with professional ethical standards, citations for previously published accounts have been provided, and the details pertaining to the author's experiences with teenage fathers have been reported in a way that protects the anonymity of the persons who were involved. Any similarity between the names and stories of the individuals described in this book and those known to readers is purely coincidental.

When Boys Become Parents

1

The Looming Crisis
America Must Confront

For the past twenty-eight years I have been on a quest to help, study, and understand boys who become fathers during their teenage years. The seeds of this venture were sown many years ago, back in 1980 when I was a twenty-two-year-old young man, fresh out of college. At the time, I was employed as a mental health worker in the inpatient adolescent unit of Fair Oaks Hospital, a private psychiatric facility located in Summit, New Jersey. I had taken a job at Fair Oaks to gain experience working with emotionally disturbed teenagers.

One summer night while I was assigned to the 3–11 shift at the hospital, I noticed that Steve, a fourteen-year-old boy on our unit, appeared quite agitated when we returned to the unit after having dinner in the hospital cafeteria. So I asked Steve if he'd like to go for a walk to blow off some steam and tell me what was on his mind. After he accepted this invitation, I took him to an outside recreational area where we played a few games of one-on-one basketball.

Although Steve was only fourteen, he was a big, strong kid who stood about five feet, ten inches tall and weighed a muscular 175 pounds. Throughout our games, he pounded his body against mine and made many aggressive moves to the basket, seeming to discharge much of his pent-up anger in the process. After a while, we took a breather and sat side-by-side in the grass next to the basketball court, where we gradually cooled down and settled into a relaxed but serious conversation.

As we both looked out toward the sunset, Steve slowly told me why he had been on the verge of exploding earlier that evening. He stated that he became upset during dinner because he had seen a woman from another unit who reminded him of his old girlfriend. As he continued with his story, I was astounded to learn that this fourteen-year-old boy was a father! Here is the essence of what he told me:

> Man, I was thirteen years old when it happened. I was dating this older chick at the time. She was nineteen and owned a car so we used to do it in her car. When she told me she was pregnant, I couldn't believe it! I thought, "How am I gonna take care of a baby?!" We talked about her getting an abortion and that's what we planned to do but she changed her mind and decided to have the baby. She kept him for about four months but then he was taken away from her because she had a drug problem. He's in foster care now . . . [pause] . . . I know I'll have him some day but right now I stay away from him because I've got too many problems of my own . . . [pause] . . . So, when I saw that other chick in the cafeteria tonight, I thought about my old girlfriend and I was reminded of all the shit we went through together.

Initially, I found it hard to believe that this boy, this confused kid, was a father. But his story was true, verified in the psychosocial records contained in Steve's file back on the unit. That night as I listened to Steve's account of his intense but brief experiences as a parent, I sensed turmoil in his voice and noticed a look of worry in his eyes. In that instant, it struck me how Steve's paternity was linked to other problems in his life. It saddened me to think that this boy had been in a position at the age of thirteen to have sex with a woman (whom I discovered to be an adult) and that his relationship with her had resulted in an unplanned and unwanted pregnancy. In later conversations with Steve, I learned that he had long-term academic problems brought on by a learning disability and a lack of structure in his home. Because his parents were often embroiled in conflict, Steve developed a habit of staying out late and running away from home at an early age. By the age of thirteen he was physically mature—having gone through puberty early—plenty handsome, and sufficiently streetwise to attract the attention of a similarly lonely and desperate person, the nineteen-year-old woman who would become the mother of his child. The intense sexual relationship they shared and the impulsiveness of their ways culminated in a pregnancy, an event that complicated their already chaotic lives even further. Because of the significant age difference between young Steve and his adult partner, legal authorities were involved in the case and criminal charges against the woman were pending.

Clearly, Steve was a kid who needed help and I extended myself to him as often as I could during his three-week stay on our unit. I had hoped to work with him longer, but he was discharged from Fair Oaks earlier than anticipated when his placement in a residential school located in Pennsylvania was arranged by his social worker. When I last heard about Steve, he had run away from the school and his whereabouts were unknown.

During my two years at Fair Oaks, I met several other boys who were teen fathers. Although all of them were older than Steve, each of them had lived troubled lives and had ambivalent feelings about being parents. All of them expressed concern for their child, but some of them had no contact with their child or their child's mother. Others maintained a relationship with their child and their child's mother even during their period of hospitalization. Some were proud to be fathers and happy to be involved in the lives of their children. Others were ashamed and experienced great conflict with their parents about their paternity. All of them admitted that they wished they had waited until they were older to become parents. As I would learn later, these varied reactions are common among adolescent fathers. And as I would also learn, most teen fathers were very different from Steve.

The memories of Steve and all of the other boys and girls I had met at Fair Oaks have stayed with me to this day. I was so moved by the lives of these teenagers that I decided to dedicate my life to helping troubled teenagers and their families. So when I left Fair Oaks in August of 1981, I set out on a professional journey that took me to graduate school and a variety of institutions whose mission is to address the mental health needs of adolescents. Over the course of the next twenty-seven years, I earned my master's degree in child and adolescent psychology and my doctorate in counseling psychology, and I was employed as a counselor or a psychologist in a state psychiatric hospital, a public high school, a university-based counseling clinic, two community mental health centers, and two private practices. I also worked as a psychologist in two prisons charged with managing and rehabilitating male youth offenders, and as a professor of counseling at Ball State University and The College of New Jersey.

In each of these different settings, time and time again I encountered adolescents who were in the throes of trying to resolve an unplanned pregnancy or struggling to raise a newborn child. Seeing pregnant and parenting teens was such a common experience that by 1990, I decided to study the professional literature on the subjects of adolescent pregnancy and parenthood in an attempt to understand why I was meeting so many teen parents and to learn what I might do to better serve them.

Adolescent Pregnancy and Parenthood in the United States

That I have met so many teen parents in my work as a counselor, psychologist, educator, researcher, advocate, and volunteer in the community is not surprising when one considers the statistics on adolescent pregnancy and parenthood in the United States. During the late 1980s and the early 1990s, the United States had the highest teen pregnancy rate of any industrialized country.[1] Even now during the early years of the twenty-first century, the United States *still* has the second-highest teen pregnancy rate among developed countries,[2] even though that rate has dropped to an all-time low in recent years.[3] Each year in our country, hundreds of thousands of teenage girls become pregnant and give birth to a baby.[4] The vast majority of these births occur out of wedlock.[5] Roughly two-thirds of the males involved in teen pregnancies are adult men who are twenty years old or older.[6] So teenage boys actually account for only about 35 percent of these pregnancies. Nevertheless, the number of adolescent males becoming fathers is substantial: each year, over 175,000 American boys age fifteen to nineteen years father a child.[7] Yet we rarely hear about these young men. As we will see in chapter 2, without question teenage pregnancy—including the hidden problem of adolescent fatherhood—remains a major social issue our nation must confront.

Too many American youth are still becoming pregnant and having children during their teenage years because our society is sexually permissive, fails to adequately prepare our nation's children for sex, and leaves them with a fragile foundation upon which they are expected to build their lives. American boys and girls are bombarded with sexual images in the television shows and movies they watch, the songs they hear, and the books and magazines they read. As a result of the pervasive influence of these images and the widespread belief among youth that premarital sexual intercourse is OK, American teenagers feel tremendous pressure to have sex. In the face of these pressures, today's youth want more guidance about sex and contraceptive use from their parents and other caring adults.[8] However, sex education by parents and professionals in the United States lags far behind that of other countries such as Sweden and France, whose track record of preventing adolescent pregnancy far surpasses America's efforts.[9] Consequently, compared to youth from most other developed countries, American teens tend to be ill equipped to deal with their early sexual encounters, placing those who decide to become sexually active at risk for sexually transmitted diseases and unplanned pregnancies.[10]

Teenagers who lack a number of the assets deemed to be essential for successful development—such as receiving support from their parents and the community, developing a sense of empowerment, having clear boundaries and expectations, making constructive use of their time, demonstrating a commitment to learning, embracing positive values, being socially competent, and forming a positive identity—are especially likely to engage in high-risk sexual behavior and other problematic behaviors that can jeopardize their futures.[11] For many young men, the clustering of numerous risk factors places them on a trajectory toward adolescent fatherhood.[12] The concentration of these risk factors is especially high in impoverished neighborhoods where very high numbers of people of color reside,[13] which helps to explain why the adolescent pregnancy, teen birth, and adolescent fatherhood rates are higher among African-American and Latino youth than among teenagers from other racial and ethnic groups.[14] These complicated issues are addressed in depth in chapters 2 and 3.

Helping Adolescent Mothers: What About Assisting Young Fathers?

As the rate of premarital childbirth to teenagers rose from the 1970s through the early 1990s, there was ongoing public concern over the detrimental effects of out-of-wedlock childbearing on teen moms and their children and extended families. Unwed adolescent mothers are at-risk to drop out of school, experience financial hardships, suffer prenatal medical complications, and exhibit inadequate parenting skills. Their children are at higher than average risk to suffer birth defects, mental retardation, and other health problems.[15] A premarital adolescent pregnancy typically sends emotional shock waves and unanticipated demands throughout the immediate and extended family that stress the family's functioning and finances.[16]

In an effort to prevent the problems associated with premarital adolescent childbearing and to assist young mothers with the transition to parenthood, numerous multifaceted service programs for pregnant and parenting teens were developed during the 1980s and 1990s. Throughout this same period, I counseled many teen mothers and their extended families. Although I was committed to helping these girls, my memories of Steve and the other teen fathers I had met during my years at Fair Oaks sparked my curiosity about the fathers of the children born to these young mothers. Who and where were these fathers? Why were they excluded from the outreach initiatives of teen parenting programs? What were their perspectives on what it meant to be a father? How could I engage these young men in counseling?

As I began to ask these questions during counseling sessions, I gradually made contact with a small number of young adult men who were the partners of my adolescent-mother clients. These young men decided to meet with me, in part, because I had earned the trust of their partners.

My initial encounters with these fathers were eye-opening experiences for me because they helped me to realize more fully a lesson I had learned many years earlier through my work with Steve: unwed adolescent paternity is often both the product and the cause of significant social problems. Furthermore, these early contacts paved the way to meeting other adolescent fathers who were the friends of my first teen-father clients. I have been helping a steady stream of adolescent fathers ever since. Their collective experiences have taught me about the complexity of teenage paternity, and they have inspired me to make the subject of teen fathers my systematic line of scholarly research. Through this research, I discovered that service programs and public policies have failed to address the problems of teenage fathers adequately, which prompted me to become a social justice advocate for this population. This book documents what I have learned from these clinical, research, and advocacy experiences, and it sets a course for changing how we treat young fathers, especially those involved in a premarital pregnancy.

Thinking Complexly about Teen Fathers

Foremost, my work with teen fathers has taught me to move beyond societal stereotypes about boys who become fathers during their teenage years. These stereotypes are widespread and they have destructive effects. For example, a common belief about adolescent fathers is that they are a callous lot who purposely exploit, seduce, and impregnate an adolescent girl and then coldly abandon her and her baby. For reasons I will explore in chapter 3, these attitudes permeate our society and explain why too many adults have little sympathy for boys who "get their girlfriends pregnant." These troubling biases persist in spite of considerable evidence suggesting that teen dads deserve much more credit than they typically receive. For example, although it is true that some young fathers have engaged in exploitive and antisocial behavior toward their partners while neglecting their children, the research literature indicates that the majority of teen fathers have a long-term, caring relationship with the adolescent mother prior to and throughout the pregnancy, and that most provide varied forms of emotional and financial support to the mother and baby during the first year of the child's life.[17] After the first year, however, the relationship between the young mother and father tends to deteriorate, and the frequency of contact between the father and his partner and child tends to decline over time.[18]

A tragic sequence and interaction of problems often cause the faltering relationship between adolescent fathers and their partners and children. To begin with, the couple must confront the emotionally draining dilemma about how to resolve the pregnancy. Should they consider abortion? Adoption? Keep the baby and marry? Keep the baby, forego marriage, but live together? Keep the baby, forego marriage, and live in separate households?[19] These weighty decisions can drive the couple apart, especially if they disagree about which option to pursue.

If the mother decides to keep the baby, then the couple and their families must address the financial responsibilities associated with raising a child, a matter that is complicated by the dire socioeconomic conditions of many teen parents. Adolescent fathers are over represented among the poor and tend to live in neighborhoods characterized by inadequate school systems and high rates of unemployment.[20] Adolescent fathers also tend to drop out of school, either before or after the pregnancy.[21] Thus, they have limited financial resources and employment opportunities, circumstances that make it difficult for them to support a family financially, even though most do try to provide some form of financial support for the child.[22] These financial hardships can strain the relationship between the adolescent parents and their respective families as they all try to cope with the crisis that is precipitated by an unplanned pregnancy.[23]

Additional problems are embedded in the tenuousness of adolescent romantic relationships. The amorous feelings between the young parents often wane and the couple discovers that they are incompatible and have irreconcilable differences. Fights between the teen parents can erupt and feuds between the families of the young parents may break out. In the face of such tensions, the adolescent father, who typically does not have custody of the baby, may be denied access to his child, and he may give up on seeking such access, either because he is unaware of his legal rights to visitation or because he can no longer tolerate the conflicts. The couple drifts apart and the father gradually loses substantive contact with his child.[24] These dire circumstances are discussed in chapters 3 and 4.

So, in the words of Bryan Robinson, a social scientist, former professor at the University of North Carolina at Charlotte, and one of the earliest champions of adolescent fathers, the experience of parenthood for most teen fathers is one of "hard truths and tragic consequences."[25] Indeed, in a series of pioneering studies conducted in the 1980s, Leo Hendricks and his colleagues from Howard University documented that teen fathers experience a variety of stresses associated with their early entry to parenthood, including relationship difficulties with the adolescent mother and her family, lost opportunities to bond with his child, financial hardships, and educational and career concerns.[26] Negotiating these difficulties while mastering the combined developmental challenges of adolescence and parenthood complicates the transition to adulthood. Hendricks suggested that young fathers could be assisted with these challenges by providing counseling and social services tailored to the needs of young fathers. Furthermore, his findings indicated that most adolescent fathers want assistance with their many concerns.[27]

In spite of the expressed concerns of teenage fathers and their desire to receive help, it appears that the needs of this population go largely unnoticed. The results of numerous studies, including several conducted by me and my students and colleagues at Ball State University and The College of New Jersey, have indicated that teenage parenting programs tend to consist of services for adolescent mothers but not for adolescent fathers.[28] Several authorities on the subject of teen fathers have argued that this neglect represents a manifestation of the societal stereotypes about adolescent fathers, which I described earlier.[29] This claim is supported by the findings of studies indicating that many service providers ignore the needs of teen fathers due to their pejorative and inaccurate generalizations about this population.[30]

In light of this inexcusable state of affairs, we are challenged to move beyond stereotypic images of adolescent fathers and to think more complexly about these young men.[31] Achieving this task is a critical first step toward helping teenage boys facing unplanned paternity. It must be followed by persistent efforts to engage adolescent fathers in services designed to assist them with their concerns and their transition to parenthood.

Why Teen Fathers Avoid Seeking Help

Recruiting teenage fathers for service program can be a difficult enterprise because they tend to avoid professional helpers for a number of reasons. Most teenage fathers are leery of professionals because they fear being treated harshly for their role in an out-of-wedlock pregnancy.[32] So they tend to shy away from people like me—psychologists, counselors, social workers, and reproductive-health-care professionals—and try to work things out on their own. Some young fathers do want the help of a caring adult, but they are too overwhelmed by the dual developmental challenges of adolescence and parenthood to seek professional assistance.[33] Guys who respond to the pregnancy by being a rock for their partner, caring for their baby, trying to complete school, and taking on a job while still trying to figure out who they are and their place in this world usually don't have the time or energy to find and utilize a professional helper. And there are other teen fathers who have been socialized to evade activities such as traditional counseling, which require intimate self-disclosure and the expression of private feelings. These young men prefer nontraditional forms of helping, such as those that are delivered through recreational and job-training programs.[34] Unfortunately, because most adolescent parenting programs are based on traditional approaches to counseling or are designed to address the needs of adolescent mothers, they don't appeal to a large number of young fathers.[35] Lastly, some teen fathers with long histories of delinquent and antisocial behavior never intended to accept the responsibilities of parenthood, so they harbor only a superficial, fleeting concern (if they care at all) for their partners and their children, and typically have little or no interest in getting guidance about fatherhood.[36]

So, too many roadblocks get in the way of teen fathers receiving the advice of a knowledgeable professional about what it means to be a man and a father. If we really want young fathers to be engaged with their partners and their children, then we must find a way to remove each of these impediments to their getting help. I examine these barriers and offer some suggestions for dismantling them in chapter 4.

Using a Male-Friendly Approach

We can help young fathers grappling with the challenges of early parenthood by relating to them with a male-friendly style. By "male-friendly" I mean several things. First and foremost, we adults must learn how to talk to boys in their language and to earn their trust by entering their worlds and adjusting what we do to what they do. So with some teen fathers, rather than expecting them to spill their guts to us in heart-to-heart, face-to-face conversations about the pregnancy and parenthood, we may have to talk with them while we're playing a game or tossing a ball back and forth, slowly exchanging vital information in the process. With others, we may have to give them something helpful to read and accept that fact that they initially might not have much to say to us as they process the content of those readings. We may have to tell them a lot about ourselves before they are ready to tell us even a little bit about themselves, especially if other adults in their lives have castigated them for their role in an unplanned pregnancy. We may have to joke and spar with them, loosening them up in the ways that boys like to loosen each other up. We must be prepared to tolerate, rather than be frightened by, their anger and vacillating moods as they try to cope with the shock and repeated crises that go hand in hand with early paternity. And we must be caring advocates for teen dads, persistently trying to help them with their difficulties at school or work and with their crucial responsibilities as a parent.[37] By taking these measures and others that are suggested in chapter 5, we will allay teen fathers' fears of being judged, identify and contact young men who are overwhelmed by unplanned paternity, and earn their trust, even the trust of young men who may be antisocial in their treatment of girls.

As a society, we must support the development of male-friendly programs for teenage fathers, such as those that are described in chapter 6 of this book, and, as is discussed in chapter 7, we must craft public policies that make the prevention of early fatherhood and the support of young men who are fathers a top priority. We must recognize that adolescent boys are not just going to come out of the woodwork and join preexisting programs for teen parents. They will especially stay away from programs through which they are immediately confronted about fulfilling their responsibilities as a father. Instead of expecting young fathers to flock to these types of flawed programs, local community leaders, concerned adults, and social service professionals must combine their resources and incorporate the types of activities and services that young men need and enjoy into the existing safety net of services that teen mothers access. For example, over the past eighteen years I have developed a psychoeducational support program for teen fathers that consists of recreational activities and providing snacks and a number of services that respond to what the young fathers identify as their most pressing needs.[38] In this program, the fathers meet one another and develop rapport with program counselors, who are typically men, through their mutual participation in recreational activities such as basketball, football, and karate. As familiarity and the comfort level among participants rise, informal discussion groups are started to facilitate group support and to identify the particular practical needs of the young fathers. A series of psychoeducational workshops are then arranged and incorporated into the recreational program. Although the content of the workshops varies from group to group, typically it includes parenting-skills training, career guidance and job placement services, and legal counsel regarding paternity issues. Regardless of the workshops chosen by the fathers and delivered by the counselors, a consistent effort is made to encourage the fathers to support the adolescent mother and the couple's baby after the trust of the young men has been earned.

If our society truly wants the tens of thousands of boys who are teen fathers to become competent, loving parents, then we must develop and furnish many more community-based, male-friendly programs geared to the needs of young fathers. Fortunately, many exemplary programs do exist, and they are featured in chapter 6 of this book.

Providing Tough Love and Healing Father-Son Wounds

Extra-special consideration, patience, persistence, and resiliency are required with the small percentage of teen fathers who have completely neglected their paternal responsibilities. Although it is easy to judge these young men and write them off as hopeless misfits who deserve punishment rather than compassion, a "tough-love" approach to counseling can foster effective paternal strivings. Many of these youth are the sons of "phantom fathers," dysfunctional men who had little nurturing contact with their children. A key to stirring prosocial paternal strivings in these boys is to help them to address the unresolved wounds in their father-son relationships. These troubled youngsters must grieve the absence of a caring father in their lives. Then they can be challenged and encouraged to create a vision of the kind of father they would like to be, the kind of father they never had.[39] The process of helping young fathers to construct healthy visions of themselves as parents is explained in chapters 5.

10 percent of the pregnant adolescents from that year placed their child for adoption due to the complicated and agonizing aspects of the adoption experience.[1] The majority (nearly 60 percent) of the pregnant teens from the early 1960s married their partners, often in shotgun weddings, which were hastily arranged and performed before the young woman began to show that she was pregnant.[2] So, back in 1960, guys like Tom faced tremendous pressure to marry when their girlfriend got pregnant. But that is typically not the case today.

Today, thousands of boys still become parents during their teenage years, including young men like Ronny, who live in a world that has changed greatly since Tom became a father in 1960. Ronny was nineteen years old when I met him in 2002. At the time, he was unmarried and had been a father for three years. I learned about Ronny from his former school counselor, who had contacted me and asked if I would be willing to help Ronny with a number of difficulties he was having with Tonya, the mother of his child. When Ronny and I talked over the phone a few days later, he was very worked up about the problems he was having with Tonya and eager to tell me about his entry into fatherhood:

Man, I was like, you know, not really tryin' to make a baby or nothin' when it happened. I was like tryin' to be cool, you know, be safe—not like those other jokers who live by me and always be doin' the nasty without no protection and not worryin' if they gonna make the girl pregnant. They be like, "Man, it's her kid now, not mine, so I ain't gotta worry about it." I didn't want to be one of those guys. So, I played it safe most of the time—you know, using condoms. But one day I made a *big* mistake man. I was just chillin' with my girlfriend one day, you know, doin' a little reefer when nobody was home at her house, and we started getting' into it and I didn't have no condom with me, so I just took a chance, you know, *and BAM!—a couple a' months later, I found out she was pregnant!!!* It musta been that one time, man, and I tell you, I started buggin' out when she told me she was pregnant. I mean, come on man, I was only sixteen years old—*sixteen years old!!! What was I gonna' do now???* I mean, I was just a kid and she was just a kid and here we was havin' a baby. Man, it was a big mess, man. We didn't know what we was gonna do. We talked about havin' an abortion, but she didn't want to do that, and I wasn't sure I wanted to do that either. So, we decided we better tell our parents. . . . I told my mom first. Man that was a tough moment! She started cryin', she started screamin' at me, *"Ronny, how could you be so stupid???"* Man, I knew she was gonna be upset because she always told me not to do nothin' stupid like the other guys in my neighborhood. Everybody runnin' around makin' babies. She wanted me to go to college, you know, make a life for myself before anything like that happened. And I went ahead and made a mess of all that. But I knew she would be OK after a while, because that's the way she is about things: upset at first, but OK afterwards. And that's how she was with this. She was really buggin' out at first, but after a while, she calmed down and helped me come up with a plan. She told me she would help me out when she can, but I had to finish school and get a job and be a good father to my baby and all that stuff. So, that's what I did. Tonya and I stayed in school, and I got me a little job at nights and on weekends at a truckin' depot washin' trucks and pumpin' gas. She got into one of these programs for teenage mothers, and they helped her out until she had the baby and then they helped her out some more after the baby was born. And I was real good, man. I mean, *real good*. I want over there [to Tonya's home] every day and saw her and my son, and we got along real good at first. I gave her money and brought my boy things, like Pampers and clothes and stuff like that. But that didn't last too long. She started accusin' me of not givin' her enough money, and then she got into this other guy, and things went down from there. I mean, things got *real bad,* man. And now I got to fight her every time I want to see my baby. And it's bad man, real bad.

Ronny's story illustrates many of the common experiences of teen-age fathers from today, which abound with teenage fathers who are rarely noticed by society. Although the teenage pregnancy rate, adolescent birth rate, and teenage fatherhood rates have all declined in recent years,[3] there are still a substantial number of boys in the United States who become fathers. From 1999 through 2003, nearly a million children were fathered by young men age fifteen to nineteen.[4] Roughly 2.4 percent of boys in this age group have fathered a child, and 6.5 percent have made a young woman pregnant.[5] Among sexually active boys, 4 percent have fathered a child, and 13 percent have been involved in a pregnancy.[6] Teen fathers like Ronny, especially those who live in poor communities, are surrounded by boys and girls who are having sex and having children, usually unintentionally but sometimes intentionally. Abortion is now a legal and medically safe option that an expectant teen can consider if she is inclined to terminate her pregnancy, provided she is legally old enough to undergo the procedure. Yet since 1994 there has been a sharp decline in the teen abortion rate.[7] Although adoption is still an option for expectant adolescents, less than 1 percent of pregnant teens place their baby for adoption today.[8] For the most part, shotgun weddings are a thing of the past: over 80 percent of teen couples who have a child remain unmarried, with the mother of the child usually retaining custody of the baby.[9] So, whereas teen fathers from Tom's era were expected to marry their partner and live together as a family, a young man like Ronny is likely to be a noncustodial father who must negotiate child support and child visitation arrangements with his partner and her family. But how did this shift in attitudes and behavior occur? What are the factors that shape the current context in which teenage fatherhood occurs in the United States? How did these factors emerge? What is the impact of these factors on young men in America?

The Sexual Revolution

During the 1960s, a sexual revolution erupted in the United States. Teenagers and young adults began to question existing sexual prohibitions, and compared to prior generations, they engaged in more open and frequent discussions about sex. Rebellious youth initiated the practice of "free love," characterized by sexual freedom and experimentation outside of the confines of marriage. Over the course of the next several decades, the acceptance of premarital sex spread from the adherents of the counterculture to the majority of young people. In addition, pornography was less stigmatized, and the media depicted nudity and sexual acts as a part of everyday life.[10]

By the late 1990s and early 2000s, the mores of the sexual revolution had taken a strong hold in our culture. Consequently, compared to youth from the 1950s, today's teenagers are more comfortable talking about sex, and they tend to believe that engaging in premarital sex is OK.[11] They also are under tremendous pressure to have sex.

The Pressure to Have Sex Is Pervasive

Although most teenagers want to hold off on having sex until they are older in caring relationships, pressure to have sex comes at them from many angles, so they feel compelled to fit in with the perceived sexual norms of other kids their age. Some of this pressure starts from within, sparked by the erroneous estimates youngsters make about the sexual escapades of their peers. Many boys and girls feel compelled to engage in sex because they think that the rate of sexual activity among their peers is higher than it actually is. In studies pertaining to this issue, "Twelve-year-old, sexually active girls thought that 80 percent of the girls their age were having sex while actually only 5 percent were sexually active. Boys' perceptions were less exaggerated but still higher than reality."[12]

The traditional masculine belief that a male can prove his manhood through sexual intercourse is a potent source of pressure for some young men to feel that they must become sexually active in order to be seen as cool. Boys who adhere to traditional views of masculinity are more likely than their nontraditional peers to be sexually experienced and to have more sexual partners.[13] Some teenage boys pester "each other to have sex, calling those who have not had sex names and bragging about having had sex."[14] These pressure tactics are seen as a way "to build up a person's own ego when in a crowd."[15] Combined with the belief that the majority of one's peers are sexually active, these pressures can prompt some young men to get sex over with so they can appear normal, as is illustrated by this statement by Lawrence, a seventeen-year-old: "Everybody out there be doin' it. So, you be like, 'Hey man, I might as well be doin' it too.' You don't want the other guys to be thinking you the only one who ain't doin' it. So, you got to go out and party and get together with somebody. Then you can say you did it and you will be all right."

Boys are not alone in their reports of being pushed to have sex: Among youth age 12–19, 82 percent of boys and 79 percent of girls report feeling pressured to have sex. "Girls say romantic partners exert the most pressure while boys said pressure is most likely to come from friends."[16] Nevertheless, in at least some communities, young men feel pressure from girls to have sex. For example, a high school boy in San Francisco reported, "Girls, especially, always want to [have sex] . . . so [if] this is what a girl wants, I [need to] prepare myself."[17]

Children and Teenagers Are Bombarded with Images of Sex

Another major source of pressure for teens to have sex is the media. American boys and girls are barraged with images of sex through various media that can form their understanding about sex: 51 percent of the teens polled by NBC and *People Magazine* reported getting information about sex from TV and movies.[18] Two teenage boys had this to say regarding the invasive presences of sex in the media: "You see it on TV; you see it everywhere—HBO, the late-night movies," says Jake of suburban Denver. "Jay-Z—a lot of his videos show him partying with a lot of girls all over him and stuff." Adds Steve Webb, twelve, of Jacksonville, Florida: "A song by Petey Pablo, it talks about all positions and stuff. My pastor was talking about that, and he said we shouldn't be listening to it." [19]

Sexual content can now fill the homes of American children and teenagers in many ways, through sexually explicit magazine ads, television shows, videos, DVDs, and Web sites. The messages often communicated through these media is that having sex is a desirable, impulsive, and rampant occurrence devoid of adverse consequences. The effects of these messages are disconcerting: exposure to sexually explicit media appears to hasten the onset and frequency of sexual intercourse among teens.[20]

According to Gary Brooks, a psychologist from Baylor University and the author of *The Centerfold Syndrome*, boys receive particularly problematic messages about sex from other males that are reinforced by the media. Boys are socialized to view themselves as sexual pursuers and girls as sexual objects. Boys are also taught that they must demonstrate that they can have sex when they are young, even if their sexual experiences are devoid of emotional intimacy.[21] In addition, boys are well aware of the dysfunctional norm that sex with girls involves a form of conquest through which the male must somehow get a female to submit to his will.[22] Increasingly, these messages are reaching a growing number of boys who have attained puberty at a very early age.

Children Are Reaching Puberty at an Earlier Age

Puberty is "the stage of adolescence in which an individual becomes physiological capable of sexual reproduction."[23] It is marked by hormonal changes, the development of reproductive organs, and the emergence of pubic hairs. For both boys and girls, there are rapid gains in weight and height. Girls develop breasts and curves, and boys start to grow facial hair, their muscles thicken, and their penises enlarge. It is a time of intense and ever-changing emotions, including curiosity, excitement, nervousness, and confusion about sex.[24] It is also a heightened period of increased sexual arousal and desire, as boys and girls develop attitudes about sex and begin to engage in sexual relations.[25]

Experts on the subject of puberty are alarmed by an increase in early-onset puberty in American boys and girls. According to Marcia Herman-Giddens, a senior fellow at the North Carolina Child Advocacy Institute, "early signs of puberty, such as breast and pubic hair development, are occurring at earlier ages than they did a few decades ago."[26] For example, in 1969 the average age of the onset of puberty for boys was approximately eleven and a half years.[27] However, today over one-quarter of all boys reach puberty by age eight,[28] and many American girls are showing signs of puberty by age seven.[29] Although scientists do not fully understand why this phenomenon is occurring, they are appropriately concerned about the impact of these changes on children. Children as young as seven or eight are not equipped to deal with the confused feelings they may have about their sexually maturing bodies. Furthermore, prior research has shown that the precocious onset of puberty is linked to early sexual activity.[30] Thus, American children are becoming sexually mature at earlier age at a time when our culture is saturated with sexually explicit information and sexually permissive attitudes.

Boys who enter puberty early in a sexually permissive culture are at risk to give in to the pressures to have sex before they fully understand the far-reaching consequences of becoming sexually active. One of the contributing factors to Steve's early introduction to sexual intercourse was his accelerated physical development. According to Steve's mom, many people thought Steve was an eighth-grader when he was only in the fourth grade. Steve reported that he took advantage of his mature looks to start having sex at age ten, even though he wasn't sure what he was doing at the time. "Sex made me feel older," he reported to me, "but it also scared me. . . . Most people don't know this about me, but there is a scared little boy inside of me that just wants to run away and hide." Like many older boys, Steve was also a victim of inaccurate and inadequate information about sex and its consequences, so uniformed about sex that he became a father even before he understood how easily he could get a woman pregnant.

Many Teenagers Still Have Inaccurate and Inadequate Information about Sex and Contraceptive Use

Unfortunately, misinformation about sex is still common. For example, some young men continue to believe "that having sex with a virgin without a condom is 'safe' (meaning that there is no risk of getting an STD, and they can ignore the risk of pregnancy), and that they could tell a girl is a virgin by just looking at her."[31] Although the percentage of sexually active teenagers using condoms has increased in recent years,[32] more than a third of teenage boys who are sexually experienced and roughly half of those who are sexually inexperienced do not understand the need to leave space at the top of a condom during intercourse.[33] And clinicians continue to report that many pregnant teens and expectant young fathers look back on the day they had the conception-causing intercourse and comment, "I thought it would be OK to do it just once without protection." These are dangerous assumptions, and their existence highlights even further that American boys need better guidance and education from knowledgeable adults regarding the facts and risks about sex.

Children and Teenagers Need More Guidance from Their Parents about Sex

Because today's youth are inundated with sexual images, feel pressure to have sex, and are reaching sexual maturity at an early age, they understandably want guidance from their parents about sex and contraception. The caring direction of loving parents regarding sexual matters can play a large role in helping boys and girls to delay having sex and to make good decisions about contraception use when they do have sex. Research shows that children raised by nurturing parents who express warmth and affection, use positive child-rearing practices, have clear but flexible rules, communicate openly about birth control, and encourage their children to delay having sex tend to wait to have sex until they are older and to use some form of birth control and have fewer sexual partners once they start having sex.[34] And the evidence also shows that most parents want to help their children to make good sexual decisions, and they do have conversations with their children about sex. For example, the results of the *People*/NBC poll indicated that 70 percent of young teens get information about sex from their parents.[35]

However, there are also strong signs that parents from all ethnic groups experience a high degree of discomfort regarding such discussions,[36] which could jeopardize the effectiveness of communications between parents and children regarding sexual information. Although conversations about sex between parents and children might occur, many parents do not convey enough guidance to teens about how to talk with a boyfriend or girlfriend about sexual concerns or about how a person knows when he or she is ready to have sex. A lack of parental guidance about sex is a particular problem for boys: parents are far more likely to discuss sex with their daughter than with their son.[37]

Anthony was one of the first teen fathers to convey to me his wish that he had received more guidance from his parents about sex. He was sixteen at the time his girlfriend become pregnant. During one of our conversations about the pregnancy, Anthony expressed disappointment about the preparation his parents had given him regarding sexual matters:

> I know my mom and dad care for me, but they never talked with me much about sex. When I was about twelve years old, my mom told me how babies are made, and then a few days later, my dad asked me if I had any questions about the stuff my mom had told me. I said "no" because I really didn't have any questions at that time. And that was the last time my parents talked with me about sex until my girlfriend got pregnant. That's when they started screamin' at me that they couldn't believe I had gotten her pregnant because they had taught me about sex and making babies and all of this other crap. But they really *hadn't* taught me much at all. . . . I wish somebody had said to me, "Anthony, don't ever go inside a girl unless you have a condom on because all it takes is just one time and you can get a girl pregnant." But *nobody* ever told me that, and here I am now, in a big mess. I just wish I had known better.

Many other teenagers feel exactly as Anthony does. According to the findings of research conducted by The National Campaign To Prevent Teen Pregnancy, "88 percent of teens say it would be easier to postpone sexual activity and avoid teen pregnancy if they were able to have more open, honest conversations about these topics with their parents."[38] Parents perceive these conversations to occur at a significantly higher rate than teens do (85 percent vs. 41 percent),[39] suggesting that parents have to pay closer attention to the frequency and content of their discussions regarding sex so that they can better prepare their children for handling sexual matters. In addition, in spite of their communications with their children about sex, parents tend to underestimate the sexual activities of their children.[40]

Formal Sex Education for Adolescents and Their Parents Is Still Inadequate

Formal sex education in schools can compensate for any gaps between what boys and girls need to know about sex and what their parents teach them. Comprehensive instruction about conception and contraceptive use and training in the coping skills to deal with sexually charged situations have been shown to reduce unsafe sexual practices among adolescents. Since the 1990s, there has been a wider provision of effective sexual education in the United States, which has played an important role in reducing the rate of teen pregnancy in recent years.[41] Nevertheless, authorities on the subject of adolescent reproductive health have concluded that the extent and quality of sex education in the United States is uneven and lags far behind that of other countries whose teen pregnancy and birth rates are far below those in America.[42] In addition, instruction that is designed to prepare parents for educating their children about sex and pregnancy prevention is very limited, yet greatly needed.[43]

Some Teenagers Do Not Have Enough Adult Supervision

Caring parents try to supervise their children's activities in order to safeguard their sons and daughters from making poor decisions. However, it has become increasingly difficult for many parents, even many loving ones, to adequately monitor the behavior of their teenagers. We live in a nation with a substantial number of dual-career couples and single working adults who have children. Due to the hours that these parents spend at their job and commuting to and from work, more and more teenagers are left to their own devices, increasing the opportunities they have to explore their sexual desires.

The level of adult monitoring can have a major influence on adolescent sexual behavior. In a study of the sexual activities of over two thousand teens attending a school-based screening program for sexually transmitted diseases, researchers reported that the proportion of teens who have had intercourse was 68 percent among those who were unsupervised for five or fewer hours per week but 80 percent among those who were without adult supervision for thirty or more hours per week.[44] Thus, teenagers with the least amount of supervision by adults engage in the most sexual activity, suggesting that some teenagers need increased supervision by responsible adults in order to deter their sexual activities.

Many Sexually Active Teens Have Difficulty Talking about Sex with Their Partners

One of the consistent concerns of young men is that they feel awkward and scared about talking with their partners about sex, even though they live in a sexually open and permissive society. Some young men do not talk about sexual issues with females because they feel "embarrassed, shy or uncomfortable; scared or afraid of rejection; and inexperienced in sex or relationships."[45] In addition, they fear "that talking will make females get angry or think that they sleep around, or that it will give females the opportunity to say no."[46] They also find it "difficult to bring up sex in the moment" because "you just want [sex] to happen . . . 'cause if you talk about it . . . it ain't going to happen."[47]

Many well-adjusted girls are reluctant and embarrassed to discuss sex with their partners. Nicole, age seventeen, who had a steady, caring boyfriend, reported to me: "I want to tell him what I am thinking and feeling about sex when we are alone, but I just can't do it. I think it is because my parents never talked about sex in front of me, so I am not used to talking about it. And I am afraid that if I tell him about some of the things that scare me that I might disappoint him. I want to be ready to have sex with him, but I'm just not sure."

If talking about sex is difficult for a girl who has a supportive boyfriend, imagine how hard it must be to bring up the subject when a girl's partner is violent and unpredictable. Related to this consideration, research shows that teenage women who have been physically abused by a boyfriend "are more likely than young women who had not been abused to be afraid to negotiate condom and contraceptive use with a partner,"[48] which increases their risk for engaging in unprotected sex and becoming pregnant.

The Number of Teenagers Who Want to Become Parents Has Been Rising

Common sense would dictate that few boys and girls would deliberately plan a pregnancy. Indeed, most mature teenagers agree with the statement, "Becoming a teen parent is one of the worst things that could happen to a 16-year-old girl or boy."[49] And studies of pregnancy intentions show that about 8 out of every 10 adolescent conceptions are unintentional.[50] Yet, a surprising number of teenagers either actively or passively allow a pregnancy to occur. For example, in his stunning book, *When Children Want Children*, Leon Dash, a reporter for the *Washington Post*, documented through in-depth interviews with adolescents from one of the poorest neighborhoods of Washington DC that numerous young couples intentionally choose to conceive a child, even though they are aware of methods to prevent pregnancy and know how to acquire contraceptives.[51]

Why would teenagers who know how to prevent conception and have access to contraceptives nevertheless choose to procreate prior to getting married? Several possible answers to this question, focused on the reasons why teenage girls become pregnant intentionally and keep their babies, have been offered: "Various psychological and socioeconomic reasons influence this decision: the need to have someone to love, to dress up, and to look nice; the belief that they will have someone who will love them unconditionally; the desire to feel like an adult; the wish to escape from parental home and be independent; to make up for their low self-esteem; and to win attention. . . . For some young women, motherhood is the only role that they perceive as possible for themselves."[52]

There is a dominant belief in our culture that boys participate in intentional conceptions for different reasons. According to this view, sexually precocious boys are cavalier and clueless about the responsibilities and hardships of early parenthood. In support of this perspective are data gathered by The National Campaign to Prevent Teen Pregnancy, which reveal that 51 percent of the boys and young men agree with the statement, "Teen boys often receive the message that sex and pregnancy are not a big deal."[53]

But the situation is not quite that simple. For impoverished teen fathers, parenthood may be one of the few marks of achievement and meaning in life. Rudy Hernandez, a sociologist and the author of the gripping report *Fatherwork in the Crossfire*, explains: "Studies show that for most poor teens, educational problems, poverty, underemployment and lack of opportunities precede teen pregnancy, and having a baby has little or no bearing on whether or not these adverse conditions change. . . . If anything, having and caring for a baby may be one of the only things that a teen living in these conditions can control and do successfully."[54]

Leon Dash shared a similar assessment after completing his compelling investigation of teenage parenthood in the inner city of Washington DC: teen fathers who are burdened by poverty consider having a child to be an achievement in an otherwise dreary future. Neither the young mothers nor the young fathers who had talked with Dash viewed a premarital pregnancy as a negative life-altering event. On the contrary, they wanted the pregnancies to happen and considered having a child to be a source of pride and meaning in their greatly troubled worlds, which were marked by poverty, crime, substandard housing, and inadequate school systems.[55] Because African-American and Latino boys are overrepresented among teens who experience these types of conditions, they are more likely than white teenagers to turn to early parenthood as a source of meaning in their lives.[56]

Cecelia Conrad, an authority in family economics, has argued that pregnancy is a rational choice for poor teenagers. Compared to upper-middle-class youth for whom higher education and great job prospects are realistic future outcomes, teens from poor communities have no incentive to delay childbearing. Furthermore, the bleak job market and limited educational opportunities play a large role in deterring boys from impoverished areas from considering marriage when their partners get pregnant.[57] Young men who have very limited incomes are not capable of supporting a family, so they tend to remain single after their baby is born, relying on extended kin to assist them and their partner with the financial care of their child. Dismal economic prospects are especially likely to discourage young, expectant African-American and Latino couples from considering marriage since they often live in communities beset by poverty.[58] Scott South and Eric Baumer, social scientists who have studied the influence of neighborhood factors on teenage parenthood, added that the difficult life circumstances in some impoverished communities foster peer norms tolerating, if not promoting, out-of-wedlock childbearing. "Much out-of-wedlock childbearing in distressed neighborhoods is, if not exactly planned or intended, at least not entirely accidental."[59]

The realistic possibility that death could come at an early age is another reason some adolescent boys deliberately choose to become parents. Howard, a twenty-four-year-old man I once interviewed in prison while he was serving a ten-year sentence for armed robbery, explained that his decision to become a teen father was linked to his fear of dying. Howard came from the poorest section of Camden, New Jersey, which has one of the highest homicide rates of any city in the country. Howard spoke with a mixture of resignation and pride as he described his decision to be a father, which was made when he was an adolescent:

> I knew about condoms and the pill and all that stuff when I was a teenager. But doc, you gotta' know what it's like out there, man. My uncle got killed. My father got shot, and he shot some people too. Guys are always running wild on the street day and night. It's crazy out there. So, you got to make your mark on this world when you can, have what you can get with a nice, little lady when you can get it. You know—start a family of your own. So, my lady and me had our kids when we was young. And that's the truth, doc. You only got so much

time to be a man in this world before your number is up and you get killed or sent to a place like this.

Howard's statement indicates that some of the important decisions of his life were guided by terminal thinking, which is a thought process characterized by a deterioration of a possible future orientation. According to the psychologist James Garbarino, author of the moving and informative book *Lost Boys*, young men like Howard who demonstrate terminal thinking are at risk to engage in many forms of risky behaviors, such as unprotected sex and violence, because they have little or no hope in the future.[60] As is discussed in chapter 7, helping lost boys like Howard to find meaning in their lives and a sense of security in the future is a key approach to preventing adolescent pregnancy and childbearing, and should be a priority of public policy.

Abortion as an Option When Teens Don't Want to Give Birth

Although there appear to be a growing number of adolescents who want to be parents, for a variety of reasons there have always been plenty of other expectant teens who would rather not bring their babies into this world. Consequently, they consider abortion.

Acceptance of abortion in the United States has seesawed throughout our nation's history: "Abortions were used frequently during the late 1800s by white women who could afford them. However, by the turn of the century, the newly formed, almost exclusively male, American Medical Association lobbied against abortion and the female midwives who performed them. As a result, states passed laws outlawing abortions."[61]

The criminalization of abortion led to the near elimination of abortion procedures by licensed medical personnel and a corresponding surge of illegal, back-alley abortions that placed women who had the procedure at great risk for medical complications. However, on January 22, 1973, in its decision regarding the case of Roe v. Wade, the Supreme Court determined that laws prohibiting abortion violated the right to privacy. Because this decision overturned all laws banning or restricting abortion, it prompted a sharp rise in the number of abortions performed by competent physicians in the United States.[62]

Since the historic *Roe v. Wade* case, abortions among pregnant teens increased during the 1970s but then declined beginning in 1980 through the 1990s:

- Abortion rates among women age 15–19 were 42.3 per 1,000 women in 1986, 37.6 in 1991, and 29.2 in 1996.[63]
- For this same age group, 45 percent of all unintended pregnancies resulted in an abortion in 1994, compared to nearly 55 percent of such pregnancies in 1981.[64]

- The most recent data suggest that between about 28 percent and 33 percent of all pregnancies (intended and unintended) among teens end in an abortion.[65]

Why has the abortion rate among teenagers declined in recent years? Part of this downturn might be attributable to the development of better contraceptive methods, such as contraceptive implants, which may have prevented more girls from getting pregnant and having to consider having an abortion.[66] There has also been a noticeable growth in the number of teenagers identifying themselves as born-again Christians who oppose abortion, as well as a resurgence of conservative values across people of many religious traditions. The influence of anti-abortion messages, particularly among devout Christian boys whose partner is pregnant, might have discouraged some expectant teens from having an abortion.[67] In addition, changes in state statutes requiring parental permission for minors to have an abortion have probably deterred some girls from terminating a pregnancy.[68]

Today Pregnant Teens Rarely Place Their Baby for Adoption

Throughout the first half of the 1900s, it was common practice to send unwed pregnant teens to special maternity homes where they were cared for until their children were born, and then those children were typically placed for adoption before the young mother was reunited with her family. Adoption services were also an essential component of family services agencies assisting women struggling with a crisis pregnancy.[69] As a result of these forms of services, women from all age groups considered adoption a viable option, especially single women who were pregnant and concerned about being ostracized for having a child out of wedlock. Since the 1960s, however, there has been a gradual acceptance of single mothers. Consequently, more and more pregnant single women have opted to carry their babies to term and to keep their children.[70]

Patterns in adoption among American women reflect these changes in attitude. For example, from 1952 to 1972, 8.7 percent of all children from a premarital birth were placed for adoption.[71] By comparison, between 1989 and 1995 only 1.7 percent of such children were relinquished for adoption, and most authorities on adoption estimate that less than 1 percent of teen mothers place their children for adoption today.[72] Thus, adoption is rarely a consideration in the pregnancy-resolution process among pregnant teenagers.

The Big Picture

Here, then, is the big picture. In the United States today, adolescent boys are growing up in a sexually permissive society and they tend to be accepting of premarital sex. Although most boys would prefer to wait to have sexual intercourse until they are older and in a stable, long-term relationship, they also are under tremendous pressure to have sex and they receive excessive exposure to sexually graphic material at a time when many of them are reaching sexual maturity at a very early age. Teenage boys are likely to have conversations with their parents about sex, but too often these discussions are infrequent and lacking in the kind of substantive guidance that can counter the inaccurate and inadequate information they have about sex and contraceptive use. Sex education in our nation's schools, though improving, is still not sufficient to prepare enough boys with the skills to handle their intimate experiences with young women. American boys spend too much time without adult supervision, and when they are alone with a romantic partner, they have difficulty expressing their values, desires, and fears regarding intimate sexual relations. A growing number of boys actually want to be teen fathers, and the utilization of abortion and adoption by pregnant teens has been on the decline. There is a growing societal tolerance for premarital childbearing, creating a context in which remaining single is acceptable, and there are pockets of extreme poverty where marrying one's partner is not a viable option for many young fathers.

The consequences of this state of affairs are very troubling. The sexual intercourse rates of American teenagers are still very high, even though they have dropped considerably since reaching their record high levels during the early 1990s.[73] Nearly half of all high school students, including 49 percent of all male students and 43 percent of all female students, have had intercourse.[74] Taking advantage of opportunities when they are unsupervised by adults, today's sexually active teens manage to have sex at all times of the day or night, and in all sorts of locations, including someone's home, cars, trucks, hotels and motels, dorm rooms, and outdoors.[75] Alarming percentages of adolescents have engaged in several forms of high-risk sexual behaviors that are linked to many disturbing outcomes:

- *Inconsistent condom use.* Although today's sexually active teens are more likely than teens from prior eras to use some form of contraception,[76] about a third don't use a condom or any other form of contraception consistently, and when that third do use a condom, they tend to use it incorrectly.[77] These boys and girls are at risk for unintended pregnancy and parenthood and infection with STDs, including HIV.

- *Early sexual initiators.* The National Campaign to Prevent Teen Pregnancy reports that "approximately one in five adolescents has had sexual intercourse before his or her 15th birthday."[78] The rate of intercourse is even higher among young adolescents from some inner-city communities. For example, in a study of the sexual behavior of students enrolled at three schools in Brooklyn, New York, investigators found that one-third of males had sex *before* they entered middle school and one-fifth of females had had intercourse *before* they left eighth grade.[79] Research demonstrates that early sexual initiators tend to engage in a long-term pattern of risky behaviors that includes having a greater number of sexual partners, more frequent sexual intercourse, and inconsistent condom use.[80] Compared to teens who delay having sex, early initiators are also more likely to force a partner to have sex, to be involved in a pregnancy, to become infected with an STD, and to smoke, use illegal drugs, and drink once a week or more.[81] Approximately one in seven sexually experienced fourteen-year-old girls get pregnant, accounting for about 20,000 pregnancies and 8,000 births among this age group each year.[82]

- *Multiple sexual partners.* The percentage of teens engaged in concurrent sexual relationships (two or more sexual relationships overlapping in time) or sequential relationships (two or more nonoverlapping relationships) is frighteningly high. In a national study of 4,707 sexually active adolescents age 15–18 years, one-third had more than one partner, concurrently or sequentially, in the past 18 months.[83] In another study, nearly 54 percent of the sexually active male students attending schools in Brooklyn, New York, had four or more partners *by the tenth grade.*[84] Teens who have multiple sexual partners have lower condom use, a higher degree of regret about some of their sexual experiences involving alcohol, and higher rates of STDs then adolescents in single relationships.[85]

- *Mixing sex with other high-risk behaviors.* It is scary to consider what some young men do during sex. Among sexually active males age 15–19, 34.8 percent reported that they or their partner were drunk or high and about 2.8 percent had injected some type of illegal drug during their last intercourse. Nearly 11 percent (10.8 percent) of these young men were always or often drunk or high during intercourse.[86]

Considering the extent of these high-risk behaviors, it is not surprising that a substantial number of American adolescent girls become pregnant each year, and about 80 percent of their pregnancies are unintentional.[87] The pregnancy rate among fifteen- to nineteen-year-old women in the United States rose sharply from 95 pregnancies per 1,000 women in 1972 to an all-time high of 117 pregnancies per 1,000 in 1990,[88] indicating that the sexual revolution resulted is unprecedented rates and numbers of pregnant adolescents. In response to the record number of teenagers—especially unwed adolescents—getting pregnant and having children, the American public and the U.S. government made the reduction of teen pregnancy a national priority during the 1990s. Consequently, there was a dramatic downturn in the teen pregnancy rate, dropping to a historic low of 84 pregnancies per 1,000 women by 2000.[89] Nevertheless, 840,000 teenage pregnancies occurred in 2000, and over 400,000 of these pregnancies resulted in the birth of a child.[90] The vast majority of these births—approximately 80 percent—occurred out-of-wedlock.[91] Furthermore, among the 33 developed countries for which pregnancy rates are available, the United States has the second-highest teen pregnancy rate, trailing only the Russian Federation, and the highest birthrate among teens age 15–17 years.[92] The United States also has exceedingly high rates of sexually transmitted diseases among fifteen- to nineteen-year-olds.[93]

So what's the big deal? Why should we be concerned that the United States has such high teen pregnancy and birth rates? The answer is obvious: Adolescent pregnancy tends to be both a consequence and a cause of numerous social problems. Within our highly sexualized culture, girls and boys who drift into parenthood face increased odds that they will never complete school, suffer financial hardships, become dependent on welfare, and struggle with the transition to adulthood.[94] The economic costs of teen pregnancy are staggering, reaching tens of billions of dollars each year.[95] What makes these outcomes so maddening is that teen pregnancies can be prevented, yet an astounding number of them occur, and most are unintentional. And many of the conceptions that are intentional are attempts by desperate teenagers to exert power and create meaning in their otherwise bleak worlds.

And what about the tens of thousands of boys who father children each year? Who are these young men? What do we know about them? How do they respond to the challenges of parenthood while they are still teenagers? In chapter 3, I answer these questions by describing the characteristics and parenting behaviors of adolescent fathers.

3

The Characteristics and Parenting Behaviors of Adolescent Fathers

Stereotypical versus Accurate Portraits

One evening during a heated community meeting regarding the problems of teenagers from an urban area of New Jersey, Sam, an influential local leader, stood up to lament the moral decline of today's youth, which, he charged, was especially evident in the sexual behavior of adolescent boys. Passionate and angry, the gentleman condemned America's teenage boys for the large number of adolescent girls who were getting pregnant and having children prior to marriage. Stirred by Sam's persuasive manner, the audience broke into a spirited round of applause, affirming everything Sam had to say, supporting his contention that we could solve our nation's teen pregnancy problem if parents would force their adolescent sons to be more responsible for their actions. In short, Sam warned, "Adults had better learn how to teach young guys to keep it in their pants" and "to stop these jokers from leaving our daughters pregnant and alone to fend for themselves and their babies."

Just three blocks away from this meeting, George, a seventeen-year-old high school dropout, bent over a sink full of steaming, soapy water in the kitchen section of a 24-hour diner, sweat dripping from his brow, while he scrubbed a large pot that had been used to boil potatoes. George was hot and he was tired, but he still had three hours to go before he could punch his time card, leave the diner, and head home to his girlfriend and their baby. By this point in his life, George had been a father for a year already and a dropout for nearly two years, a young man from a poor neighborhood who never really felt that there was any point to completing his education. Although he had not succeeded in school and he liked to smoke marijuana, he now worked sixty hours a week, splitting his hours between the diner and a gas station where he pumped gas year-round, bearing the blistering heat of the summer and the numbing cold of the winter, to pick up some extra cash so that he "could take care of my boy and my little lady."

About eight miles to the southeast, James, a nineteen-year-old, sat in his prison cell wondering about what had become of his life. By age eighteen, he had spent the better part of the prior seven years in one type of juvenile correctional facility after another. When he was just eleven years old, he stabbed a teacher in the face with a pencil. He had stolen numerous cars between the ages of twelve and seventeen during his brief releases from youth prisons. Over the course of his teen years, he had abused all kinds of drugs, frequently got loaded on vodka, and liked to score in bed with lots of girls. He had gotten at least four teenage girls pregnant, two of whom gave birth to his children, a son and a daughter, who were being raised in separate households while James completed his current ten-year sentence for shooting a man during the holdup of a convenience store. The odds were that James would not see his children for a long, long time, if ever again, because their mothers wanted nothing to do with him, and James had priorities other than his children on his mind, such as his attempt to organize an appeal of his conviction for aggravated assault.

I knew all three of these individuals—Sam, through our mutual work on local teen tasks forces, and George and James, who were young men I had counseled through my work as a psychologist—and their respective stories tell us a great deal about how society views adolescent fathers and the varied ways different boys respond to the advent of fatherhood during their teenage years. We live in a country that has historically embraced Sam's view that most sexually active boys, particularly those who get a girl pregnant or become a teen father, are irresponsible and self-centered delinquents like James. Consistent with this viewpoint, young men like George—who did everything in his power to be a responsible partner and parent once his girlfriend became pregnant—are considered to be a rare exception among the legions of boys who are allegedly responsible for the teen pregnancy problem that has challenged our nation for the better part of three decades. But is this an accurate point of view? To what extent are teenage boys responsible for the hundreds of thousands of pregnancies and births to adolescent women in the United States each year? Are most young fathers like James, an antisocial youth who appears to have little regard for others, including the mothers of his children and his babies? What can we accurately conclude about the characteristics and parenting behaviors of teenage fathers?

The Origins of Stereotypes about Teenage Fathers

Most people like Sam don't realize that many of their perceptions about teenage fathers are misconceptions. These mistaken beliefs are rooted in observations people have about certain types of sexually exploitive adult men who father children born to unwed adolescent girls, which are then attributed to adolescent fathers. Understanding how these stereotypes about adolescent fathers were formed and debunking them begins with an explanation of the complex challenges that are associated with ascertaining the ages of the males whose children are born out of wedlock to teenage mothers.

It is difficult to obtain precise figures about the ages of unmarried males who father children because only 69 percent of these men eventually establish paternity[1] and because many unmarried women (40 percent to 50 percent) do not provide information regarding the fathers of their baby on birth records.[2] Teen mothers are especially likely to conceal the identity of the father from birth records because they either don't get along with the father, have concerns about visitation issues with the father, don't see any point to acknowledging the father's paternity, or the father doesn't want to be involved or doesn't believe the child is his.[3] His partner's parents can also play a role in his partner's decision to conceal the father's identify. In some cases, they might not want the young man to know he is the father because they consider him to be unfit for parenthood, so they convince their daughter to claim she doesn't know who the father is. In other instances in which the father of the child is legally an adult (eighteen years old in all but two states) but the young mother is still a minor, the adolescent mother and her parents might decide to hide the father's identify in order to prevent the father from being charged with statutory rape law violations.[4] As a result of these practices, we must rely on national survey data, rather than birth records, to try to estimate the ages of men who father the children born to adolescent mothers and to get a handle on the circumstances associated with these births.

The findings produced from several of these surveys are shocking and they are contrary to the beliefs of Sam and other people who agree with Sam's point of view: *adult men, not teenage fathers, are responsible for the majority of births to adolescent women, and these older men are much more likely than adolescent boys to force their partners to have sex.* For example, data obtained from the National Maternal and Infant Health Survey, which is a survey of mothers conducted by the National Center for Health Statistics, revealed that only 35 percent of the males involved in adolescent pregnancies are teenagers. The other 65 percent are men age twenty years or older.[5]

Similarly, investigators analyzing 45,500 teen births in California found that about two-thirds of the fathers were adult men who were no longer in school and were, on average, more than four years older than the teen moms. Adult men were also responsible for a surprisingly large percentage (approximately 47 percent) of births to fifteen-year-old girls.[6] In another California study examining the age of the fathers of children born to 12,317 very young mothers from 1993 through 1995, investigators found that adult men were responsible for nearly 27 percent of the births to adolescent girls *younger* than age 15. These men were on average 8.8 years older than the girls.[7]

The age gap between sexually active girls and their male partners is not limited to very young adolescent girls: 53 percent of *all* sexually active teenage women had intercourse for the first time with a male who was from two to eight or more years older.[8] Furthermore, over half of the partners of pregnant teenagers are at least three years older than the pregnant teen,[9] and nearly 57 percent of the women who become pregnant with their first sexual partner are involved with a man who is at least two years and as many as eight or more years older.[10]

Jacqueline Darroch, David Landry, and Selena Oslak of the Alan Guttmacher Institute, a nonprofit organization focused on sexual and reproductive health research, policy analysis, and public education, expressed concern for young teenagers who are involved in sexual relationships with much older men: "The more than 100,000 women younger than 18 whose sexual partner is six or more years older have much greater chances of becoming pregnant and having a baby than do other minors whose partner is closer to their age."[11] To support this observation, the authors noted that the pregnancy rate among fifteen- to seventeen-year-olds whose partner is six or more years older is nearly four times as high as the pregnancy rate for those whose partner is no more than two years older. The fact that "pregnancy rates are clearly highest for the teenage women with the oldest partner" is troubling to the authors "because it raises the concern that the age difference may make it more difficult for young women to resist pressure to have sex and to become pregnant."[12] Stating the same concern, Sharon Nichols and Thomas Good, authors of *America's Teenagers—Myths and Realities,* warned that our society had better realize that "many pregnancies happen because young females are vulnerable to the persuasion and threats of older men."[13] Consequently, Nichols and Good argued, we must do a better job of educating young men and women and their parents about the predatory behavior of older men, and we have an obligation to help teenage girls who find themselves in sexually abusive relationships with adult men.

Mike Males and Kenneth Chew, a pair of researchers from the School of Social Ecology at the University of California, Irvine, echoed these opinions in their analysis of data from California, noting that not only are most of the partners of teen moms adult men, but also "the younger the mother, the wider the partner age gap."[14] For example, among teen mothers whose partner was an adult male, the median age of eighteen-year-old mothers was about four years younger than the adult males, but for ten- to fourteen-year-old mothers, the gap was nearly seven years. The authors concluded, "What we call school-age childbearing is predominantly a teen-adult phenomenon."[15] The authors commented that the gap between young teenage girls and adult men "is especially significant because teenage mothers with much older partners are disproportionately the childhood victims of sexual assault by adult men."[16] Consequently, policy makers who hope to reduce the teen pregnancy and birth rates must consider the possible role of sexual coercion and abuse in early childbearing. "If prevention of early childbearing is the goal, then the predominant involvement of much-older adult males in the sexual assault of children, the initiation of young adolescents into sex (often by rape), and the impregnation of school-age females in voluntary relationships must become central in research and policy."[17]

These warnings must be heeded because forced sex is more likely to occur with girls who have adult sexual partners than those who have younger mates. Sexually active young girls involved with older men (seven or more years older) are twice as likely to experience some type of sexual coercion during first premarital intercourse than girls who are involved with a male who is the same age or younger.[18] In addition, the likelihood that a child-abuse investigation is initiated increases as the gap in age between an adolescent mother and her partner widens.[19]

It must be acknowledged that not all sexual relationships between younger girls and adult men are coercive. For example, within Hispanic culture, Latinas are encouraged to find older men, who are believed to be more settled and responsible. So, it is both common and socially acceptable for young Latina women to partner with a man who is six or more years older.[20] In his investigation of young Chicano fathers, the sociologist Rudy Hernandez provided vivid descriptions of relationships between younger women and much older males who "took care of their business," meaning that they were very supportive of their partners and loving fathers to their children.[21] Thus, healthy relationships between older males and younger females are possible, even though the likelihood of exploitation is higher among such couples.

And what about teenage fathers? The research shows that adolescent fathers are responsible for only a third of the births to teen mothers and they are less likely than adult men to sexually coerce their partners. But if this is the case, how come they have such a bad name with people like Sam and those who agree with Sam's portrayal of young fathers? Bryan Robinson, author of the groundbreaking book *Teenage Fathers*, argued that our impressions of how adolescent fathers relate to their partners often gets confused with facts about older men who maltreat much younger girls. Robinson documented that certain myths about teenage fathers can be traced to a few highly influential publications in the psychological, psychiatric, and sociological literature during the 1940s and 1950s when all unwed fathers, regardless of age, were lumped together for analysis and discussion. Based on "insufficient data, a handful of anecdotal cases, [and] historical stigma," the authors of these early writings portrayed teenage fathers as social misfits who had little regard for anyone but themselves.[22] The media latched onto this negative image of adolescent fathers and helped to perpetuate it in the public's eye. As a result, there are widespread beliefs that teen fathers are "Don Juans," "Super Studs," and "Phantom Fathers" who move from one damaging sexual conquest to the next, fathering a series of children and then abandoning their partners and their children to fend for themselves.[23] Robinson criticized the perpetuation of these myths because they are untrue and have the effect of turning people away from young fathers who need help. Investigators from the Texas Fragile Family Initiative, one of the largest studies ever conducted on adolescent and young-adult fathers, expressed a similar concern based on their data pertaining to over 1,100 young fathers. These researchers reported that 93 percent of the fathers from the Texas study had children with a single female partner and 73 percent saw their children either daily or every few days.[24] Clearly, these young men do not fit societal stereotypes about teen fathers. Nevertheless, pejorative images of adolescent fathers live on.

Instead of promoting these stereotypes, Robinson urged social scientists and helping professionals to recognize the tender age at which teen fathers become parents, and he emphasized that young fathers need compassionate assistance with the many hardships associated with adolescent paternity. Indeed, the 173 teen fathers who participated in one recent study were very young, with an average age of 14.9 years at the time of their first child's birth. These boys experienced numerous problems and they wanted parenting training, job training and employment opportunities, and relationship counseling to help them with their child-rearing responsibilities.[25] In order to help young men like these with their transition to fatherhood, we must move beyond our simplistic notions of adolescent fathers and create an accurate and complex portrait of this population. The remainder of this chapter provides this complex portrait by summarizing what we know about the characteristics and parenting behaviors of teen fathers. This information verifies that although antisocial young men like James appear to represent the boys who father children during their teenage years, the majority of adolescent fathers are like George, struggling to be good fathers while facing incredibly difficult circumstances.

Young Men at Risk

George and James are just two of many thousands of young men in the United States who have a fragile foundation upon which they are attempting to build their lives. The life circumstances of boys like George and James are devoid of the types of assets that have been shown to increase the odds that a boy will enter adulthood with a bright future. These assets, including external assets such as receiving strong support and validation from adults, and internal assets such as having a strong commitment to learning and having positive values that foster good decision-making, have been shown to promote resiliency in the face of adversity, inoculate youth from engaging in high-risk behaviors, and foster the development of personal competency.[26] In the absence of these vital assets, boys like George and James are prone to engage in a number of high-risk behaviors that can jeopardize the quality of their future.[27] The fabric of their lives is filled with risks, each of which can complicate their development, and when clustered together, can set them on a rapid course toward becoming teenage fathers.[28] Among these many risk factors is poverty.

The Harsh Socioeconomic Realties of Today's Teen Fathers

Although George and James responded in vastly different ways when they became fathers, they shared several common characteristics, including that fact that they both came from poor families residing in a highly depressed urban area. George's family lived from paycheck to paycheck earned by his father, an unskilled construction laborer who barely made enough money to support his family, which consisted of his wife, George, and four other children. During periods of unemployment for George's father, money would be so tight that the family would have to survive on water, bread, and meager portions of a generic brand of tuna fish. The situation was even worse for James. He hardly knew his father, who was serving a life sentence in a state prison for murder, and his mother depended on welfare as her only means to provide for her three children. Toward the end of nearly every month, James's mom would run out of cash, and James and his siblings would go hungry for days at a time. Often, there was no heat or hot water in the building where James and his family lived, and his home was rat- and roach-infested. Gangs roamed the streets in the areas where both boys lived. Most of the neighbors near George and James lived under similarly dire circumstances, struggling to stay alive in environments where poverty and crime were rampant and opportunities for work and a ticket to a better life were not to be found.

The harmful impact of poverty on boys like George and James cannot be overstated. Commenting on the physical, social, and psychological conditions associated with being poor, Gary Evans of Cornell University observed:

> Poor children confront widespread environmental inequities. Com-
> pared with their economically advantaged counterparts, they are
> exposed to more family turmoil, violence, separation from their fami-
> lies, instability, and chaotic households. Poor children experience less
> social support, and their parents are less responsive and more author-
> itarian. Low-income children are read to relatively infrequently, watch
> more TV, and have less access to books and computers. Low-income
> parents are less involved in their children's school activities. The air
> and water poor children consume are more polluted. Their homes are
> more crowded, noisier, and of lower quality. Low-income neighbor-
> hoods are more dangerous, offer poorer municipal services, and suffer
> greater physical deterioration. Predominantly low-income schools and
> day care are inferior. The accumulation of multiple environmental
> risks rather than singular risk exposure may be an especially patho-
> genic aspect of childhood poverty.[29]

Rates of teenage fatherhood are highest among boys like George and James who are raised in the suboptimal conditions found in poor neighbor-hoods. Research has established that there is a clear link between teen father-hood and impoverished families and neighborhoods.[30] For example, data from the National Longitudinal Survey of Labor Market Experience—Youth Cohort indicate that teen fathers are twice as likely to come from poor families than are non-fathers.[31] Across different racial and ethnic groups, relationships between the rates of teenage pregnancy and adolescent parenthood and com-munity poverty remain statistically significant.[32] As exposure to a number of factors (such as being raised in a single-parent family or living in high-crime areas) that are common in low-income neighborhoods increases, so too do the odds that a young man will become a father while a teenager.[33]

Poverty among African Americans and Latinos is a major reason why adolescents from these cultural groups are overrepresented among teen-agers who become parents. Over one-quarter of Latino and approximately one-third of African-American children under the age of eighteen live in poverty.[34] By comparison, nearly 11 percent of non-Hispanic white children are poor.[35] Thus, substantially higher percentages of African-American and Latino teenagers are exposed to the harmful conditions linked with a life of poverty that raise the risk for teenage pregnancy. Not surprisingly, the higher poverty rates of African-American and Latino youth are associated with relatively high teen pregnancy and birth rates among these teenagers: The teen pregnancy rate among African Americans (134.5 per 1,000 teenage girls) and Latinas (131.5 per 1,000 teenage girls) is more than two and a half times the teen pregnancy rate for non-Hispanic Whites (48.2 per 1,000 teenage girls).[36] The teen birth rate for African Americans and Latinas is also significantly higher: 63.3 per 1,000 African-American teenage girls and 82.6 per 1,000 Latina teenage girls, compared to 17.3 per 1,000 non-Hispanic white girls.[37] In addition, higher percentages of sexually active African-American (19 percent) and Latino (21.1 percent) males than non-Hispanic white males (9.1 percent) age fifteen to nineteen have caused a pregnancy.[38]

Many boys from underprivileged areas who accurately sense that their life options are limited may view fatherhood as one of the few adult roles they can achieve in life.[39] Consequently, they may deliberately father a child or not take consistent steps to prevent a pregnancy. Also, they are likely to experience academic difficulties and to drop out of school.

Problems with Completing School

James had not completed school and was still working on his GED when I met him in prison. He had posed numerous behavior problems in the classroom as a boy, and his disruptive behavior continued into adulthood. His prison records indicated that he had been written up on disciplinary charges for violating rules during GED classes, and his teacher told me that she thought James had no intention of completing his GED but was attending classes in order to try to make a favorable impression for the judge during his appeal of his sentence. When I asked James about his educational record, he shrugged his shoulders and had this to say: "What difference does school make, man? Sure, guys like me could go to school and get a little diploma and show it off to our mommas and make them proud, but it ain't gonna make no difference in our lives. Life is still gonna be crazy whether you got that diploma or not. So, I didn't waste *my* time with school. And, I probably will get my GED one day because I'm in here and I got nothin' better to do. But that ain't gonna make no difference in my life either."

Although George was a very hard worker and a responsible human being, he shared James's pessimistic attitude about education. George dropped out of school the day he turned sixteen and had no plans to return to school to complete his education. While James's academic problems were due to his chronic impulsive and aggressive tendencies, George's educational difficulties were the result of a significant learning disability and the feeling that he never fit in at school:

> Reading was always tough for me, doc. I remember the first year I was in school and all the kids around me started reading books, I couldn't keep up with any of them. And that's how it was for me from then on. I just couldn't get the hang of reading, and I never really liked trying to

learn to read either. I felt the same way about homework—I was never really any good at it, so I didn't bother doing it. Besides, what difference would it have made? My dad had a high school education, but it didn't get him anywhere. He's a good man, and he did everything he could to take care of us, but his education had nothing to do with that. And I knew getting an education wasn't going to help me either, especially with all the problems I had reading and keeping up with the other kids in school. But I've always been a quick learner when it comes to doing things with my hands, so I decided a long time ago that I was going to try and get ahead by getting a job and putting my money away before I had a family. But then I went and had a kid by mistake, so now I got to take care of that and try to get ahead while I'm caring for my little lady and our kid.

Like James and George, teenage fathers have increased odds that they won't complete high school.[40] More than one-third of adolescent fathers but only about 12 percent of non-fathers fail to complete high school or complete a GED.[41] Teen fathers also complete fewer overall years of schooling[42] and are less satisfied with their educational experiences.[43] In one study of 206 at-risk boys, which included 35 youths age seventeen to nineteen who were fathers, the strongest predictor of fatherhood in the sample was poor academic performance.[44] In both rural and urban areas of the United States that are impoverished, academic failure is an especially salient experience for boys who become fathers. Over half the youths who enrolled in several special programs for low-income, young fathers, including the Fathers Forever Program in Buffalo, New York,[45] Operation Fatherhood in Trenton, New Jersey,[46] the Public/Private Ventures Young Unwed Fathers' Pilot Project,[47] and the Maine Young Fathers Program,[48] had neither finished high school nor completed a GED.

Teen fathers drop out of school at different points in their lives and for different reasons. Some boys, such as George, subsequently drift into parenthood, whereas other males in school at the time of their partner's pregnancy are poor achievers or disconnected from the school environment, and the pregnancy serves as the culminating event for them to leave school.[49] A portion of young men from both groups are juvenile delinquents like James, whose many problems, including school drop-out and early fatherhood, are linked to an antisocial lifestyle that includes the abuse of drugs and alcohol.

Delinquency, Substance Abuse, and Teenage Fatherhood

There is a widely held belief, expressed by people like Sam, that teen fathers are antisocial deviants.[50] Contrary to this perception, the majority of teen fathers are law-abiding people. Nevertheless, there is extensive evidence documenting that boys who are involved in drug use, drug trafficking, gang activity, and other delinquent behaviors that can lead to incarceration are more likely to become teenage fathers than their non-delinquent peers. Here is an overview of that evidence:

- Researchers studying the criminal records of a sample of youth in Oregon documented that adolescent fathers had more than twice as many juvenile arrests as did non-fathers. The fathers were also more likely than non-fathers to use drugs and tobacco and to fail to complete high school.[51]
- In 1999, a team of investigators found that 20 percent of males committed to several juvenile centers in the Richmond, Virginia, area had fathered at least one child;[52] by comparison, only about 7 percent of all boys age fifteen to nineteen in the United States had fathered a child at the time the study was conducted.[53]
- Of the 506 inner-city students who participated in the Pittsburgh Youth Study, 12.3 percent were fathers, and the fathers were more than twice as likely to be delinquent as non-fathers. In addition, the fathers tended to continue to engage in serious acts of delinquency, such as car theft, breaking and entering, strong-arming, attack to seriously hurt or kill, or rape, as well as property offenses, frequent drinking, and drug dealing *after* they became parents.[54] In other studies, investigators found that both drug- and non-drug-related crime by adolescent fathers *increased* after the birth of the child.[55]
- There is an association between teenage parenthood and being diagnosed as having a conduct disorder (a pattern of behavior in which the basic rights of others or major age-appropriate societal rules are violated),[56] an oppositional defiant disorder (a pattern of defiance, argumentativeness, and disobedience toward authority figures), or a drug- or alcohol-related disorder.[57]

Delinquent youth are more likely than well-adjusted boys to become teen fathers because they engage in numerous unhealthy and dangerous behaviors—including high-risk sexual encounters—at an early age, and they tend to have deviant friends who support their involvement in risky and antisocial activities. For example, boys who anticipate initiating sex tend to use more alcohol and marijuana and to associate with peers who are sexually active, have gotten someone pregnant, use alcohol, and have been in jail.[58] Boys who have been involved in a pregnancy often show a cluster of other health-risk and problem behaviors referred to as a "risk behavior syndrome."[59] These behaviors include being in fights, drinking while driving, cocaine use, regular use of cigarettes, early initiation of sexual intercourse, and having multiple sexual partners. The risks some of these boys face are astounding. For example, compared to a group of peers who had never been involved in a pregnancy, one sample of inner-city boys between the ages of twelve and eighteen were fourteen times more likely to report three or more sex partners in the last year, more than five times as likely to report a sexually transmitted disease history, more than three times as likely to test positive for drugs, and more than two and a half times as likely to be inconsistent or nonusers of condoms.

So, delinquent boys who become fathers tend to live life on the edge. They engage in unconventional behavior and they don't fit in with conventional boys their age, which may lead to more frequent interactions with other disaffected peers who approve of their risky and problematic behaviors, thereby spurring participation in even more unsavory activities, including criminal behavior, substance abuse, and unsafe sexual practices.[60] Compared to other teen fathers who are not delinquent, these types of boys are poor candidates for parenthood, for they tend to neglect and harm their partners and their children as part of an overall pattern of antisocial behavior that can land them in jail, as was the case with James.

The Role of Physical Abuse, Neglect, and Forced Sexual Contact in Early Fatherhood

Various forms of dysfunction run high in families headed by parents who neglect or beat their children. Among the children raised in these families, boys are much more likely than girls to be victims of violent forms of punishment, which not only cause physical and psychological damage, but also limit their opportunities to witness, experience, and develop positive interpersonal skills.[61] Consequently, they may not be socially equipped to ask friends and adults questions about sex and contraception use, or to form the type of supportive, open relationships with girls that can help them to negotiate safe sexual practices during intimate encounters. At the same time, they may be hungering for intimacy, if not desperate for it, which can lead to their plunging quickly into sexual relationships with girls without taking the necessary precautions to prevent a pregnancy. Under such unfortunate circumstances, fatherhood can loom just around the corner.

Although there are a disproportionate number of teen fathers like James, who are the victimizers of others, there are also a heartbreaking number of young fathers who have been the victims of some form of neglect or abuse. In a longitudinal study that included 240 boys, a team of investigators led by Ellen Herrenkohl of Lehigh University found that adolescent boys who had been both physically maltreated and neglected as children were significantly more likely to be teen fathers than boys who had been neither abused nor neglected. The physical abuse documented in this investigation included being slapped or hit resulting in a bruise, being hit with a paddle or stick, and being burned, while neglect included emotional and physical neglect. Nearly one-third of the abused and neglected boys but only 5 percent of the non-abused or non-neglected boys were young fathers. The authors also found a significant relationship between sexual abuse and teenage fatherhood: nearly 30 percent of the sexually abused boys but only about 15 percent of the non-abused boys became adolescent fathers.[62]

Boys who have been the victims of sexual assaults are significantly more likely than non-abused boys to report getting someone pregnant. Analyzing data pertaining to teens from Massachusetts, which were obtained from the Youth Risk Behavior Survey, a group of researchers headed by Natalie Pierre of Children's Hospital of Boston calculated that 12 percent of the 824 sexually active males in grades 9–12 participating in this study had gotten a partner pregnant, and 8 percent had been forced by someone else to have sexual contact against their will. "Of those who reported forced sexual contact, 36.4 percent reported having been involved in a pregnancy; of the males who did not report a history of forced sexual contact, 9.4 percent were involved in a pregnancy."[63] Similar findings were reported in studies involving adolescent boys from Vermont,[64] which was focused on boys who had been forced to have intercourse against their will, and from Minnesota, which involved boys who had suffered incest or nonfamilial sexual abuse.[65] The Minnesota study was especially sobering, yielding very disturbing figures from two surveys, which were collected from more than 25,000 teenagers in 1992 and again in 1998:

- In 1992 among sexually experienced adolescents, 22.8 percent of boys who had been the victims of incest, 22.3 percent of boys who had been victimized by a nonfamily member, and 61.4 percent of boys who had suffered both forms of abuse had been involved in at least one pregnancy, compared to only 10 percent of boys who have never been abused.
- The same trend was found for the 1998 data: 27.1 percent boys who had been the victims of incest, 23.5 percent of boys who had been victimized by a nonfamily member, and 31.3 percent of boys who had suffered both forms of abuse had been involved in at least one pregnancy, compared to only 8 percent of boys who had never been abused.[66]

Comparing their results from Minnesota to the findings from Massachusetts and Vermont, Elizabeth Saewyc and her colleagues from the University of Minnesota School of Nursing concluded that the "similarity of findings suggests that the relationship between teenage pregnancy and sexual abuse is not limited to one geographic region, or racial or ethnic group, and is relatively consistent over time."[67] Moreover, these authors observed that the link between being the victim of child sexual abuse and later being involved in a teen pregnancy is especially strong for males.

Why is this case? Why are sexually abused males at greater risk for involvement in a teen pregnancy than sexually abused females? Saewyc and her coauthors offered the following three explanations:

> The first pertains to family environment. Sexually abused adolescent males tend to report more dysfunctional family environments than abused adolescent females do—including greater likelihood of substance abuse and domestic violence, regardless of whether the abuse was incest or nonfamilial abuse. If they are less likely to have supportive families who can help mitigate the trauma of sexual abuse, then they may be more likely to use negative coping methods—such as substance abuse, running away, and risky sexual behaviors—that put them at risk for teenage pregnancy involvement.
>
> The second explanation is based on culturally prescribed gender expectations. . . . Societal messages about masculinity and sexual behavior tend to portray males as the initiators of sexual contacts, and young men are expected to take the dominant role in sexual relationships; but a male youth who has been victimized has had that control taken away, and this may challenge his sense of masculine identity. Fathering a child is a potent symbol of masculinity and could restore the abused teenager's sense of identity.
>
> To complicate the process for adolescent males, the majority of sexual-abuse perpetrators are adult men, regardless of the victim's gender. Same-gender sexual abuse may create confusion about sexual identity, especially since sexual identity develops during adolescence, and a homosexual or bisexual orientation carries additional stigma in U.S. society. Fathering a child is one way to counter appearances of sexual minority status.[68]

Self-Esteem and Teenage Fatherhood

A common assumption about boys who become adolescent fathers is that, due to deep-seated feelings of inadequacy, they impregnate young women in an attempt to boost their self-esteem.[69] However, this is a mistaken impression. Early research on the psychological makeup of teenage fathers, which was conducted during the 1970s and 1980s, documented that problems of self-esteem were the consequences, rather than the cause of, early fatherhood.[70] More recent research shows that the relationship between self-esteem and adolescent parenthood is complicated and varies from population to population. For example, on the whole, the self-esteem of

African-American boys does not appear to be affected by teenage fatherhood, perhaps due to greater acceptance of adolescent childbearing in some African-American communities.[71] By comparison, the self-esteem of white boys[72] and boys with high educational ambitions[73] tends to take a downturn when they father a child during their teenage years. For white boys, this effect is probably related to the historical stigma that has been associated with premarital adolescent childbearing among white Americans. For educationally ambitious youth, the onset of fatherhood may be viewed as an impediment to the achievement of education goals. High-achieving males may suffer a wound to their self-esteem because they have disappointed themselves, their family, teachers, and other community role models by becoming a father before the completion of high school and college.[74] So, although self-esteem does not appear to play a significant role in young men becoming fathers, it does tend to decline after the onset of fatherhood, probably due to the many stresses associated with becoming a parent prematurely.

Locus of Control and Teenage Fatherhood

The relationship between locus of control and adolescent fatherhood is also complicated. Locus of control refers to a person's sense of control over his or her behavior. People with an internal locus of control perceive themselves to be in control of events in their lives and to be able to make changes in their world; people with an external locus of control consider external forces, including other people and the environment, to control life events. Higher scores on measures of locus of control reflect a greater internal locus of control.

Locus of control has been a frequent subject of research pertaining to adolescent fathers, and although the findings have been mixed,[75] most of the data suggest that teen fathers tend to have an external locus of control. Yet compared to adolescent mothers, teen fathers tend to have higher internal locus of control scores.[76] Thus, it appears that boys and girls who become teenage parents typically feel controlled by forces and events in their external worlds, and this experience is stronger for teen mothers than teen fathers.

How an external locus of control can contribute to a young man's entry into fatherhood is not clear. Boys who have a higher degree of external locus of control might become parents in an attempt to experience a sense of mastery over their environments.[77] A more plausible explanation is that young men who feel powerless to control their environments might be less likely to take the kind of responsible actions that could prevent a pregnancy than do boys with a high internal locus of control. Indeed, there is evidence that boys with an external locus of control are less likely to use contraceptives during sex.[78] Consequently, it appears that young men who have an external locus of control may not fully recognize the implications of sexual risk-taking, which places them at risk to become fathers at an early age.

Psychiatric Illness and Teenage Fatherhood

It must be emphasized that most teenage fathers are reasonably well-adjusted human beings who are not very different from non-fathers in terms of their mental health. Nevertheless, there is a significant association between being an unmarried teenage father and having a psychiatric disorder. Among teen fathers who have a psychiatric illness, the illness tends to exist prior to the pregnancy, rather than arising in response to it. Thus, adolescent boys with psychiatric disorders have increased odds of becoming teen fathers. In particular, boys with anxiety disorders, addictions, affective disorders (e.g., depression), and conduct disorders are at risk to become parents out of wedlock.[79] The authors of the study in which these findings were reported, headed by Ronald Kessler of the Harvard Medical School, hypothesized that the low self-esteem and insecurity associated with anxiety and affective disorders might "lead some young people to become attached to the first seemingly secure romantic partner available to them," which could result in a rush into intimate sexual relationships that places the couple at risk for pregnancy.[80] The authors also surmised that the link between teenage fatherhood and conduct disorder, which is the psychiatric diagnosis given to youth who engage in antisocial behavior, "could be due to the acting out often associated with that disorder."[81] The association between becoming a father and having an addiction is probably due to a loss of inhibition and rational planning experienced by addicted teenage boys when they are under the influence of drugs or alcohol, which raises the risk that they will fail to use contraception during sex.[82]

Multiple Risk Factors and the Entry into Early Fatherhood

The evidence I have reviewed thus far indicates that teenage boys who are poor, experience academic difficulties, drop out of school, engage in delinquent behavior and substance abuse, have been the victim of physical or sexual abuse, have an external locus of control, or suffer from a psychiatric illness are significantly more likely to become fathers prior to age twenty than are boys who do not have these characteristics. Other findings indicate that several family factors are also linked to early fatherhood. For example, the less connected a boy feels to his family, the greater the odds that he will be responsible for a conception.[83] A boy is also at increased risk for impregnating a partner and becoming a father if:

- He is raised by a single parent
- His mother had her first birth at an early age
- One of his parents is depressed
- His family lacks social support
- His parents do a poor job of monitoring his whereabouts
- His family has gone through numerous transitions (such as the movement in or out of the home by a mother, father, or their romantic partner)[84]

According to a special report issued by the U.S. Department of Justice, the probability a young man will become a teen father gets higher as exposure to risk factors accumulate:

> As the number of risk factors increases, the prevalence of teen fatherhood increases too, rising slowly at first. By the time a youth accumulates five or more risk factors, the teen fatherhood rate "virtually explodes." . . . Almost a third of those with five risk factors and almost half of those with six or more risk factors become teen fathers. Although it is clear that teen fatherhood is not a function of any single factor, when a young man faces numerous and often interacting risks, the chance that he will become a teen father jumps dramatically.[85]

Understanding the cumulative impact of these risk factors helps us to get a clearer picture about how some boys, like George and James, become fathers. Katherine Pears and a team of investigators from the Oregon Social Learning Center proposed that certain family dynamics interact with other factors to set into motion a series of events that can propel a boy toward early fatherhood. Specifically, boys born to young parents may grow up with the perception that early parenthood is an acceptable life experience. Boys from poor, working-class families, who are also likely to cope with more family transitions and to be raised in single-parent homes, "may perceive themselves as having fewer educational and income opportunities. Thus, they many not take the steps to prevent parenthood that a youth with greater opportunities might take." Also, "Becoming a father may be viewed as an adult behavior that can be successfully accomplished,"[86] particularly if the boy has experienced school failure. When boys who view the world in this way have parents who do not provide effective monitoring, there is a heightened risk that these youth will engage in unsafe behaviors, such as substance abuse, antisocial activities, and risky sexual relationships, especially if they live in neighborhoods where there are high levels of substance abuse, delinquency, and sexual intercourse by teens. Collectively, these factors set the stage for a young man to become involved in a pregnancy during his teenage years.

The life stories of George and James illustrate how multiple risk factors can place a boy on a trajectory toward adolescent parenthood. Both boys were poor, they had a history of academic difficulties, and they were the sons of mother and fathers who had become parents at an early age. James was also alienated from his family, received little guidance from his mother, had virtually no contact with his father, and his mom had moved through a series of relationships with men whose presence was a disruptive factor in James's life. Both George and James had smoked pot on a regular basis, and James had developed the additional habit of abusing vodka and many other types of drugs, including speed and cocaine. James also was well on his way to becoming a career criminal. Based on what we know about the risk factors for teenage fatherhood, it is easy to see that George was at high risk to become a teen father, and that James seems to have been destined to become one.

As he approached his twenties and faced an extended period of his life locked in prison, it was doubtful that James would have any substantive contact with his two children for the next ten years. But George was enjoying a relationship with his baby son every day, sharing a life with him and the boy's mother as he moved back and forth between his modest home and his two jobs in the diner and the gas station. As we shall see in this next several sections of this chapter, research on the paternal behaviors of young fathers suggests that most teen fathers are a lot more like George than James in their initial commitments to their partners and their children, in spite of their subpar parenting skills.

The Parenting Behaviors of Teenage Fathers

Most adolescent boys are ill prepared to be parents, and those who become fathers during their teenage years report their lack of readiness to parent and their regrets about becoming fathers too early in life. One teen father, who had participated in an interview with Constance Dallas and Shu-Pi Chen of the University of Illinois in Chicago, shared this viewpoint about being a father at a young age: "The older father has it better. They can offer a whole lot more. They've been through everything that we're going through now except that we're having children at this age. They've been through everything that we're going through now so I believe they would know more. I wish I had waited until a later time, to be more cautious, to wait until I was older and had more experience."[87]

Both young mothers and young fathers lack an understanding of developmental norms for children, and they tend to have unrealistic expectations about how often infants cry and to use physical discipline with their children.[88] These knowledge and skill deficits can be reduced if not eliminated through systematic instruction on how to care for a child properly. However, historically the response of social-service agencies to provide parenting skills training to teenage fathers has been glaringly dismal.[89] Without such instruction and the social support for fathers to be more involved in direct child care, adolescent fathers are apt to remain deficit in their understanding of child development and to abide by traditional gender-role expectations, which prescribe caretaking roles to females and provider and protector roles to males. Consistent with these expectations, adolescent mothers and their families typically shoulder most of the duties associated with caring for a couple's baby.

When young fathers do interact with their children, they demonstrate a mixed performance in their demonstration of parenting behaviors. Adolescent fathers raised in high-crime areas tend to engage in negative and coercive control tactics that are associated with the development of problems in children, such as antisocial behavior. However, adolescent fathers also tend to provide relatively high levels of positive, instructive guidance when their children attempt to complete cognitively-oriented activities, such as helping a child to read or responding to a child's inquiry about the world and how things work.[90]

It is understandable that adolescents, both boys and girls, would have inadequate knowledge about child development. But why are teen fathers more likely than teen mothers to use coercive control as a child-management strategy? One reason has to do with the way boys are raised. Parents are much more likely to use hitting, spanking, and other tough tactics as a form of discipline with their sons than with their daughters, thereby teaching boys that violence is an acceptable method for dealing with children.[91] Boys who are raised under these physically punishing conditions are likely to repeat the pattern of harsh parenting with their own children. It is also possible that hostility expressed by teen fathers toward children could be a form of spillover from conflicts between the young couple. Related to this latter idea, Paul Florsheim and his colleagues from the University of Utah examined the quality of the relationships of thirty-five couples who were teen parents and the impact of relationship quality on child rearing. The authors found that high levels of hostility between adolescent mothers and fathers were associated with lower levels of both maternal and paternal nurturance of children. This effect was even stronger among couples who lived together, suggesting that living with a partner with whom one has conflicts tends to have a particularly detrimental influence on parenting.[92]

Thus, conflicts between adolescent parents could have a "cascading, negative influence" on their children.[93] But how common is it for teenage parents to have conflicts? Overall, how do teen fathers relate to their partners and children?

Relationships between Teen Fathers and Their Partners and Children

As was mentioned earlier, a popular conception about teenage fathers is that they shrewdly seduce and impregnate a girl, and then they swiftly ignore their paternal responsibilities. However, most of the evidence regarding the length of the relationship between young parents prior to conception contradicts the notion that adolescent fathers are cold, manipulative, and irresponsible. Nearly three-quarters of teenage mothers report they were in a committed relationship with their partner at the time they became pregnant.[94] In a study by Katherine Pears and her colleagues of the Oregon Social Learning Center, the average length of the relationship between fathers age fourteen to twenty-one and their partners was twenty months, which suggested that "many of them had relationships of almost a year before the conception of the child."[95] In another study of thirty-one adolescent couples age nineteen or younger, David Moore and Paul Florsheim of the University of Utah calculated that the couples had been dating, on average, for approximately seventeen months. Thus, many young fathers enter a committed relationship prior to parenthood.

What helps young fathers to maintain these early commitments? According to a growing body of research evidence, "the quality of the father's relationship with the mother early on in the pregnancy is an important predictor of continuity."[96] Regardless of romantic attachment, fathers who have a harmonious relationship with their partner are more likely to be involved with her and her children than those whose relationship is riddled with conflict.[97] It also appears that a young father will be involved with his child if he has earned the respect of the maternal grandparents, who can play a key role as a gatekeeper to their daughter and grandchild.[98]

Understanding and respecting the gatekeeper power of the young mother and her parents is crucial for teen fathers because only about half live with their child shortly after the child is born,[99] and even less reside with their child several years or more after the child's birth.[100] Furthermore, very few fathers have legal custody of their children, so they must be able to show their partner's family that they care for their child if they want to remain involved their child's life.[101]

Demonstrating such care is a common value of many adolescent boys. Related to this desire, a recurring theme expressed by teenage guys is that a man must fulfill his duties. For example, here is what a team of investigators headed by Arik Marcell of the University of Maryland School of Medicine observed among a group of inner-city adolescent male students:

> The students defined a man as a leader, one who takes responsibility for his actions, morals, emotions, wife, family, job and home; one

who want to be noticed and liked by others; one who stands up for what he believes; and one who is mature and strong, not only physically but psychologically. . . . When participants were asked to define a responsible man, their most emphasized responses were that such a man takes care of his family, has a good job and handles his business. He "has a plan for [his] family . . . not only for [him]self" and "knows his priorities."[102]

These students also reported that a man who gets his partner pregnant "would have to support the child and her family," even though he might be stressed or in trouble with his family for his role in the pregnancy.[103]

Caring teen fathers support their partners in various ways during the pregnancy and the birth of their child. Most teen fathers give their partners gifts, provide them with transportation, join them for visits to the doctor's office during the pregnancy,[104] assist their partner during labor, and visit the baby in the hospital nursery.[105] One young father shared his feelings regarding the experience of his child's birth: "I just think a father should be in there, to go through the experience, you know, to see what the mother goes through. And really, when you're in the operating room or the birthing room, that really starts it all. It's like you see your son or daughter come out and you're there, and that's where everything starts."[106]

After the baby is born, most adolescent fathers provide their partners with cash or some type of necessary item, like furniture, diapers, clothing, and food.[107] Teen fathers who neither live with their partners nor have custody of their child but want to be involved with their baby tend to visit their child in intervals ranging from every day to once a week. These same fathers report having close relationships with their child, providing child care for periods ranging from a few days to a few months, and demonstrating numerous caring behaviors, such as feeding, changing, bathing, and playing with the baby and taking the baby to the doctor or hospital.[108] Teen fathers also serve as an important source of emotional support for their partners,[109] and they tend to see themselves as the primary disciplinarians of their children.[110]

Young fathers who make an earnest attempt to be good parents and partners state that a father must "take care of his business"[111] and "be there" for his child.[112] Both expressions mean that a man fulfills his paternal responsibilities in an ongoing manner. One adolescent father explained it this way: "I think the most important thing is for me to be there for my daughter. I need to give her love and understanding. A father is one who make[s] you smile. Being a father means being there for everything."[113]

Some teen fathers react in a heroic manner when they learn that their girlfriend is pregnant. Consider the response of Beto, a teen father from a poor barrio in Michigan, to his partner's pregnancy: "By the time Beto was in the eleventh grade, he was pretty much working full time, going to school and making sure that his siblings were going to school. This is when his girlfriend became pregnant for the first time. He quit school and moved his girlfriend into his mother's house. After the baby was born he had an elaborate wedding."[114]

Many young fathers express their support for their partners even though the couple chooses not to marry. For example, Rudy Hernandez, described the devotion of a twenty-four-year-old man named Jesus, who had become a father at age eighteen. Jesus was the father of two daughters, one six years old and the other two years old. His girlfriend was pregnant with their third child. Although the couple had no immediate plans to get married, they considered themselves to be an exclusive and committed couple, and Jesus expressed his passionate dedication to his partner and their children: "I love my vieja [girlfriend]—I'd kill for her. My children, I'd kill for them and die for them all in the same day—I'd take the food right out of my mouth so they could eat. I can't imagine it being any way else for a man. He's not like that, he doesn't take care of business—he's no man."[115]

Father involvement and support has many benefits for adolescent mothers and their children. Adolescent mothers who sense that their partners support them tend to report greater life satisfaction, lower levels of depression and psychological distress, and higher self-esteem than mothers who lack such support. Father support also appears to bolster the child-rearing skills of adolescent mothers, and to foster healthy emotional, cognitive, and social development in the child, especially if the child and the father perceive their relationship to be close.[116]

Being a loving and responsible father also has benefits for teen fathers themselves. For example, fatherhood tends to trigger a growing maturity in teen fathers. Compared to their non-father peers, teen fathers tend to show greater involvement in socially productive activities, such as serving as volunteers in their communities.[117] Many are elated when their child is born, as is illustrated by this testimony from a teen father: "It kinda gives you, it's a . . . it's an unexplainable feeling. Like when I was in the delivery room and he came, and he was there, you know, and he looked at me . . . it was like, you're in awe. That's the best way I can say it, you're in awe! You're like, wow! He looks at you and your body like tingles . . . it's almost like catching the Holy Ghost or something!"[118]

The joy associated with fatherhood continues well after the child is born. According to Allen and Doherty of the University of Minnesota, the ten teenage fathers who participated in their study "used spiritual metaphors to describe their becoming and being fathers. ET [one of the participants] referred to his daughter as 'a gift from God' and described his becoming a father as a 'blessing,' something that had changed his life for the better. Others cited parental obligation as having brought purpose to their lives. Despite regrets about the timing of their transition to parenthood, most of the group felt capable of 'being there' for their children."[119]

Satisfaction about fatherhood continues well into adulthood for many teen fathers. Results from the National Survey of Families and Households indicate that "men who are adolescent fathers reported greater satisfaction as adult parents than men who fathered as adults."[120] Happiness about fatherhood appears to flourish even though adolescent fathers are also at risk for depression, which is a by-product of the stresses associated with becoming a father at an early age. It is believed that the fulfillment a father experiences as a parent helps him to persist with his parenting duties when he is struggling with depression.[121]

A small percentage of teen fathers show no joy about becoming a parent, however, and they have no intentions of supporting their partners and children. For example, Andres, a young man who became a father at age nineteen, described how he did everything is his power to avoid acknowledging his paternity: "I ended up in court for non-payment of child support. I was 19 years old and being threatened with jail time if I didn't make good with some cash. Well, a paternity test was done, and it ended up that the kid was mine. I knew all along that the kid was mine. But, I didn't want to admit it because things were going so smoothly for me."[122]

Unfortunately, although most teenage fathers have committed, romantic relationships with their partners prior to the pregnancy, a substantial percentage of them gradually reduce their contact with and their support of their partners and their children over time. In my prior analysis of numerous research studies pertaining to this subject,[123] I determined that approximately two-thirds to three-quarters of the teenage fathers from various studies had regular contact with their partners during the pregnancy and had supported their partner and the baby in various ways at least through the first year of the baby's life. However, somewhere between only one-fifth and one-third of all fathers were still substantially involved in the lives of the partner and child three years after the child's birth. Other scholars have reached the same conclusion as I did: the relationship between young fathers and their partners tends to weaken over time.[124] For example, based on their review of related research, Christina Gee of George Washington University and Jean Rhodes of the University of Massachusetts-Boston estimated that at least half of teen fathers were still involved with their partners during the second year of the child's life. However, in one study in which longitudinal data were collected, only "26 percent of adolescent mothers reported close (defined as frequent and emotionally positive contact) relationships with their child's father at 3 years postpartum, [and] this percentage declined to

12 percent at 6 years postpartum."[125] Reporting their own data from a study of social support, social strain, and relationship continuity of adolescent mothers, Gee and Rhodes again found that the adolescent mothers perceived their partner's support to decline from the time of the birth of the couple's child through the first three years postpartum. At childbirth, 51 percent of the mothers had identified the child's father as a significant source of social support, but only 27 percent stated the fathers were a part of their social-support networks by the third year postpartum.[126]

Why do teen fathers tend to reduce their contact and withdraw their support for their partners and their children over time? Answering that question requires an extensive analysis of the many stresses and strains associated with becoming a father while a teenager, which are the subjects I address next.

4

The Service Needs of Adolescent Fathers

Addressing Hardships and Societal Neglect

Life was never easy for William. He was the youngest of three children raised by a single mom in a rough inner-city neighborhood. She did her best to provide for her two sons and her daughter, working as a custodian for the local school district. Like most good parents, she had positive dreams for her children, hoping they would complete high school, go on to college, and get a decent job so they could have a better life than she had had. But things didn't work out that way for any of her children, including William.

William's older brother got involved in a gang at an early age, and by the time he was an adult, William's mom sent the brother packing, telling him that he could no longer live under her roof as long as he continued to run with his "evil" friends. William's sister got pregnant at age fifteen and had a baby out of wedlock at age sixteen. She kept her child, continued to live with the family, and spent the next nine years of her life in a state of constant conflict with William's mom. Initially, William seemed to be headed in a different direction than his brother and sister. During his early elementary school years, he was a "B" student and he rarely got into trouble. His mom thought he had potential, but something happened to turn his early forward progress out of kilter. Around the fourth grade, he mysteriously became moody and oppositional toward his mother, and he lost interest in school. Although he never became an outlandish delinquent like his brother, he nevertheless changed for the worse, and he just seemed to go through the motions of life until he fathered a child at the age of seventeen.

William was no idiot. He knew that a guy could get a girl pregnant by having sex just one time if neither the guy nor the girl used a reliable form of contraception. So, most of the time when he had sex with his girlfriend, Anita, he used a condom, and the two managed to avoid causing a conception for about six months of sexual relations. But inconsistent condom use is a dangerous game to play, especially when a couple like William and Anita likes to smoke a little marijuana while making love with each other. The young lovers eventually discovered the cost of their inconsistency when Anita got pregnant just before she turned seventeen.

William was blown away when he got the news. He knew his mom would "freak out," and he knew that Anita's mom would too. So, he decided right away that he would drop out of school and get a job to support Anita and the baby. "After all," he told himself, "I'm not getting anywhere in school anyway." So, he and Anita dealt with the uncomfortable moments when they had to tell both single mothers about the pregnancy and their decision to keep the child. These were not happy moments for either family. William's mom was crushed. She had considered William to be the "last hope" among her children, and now he "had ruined his life." Anita's mom reacted pretty much the same way, and she was furious at both teenagers for their irresponsible behavior. Anita's mom made some nasty comments about William's mother and her family when the two got together to talk about the pregnancy, and those remarks set the stage for years of icy resentment between the two families that would never melt away. Nevertheless, both kids gave their relationship their best shot, and for a while they responded to their difficult situation in admirable ways. Anita continued to attend school until her baby was born, and William got a part-time job in a local department store. He also "sold weed here and there" to pick up some extra cash, and he kept about half of his money and gave the rest to Anita.

Shortly after their daughter, Annuncia, was born, things took a turn for the worse. The department store folded, and William was out of a job. This cut into the amount of money he could give to Anita, which further ignited her mother's anger toward William and his family. Soon visitation with Annuncia became a problem. Anita started to side with her mom, and she told William he had better start to "put up or shut up" when it came to providing for his baby or else he would not be allowed to see her. She was also upset with William because she had heard a rumor that he now had his eye on another young woman who lived in their neighborhood. Now, Anita didn't want anything to do with "a man who prefers a home wrecker over me." William's subsequent visits to Anita's home often deteriorated into shouting matches that started between him and Anita and were escalated by Anita's mother. In one of those instances, the police were called, and William was ordered to go home or he would be tossed into jail.

By the time Annuncia was twenty months old, William was rarely seeing his daughter. Also around this time it became clear that something was wrong with Annuncia, who had been born six weeks prematurely. Her pediatrician had been concerned since Annuncia's birth that the she might suffer later difficulties due to her early delivery. True to these fears, Annuncia demonstrated delays in her motor skills and language development, which became a constant source of worry for both families. William was not equipped to deal with this setback. He felt helpless, and he saw his situation as being beyond his power to control. At one point, he decided he needed help from someone who might be able to give him answers regarding his complicated situation. But to whom could he turn? His father had never been a part of his life, so William knew he could not rely on him for any paternal guidance. And he dared not seek the advice of his wayward brother, whose judgment was not even worth considering. Desperate, William remembered seeing a highway billboard featuring a toll-free hotline for people in crisis. He walked to the highway, wrote down the number, and made a call to the hotline from a pay phone located outside a convenience store. The woman who answered the phone was a nice person, but she didn't know of any phone numbers for programs for teen fathers to give him. But she did suggest to William that he try calling his local mental health center so that he could talk to a counselor there about his problems. William scribbled down the number for the agency as the crisis operator recited it to him, but he later threw the number out, fearing that he would appear to be some kind of a nut case if he were to be seen going to a psychiatric facility for assistance. That would be his last attempt to get help for many years. Temporarily, he gave up on visiting his daughter, and he became a stranger to her.

Several years later, I received a call from William late one night while I was working in my office at The College of New Jersey. His mom had gotten my number from a friend of hers who had enrolled in one of my graduate courses in counseling a few years earlier. William sounded scared, and he rambled a bit as he awkwardly asked me if he could come to me for counseling. I told him how much I appreciated his call, and quickly assured him that I was confident I could help him because I had learned quite a bit about guys who become fathers at an early age. This little bit of information seemed to convince William that I was a person whom he might be able to trust, so he agreed to meet me the following week for what would be the first of over two dozen sessions we would have over the next two years. During that period of time, I learned William's life story, including the details that I have just shared. We explored the many issues that had placed him at risk for becoming a father and the forces that had contributed to his gradual withdrawal from his daughter, Annuncia. We established a plan for ending the feud between Anita and him and for resuming his relationship with

Annuncia. Many months later, after numerous ups and downs associated with implementing this plan, we celebrated together the day Anita granted him the first of many visits that allowed him ever so slowly to re-engage his daughter in his life.

Like William, most teenage fathers grapple with a host of hardships, including the adverse circumstances that play a role in their becoming fathers, and the difficult experiences associated with being an adolescent parent. Typically, sexually active boys are stunned when they learn their partner is pregnant, and they are flooded with a wide range of unsettling emotions as they try to cope with the demands of fatherhood. Many boys who are already disillusioned with their educations view fatherhood a compelling, final reason to drop out of school, and other boys who might want to complete school find it impossible to do so in light of the increasing hours they spend in the work force and attending to their children. Their work histories tend to be problematic and marked by limited career options, sporadic employment, and employment in informal jobs and the underground economy. Consequently, it is common for teen fathers to have difficulty supporting a family financially, which makes them poor candidates for marriage. Due to their limited economic resources, adolescent fathers typically struggle to make either formal or informal child-support payments, which is a major source of tension between teen fathers and their partners and their partners' families. Conflicts over finances and a number of other issues take their toll, and the majority of teen-parent couples eventually break up. Amid these conflicts, teen fathers are often denied access to their children, particularly when a young father fails to pay child support or if he demonstrates an antisocial lifestyle. Young men who make an earnest effort to be good fathers experience profound stress when they are prevented from seeing their children, and worry about the well-being of their children is a common concern. Compared to children born to adult couples in their twenties, the children of teen fathers are more likely to be born prematurely, to die or suffer some type of serious injury while babies, to have cognitive deficits, and to rely on public assistance once they reach adulthood.

Although teen fathers want help with the many problems associated with early paternity, it is common for them to tackle the challenges of fatherhood without sufficient guidance about what it means to be a man or a father. Although adolescent fathers identify their mothers as a primary person they can turn to for help, a troubling percentage of teen fathers face the challenges of fatherhood without the caring direction of an adult male or the substantive support of their peers. Some young fathers have extremely dysfunctional parents whose behaviors complicate the transition to parenthood for these young men. The majority of teen fathers need and want preparation for fatherhood, skills to enhance their relationships with their partner and their partner's family, career counseling, job skills training and placement, legal advice regarding paternity matters, and mental health services. Nevertheless, they tend to be disregarded by health, educational, social service, and mental health professionals or treated in ways that devalue their roles as parents. Many young fathers also avoid using professional services due to fears of prosecution and traditional masculine hang-ups about seeking help, while others are simply too overwhelmed by their circumstances to utilize services.

In this chapter, I chronicle these problems and document the historical disregard of teen fathers by society, beginning with a description of the emotional impact of an unplanned pregnancy on the lives of teenage boys who become parents.

Shock, Stress, Worry, and Depression

Approximately 51 percent of boys age twelve to nineteen have never really thought about what their life would be like if they were involved in a pregnancy as a teenager,[1] suggesting that an unintended pregnancy would be a big shock to many boys. Indeed, it is common for expectant teen fathers to be stunned when they learn that sex with a girlfriend has resulted in a pregnancy. As one teen father stated: "When you're having sex, you aren't thinking about this [pregnancy], what's going to be the result. You don't be thinking about drawing back at the time. Then you're thinking about, 'I got a kid on the way.' It's instant man! And it ain't nothing you can do about it. That's just how it is."[2]

Adolescent males who have considered the implications of a pregnancy typically view an unintended conception as a significantly stressful life event. Boys from two high schools in San Francisco reported that there were serious consequences for getting a partner pregnant, including becoming upset and stressed and getting in trouble with parents.[3] Considering what it would be like for a young man in this situation, the boys responded, "His life would be messed up,"[4] and the pregnancy would prevent him from achieving his life goals.[5]

The reports of teen fathers verify that adolescent fatherhood can be a highly stressful life experience from the teenage years into adulthood. Meeting the demands of fatherhood can be shocking and taxing, which was the case with this teen father: "I didn't think there was this much responsibilities. I mean, there's hundreds of 'em! Some weeks I plan for me and [my child] to do somethin' the whole week and it's like, and I didn't know in between he was going to wet his clothes, and now I gotta change him, and I gotta do this, and I gotta [do that]."[6]

Compared to their non-father peers and older fathers in their twenties, adolescent fathers show more symptoms of depression.[7] Young fathers also have significantly less general life satisfaction, overall social support, community satisfaction, and friend support than do non-father peers.[8] Self-esteem, typically healthy before the pregnancy, can plummet after the onset of fatherhood.[9] Stress and depression are likely to grow worse after the birth of the child and to persist into adulthood as the young fathers attempt to cope with the many twists and turns in their relationships with their partners and their families.[10] Feelings of anger, sadness, nervousness, tension, and helplessness are common.[11]

What problems are the bases for these emotional difficulties? Teen fathers worry about a number of concerns, such as addressing relationship conflicts with their partners, having access to their children, meeting their financial obligations due to a lack of money, completing school, finding a job, and being competent fathers.[12] It is also common for young fathers from bad neighborhoods and those who are involved in drugs to experience difficulties with their families and the police.[13] Some report that the judicial system is unfair when it comes to supporting paternal rights, and they complain that their former partner or wife shows a lack of respect for their role as fathers by denying them visits with their child.[14] Many lament the absence of a father role model to guide them during this difficult period in their lives.[15] Others are confused about how to establish paternity, and they feel that social-service institutions devalue fathers by excluding them from services and from important decisions that affect the well-being of their children.[16] A handful express disbelief that the child is theirs, or they have trouble with the fact that the child is not of the sex the father had desired.[17] Because these problems can impede father-child involvement, an in-depth analysis of these issues follows.

School and Employment Difficulties and the Underground Economy

Teen fathers tend to have the lowest educational expectations and aspirations in comparison to other males, and they are about three times more likely than non-fathers to drop out of school.[18] Maureen Pirog-Good of Indiana University, the author of a major national study regarding the educational outcomes of teen fathers, believes that the majority of teen fathers probably lag behind other boys in school achievement prior to the onset of their partner's pregnancy. Although some young men drop of school and later become adolescent parents, it is more common among the young men who eventually become teen fathers to be disillusioned with school prior to the births of their children and to become even more dissatisfied with their education after becoming parents.[19] Thus, the boys who become teen fathers are typically like William—well on their way to dropping out of school, and deciding to do so after they become parents.

The amount of hours a teen father spends at work while still a student could play a role in his decision to drop out. Youths who leave school are more likely to have worked twenty-one hours or more per week than students who complete school.[20] Finding a job providing substantial hours of employment may make working a higher priority than school for teen fathers and prompt them to leave educational programs,[21] as was the case with Andrew, an eighteen-year-old teen father: "When I got a job on the night shift at the foundry, I didn't have time to stay in school any more. Besides, what difference would it've meant? I wasn't doing squat in school, and I was tired all the time from work and running back and forth between my house and my kid's house where he lives with his mother. Somethin' had to give, so school was it."

The failure to complete high school typically has a detrimental impact on a young man's work history. Men who drop out of school tend to have high job turnover rates as they drift from job to job over the course of their lives.[22] Compared to other males who complete high school or college, dropouts experience higher rates of unemployment[23] and longer spells of being out of work.[24] Not surprisingly, teen fathers who have dropped out of school experience similar employment difficulties,[25] and many of them, like this young man, can become hopeless about having a successful career: "I just give up on everything. . . . I know that sounds like suicide, but that's not really what it is, I just have those thoughts sometimes. . . . Whenever I don't have a job . . . or get into some bad luck . . . [I also have] devious thoughts . . . [about] how to get money . . . but then I don't wanna go to jail, so I sit and do nothing."[26]

Dropping out of school increases the odds that a young father will have difficulty providing for his partner and child over the long term. The educational disadvantages of being a dropout result in fewer and less-lucrative opportunities in the labor market in adulthood, which gradually yet steadily reduces the ability of the father to support himself and his child as the youth ages.[27]

Although some teen fathers who are school dropouts express an interest in obtaining their GED as part of their plan to improve their life circumstances, they also find it difficult to either enroll in or complete GED programs due to their work responsibilities and complicated lives.[28] Other teen fathers, particularly those with impoverished backgrounds, view working toward a GED to be a waste of their time. For example, Beto, a young father interviewed by Rudy Hernandez in his riveting study of Chicano fathers, was well on his way to giving up on school when he learned that he was about to become a father. So, once his girlfriend got pregnant, he dropped out of school to care for her and their baby, as well as his younger siblings. He proclaimed that he had seen no value in going back to school to complete his education: "For what? My carnal [brother] graduated and he's working at the same place I am. He's four years older and I got him the job there. Really, I think my carnal is the only vato [dude] there who graduated. So I go to adult ed . . . so what? You think that if I went to adult ed people are going to line up to give me $100,000 a year job? Adult ed is useless."[29] For young fathers like Beto, GED classes must be coupled with training for the types of jobs that will realistically improve the life circumstances of young men, or else those classes are likely to be sparsely attended.

Although boys and girls from all socioeconomic levels become parents during their teenage years, adolescent parenthood is concentrated among the poor. Few writers have communicated this point as vividly as Rudy Hernandez: "While poverty and limited opportunities may, in part, be perpetuated by teen pregnancy, the fact is that 38 percent of all teens live in poverty and *that* 38 percent is responsible for 83 percent of all teen pregnancies."[30] Hernandez argued that poverty and bleak employment prospects play a key role in the rising number of Latino fathers who don't marry: "Jobs that require even minimal training are being relocated outside city limits, creating highly concentrated pockets of poverty in inner cities—barrios—where most Latinos live. . . . Moreover, increasing unemployment has seriously decreased the number of marriageable men and consequently there is a rise in female-headed households."[31]

Poverty and employment difficulties are common facts of life for teen fathers across racial and ethnic lines. Investigators working in a special service program for young fathers in rural and urban parts of Maine documented that the majority of the fifty-three primarily white men seeking assistance with their fatherhood needs were poor and out of work.[32] Chicano adolescent fathers from several urban areas in Michigan reported similar difficulties as they valiantly attempted to take care of their fatherhood duties in the face of grinding poverty and slim job prospects.[33] Poverty and chronic unemployment are also harsh realities for hundreds of inner-city African-American males who have fathered children with adolescent mothers.[34]

The dismal life circumstances of some teen fathers are almost too horrible to be true, yet they are all too real. For example, a group of thirty-five teen fathers who were the focus of the Oregon Youth Study had attended schools with the highest rates of delinquent episodes. There was a tendency for these boys to live in poverty and in single-parent homes. School failure, poor monitoring by parents, substance abuse, and risky sexual behavior were common, and it appeared that most of the boys had abandoned any hope of having legitimate employment.[35] It is hard to imagine trying to be an effective parent under these conditions.

In the face of these types of hardships, many young men turn to illegal activities either as a primary or secondary source of income. Rudy Hernandez explained:

> Increasingly unemployment and shriveling opportunities for even poorly paid jobs also have forced many Latino youths to wander in and out of the underground economy in order to contribute to their families' financial stability. . . . Nearly all studies of contemporary barrio youth life (read: gang literature) support the notion that young Latino men turn to "street culture," informal—oftentimes illegal—economy, as a means to eke out an existence and earn respect in the absences of many viable opportunities. . . . These alternative forms of "getting over" usually mean getting exploited by older men who have them "selling wares" for low pay, working long hours and in dangerous conditions and with the constant risk of imprisonment—hardly the hands-over-fist of cash that the media would lead us to believe is inherent to selling drugs.[36]

A pattern of illegal activity and exploitation by older men is common in many of our nation's troubled communities. Like the teen fathers from the barrios of Detroit, Lansing, and Adrian, Michigan, which were the areas where Hernandez did his research, numerous teenage African-American, Latino, and white teen fathers across America have been engaged by older men to engage in the drug trafficking industry. One young father explained how the drug trade worked in his neighborhood: "Where I lived at it was just a natural thing that . . . the older guys get you connected up or if an older guy admired a young guy, a young boy, which they call us young boys and old heads, that's how it is. . . . If they admire a young boy, the old heads take him under, you know . . . have him on a corner to sell or might have him go deliver something or take something to somebody. . . . It's good money."[37]

Working in the underground economy provides financially strapped adolescents and young adult men a way to live up to the masculine expectation that a man is a reliable provider. Indeed, the majority of the fathers Hernandez interviewed sold drugs to supplement their incomes and saw their work in illegal activities as *just one of many* ways they were trying to be responsible men who cared for their partners and their children. Beto, one of those fathers, expressed pride at being able to provide for his family through a combination of legal and illegal employment: "I'm doing good. I work two shifts and I have a little jale [selling marijuana and cocaine] on the side. So, my vieja [partner] and my babies have everything they need."[38]

Because legitimate forms of employment are very limited and pay only the minimum wage, some fathers view participation in the drug trade as a necessary source of income. As one father put it, "All I can do is these stupid ... jobs making minimum wage—that's why I gotta do stuff on the side."[39]

Because drug involvement is linked to many dangers and poor outcomes, such as violence, addiction, and incarceration, it can serve as a barrier to father involvement. Indeed, 53 percent of 173 teen fathers from one urban area reported that their drug involvement impaired their ability to provide care for their children.[40] Nevertheless, teen fathers from poor inner cities may feel pulled into the world of illegal drugs in spite of its dangers and its impact on father-child relations: "Job scarcity in impoverished communities makes drug dealing the only viable economic option for many youth. Thus, a teen father's involvement in drug dealing paradoxically may allow him to contribute financially, even as it draws him into a world incompatible with healthy child rearing."[41]

Most teen fathers appear willing to work, and they will consider a wide range of options—both legal and illegal—to improve their economic circumstances. The majority of teen fathers (nearly 84 percent) would work even if they could live comfortably without working.[42] In addition, teen fathers are significantly more likely than non-fathers to report that they are willing to enter job training and apply for food stamps.[43] Furthermore, it is common for adolescent fathers to take on a variety of informal jobs, such as painting houses and washing cars, to earn money.[44] Teen fathers also are significantly more likely than non-fathers to endorse the belief of resorting to shoplifting if unable to support one's family.[45] So, boys who become parents while teenagers are, on the whole, an industrious bunch who are eager to enter the labor market, but are willing to turn to illegal means to survive.

Although it appears that most of the teen fathers who enter the drug trade and other forms of criminal activities do so only as a last resort, it must be acknowledged that a small percentage of those who commit crimes thrive on exploiting and manipulating others and rebelling against all forms of authority. Because these particular young men have serious character disorders, they resort to theft, robbery, drug distribution, and violent behavior even when they have opportunities for gainful employment. For them, breaking the law is a way of life, and they show little desire and capacity for legitimate work. So, their problems in the world of work are of their own doing.[46]

Whether teen fathers enter the labor market and then decide to have children or having children causes them enter the labor market, it is clear that teen fathers tend to enter the labor market earlier and have less long-term success than their non-father peers. Although they start working earlier than non-fathers do, adolescent fathers are at a clear disadvantage by the time they reach their mid- to late twenties, at which time they spend more weeks out of the labor force, spend more weeks unemployed, and earn less income.[47] Keeping a job year-round is an especially demoralizing problem for unwed teen fathers, for they are about 60 percent less likely to work year-round than are comparable men who never had children before marrying.[48] In light of these employment and earning difficulties, it is not surprising that adolescent fathers have trouble keeping up with their child-support payments.

Difficulty Meeting Child-Support Payments

Poor family backgrounds, dismal employment histories, and economic hardships make it difficult for many teen fathers to make full child-support payments to their partners, even when they want to be good providers for their child.[49] One nineteen-year-old father had this to say to me about the problems he had financially supporting his child: "It's tough out there, man. You be trying to get your little job, you know, and the one you get don't pay you enough to ever get ahead on nothin', man. It's like I wanna buy this and I wanna buy that for my baby, and give my baby's momma some money, but sometimes all I can do is just scrape a little bit a' money together and that's it, man."

Impoverished teen fathers often attempt to compensate for their inability to furnish formal child-support payments in a number of informal ways. The father may live with his partner and provide child care for periods ranging from a few days to a few months.[50] As often as they can, the majority of teen fathers contribute cash or necessary living items to both mother and child.[51] Most also help the mother of their child in other ways, such as providing them with emotional support, transportation, and gifts while the mother is pregnant and after the baby is born.[52]

Young men who have limited incomes and try to support their partners and children in informal ways will sometimes make sure that their efforts are visible so that others can see that they are fulfilling their obligations, as is evidenced by this father's proclamation:

Yup, when I buy things myself and carry 'em over it's better because then . . . you know how neighbors be all nosy, into everybody's business and everything. . . . Like they always be sayin' this child's father don't do nothing for him and I only seen that child's father bring Pampers over to the house one time, you know. . . . They be countin' and sayin' whether this man or that man deserve respect . . . on account of what they see from their porches and stuff. . . . And like I don't want that kinda reputation to bounce offa me and my family. . . . So I just buy the things my daughter needs and make sure at least somebody sees that I brought the baby somethin'.[53]

Making these types of demonstrations of support increase the odds that a father's paternal rights will be respected, in spite of his financial limitations.[54] Nevertheless, the financial hardships of many teen fathers make them less suitable candidates for marriage. When their limited economic resources impact their ability to pay child support, they not only can get in trouble with child-support officials, but their relationships with their partners can deteriorate and access to their child might be denied.

The Teen Father's Relationship Problems with His Partner

The economic hardships of teen fathers set the stage for problems in their relationships with their partners, beginning with the decision about whether or not the young couple should marry. Marriage tends to be neither a preferred nor a successful option for adolescent parents, and a primary reason teen fathers don't marry their partners is because they lack the financial resources to support a family. Too many young fathers have employment difficulties.[55] As a result, teen fathers worry all the time about how they are going to earn enough money to sustain a family.[56] The limited earning power of these young men is a major factor in the couple's decision not to marry. In his classic longitudinal study of adolescent parents, Frank Furstenberg of the University of Pennsylvania found that most of the adolescent mothers in his study wanted to marry the father of the child *if* and *when* they thought he would be capable of supporting a family.[57] The fact that couples who have the financial resources to support a family appear to prefer marriage as a form of pregnancy resolution is further evidence of the importance of economic factors in considering marriage.[58]

Approximately 89 percent of first-time teen mothers become pregnant outside of marriage, and only 16 percent of them marry before the baby is born.[59] When teen parents do make the decision to marry, they face tough odds that the marriage will survive. Adolescent marriages have greater discord than do adult marriages,[60] and the divorce rate is greater for teenage than adult couples.[61] Cohabitational arrangements of adolescent couples are also very fragile, usually ending in a separation.[62] Overall, relationships between adolescent parents are unstable and they deteriorate over time.[63]

Why do the marital bonds of teenage mothers and fathers tend to fray? Adolescents entering marriage are unlikely to have a clear understanding of the strains that can occur in a marriage or of the sustained effort and commitment that are required to make a marriage succeed. So, unrealistic expectations about the marital relationship might contribute to the demise of marriages among adolescent couples.[64] Forced marriages between incompatible and very young teens to legitimate a pregnancy are particularly apt to end in divorce and are especially prone to be unhappy and characterized by low income.[65] In addition, many young parents may have a number of social, psychological, familial, and economic problems that predispose the couple toward distress, and the responsibilities of parenthood can exacerbate these difficulties.[66] For example, fulfilling parental and marital duties might impede the educational progress of teenage parents. Adolescent mothers who leave their families to reside with the father of their child are less likely to achieve their educational aspirations than those mothers who remain with their families.[67] Also, for teenage fathers, living with the child (and presumably with the child's mother) is directly related to adverse educational consequences.[68] The failure to complete high school can worsen the economic prospects of the couple and further stress their relationship. Finally, welfare policies might undermine marriage for some young couples. In certain circumstances, an employed father who decides to marry or live with his partner can hurt his family financially if the mother is receiving public assistance; according to welfare policies, his marriage to the mother or his presence in the home could result in the reduction or termination of Temporary Assistance for Needy Families (TANF) (welfare) and Medicaid benefits.[69] Consequently, some couples who decide to live apart for economic reasons report a withering away of the emotional connection between them because they "can't live like a normal family."

Whether they marry or—as is more commonly the case—remain single, expectant teenager mothers and fathers are often on rocky ground, which helps to explain why so many young couples involved in an adolescent pregnancy tend to break up. Expectant teen parents tend to engage in problematic patterns of relations. For example, compared to non-expectant teen couples, expectant adolescent couples engage in significantly higher rates of hostile interpersonal interactions and significantly lower rates of warm interactions. Young expectant couples also demonstrate higher rates of demand-withdraw patterns of behavior, which are characterized by one partner exerting control and pressure for change and the other partner maintaining a position of autonomy by avoidant withdrawal and distancing.[70] The demand-withdraw pattern is associated with poor conflict resolution, discord, and dissatisfaction in the relationship, which "may compromise the couple's ability to successfully navigate the transition to parenthood, raising the risk for several problems, such as negative parenting behavior, unstable family environments, and paternal disengagement."[71] These negative behavioral patterns "may be due to the stress associated with adolescent pregnancy."[72] The sources of this stress probably include "the various financial, interpersonal, and social pressures associated with the onset of parenthood, as well as the ambivalent feelings about the prospects of becoming a parent."[73]

A wide range of issues could contribute to dysfunctional relationships between teenage mothers and fathers. Adolescent mothers often attribute their relationship difficulties to "problems with their male partners ranging from disappointments over unmet expectations for financial and child-care assistance to serious conflicts, difficult break-ups, and physical and sexual assault."[74] In comparison, teen fathers consistently report that disputes with their female partners over child rearing, child support, and visitation are significant sources of strain in the couple's relationship.[75] It also appears that a high number of stressful events in the life of the adolescent mother, such as the death of a family member or friend, or the divorce or separation of her parents, can loosen the bonds between her and the baby's father.[76]

Problems with Visitation and Access to the Baby

A consistent source of significant stress for adolescent fathers is that they are denied access to their child by their partner and her parents.[77] For example, seven (30 percent) of the fathers participating in one study "reported that involvement with their children depended on the child's mother and/or her family members; 3 of these stated that the child's mother and/or mother's family prevented their involvement currently."[78] A teenager who was interviewed in another study by William Allen and William Doherty of the University of Minnesota described how difficulties between him and his child's mother affected the quantity and quality of time he spent with his son: "Well, like when me and [partner] weren't fond of each other, it kept me and my son apart. She would always [say], 'I don't want to see you today,' or I would want to see my son, and me and her were fightin'. I would say, 'Well I'm comin' over' . . . and she'd say, 'No, you don't,' and leave. And I would come over there and she'd be gone."[79]

Other fathers reported to Allen and Doherty that they would sometimes receive verbal abuse and threats from their partner's family when they tried to visit: "Another young man detailed how after trying repeatedly to see his child and the child's mother, he was chased at gunpoint from her father's house by some of her relatives."[80]

Teen fathers might disengage from their partners because of the discomfort they experience when visiting a partner who is romantically involved with another man or because they sense that the new man in the mother's life has taken on the role of surrogate father for the mother's child.[81] As the following young man's report illustrates, the presence of another man in a former partner's life can make it very awkward for a father to enjoy visits with his child: "You don't want somebody else to come in and then your son or daughter will call them 'daddy.' You'll come visit and want to spend time with your child and you can't because your girlfriend says, 'I got somebody else over here.'"[82]

Since most teen mothers are unmarried and many of them live with their single mothers, the maternal grandmother is seen as a crucial gatekeeper to her daughter and her baby. Consequently, if adolescent fathers want to have regular contact with their children, they must develop positive relationships with the maternal grandmothers, probably before the birth of their infants, or else they may jeopardize their chances for getting to see and know their child well.[83]

Several factors, including a young man's ability to support his child financially, the quality of his relationship with his partner and her parents, and his competency as a father appear to determine if he is granted access to his child.[84] Some maternal grandparents will honor the paternal rights of an adolescent father who treats his partner and child in a loving manner, even if his ability to pay child support is severely limited.[85] In other cases, however, he is presumed by the family to be unfit and prevented from seeing his child even if he makes required child-support payments and makes an effort to remain engaged in his child's life.[86] Sometimes a teen mother may even disavow the paternity of a father during periods of estrangement. This decision may or may not have anything to do with his performance as a parent. The mother may use access to the child as a ploy to coerce the father to remain romantically involved with her or as a way to punish him for the end of their romantic relationship.[87] In very severe cases, referred to in the clinical literature as parental alienation syndrome, the mother successfully turns the child against the father through covert or overt manipulations that result in the destruction of a warm and loving father-child relationship.[88]

Fathers who are denied access to their children, particularly those who are the targets of parental alienation, report feelings of extreme frustration, anger, and worry.[89] In a qualitative investigation of non-custodial males who wanted to be engaged with their children, Ron Lehr and Peter MacMillan, a pair of researchers from Canada, documented that the experience of forced separation from one's child is extremely stressful for caring young fathers. Many of the eighteen low-income or unemployed fathers who participated in this study, including a sample of teen fathers, felt that their partners had little respect for their rights as fathers and low confidence in their ability to care for a child properly. It seemed that nothing they did was ever enough to please their partner or her family. The fathers reported considerable amounts of interference from the maternal grandparents. The fathers also had little faith that the courts were ever on their side, as was evidenced by their statements about the legal system:

"My biggest frustration is the law."

"I do not have a positive hope that I will win in the court room."

"In court, I already have the attitude that I am going to lose."

"The judge doesn't seem to care."

"Any accusation against the father is automatically taken as guilty until proven innocent."

"There's only three things a father can do to win custody of a child: if the mother abused the child, does drugs, or is an alcoholic."

"Judges still side with the mother because they still believe that the child should be with the mother."

"In court, the mother does not have to prove that she is innocent."

"In the field of parenting, we are not equals at all. When it comes to parenting, we are considered inferior."

"It is assumed that the mother is gonna be a better parent all around."

"From day one, I have been on the defense the whole time."

"What she said was gold and what I said was mud. I got tired of defending myself. This was about our fifth battle over access."

"An accusation takes me forever to clear up and then there are 10 more waiting for me."

"I find it a lot of pressure fighting for access to my kids all the time."[90]

Teen fathers who experience these types of roadblocks to their children sometimes give up on fighting their partners in court and abdicate the right to visit their child. Others, such as this young father, respond by cutting off payments of child support: "They tell me, 'Stay away but send money.' But I ain't sendin' nothin' if I can't see my baby boy!"[91]

Tragically, after extended periods of fruitless efforts, some young men give up trying to maintain a father-child relationship and wall off their feelings for their child in an attempt to protect themselves from additional heartache. Tom, a twenty-year-old, did exactly that:

I was sixteen when my baby was born, but from day one my girlfriend and her mother never wanted me around. They had some other guy in mind for her, so that left me out of the picture. I talked with 'em about it, brought 'em and my baby gifts, fought with 'em about it, and took 'em to court about it. And nothin' worked—NOTHIN' MAN! At first, I kept tellin' myself, "I gotta keep tryin'"—you know, for my baby's sake. But then I was like, "Man, you just can't win—you just can't beat the system." Everybody is against you. So, I just gave up and stopped thinkin' about him [his son]. And I try not to feel anything anymore because I just get too stressed out when I do.

The children who are the victims of parent alienation syndrome suffer in numerous ways. One young woman expressed to me her sense of bitterness after she and her father managed to develop a relationship during her adult life after years of suffering a separation that had been forced upon them:

I had no idea when I was growing up that my father was actually a decent man. My mother always had nothing good to say about him and I was never allowed to see him, even though I knew he tried to get in touch with me from time to time. For a while, I believed my father was some kind of monster or criminal who wanted nothing to do with me. But as I got older, I started to realize there were some things wrong with my mom, and when it was time for me to go to college, my dad finally found a way to get in touch with me there. At first I wasn't sure I wanted to see him, but a part of me was curious to know him and to find out why he was never there for me. So, I decided to meet him one time at a diner near my school. When I did, I was really scared and I had a lot of anger inside of me, and I let him have it shortly after we sat down together. But then he began to cry and he told me all of the things he went through—how he had been a teen father . . . how crazy my mom got . . . how he wasn't allowed to see me no matter how hard he tried . . . the money he spent on the lawyers and the courts. . . . I heard for the first time his point of view on the whole thing that happened between him and my mom. And it left me bitter that I never had the chance to have my father when I was a little girl. So, I am making up for lost time, now, and my dad and I have a good relationship. Even though we live in different states, he talks with me on the phone once a week and we email each other just about every day. . . . It's nice to have him in my life, to be able to say as other people do—that I have a father.

The severing of the father-child relationship is a great injustice to young men who demonstrate sincere efforts to be good fathers. Creating roadblocks between a caring father and his child can result in the termination of child support and lost opportunities for a child to grow up with the love of his or her biological father. However, it must be emphasized that a young mother and her family are quite justified for trying to keep a father at bay when he displays a cavalier and antisocial lifestyle. Some teen fathers are the architects of their own misery because they act in a self-centered manner that jeopardizes their relationships with their partners and children. Ron Lehr and Peter MacMillan observed this pattern among a portion of the young men who had participated in their support group for single fathers: "Some of the young fathers acknowledged they were not always good husbands nor good fathers. Some of them suggested that they contributed to their own difficulties by wanting to maintain a lifestyle similar to the one they had prior to having a child."[92]

A young father who was serving a ten-year state prison term for a variety of assaults, robberies, and drug convictions once shared regrets about his antisocial and promiscuous lifestyle during a psychotherapy session with me: "Man, I was always running wild on the streets, hanging out with my associates, getting into all kinds of crazy shit, when I should have been staying at home with my lady and my kids. And I always had to have another girlfriend on the side, you know, for some extra fun. . . . And look at where it got me—in here, and my lady's out there now with some other guy and I don't see my kids and they don't want to see me."

Although the responsibilities associated with fatherhood inspire some delinquent youth to give up antisocial activities,[93] it appears that most antisocial youth who become teen fathers actually grow to be *more* delinquent after the onset of fatherhood.[94] While an increase in some criminal activities may be associated with efforts to provide for a child, it is also likely that the intensification of delinquent behavior represents the ongoing development of an antisocial lifestyle characterized by a lack of empathy, the exploitation and manipulation of people, and the chronic violation of the rights of others through crime. It is an adaptive response on the part of loving parents to try to protect their daughter and grandchild from the potentially destructive influences of a teen father who shows this pattern of development. In these types of situations, the gate-keeping function of the family is to keep a deviant young man from doing harm to the daughter and her child. Thus, due to his own dysfunctional behavior, the father undermines any chance he might have had to a healthy bond with his child and to enjoy the privilege of being a truly engaged, loving father. Helping him to see the error of his ways must be a central focus of psychotherapy with such a young man.

Problems of the Children of Teen Parents

Approximately 86 percent of teenage fathers have a partner who is between the ages of fifteen and nineteen.[95] So the vast majority of these partners are teenage mothers. The children of these teen-parent couples are at risk to have a number of difficulties during childbirth, early childhood, and adulthood:

- According to national data regarding neonatal deaths, babies born to teen mothers age fifteen or younger are about four times as likely to die within their first year of life than were babies born to women age twenty-three to twenty-nine. Also, compared to babies born to women in their twenties, babies born to adolescents age sixteen to seventeen are three times more likely to die, and those born to adolescents age eighteen to nineteen are two and a half times more likely to die.[96]

- The sons and daughters of thirty-five adolescent fathers in a study conducted in Oregon were significantly more likely than children born to adults (age 20–42 years) to have premature births and to suffer some type of serious injury.[97]

- The daughters of teen mothers are nearly four times more likely to receive public financial support than the daughters of older women (twenty-five years old and above).[98]

- Compared to children born to older women, the children of teen mothers tend to score lower on tests of cognitive ability.[99]

Because teen parents tend to have poor child-rearing skills and experience a great deal of stress, there is public concern that they are at risk to abuse their children. However, based on her comprehensive review of research studies on child maltreatment and her analysis of statewide data from maltreatment reports in Illinois, Carol Massat of the University of Illinois at Chicago reported that adolescent parents are not overrepresented among maltreating parents or among parents of children in out-of-home care. Consequently, Massat concluded that the widespread belief that teen parents are more likely than adult parents to abuse their children is a myth that is deeply entrenched in our culture. Furthermore, she stated that the mechanism that seems to be producing negative outcomes for the children is not age alone. Other factors, such as low education levels, single-parent status, unshared responsibility for child care, and low socioeconomic status, which are correlated with adolescent parenthood, seem to be producing the negative outcomes for children of adolescent parents. These factors, she argued, have the net effect of reducing access to quality health care and viable career options, thereby increasing the risk of negative outcomes for children.[100]

Father Absence and Father-Son Wounds

A boy has a natural inclination to identify with his father, to appreciate his presence, and to seek his guidance.[101] Tragically, in communities where there is a high teenage pregnancy rate, there also is a high degree of father absence and dysfunctional fatherhood, which means that many male youths in those communities face their journey through life without a father or with a bad one. The frequency of father absence and father wounds in the lives of teen fathers is heartbreaking:

- 44 percent of the 173 teenage fathers from one urban setting reported that they had no father as a role model and that the absence of a caring father was a barrier to their involvement with their own children.[102]
- Debra Klinman, the project director for the Teen Father Collaboration study, which included approximately four hundred teenage fathers nationwide, reported that teenage fathers tend to have phantom fathers who are rarely present in their sons' lives.[103]
- In an investigation by Leo Hendricks of Howard University, 35 percent of twenty unwed, adolescent fathers reported living in father-absent homes.[104] In a later study by Hendricks, 40 percent of forty teenage fathers were raised in father-absent homes and about 70 percent of this sample reported that they felt closer to their mothers than to their fathers when they were growing up.[105]
- Janet Hardy and Laurie Zabin of Johns Hopkins University reported that the majority of the seventy-two teenage fathers from their study who were not living with the mother and child resided in single-mother households.[106]
- In his ethnographic analysis of young fathers from several inner-city neighborhoods, Mercer Sullivan discovered that only two of the eleven adolescent fathers from his study had grown up in households with father figures present, none of them had lived with their fathers for any extended period of time, two had been completely abandoned by their fathers, and one of the boy's fathers had murdered the boy's mother.[107]

It is common for teen fathers to take on many of the paternal responsibilities in their households because their own fathers were ineffective parents or were absent from their son's lives. Boys placed in the position of being a child parent understandably have low regard for their fathers. Five out of ten teen fathers from an investigation by Allen and Doherty gave their father a rating of 5 or less on a scale ranging from 0 = terrible to 10 = excellent. (Two gave their father a rating of 0.) One young man from the study shared the following sad commentary about fatherhood in his world: "I don't want my son growin' up like I did. There's a lot of kids who don't have fathers, or if they do have fathers they're in jail or on drugs or not working or don't care about anything else. . . . So what [if] they're a father. If you look at it, there's probably more dads out there that's not doin' what they should be doin' for their children than there is dads doin' everything they can."[108]

Six out of the seven young Chicano fathers interviewed by Rudy Hernandez had bad experiences with their own fathers, who were either absent from or abusive or neglectful toward their partners and children. A sampling of their stories conveys the range of father-son wounds these boys experienced.

One young man, Jesus, reported that his father repeatedly abandoned the boy's mother and children, only to return periodically and take charge of the house as though he had never left. Another boy, named Junior, reported that his father was a drunk, had an explosive temper, and was unfaithful to Junior's mother. A third boy, Beto, expressed outrage about his father, who had left his family for Texas to find work, started a second family there, and never came back to Beto and his family.[109]

Sadly, a boy can be hindered by the absence of a father or by the influence of an ineffectual one. Inadequate fathering is associated with low intellectual achievement, poor self-control and sexual confusion in sons.[110] A boy who lacks a father or a significant adult male role model in his life is likely to suffer from an inability to know his place in the world.[111] In an effort to define his maleness, he may imitate the behavior of other males, including other boys from the streets, who may communicate a message that he must become aggressive, violent, and a sexual exploiter to be considered masculine.[112]

Young men are profoundly affected by the absence of their fathers. They feel angry, hurt, and unimportant due to what they perceive to be parental unconcern and disinterest. Some can spend an entire lifetime mourning the absence of a caring father in their lives. Others, such as this seventeen-year-old teen father named Danny, demonstrate a determination to stop a tradition of child abandonment in the family: "I've got to stop the cycle—you know what I mean? I got to make sure that my kid knows me so that he don't grow up to abandon his kid like my father abandoned me and like his father ran out on him."

Unfortunately, although some teen fathers make a valiant effort to break the cycle of father absence with their children, having an absent father appears to increase the odds that a boy will forsake his paternal responsibilities. Poor fathering skills can be passed from father to son from generation to generation in families.[113] In a special report on the role of fathers in their children's lives, the National Institute of Child Health and Human Development concluded, "When fathers are not present in their children's lives, their sons are more likely to become fathers themselves when they are teenagers and to live apart from their children."[114] Some teenage fathers not only replicate the experience of father absence with their own children, but they also imitate other forms dysfunctional behavior that had been modeled by their own fathers. Consider the experience of Chris, a twenty-nine-year-old inmate, who described his father to me: "My old man was always out runnin' the streets, runnin' his games, droppin' in and out of my life and in and out of jail. And look at me—I ended up just like him, sittin' here in a jail cell, hoping that my kids will visit me on weekends and knowin' that ain't never gonna happen."

Dysfunctional Mothers and Mother-Son Wounds

Although the majority of adolescent fathers identify their mothers as the person they are most likely to turn to for assistance with the unplanned pregnancy,[115] some of them have very dysfunctional mothers who react in a pathological manner in response to the son becoming a father. For example, there are documented cases of single mothers who were unable to provide any reliable supervision for their children because of their addiction to drugs or involvement in prostitution. This lack of structure played a role in the children's risky sexual behavior that culminated in unplanned pregnancies.[116]

Many teenage fathers raised by dysfunctional mothers have described to me their deep resentment toward their moms for not making better choices in their lives and for "allowing all sorts of jokers to take advantage of her." In some families, single mothers cope with their loneliness by clinging to their sons and making them dependent and captive to the mother's emotional needs. Clinical experience suggests that these mothers experience an irrational sense of betrayal upon learning about the boy's role in an adolescent pregnancy, and in response give him a choice of denying his paternity or leaving the mother's home. In other instances, mothers have communicated to their sons an implicit message that "you can do no wrong." For example, in a television news interview, the mother of an adolescent boy expressed her support for her son who was a member of the gang, "The Spur Posse." Members of this gang espoused a cavalier sexual attitude toward adolescent girls. The mother denied any wrongdoing on the part of her son and accused the girls who were sexually involved with gang members of willful seduction and promiscuity. Essentially, by making this statement this mother gave her son permission to exploit girls and to not worry about the consequences of his behavior.

Lack of Understanding and Guidance about Fatherhood

One of the most important factors impacting a boy's response to becoming a parent during his teenage years is his notion of fatherhood and what it entails, and these notions vary greatly among adolescent fathers. Boys who have a good idea about what it means to be a father usually are determined to provide for their children in a consistent, dedicated manner. They emphasize that being a good father involves keeping a focus on one's family, being there for one's child and partner, taking care of responsibilities, and showing love.[117] However, other young fathers generally lack an understanding of appropriate fatherhood behaviors, and they tend to "perceive occasional visits with their children as more than minimal involvement."[118] They have poor parenting skills and demonstrate that their approach to fatherhood is that of controlling their children through coercive measures, such as harsh physical punishment.[119] They disappoint their partners by not helping enough with parenting duties.[120]

There are several reasons why some clusters of teen fathers are naïve about fatherhood. As was mentioned earlier, a disproportionate number of young men were raised without a father, or their own father or mother was a poor role model of what it means to be a parent. Although some samples of teen fathers have received emotional, social, and financial support from their families for their efforts to be good fathers, especially their mothers,[121] other young men have reported that no one in their life provided them with advice about fatherhood. They lament their poor understanding about how to be a father and the absence of any loving instruction about what father-hood means.[122] Thus, too many young men lack the wisdom of a caring adult to guide them during their journey to fatherhood.

Altered Peer Relationships

Although fathering a child prompts no changes in the time and manner some young men spend with their friends, teen fathers who accept their paternal responsibilities report that early fatherhood greatly affects their relationships with their peers. They are often left behind by their friends, or they feel out of place when they do attend parties and other social events for teenagers.[123] A consistent theme expressed by responsible teen fathers, such as this nineteen-year-old, is that taking care of a child supersedes going out with friends to have a good time: "One of the stresses I have is having to make sure I can provide for my family and feed them and buy all the diapers and everything I need and make sure I have the money for them to take care of all that. . . . I miss going out with the guys and a lot of my friends. But then I don't worry about who's got the party and where's everybody going. I know where I'm going to be at night now—at home."[124] Many teenage fathers want the support of their peers during the fatherhood experience. For example, 23 percent of the 56 teenage fathers interviewed by Leo Hendricks indicated that they were likely to turn to their peers when they needed help with a problem.

In spite of this need for peer support, however, adolescent fathers may be unlikely to receive it. Teenage fathers consistently report feeling socially isolated from peers, perhaps because the social limitations imposed by parenthood preclude sufficient peer interactions.[125] The loneliness of young fathers may also be related to an unwillingness or inability of peers to offer their support.[126] Sometimes teen fathers experience painful judgments by their non-father peers. One young father reported: "You [the adolescent father] feel that you're not as important as before you had the kid. Because when you got a kid, you're accepted but it's like you got a strike against you or something. They [peers] don't say nothing to you at school. It's like it's a strike against you to them. You got kids so you can't go to the show with them all the time. Always the kids come first!"[127]

Not all teen fathers place the needs of their children over the desire to be with friends, however. At times, the normal adolescent desire of the teenage father to socialize with other adolescents may conflict with the social obligations of parenthood. Demands from one of these theaters in his life can interfere with his satisfactory acclimation to the other. For example, the desire to date and to socialize may distract him from fully investing himself in his child and partner and retard his growth as a father.[128] A forty-six-year-old man I interviewed in prison shared this account of how he allowed his relationships with his friends to distract him from investing in his wife and daughter during his teen-father years: "My first old lady was really sweet and a darn good mother. But back then [when he was a teen father], I was too much into my macho bullshit to realize how good I had it. I always had to be hangin' out with the guys, hittin' the bars, foolin' around, and seeing what kinda trouble I could get myself into. . . . I hardly saw my daughter when she was young, so that's why wife divorced me when my kid was just two. I had a good thing in her [his former wife] and I blew it."

The Services That Teen Fathers Need

Teen fathers want emotional support during the transition to fatherhood, and information, practical help, and counseling to address problems with their partners, families, and communities.[129] The most frequently requested services include job referrals, vocational education, job readiness, parenting education, GED classes, legal advice regarding paternity establishment and child-support orders, medical treatment, mental health counseling, relationship counseling, and child-care assistance.[130]

Research has demonstrated that adolescent fathers are most likely to participate in a service program for fathers if it includes employment services. For example, among the hundreds of young fathers who participated in services provided by the Texas Fragile Families Initiative, 76 percent were attracted to their local fatherhood program because they wanted help finding a job and they believed that the program would help them secure employment.[131] Thus, career counseling, job training, and job placement services must be a central component of adolescent-father programs in order for them to be a success.

From a young father's perspective, employment-related services are essential. Most young men and their partners consider the provision of child support to be a primary responsibility of fathers. Employment difficulties can prevent a young man from being able to provide child support, which can be a source of considerable strain between him and his partner and her family, and a reason why they deny him access to his child. Consequently, many adolescent fathers might "assume relationship problems can be fixed by employment"[132] because partners and their families are more likely to recognize the paternal rights of a young man who works and provides them with consistent child-support payments.

The nature of the employment market is another reason why teen fathers must receive competent career and employment counseling. The job market for young fathers is extremely limited. Historically the unemployment rate is higher for younger men than older men.[133] To make matters worse for teen fathers, boys and young adult men seeking jobs tend to have very limited skills, while the market for low-skill workers has been declining due to structural shifts in the U.S. economy and the relocation of unskilled and semiskilled jobs abroad.[134] This shift has resulted in lower employment rates and a declining quality of life for low-skill workers.[135] Consequently, in order be more competitive in the job market, teen fathers must earn degrees in higher education or obtain some form of advanced technical training that will enable them to find jobs that will produce incomes that will help them to rise out of, or not fall into, poverty levels of existence.

Considering that teen fathers are overrepresented among adolescents who have been abused, have a psychiatric illness or substance-abuse problems, and engage in antisocial behavior, various forms of mental health counseling should be another essential components of teen-father programs. Mental health counseling sometimes has to be the first line of intervention because "some young fathers may need to receive counseling for more serious problems before they can accomplish other tasks."[136]

Counseling to enhance the relationships between teen parents is also essential. Teen fathers must be taught how to use empathic and problem-solving skills so that they can enjoy positive interactions with their partners. Couples counseling and multi-systems therapy are required to address serious conflicts that emerge between adolescent fathers and their partners and their families. Young fathers also need various forms of legal counseling to inform them about their responsibilities regarding child support and their rights regarding child visitation and custody.

Last but not least, young fathers need guidance about what it means to be a man and a father. Preparation for parenthood must include activities designed to clarify attitudes about masculinity and fatherhood, parenting-skills training, and family-planning information to prevent additional unintended pregnancies.

Why Teen Fathers Don't Get the Help They Need

Too many teen fathers don't get the help they need from professional health care and social-service professionals. There are several reasons why this is the case.

Harmful Stereotypes and the Exclusion of
Teen Fathers from Service Programs

In spite of the well-documented fact that the majority of teen fathers want help with the transition to parenthood, for decades most school-based and community-based teen parenting programs have offered more services to teen mothers than to teen fathers, and many programs have no service components whatsoever for young fathers.[137] In addition, practitioners have not understood the kinds of services teen fathers need,[138] and practitioners in training tend to have ethnocentric stereotypes about the needs of teen fathers from different racial and ethnic backgrounds and how to treat them.[139] On the basis of these well-established service biases, professionals and society give teen fathers the following mixed message: "We expect you to be a responsible parent, but we won't provide you with the guidance on how to become one."[140]

In his classic book, *Teenage Fathers,* Bryan Robinson surmised that teen fathers are overlooked by service providers due to the destructive influence of pejorative myths depicting these young men as macho, cool super studs and Don Juans who sexually exploit their partners and then become phantom fathers after their child is born.[141] Carolyn Cutrona and her colleagues of Iowa State University shared a similar assessment:

> The fathers of infants born to adolescent girls are more often viewed as "culprits" than as potential contributors to the well being of the young mother and her child. . . . They are overlooked as potential resources for a variety of reasons. These include assumptions that the mother-infant relationship is primary, that the influence of fathers is minimal during the first months of a child's life, that men who impregnate adolescents are generally unsavory characters, and that such men have little interest in either the young mother or their offspring.[142]

Teen fathers are well aware of societal stereotypes about them and report that they feel stigmatized by society.[143] Some of these boys begin to believe the consistent message from others that they are not suitable fathers, so they feel unworthy to receive help.[144] One young man expressed his dismay regarding the biases that people have about adolescent fathers: "We are not all hanging out trying to make babies, then leave the baby and the mother, and brag about it, but there are many of us who do care, and try to do the right thing for our child. It is these young fathers that need to be heard about more than those that do not do anything for their child except fade away."[145]

Counselors and social and health-care workers must confront and divest themselves of harmful stereotypes about teen fathers,[146] think complexly about these young men, and keep an open mind about serving them.[147] As the information in this book has demonstrated, although some teen fathers behave in callous and cavalier ways toward pregnancy and childbirth, most teen fathers care about their partners and their children, and the confluence of numerous stresses contributes to a gradual deterioration and severing of ties between a substantial percentage of teen fathers and their partners and children. Providing assistance to teen fathers will reduce the number of them who withdraw from their partners and children, while opening up the various emotional, social, and economic resources of the teen father's family to the adolescent mother and her family, which can enhance the well-being of the couple's child.

Policies and Procedures Devaluing the Role of Fathers

Adolescent men who want assistance with the transition to fatherhood verify that services for fathers either don't exist or they are not delivered in a manner that is responsive to the needs of men. One group of young fathers from an urban area expressed frustration that there were many services in their city, "but practically none were for men. . . . In addition to the expressed lack of services, these men felt intimidated by and discriminated against by service agencies for women."[148] The following testimony is a disturbing example of the way the system sometimes mishandles and maltreats adolescent fathers. The young man had taken his son to the hospital, where the boy had been admitted for some type of bite on his face:

> When I call up there or when I went back there, they tell me I can't even see my son. They took him and told me, "Even though you're the father we can't tell you nothing. We have to notify the mother, let her know her son is here, let her know who brought him." Even though I'm the one who brought him. Later, when I asked the county about the report concerning the bite marks, they told me, "We can't tell you anything; that information is confidential." [After a pause, with a perplexed look on his face, he said,] I'm the one who made the report.[149]

Young men who are treated in this manner are understandably alienated from the very institutions that are supposed to help children and families.

Programs Are Underfunded and Understaffed

Another problem with service programs for teen fathers is that too many of them are underfunded and understaffed. Many communities struggle to provide even the most basic-level services to the neediest of citizens because human-service agencies are underfunded and their workers are overburdened with huge caseloads.[150] Schools and clinics that provide reproductive-health services to teenagers are also challenged to meet the needs of young parents in the face of shrinking resources. Considering that programs that involve young men typically are "budded off" from existing services for young women, many institutions have very few resources to divert current employees or add new ones to programs targeting teenage fathers.[151] So even though staff members may be very dedicated to helping young fathers, there may not be enough personnel to address all the needs of program participants. This was the case with the highly admirable Fathers Forever Program (FFP), an innovative service project in Buffalo, New York, consisting of academic, employment and life-skills training for low-income fathers age sixteen to twenty-one. Although FFP professionals often went far beyond their formal roles and provided various forms of informal assistance and counseling to FFP participants, some of the participants "needed more socioemotional support than the program could offer."[152] If programs are not sufficiently staffed, young men can get the feeling that their needs don't really matter.

Female-Oriented Services

The female orientation of teen-parent and reproductive-health programs is another reason young men don't participate in programs. Many clinics are just not well suited for boys and men: "The physical spaces (i.e., images on the walls, waiting and examining room reading materials) are typically geared to women, most of the clients are women and programs are typically staffed by women. In regard to men and the clinic, a female Hispanic clinic worker said: 'They don't feel comfortable in having to go in there.'"[153]

Numerous adolescent fathers who were interviewed by Leo Hendricks rendered the same opinion. Overall, these young men viewed reproductive-health services and teen parenting programs as female oriented and they did not feel comfortable turning to professionals in these settings for help.[154] Consequently, helping professionals should transform their work settings so that they become environments in which males can feel more at home. In particular, posters and reading materials must include images and subjects that appeal to young men, and helping professionals must learn how to talk to young men about the topics that interest them in a manner that reflects male ways of relating, such as discussing sports and having conversations side by side rather than face to face.[155]

Fear of Prosecution and Loss of Welfare Benefits

It is common for some young men to avoid professional helpers because they fear their participation in service programs will lead to their being turned in to authorities on statutory rape charges. Young men who have reached legal adulthood—age eighteen or above—face the potential of being charged with statutory rape or statutory sexual assault if they have had sexual relations with a minor. For example, a current Pennsylvania law states that "a person commits a felony of the second degree when that person engages in sexual intercourse with a complainant under the age of 16 years and that person is four or more years older than the complainant and the complainant and the person are not married to each other."[156]

Statutory rape laws vary from state to state:

> Statutory rape is illegal sexual activity between two people when it would otherwise be legal if not for their age. The actual ages for these laws vary greatly from state-to-state, as do the punishments for offenders. Many states do not use the actual term "statutory rape," simply calling it rape or unlawful sexual penetration. These laws rarely apply only to intercourse, but rather to any type of sexual contact. Dating someone without sexual contact cannot be considered a form of statutory rape, and is almost never illegal.
>
> All states have an "age of consent, or an age at which a person can legally consent to sexual activity and can then no longer be a victim of statutory rape. . . . Statutory rape charges can be brought up by the victim, parents of the victim, and in most states, they can be raised by the state. California has been a major example of this, filing charges against fathers of pregnant women, at the protest of both the women and the parents of the involved parties.[157]

Many teen fathers age eighteen and nineteen are very leery about using service programs because they fear that program officials might file statutory rape charges against them. This concern is particularly common in the Hispanic culture because it is quite customary for Latina teens to have relationships with much older men. Therefore, Latinas "may be reluctant to give information about their partner for fear that he will be arrested."[158] Furthermore, "although the father might be active in the lives of the teenager and her child, often he is socially invisible to avoid legal repercussions."[159]

Another deterrent to participation in fathering programs is concern about being identified and prosecuted for failure to meet child-support obligations, which could also be coupled with a loss of welfare benefits for a young man's partner. Welfare-dependent couples sometimes conspire to maximize their economic resources by hiding the identity of the father, which prevents the father from having to make official child-support payments while allowing the mother to collect welfare. Although this behavior is illegal, couples who have destitute lives consider this collusion to be a necessary survival strategy. Historically, the collection of formal child support from the father could result in reduced welfare benefits. Typically, the loss of these benefits adds to the hardships of young parents struggling to make it in a world of poverty.

The wisdom of policies that lead to the prosecution of some young men who happen to be older than their partners or are trying to find a way to cope with crushing poverty needs to be reevaluated. Public policy designed to protect girls from sexual abuse by adult men and economic abandonment by deadbeat dads must also encourage, rather than deter, father involvement in the lives of their children and in programs that can help them to be better parents. These issues are explored in more detail in chapter 7.

Misogynist and Antisocial Orientations

Adolescent boys who view girls as sexual objects or who have developed an antisocial lifestyle often couldn't care less about the availability of teen fathering programs because they have no intention of meeting their paternal responsibilities. For example, one teenage boy featured in the documentary *Not Me* unabashedly explained his shallow feelings for girls, the ploys he used to seduce them, the manner in which he dumped them, his total disinterest in considering that he may have fathered a child, and his belief that it is solely the girl's responsibility to care for a baby.[160] During the 1990s, "The Spur Posse," a gang of young men from Lakewood, California, espoused the practice of awarding points to gang members for sexual conquests. Gang members showed no concern for girls they exploited and had no interest as to whether or not the girls got pregnant. Such actions are intolerable:

> The behavior of the members of "The Spur Posse" and other boys disinterested in the wellbeing of girls raises very serious questions about how some males are socialized to view and treat females. Addressing this issue is paramount in the effort to end the exploitation of women in a patriarchal culture. Men can take the lead in this effort by redefining masculinity to include those valuable aspects of traditional masculinity while eliminating those that are obsolete and dysfunctional. . . . As a part of the reconstruction of manhood, adults must teach impressionable boys to value and practice socialized, nonsexist ways of relating to women. Clearly, this undertaking has tremendous potential for training males to act with responsibility and consideration toward the mother and baby should they discover that they have become parents as adolescents.[161]

Self-Defeating, Traditional Male Attitudes about Receiving Help

Some teen fathers have difficulty accepting help even when they know that help is available due to the belief that men must be self reliant. Young men with a traditional sense of masculinity view asking for help to be a sign of weakness and inconsistent with the image of a man as someone who is tough and in control of his emotions.[162] Teenage fathers who embrace this perspective believe that males should handle health issues by themselves. They also contend that males "tend to delay getting care and instead wait to see if the health problem will 'just pass,' in contrast to females who tend 'to take care of problems as soon as they see them.'"[163] The influence of such traditional views about seeking help appears to cut across age, ethnic, and racial lines.[164]

In order to overcome the powerful influence of these attitudes, service providers can help traditional young men to reframe their conceptions about receiving help. For example, they can challenge teen fathers to "step up to the plate" and "be man enough" and "courageous enough" to get help.[165] In addition, professionals can "create alternative, nontraditional forums that reduce blows to men's self-esteem by changing the context of help seeking."[166] For instance, health care and counseling services can be components of recreational and employment programs that teen fathers with traditional masculine beliefs are likely to use without feeling embarrassed.[167]

Overwhelmed Fathers

Some teen fathers are so overwhelmed by their parenting duties and other problems in their lives that they don't have the emotional stamina to utilize professional assistance. In a series of case studies appearing in *Multicultural Counseling with Teenage Fathers,* I documented that several teen fathers were difficult to engage in counseling because their lives were so complicated and their families were troubled by a multitude of problems.[168] Similarly, Kathleen Kost of the State University of New York at Buffalo noted that over half of the fathers who had enrolled in the Fathers Forever Program did not complete the program, probably due to educational problems, criminal activity, homelessness, a lack of sufficient support in the young men's lives, and the hopelessness these men had about their futures.[169] Consequently, persistent and varied forms of outreach and intensive support and mentoring are necessary in order to recruit and retain young fathers in counseling and service programs. In chapter 5, I describe these approaches to helping, as well as numerous other considerations associated with the process of assisting adolescent fathers.

5

Helping Teenage Fathers

The Process of Engaging Young Fathers and Assisting Them with the Transition to Parenthood

Before Ralph became a father at age eighteen, his life was in fairly good shape. He was about to graduate from high school, he had been accepted for admission to a state college, and he was very much in love with his girlfriend, Angela, who was also about to graduate and head off to nursing school. Although the couple was young, they were committed to each other, had engagement plans, and dreamed of sharing a life together once they completed college. Their families shared similar values and had forged close ties. So when Angela became pregnant, although the two families experienced an intense period of shock, they quickly rebounded from the crisis and rallied around their children, helping the youngsters to modify their life plans so that they could marry, care for their baby, and complete their educations at a slower but steady pace.

During the early stages of the crisis pregnancy, Ralph and his parents called a social worker who was associated with a local teen pregnancy task force for guidance to help Ralph adjust to his new parental responsibilities. Recognizing that the two families involved in this pregnancy had many strengths and were quickly mobilizing their resources to help Ralph and Angela, the social worker determined that what Ralph most needed was encouragement and advice from another male who had been through similar circumstances. She referred Ralph to a mentor father program, where Ralph was connected with a man in his late thirties who had become a father when he was just sixteen. The relationship formed between the mentor and Ralph, combined with the healthy support of the two families, was all that was necessary to get Ralph through the crisis and onto a course of action that would assure a bright future for him, Angela, and their baby.

Although the professional process of helping Ralph was straightforward and simple, it is rarely that easy with many teenage fathers, especially with boys like Jamie, who at sixteen was about as confused as a young man could be, and was holding on to his life by a thread. While other boys his age were attending school, dating girls, and eagerly talking about their favorite football team, Jamie spent most of his waking hours thinking of the many ways he could kill himself. His life had been a living nightmare, and he saw ending it as his only route to relief.

Jamie's life was chaotic since the day he was born. He was a member of a disturbed family that few people would want to know and even fewer people could manage to survive. His father, Mr. V., was a brute who believed that best way to raise his son was to break him. His mother, Mrs. V., was an alcoholic whose vision of reality was distorted by an ever-present, gin-induced haze that kept her from noticing her husband's penchant for going into a rage. Together, Mr. and Mrs. V. gave Jamie a clear message that their home was not a safe place for a child. So at a very early age, Jamie found a new home for himself out on the streets.

It was in the streets that Jamie began to smoke reefers at age eleven and was "befriended" at age thirteen by a middle-aged man from his neighborhood, who was an expert at recognizing boys who were ripe for exploitation. After gradually earning Jamie's trust over the course of several months, the man molested Jamie one day while the two were alone in the man's home. The assault he suffered at the hands of this man, like the abuse he had endured in his home, was a trauma he chose to hide from the rest of the world as he tried to find his way in life, a damaged boy with a wounded spirit lacking direction.

Jamie's efforts to hide his pain did little good, however. So he increased his use of pot and turned to girls for casual sex as his way of managing his demons. But these tactics made his already-troubled life even more troubled: Jamie grew more depressed, his grades declined in school, and by age sixteen, he had fathered a daughter. He was also on the verge of killing himself.

A loving teacher played a crucial role in saving Jamie's life. She recognized that he was not achieving his fullest potential as a student, and she noticed his dark moods and deep melancholy. Whereas other educators considered Jamie to be a screw-up, she realized he was a troubled soul and a bright kid who desperately needed help. So she called Mrs. V. and urged her to seek help for Jamie from a psychologist who was knowledgeable about teenage fathers. Mrs. V. ignored this request until her husband suddenly took his own life, locking himself in the family's garage and shooting himself in the head during the early morning hours while his family slept. Rocked by the loss of her husband and fearing that she might lose Jamie too, Mrs. V. contacted the psychologist and arranged for Jamie to go for counseling.

Fortunately for Jamie, the psychologist knew how to establish rapport with young men who are reluctant to see a counselor. He talked to Jamie in a male-friendly manner, discussing with him his interests and his most pressing concern, which was trying to figure out how he could be a good father at such a young age. Responding to this matter, the psychologist worked with school officials to get Jamie placed in a co-op program that allowed him to spend part of the school day working in a supermarket. The psychologist arranged for Jamie to watch videotapes on parenting skills, and the two discussed his reactions and questions about what it means to be a good father. Subsequently, Jamie used these skills during his visits with his daughter, Rachel, and her mother, Alice. The psychologist gradually bridged from these urgent fatherhood issues to other problems, such as Jamie's self-defeating use of marijuana and his unsafe sexual practices. The trust that the psychologist earned by helping Jamie with his fatherhood concerns allowed him to explore these more sensitive issues with Jamie, which prompted Jamie to reveal details of his traumatic past, including the physical abuse by his father and the sexual assault by the neighbor, who by this time had hung himself after being sent to prison following a conviction for an assault of another boy. The psychologist helped Jamie to see the link between these traumas, his drug use, and his sex practices. The psychologist taught Jamie alternative coping skills, such as progressive muscle relaxation for handling stress, as well as strategies for handling sexual encounters and practicing safe sex. He also guided Jamie through a series of negotiations with Alice and her family regarding child visitation and child support so that Jamie could remain a supportive person to Alice and Rachel. Throughout these negotiations, Alice's parents, Mr. and Mrs. T., began to notice the efforts Jamie was making to be a good father, and they responded by becoming a major source of support for him, further nurturing his attempts to fulfill his paternal responsibilities. The combination of these interventions and sources of support helped Jamie to embrace his duties as a father, reengage himself in school, and set his sights on going to college as a business major with the hope of becoming a manager in a supermarket.

The interventions that were used to assist Ralph and Jamie with their respective issues represent two extremes along a continuum of helping teenage fathers. Young fathers like Ralph, whose promising future was merely delayed by his early entry into fatherhood, need a minimal level of professional assistance during the transition to parenthood. Other adolescent fathers like Jamie, whose traumatic life was further jeopardized by his becoming a father, require a much wider range of services provided by various forms of professionals in order to help these young men make a successful adjustment to the demands of fatherhood. Between both extremes, the process of helping adolescent fathers is often demanding and complicated. As was documented in chapter 4, teenage fathers tend to have numerous adjustment difficulties that call for a multifaceted approach to helping. As was the case with Jamie, the process begins with trying to figure out ways to establish rapport with a young man who may not be trusting of counselors. There is a never-ending shifting of priorities as new issues emerge both before and after the birth of the baby. Throughout the prenatal and postnatal stages of counseling, the young father needs help learning how to be a good parent and dealing with concerns pertaining to his child, his family, his partner's family, school, and work.

The purpose of this chapter is to describe the process of engaging young fathers and assisting them with their many concerns. Whether you are a professional from the social-service or health-professions fields or simply a concerned adult interested in the subject of adolescent fatherhood, the information provided in this chapter can help you to understand the issues, challenges, and practices associated with helping teenage fathers, beginning with the task of reaching out to teenage fathers and earning their trust.

Outreach with Teen Fathers

Teenage fathers are often reluctant to use formal services because they fear those services will either not address their needs or they will be staffed by adults who have a pejorative view of young fathers. Consequently, it is essential that organizations whose mission is to serve adolescents use intensive, sensitive methods to identify, reach out, and earn the trust of the adolescent fathers who reside in their communities.

Unfortunately, many institutions fail to support extensive outreach by their social-service and health-care professionals with teen fathers due to biases about helping this population or a lack of understanding about what young fathers actually want and need from service providers. One of the most insurmountable obstacles hindering outreach work with boys who have fathered children is organizational ambivalence about helping teen fathers.[1] For example, sometimes top-level administrators pay lip service to assisting young fathers for public-relations reasons while sending an implicit message throughout an organization that teen-father programs are not a priority or that teen mothers rather than teen fathers should be the ones receiving services. These anti-male sentiments can permeate an agency and ultimately undermine the staff ostensibly hired to work with male teenagers.[2] In order to create a genuine culture of caring for teen fathers, everyone involved in the program, including executive personnel and service workers, must communicate to the community and the young fathers within it that fathers really matter and that teen-father programs are an integral part of the organization, rather than a second-rate appendage.[3]

Efforts to recruit young fathers are often successful when programs have certain features and incentives. When asked for their opinion about what is required to get teen fathers to participate in parenting programs, adolescent boys recommend using peers to recruit young men for services because males "will listen to peers before they'll listen to adults."[4] Teenage boys also recommend that program developers offer incentives that will enhance the appeal of programs and increase the odds that young fathers will use them.[5] For example, teenage fathers have reported that the provision of free and confidential STD testing, employment counseling, and legal counsel regarding paternity matters would motivate them to use programs for young fathers.[6] Other appealing features of successful programs have included providing free meals during program activities, free transportation to and from the program, information about childbirth and parenting, and paraprofessional peer counselors to facilitate group meetings.[7]

Roy, a participant of an inner-city multifaceted service program for young fathers, verified for me how certain features of the program had appealed to him:

> When this guy first told me about the program, I was skeptical—you know—not sure if this would be all right for me. I mean, the first thought in my mind, you know, was "are they gonna come after me with all kinds of lectures about how I should be a good father and all that?" But they didn't do that. They was like, look, we got some services that can make your life better. We can help you take care of your baby. We can help you find a job. We can hook you up with other guys who been through what you been through. And we can answer your questions about bein' a father, and all that stuff. So, I decided to give it a try, and it was all right. I got the feeling that they cared about me and the other guys who were in the program. So, I kept coming back.

One of the key factors in getting boys like Roy to even consider enrolling in a program is the type of outreach strategies that are used to make contact with them and to earn their trust. Whether outreach is conducted by professionals or peers, it is crucial that outreach workers visit places where young men like to socialize, such as ball courts, community centers, pool rooms, street corners, and barbershops.[8] One professional affiliated with a support program for single fathers was successful recruiting participants by using a very informal approach that involved meeting with them individually in their communities over a cup of coffee.[9]

Adolescent mothers can be excellent recruitment allies, especially if they want their partner to get help.[10] Thus, outreach workers should consider developing collaborative relationships with professionals who provide services to teen mothers for the purpose of recruiting young fathers. Obstetrical-gynecological and Planned Parenthood clinics and pediatric offices are ideal settings for developing helpful referral sources.[11] Other potential referral sources include physicians, school counselors, teachers, coaches, administrators, clergy, police officers, and staff at vocational training centers, GED programs, and recreational centers.[12] Teenager fathers who have already invested themselves in some sort of program are also good sources of information and influence for getting other young fathers to participate.[13]

Schools are logical locations to reach young fathers who are dividing their time among school, work, and their families. School nurses "could provide information about pregnancy and parenting to all high school students, some of whom may be fathers. School staff who have trusted relationships with students could identify adolescent fathers to participate in support groups during lunch breaks or study periods."[14]

Public-service announcements and advertisements are useful tools for getting the word out about teen-father programs. Professional helpers can work with the media to create commercials about service programs featuring teenage boys talking realistically about their experiences as fathers and the help they have received from a particular program.[15] All forms of advertisement should include language that appeals to young men and be stated in words and expressions they can understand.[16]

The First Contact with a Teen Father

Adolescent fathers tend to be the victims of discrimination from adults who come into contact with them. Sometimes teen fathers are "simultaneously rejected and ignored, disparaged and excluded, condemned and punished" for their role in the pregnancy.[17] Because many teen fathers fear that they will be judged by counseling and social-service professionals, they are unlikely to utilize even the best-designed service programs, and they can appear wary and be elusive when professionals contact them.

Adolescent fathers would find it easier to use services if adults were helpful and nonjudgmental.[18] They also prefer working with providers "who are trustworthy, pay attention and are nice to them, with whom they will feel comfortable talking and with whom they can talk one-on-one."[19] Therefore, it is imperative that helpers divest themselves of harmful stereotypes about teen fathers and employ persistent outreach and rapport-building strategies with adolescent males facing early paternity.[20] Most importantly, outreach workers must convey a caring and nonjudgmental manner when they approach teen fathers for the first time.[21]

First impressions can make or break any attempt to earn the trust of a young father. In order to prevent the initial contact with a teen father from becoming a disaster, there are numerous mistakes professionals must try to avoid. It is prudent to refrain from focusing on a young man's failures because doing so "may discourage men from self-disclosure."[22] Topics about sexual and parental responsibility also should be avoided until a strong degree of trust has been established.[23] Asking many questions during a first interview also can cause some teen fathers to clam up because they associate frequent questioning with interrogations they have experienced with other adults, such as parents who grill them about their role in the pregnancy, or police and other law enforcement personnel who investigate crimes that might have involved the young father.[24] Professionals who ask too many questions may remind a boy of prior experiences of forced participation in counseling and psychological evaluations that were viewed by the youth as attempts "by shrinks to mess with my head."[25]

Because some young men have had negative experiences with counselors, psychologists, health-care workers, or adult authority figures, and fear that information obtained by professions might be used against them, a critical task during the initial stages of the helping process is to explore the teenage father's view about counseling. Through this process, misconceptions about the purpose of counseling can be corrected, and assurances about confidentiality can be given.[26] For example, when I started counseling with Rickie, an eighteen-year-old father in prison, I explained to him that anything other than plans to hurt himself or someone else would be kept strictly between us, so there was no way officials could use our therapy sessions as a tool to discipline him. Furthermore, I told him that I was there to address *his* needs and to see if I could help him to find ways to achieve a more satisfying life. This information enlightened Rickie about counseling, and he proceeded to spend months talking with me about problems with his family and concerns about his daughter.

Sometimes it is necessary to arrange first meetings at the young father's residence, at a recreational center, or some other familiar turf in which the adolescent feels comfortable.[27] This conveys to the teenager that the counselor is willing to enter the boy's world and comprehend its realities. I have found it particularly helpful to relate to youths like Jamie in a "male-friendly way," which involves employing the natural methods boys use to become friends, such as taking turns shooting baskets, tossing a football back and forth, walking side by side down the street, sharing a snack at a fast-food restaurant, telling jokes, and talking about sports and music.[28] It is a good idea to understand the slang expressions young people use, to be knowledgeable about recent events in the local community, and to create a male-friendly office environment by displaying sports magazines and offering the young man a soft drink and engaging him in nonthreatening, casual conversation during initial brief encounters. "Moreover, trust, rapport, and constructive communication are likely to be established more rapidly . . . when the young father and clinician sit side-by-side rather than opposite each other."[29] This seating arrangement tends to reduce suspicion. I have found that wearing a long-sleeved shirt and rolling up my shirtsleeves when talking with a teen father conveys to the youth the implicit message that I am ready to work for the youngster.[30]

Taking a positive stance is an effective starting point for earning a teen father's trust.[31] Communicating one's readiness to serve as an advocate for the young man and explaining how he will be helped to navigate social-service, legal, medical, educational, and employment systems are other effective strategies for establishing instant credibility.[32] Rapport is enhanced when the helper is willing to maintain a flexible agenda and a readiness to respond to what the young father identifies as his most pressing need. For example, teaching him parenting skills may have to take a back seat temporarily to helping him find a job or getting him legal advice regarding his rights as a father. Focusing on strengths and directing a young man toward desirable solutions for his problems can also be beneficial. For instance, counselors can ask a few of the following nonthreatening, positively oriented questions:[33]

What do you want most for your child?

What kind of relationship would you like with your baby?

How would you like things to be between you and your partner?

In what ways do you like to help your partner?

What steps would you be willing to take to help you get a job?

What are the conditions that would help you to return to school?

What are your strengths or best qualities?

A good way for helpers to end the first contact with a young father is to provide him with their card so that the young man has the helper's name and contact information. It is also a good idea to note the hours of availability on the back of the card so the young man knows when he can call if he wants to make a follow-up contact with the helper.[34] Stress with the young man that you would like to meet with him again, obtain his phone number or some other means of reaching him, and determine when it would be convenient to contact him in the near future. End the first session by thanking the young man for his time, and promise to give him a follow-up phone call or visit.[35]

Professionals who use these outreach strategies are usually able to break through the wariness teen fathers have about helping professionals.

Hussein, a seventeen-year-old, described the impact of the first meeting he had with an outreach worker who had employed male-friendly outreach methods with him:

> When I first saw that guy [the outreach counselor], I said to myself, "I ain't never gonna tell this guy nothin'." But then he talked to me in a real respectful manner while we was shootin' basketball, and I could tell he cared about me even though the guy didn't know me. And I went from believin' I would just throw him a bone [humor the counselor] to get rid of him, to feelin' like this guy might really understand me and be able to help me. So, I decided to come back, and he's been great to me ever since. . . . I don't know what kind of a father I would be if I didn't have him.

The Role of the Case Manager

In the mental-health fields, a case manager is a professional who oversees the provision of services for a person needing some type of assistance, making sure that the person's needs are addressed, and monitoring the person's progress. Experts on the subject of adolescent fatherhood stress the importance of assigning case managers with teen fathers because these young men tend to have so many needs and require the direction of a caring professional to help them negotiate social-service, health-care, educational, and legal systems. The staff employed in the Aroostook County Action Program (ACAP), which was one of the sites of the Maine Young Fathers Project, recommended that case managers for teen fathers be men: "ACAP [employees] felt that is was to their disadvantage having a female case manager. Although she was able to provide a female point of view to the clients, she also felt that a male would be able to make more impact about relationship issues and parenting."[36]

Another crucial issue pertaining to case management is having full-time employees assigned to father services. The ACAP staff expressed dismay over the part-time status of the one case manager assigned to assist the young fathers in the Maine project,[37] and professionals in other programs have reported being overwhelmed by the needs of the fathers they have served.[38] Related to the issue of organizational support discussed earlier, teen-father programs must be sufficiently staffed if they are going to address the needs of adolescent fathers adequately. In order to meet those needs, the case manager must be allotted enough time and resources to guide a young father to needed services and to offer him key emotional support as he deals with the ups and downs associated with becoming a father at an early age. In effect, the case manager must act as a caring broker of services who works as an assertive advocate in securing services such as family-life education, job training, and family counseling for teen fathers.[39]

Maintaining Long-Term Rapport with Teen Fathers

Helpers can maintain rapport with young fathers and increase the odds that they will continue to participate in counseling and parenting programs by assisting them with their ongoing practical needs. For example, case managers from one program helped to ensure that teen mothers and fathers attended parenting skills sessions by contacting them about classes, transporting them and their babies to and from classes, and giving them useful gifts, such as music tapes they could play with their babies.[40]

Rudy Hernandez, the author of *Fatherwork in the Crossfire,* reported that he went to great lengths to earn and maintain the trust and respect of Chicano teen fathers. His tactics are good examples of the extent to which professionals sometimes have to go in order to sustain an ongoing relationship with young fathers and the other key people in their lives: "I assisted one of my informants [a teen father or a friend or family member of a teen father] in changing a bad engine in his car. I accompanied another on a trip to visit his older brother in prison. I also assisted an informant in repairing a broken water heater at his mother's house. During these sessions, we traded anecdotes and stories about barrio life that sometimes turned nostalgic."[41]

Hernandez's approach also illustrates that professionals must observe, and adapt to, the relational style of the teen father. Counselors, social workers, psychologists, and health-care professionals tend to be comfortable with intimate self-disclosure. However, boys who have a traditional male relational style tend to express themselves through action, rather than words. These young men might recoil from a helper who abruptly encourages the expression of private thoughts and feelings. Consequently, the helper might have to adjust his or her relational style so that it matches that of the teen father. In addition, the helper must learn to judge how thoroughly the youth is willing to focus on personal issues at any given moment. For example, it may be necessary to approach personal issues cautiously and to view a counseling session as a vehicle for providing the client with information pertaining to his concrete needs, such as how to obtain a job or legal advice or facts about parenting and child development. Over time, the helper should look for windows of opportunity during which the young man is less reticent to disclose his emotional issues. Often, these opportunities are likely to emerge under the guise of a joke by the boy, or a passing comment that is shared by the youngster in the context of some other activity, such as tossing a football back and forth. When these opportunities emerge, the helper is likely to acquire important information by mirroring the client's manner of expression, such as joking with him and engaging him in some good-natured ribbing. Of course, with boys exhibiting a nontraditional male relational style, a more direct exploration of personal events is usually possible.[42]

Being considerate of and responsive to the cultural background of a boy is another crucial factor in the maintenance of rapport with teen fathers. For example, although wanting to learn parenting skills or getting a job are concerns that cut across racial and ethnic lines, African-American teen fathers might also need assistance to address institutional barriers associated with various forms of prejudice,[43] such as the racism and sexism this young man reported:

> I know for sure that there's discrimination. . . . Not long ago, when my son's mother and me was still together . . . every job we go to, we applied for the same jobs. Me and her had the same references and everything because me and her worked the same jobs before. . . . She hadn't had no high school diploma and I hadn't neither . . . and she was always the first one to get hired. And I think people just usually look at young black males like we not responsible. . . . We just so stereotyped that sooner or later, even if they do give us a job, we gonna quit or we ain't gonna do exactly what they want, you know, or we ain't gonna carry out things the way they supposed to be carried out. . . . Whereas a female I think they look at them as more understadin' . . . more obedient. . . . They think all young black males ain't got no discipline. . . . I can't exactly say what it is but I just feel we always have that barrier against us because we're young and we're black men.[44]

Professionals who are uncomfortable or incapable of discussing racial issues are likely to be rejected by African-American adolescent fathers for whom racism is a salient issue.[45] Helpers must also be attuned to culturally salient issues for non-Hispanic white and Latino boys. Because having a child out of wedlock still carries a strong stigma in non-Hispanic white communities, helpers working with white teen fathers may have to help them to resolve their feelings of shame and embarrassment about the pregnancy.[46] Professionals must be prepared to help Latino adolescent fathers with their conflicts between the traditional gender roles emphasized in the Hispanic culture—particularly among young Latino men who have recently entered the United States from a foreign country—and the pressure from the mainstream American culture for men to take on more flexible gender roles.[47]

Sally Brown, the author of *If the Shoes Fit,* the final report pertaining to the Maine Young Fathers Project, offered several considerations regarding making and keeping appointments. First, she recommended that practitioners be available in the evenings and weekends if possible, since these are the only times some fathers are available to go to agencies for services. Second, she found that the many of the boys and men who had participated in the Maine Young Fathers Project were not very good at following through on making and keeping appointments. Thus, she advised counselors to be persistent in their efforts to serve young fathers, even though they may feel frustrated with some of the young men they are trying to help. She also noted that patience and determination frequently prove successful in engaging this population in counseling.[48]

Perhaps the most important message a helper can convey repeatedly to a teen father is that he or she is willing to serve as an advocate for the client over the long term. Such a commitment is likely to engender a foundation of trust that can sustain a therapeutic relationship through the prenatal and postnatal crises commonly experienced by young men involved in an unplanned pregnancy.[49]

Helping Teen Fathers during the Prenatal Period

During the prenatal period, an expectant teen father needs decision-making counseling as he and his partner try to determine how they will resolve the pregnancy. If the young father is still enrolled in school at the time, he also may need assistance with the decision to remain in school or to drop out. In addition, he requires guidance about what it means to be a father and education in parenting skills.

Pregnancy Resolution Counseling

For most teenage boys, being involved in an unintended pregnancy would represent a scary crisis filled with many tough decisions. An expectant teen father struggling to resolve a crisis pregnancy

> must contemplate a variety of options, each of which may pose an emotionally and morally laden conflict: Should he persuade his partner to have an abortion, or should he urge her to carry the baby to term? If the child is born, should the couple keep the baby or give the infant up for adoption? If they keep the child, should they marry? If they marry, should they live on their own or with parents or relatives? If they don't marry, who should have custody of the baby? If the father is excluded from decisions regarding abortion and adoption, or if he chooses or is placed in a noncustodial role, what are his legal rights and obligations? What does unmarried, custodial fatherhood entail?[50]

Dealing with all of these dilemmas can make a boy's head spin or sink him into a state of depression. A young father from the Public/Private

Ventures program shared this account of his experience during the early months of his partner's pregnancy: "When I found out she was pregnant, I just stayed in my room and didn't talk to nobody for weeks. . . . Well, it was more like months. . . . That depression state lasted for about two months. I thought I was going crazy."[51]

Some expectant teen fathers and their partners respond to a crisis pregnancy with extremely bad judgment. For example, in 1993 Garcia, an eighteen-year-old expectant teen father, and his seventeen-year-old pregnant girlfriend, fearing the reactions of their parents, decided they would try to hide the pregnancy and after the baby was born, report to their relatives and the authorities that they had purchased the baby from a drug user to get the baby away from him. After the young mother gave birth at home by herself, the couple told this concocted story to the police, but later admitted the tale was not true.[52] In another sensational case that made national headlines in 1996, Brian Peterson and Amy Grossberg, who were teenagers at the time, were charged with first-degree murder for the death of their newborn baby boy. The teenagers had concealed the pregnancy and delivered the baby on their own in a motel room in Newark, Delaware. After the baby was born, the couple went into a panic and disposed of the baby in the motel garbage dumpster. When the baby's body was discovered and linked to the couple by the authorities, they were arrested and charged with murder. In 1998 both Peterson and Grossberg pleaded guilty to manslaughter and received eight-year sentences, for which they both spent more than two years in prison before they were released to complete the remainder of their sentences on parole.[53]

These extreme cases illustrate how desperate expectant teens can get while trying to resolve an unintended pregnancy without the counsel of a wise, caring adult. Because both the young mother and the teen father are involved in the decisions associated with the pregnancy, it is advisable to work with the couple until they have determined how they will handle their situation. Expectant teen parents need compassionate guidance about considering all of the options available to them. Because the dilemmas associated with resolving the pregnancy are value laden, professional counselors must examine their attitudes and feelings about premarital pregnancy, abortion, adoption, adolescent marriage, and out-of-wedlock childbirth.[54] Counselors have an ethical obligation to respect the values of their clients and to refrain from imposing their own preferences on teen parents as the couple attempts to decide on a course of action.[55] It is recommended that counselors assist the couple to clarify their values pertaining to each of the possible options for resolving the pregnancy and to evaluate carefully the pros and cons of those options before a decision is made.[56] Any counselor who is unable to abide by these guidelines has an ethical responsibility to discuss his or her biases with the couple and to refer them to another professional who is capable of respecting the couple's values.[57]

While assisting the expectant father with these decisions, the counselor must remember that the pregnancy-resolution process will be greatly affected, if not completely determined, by the expectant adolescent mother and her family. Furthermore, if the expectant father has informed his family of the pregnancy, they are also likely to exert influence on the decision-making process.[58] Moreover, if the couple is considering abortion, the expectant teen mother may be required by law to notify her parents and obtain their permission to have an abortion before the procedure can be performed.[59] Therefore, it is recommended that the counselor explore with the client his willingness to involve all of these parties in the decision.[60] The ramifications of notifying both families versus keeping the pregnancy a secret must be discussed as well.[61]

Jeanne Warren Lindsay, author of *Crisis Counseling with Pregnant Teens,* observed that most parents are helpful to expectant teen parents after the initial shock of the pregnancy has passed.[62] Therefore, it is advisable to obtain permission from the young couple to solicit the input and support of their families during this emotionally draining time. When counseling these various parties,

> it is common for the young couple's parents to express strong feelings of hurt, anger, and disappointment to the couple for the pregnancy. The counselor must empathize with these feelings while directing the families toward taking constructive action whether it pertains to making arrangements for an abortion, adoption, or who will have custody of child. In addition, the counselor can gently help the families to reframe how they view the pregnancy; instead of seeing the pregnancy solely as an irresponsible act on the part of the couple and as a burden on the family, the family can be encouraged to entertain the love and hopes and dreams that they have for the baby. Recruiting the support of extended family members and trusted members of the community, such as a local minister or close neighbor, can also to help the families feel less overwhelmed by the pregnancy and more positively directed toward the future.[63]

In order to be an effective resource for expectant teens and their families, counselors must know the pros and cons and legal considerations pertaining to abortion, adoption, common-law and traditional marriages, and noncustodial parenthood. Because it is beyond the scope of this book to discuss each of these subjects in detail, the reader is referred to one of my earlier books, *Multicultural Counseling with Teenage Fathers,* for an in-depth analysis of these topics as they relate to pregnancy-resolution counseling with adolescent fathers.[64]

Crisis Educational and Career Counseling

The onset of an intended pregnancy can create dilemmas for expectant teen fathers about staying in school. As was documented in chapter 3, boys who become involved in a premarital conception tend to have preexisting academic difficulties, and the pregnancy becomes an added reason to drop out of school. They also may be under considerable pressure to earn money to help support their partner, as was the case with this young man: "I didn't know what to do, but I had to do something before I . . . well, I don't know what I mighta done. . . . I was so depressed. So I knew like I had to get a job. I had to get money. So I started working myself to death."[65]

The failure to complete school can seriously limit a young man's future opportunities and earning potential over the long term. Consequently, helping professionals, especially school counselors, should try to employ the following measures to help a young father to stay in school: Refer the client to an in-school support program for expectant and parenting teens; place him in an alternative school that has cooperative work placements with local employers; and enlist the assistance of the extended family in the form of financial support or providing child care while the teen parents complete school.[66]

Some young fathers will drop out of school even when school personnel make an effort to keep them enrolled, and others have left school before becoming fathers.[67] Because these fathers must find employment in order to support their children, an orientation to the world of work that includes training in job-readiness skills, such as how to apply for and keep a job and communicate effectively, as well as training for specific occupations, is an essential service during the prenatal period.[68] As this young father testified, the benefits of these services can be quite striking:

> The job-readiness workshops and the program helped me develop my skills job-wise . . . especially like my interaction skills because that was something that I really had to develop because I always been the type that really didn't want to talk to too many people. Because like my jobs that I had in the past, it was all like a leave me on my own job, just tell me what to do and then you just go about your business, because I didn't like supervision where somebody watch you all the time. I'd just up and leave those jobs where I had to talk to somebody or something like that. . . . So when I came to the young fathers program it sort of changed me. . . . I wasn't used to people lookin' at me dead in my face and you know asking me questions and wanting me to

talk back to them. . . . So, how to talk to people . . . that really helped me a lot as far as my training and skills that I really needed.[69]

Preparation for Fatherhood

An unintended pregnancy sparks a developmental crisis for many expectant teen fathers because they are suddenly confronted with the realization that they are about to become parents and undergo major changes in their lives. During the prenatal phase, they think a great deal about what it means to be a man and a father. Nick, a seventeen-year-old, remarked:

> One day all I was worried about was getting my homework done, playing sports with my buddies, and dating girls. Then the next thing I knew I was about to become a father and I was just a kid myself. I never thought about all this fatherhood stuff before and then it really hit me how important the job is. I saw I had this big job to do *and I was really scared.* I mean, I started thinking about stuff I never thought about before—my girlfriend would be having a baby, I'd be seeing the birth of my baby—*my baby!* . . . and I'd have to get a job and be caring for a baby real soon. . . . It really got to me, worrying about all this stuff.

Young men facing impending responsibilities of parenthood report that they need support regarding their fatherhood concerns during the prenatal phase.[70] Many ponder questions such as, "Am I ready to be a father?" and "What does a good father do?" Therefore, expectant teen fathers can benefit from advice about being a father through the guidance of professional counselors, adult mentors, or peer support groups.

During the 1990s, several colleagues and I developed an educational support-group program that is designed to help expectant teen fathers and young men who are already fathers prepare for parenthood.[71] The purpose of the group is to help young men address their feelings about being a teen father, clarify what it means to be a man and a father, and learn parenting skills and methods to prevent other unintended pregnancies. A central theme permeating all of these activities is the father's role in supporting his partner during and after the pregnancy. Young fathers develop rapport in the group by participating in recreational activities and sharing meals together. The young men have discussions about masculinity and the responsibilities of fathers, including conversations about their own fathers and whether or not these men were good role models of fatherhood. The participants identify the goals they have for themselves as fathers and how they intend to care for their children. Formal training in parenting skills is provided, and family and life management and family-planning strategies are taught, including coping skills young men can use to avoid additional unplanned pregnancies.

Fathers who join the group during the prenatal stage share their reactions to the pregnancy and use the assistance of their peers to develop a vision of the type of father they want to be. Expectant fathers also have the opportunity to witness fathers who already have children practice parenting skills. These observations allow the expectant fathers to get some idea of what good parenting involves, and they have the chance to refine their parenting skills with their own children during the postnatal stage of counseling.

Teaching about fatherhood in psychoeducational support groups is preferable over other approaches because of the benefits acquired from the perspectives and support of peers. As one participant from the Public/Private Ventures Young Unwed Fathers Pilot Project commented: "There's no pressure on you and you can hear a lot more sides to your problems. . . . But with yourself you can only hear one side, that's your side, because you agree with your side. And that's what I like about the program . . . cuz a lot of times I hear some things that these guys talk about that I'm going through. And I talk to them and I listen to what I told them."[72]

Feedback from teen fathers about support groups suggest that the participants develop positive perspectives on fatherhood, effective parenting skills, responsible sexual attitudes and behaviors, and most importantly, satisfying relationships with their children.[73] In addition, participation in support groups enhances the odds that young men will formally establish paternity.[74]

Responding to the Couvade Syndrome

Occasionally, expectant teen fathers who are intensely worried about the well-being of their partners during the pregnancy have been known to experience a cluster of somatic symptoms that are referred to in the medical literature as the *couvade syndrome*.[75] This stress-related reaction consists of the manifestation of physical aches and pains and anxieties about the birth and delivery of the baby.[76] The young man may feel acute anticipatory anxiety about his role during labor and childbirth. At the same time, he has empathy for his partner and typically attempts to be sensitive to the expectant mother's needs.[77]

I have employed several successful interventions with four adolescent boys affected by the couvade syndrome. All four of these young men recovered from physical ailments and intense anxieties after they were informed that their symptoms are common among men during the prenatal period, received training about the childbirth process, and were taught specific strategies they could use to support their partners throughout the pregnancy and during labor and delivery.[78]

Preparing expectant teen fathers for the labor experience of their partners can help to prevent the onset of the couvade syndrome or minimize its impact. A youth who is welcomed by the mother as a labor partner should be encouraged to join his partner in learning about the Lamaze method or some other form of birthing training. Expectant young fathers who have unstable, conflicted relationships with their partners may not be allowed by the partner and her family to be present at delivery. It is recommended that these boys receive some training about the birthing process to help allay their fears about the event and to assist them in understanding the experience their partners go through during the delivery of the baby.[79]

Supporting the Adolescent Mother during the Pregnancy

Educating expectant teen fathers about the needs of their partners can help these young men to be more supportive of the adolescent mother during the pregnancy. Boys tend to be naive about the health risks associated with early childbearing, so they need to be encouraged to help their partners to get adequate prenatal and postnatal medical care.[80] In addition, "training in empathic listening skills and specific comforting behaviors can empower the client to be an important source of emotional support for his partner during the suspenseful months prior to the delivery and well into the postnatal period."[81]

Counseling during the Postnatal Period

Although counseling during the prenatal stage can help a young father to weather the many storms generated by a crisis pregnancy, old issues may linger or reemerge, and new concerns and crises can erupt at any time. Counseling and education to address postnatal fatherhood challenges, ongoing family problems, long-term educational and career considerations, and a variety of mental health and behavioral issues must be provided.

Postnatal Fathering Skills Training

Given the relatively poor parenting skills demonstrated by teen fathers, it is recommended that they receive early assistance "on all aspects of raising healthy, socially skilled children,"[82] including "skills-oriented parent education programs that will help them fulfill their roles as providers, caregivers, and nurturers of their children."[83] By learning and practicing good child-rearing skills, young fathers can have a direct, positive impact on their child's development, and they might also foster indirect benefits for their child by using their knowledge about parenting to support their partner's child-rearing behaviors.[84] Thus, it is recommended that during the postnatal period, discussions about what it means to be a man and a father, which were described earlier, be supplemented by direct training in parenting skills. Excellent parent-education curriculums that are geared toward fathers are available from the National Fatherhood Initiative,[85] the Manpower Demonstration Research Corporation,[86] and the National Family Preservation Network.[87]

Evaluating the Family Caregiving System

The parenting behaviors of adolescent mothers and fathers are shaped long before a child is born by longstanding patterns of family interactions. When a family has a well-established tradition of trust and mutual respect and support, a responsive family caregiving system emerges, characterized by a form of shared responsibility for the child in which the grandparents assist with child care while fostering the ever-developing child-care skills of the young parent.[88] In this type of family system, role sharing develops, and the grandparents and teen parent help each other attend to the needs of the baby in a mutually supportive and flexible manner.[89] Fortunately for Jamie, whose difficult and complicated entry into fatherhood was described earlier in this chapter, Mr. and Mrs. T. promoted a responsive family caregiving system with Jamie and Alice, which promoted the shared care of baby Rachel by everyone in the family.

By comparison, other families have much different patterns of interactions that set the stage for trouble when it comes to handling the addition of a child born to a teenager in the family. Some families practice role-binding in which the teen parent takes on sole responsibility for child-rearing duties, while other families engage in role-blocking in which either the adolescent parent abdicates the parenting role or it is usurped by the grandparents.[90] Families with preexisting punitive, hostile, and disengaged patterns of behavior respond to the birth of the baby with "adversarial relations" whereby there are frequent disputes about child care, the absence of effective guidance about child rearing, and the emergence of poor parenting behavior by the teen parents.[91] Because these patterns play a crucial role in how teen mothers and fathers approach parenthood, practitioners are urged to assess the family climate prior to the onset of parenting-skills training with teen mothers and teen fathers and to intervene with families who demonstrate role-binding, role-blocking, or adversarial relations. The counselor's role with such families is to address "conflicts in ways that demonstrate worth and dignity of family members while working to create more options and flexibility in the caregiving situation."[92]

Boys who are involved in an unintended pregnancy are rarely ready to be fathers and they worry about how to take care of a baby. A sixteen-year-old named Keith shared this account of his struggles: "I was shocked and I was depressed because I was only fifteen when my girlfriend got pregnant. And then when my son was born I was afraid to hold him—I was scared that I might hurt him or drop him because he was so small. I didn't know about changing diapers and giving him formula and all that stuff. . . . Sometimes, I feel like I'm his older brother because I'm not really old enough to be a father, *yet I am his father. . . .* It's scary and I'm not always sure what I'm supposed to do."

Fathering-Skills Training with Peer and Adult Mentors

Boys like Keith are understandably unsure about how to care for a baby, so they need training in child-care skills. An innovative approach to helping young fathers learn parenting skills while addressing their fears and doubts about child care is to use peer mentors as trainers: "Using competent adolescent parents as role models or peer counselors may help build confidence in other adolescent parents. Because social interactions with peers are very important to adolescents, young parents may benefit more from hearing another adolescent parent attest to the importance of learning child development. . . . As one adolescent parent . . . stated, 'It's great to talk to someone who is in this situation.'"[93]

The use of peer or adult mentors during parenting-skills training may be particularly important for teen fathers who have absent or abusive parents or who are estranged from their family of origin. Teen fathers who were abandoned by their own fathers and have little idea of what it means to be a good father can benefit from the guidance of another male who can serve as a role model worthy of emulation.

Males who are chosen to be either peer or adult mentors of young fathers should be good role models who themselves have established paternity with their own children, provide emotional and financial support to their children and their partners or wives, and actively share child-rearing responsibilities.[94] An obvious advantage of using boys and men who have these qualities is that they are veteran parents who can share with expectant fathers their views on how they handled prenatal crises and how they view their roles as fathers now that they have a child. Peer and adult mentors can advise boys who are new to fatherhood about handling difficult parenting challenges, such as caring for a colicky baby or juggling parental, work, and school duties. In addition, it is very instructive when a veteran father brings his child to parenting-skills training sessions to demonstrate particular skills, such as comforting, feeding, changing, playing with, and loving his baby. Peer and adult mentors are also good at confronting young fathers who neglect their paternal responsibilities. As is illustrated by this young father's report, a youth is likely to accept constructive criticism about irresponsible behavior if it is posed by peers or respected adult mentors:

The leaders and the other fathers in the group, they some different kind of people that I ain't never run across before in my life. They challenged my bullshit, and after a while, they just flat out wouldn't accept it. . . . It made me think about the way that I just keep making the same old mistakes over and over and using the same sorry excuses. . . . The boys in my posse couldn't never do this. . . . They couldn't call me on nothing cuz they be just doin' the same things as me. I can't hardly believe it, but I'm seein' some changes in myself . . . getting my priorities straight.[95]

Successful confrontations with irresponsible teen fathers can be paired with discussions about the difficulties of young mothers as a way to promote empathy for their experiences. The emotional reactions of teen mothers to parenthood are remarkably similar to that of young fathers: teen mothers report feeling shocked, overwhelmed, depressed, alone, abandoned and betrayed, yet determined to be good parents. [96] Practitioners can use the group process to help young fathers learn about and acknowledge the many difficulties experienced by teen mothers and to generate ideas for how they can be more supportive of their partners. Again, the modeling of appropriate behavior by some group members can be a powerful tool in promoting similar behavior by other group members.

A final benefit of group parenthood training is that the supportive atmosphere of the group can foster the psychological well-being of the group members. Ron Lehr of Acadia University and Peter MacMillan of the University of Northern British Columbia interviewed eighteen young men who had participated in a support group for young fathers. These fathers enjoyed talking to the other members of the group about their problems and parenting concerns:

The act of sharing with other men proved very empowering because they said it helped them understand their own experiences more, gave them a feeling that they were supported, and gave them courage to continue in their commitment to their children. They also reported that listening to other men gave them more understanding and respect for relationships as well as a better understanding of how to more effectively handle their own problems. One father proclaimed: "Fathers' programs give fathers a better understanding of how to deal with problems and issues." The fathers also indicated that this program helped them develop a more positive and optimistic outlook, helped them get in touch with their feelings, helped them keep their focus on their children, and, overall, increased their self-esteem: "I'm basically getting out of it what I wanted which is to feel better about everything." "This program is reinforcing my self-esteem, knowing that I was a good father and still can be." "Nobody that knows me has ever said in the slightest that I was a bad father, but what I got out of this was the feeling that I was [a bad father] until I started coming here."[97]

Coeducational Parenting-Skills Training Groups

A relatively novel idea of teaching parenting skills to teen fathers is the provision of coeducational parent education programs. For example, The Attachment Teen Parenting Program (ATPP) is a ten-week coeducational parenting program for teen mothers and fathers and their babies. Program coordinators create a safe, therapeutic environment by emphasizing three rules—maintaining group confidentiality, respecting the experiences and feelings of group members, and focusing on the baby's needs. The group has a consistent, predictable, and understandable structure, beginning with an opening ritual during which rules are reviewed and participants share their current feelings and engage in an icebreaker activity (e.g., describing some recent experience with one's baby). Next, the parents learn and practice with their own child parenting skills that involve structuring (helping one's baby to feel safe), challenging (stimulating the baby's learning in developmentally appropriate ways), enjoying (having fun with one's child), and nurturing (holding, touching, feeding, and comforting one's baby in a loving manner). Following the structuring and challenging activities, a snack is provided, and then enjoying and nurturing activities are initiated. After all the parenting-skills activities have been completed, the young parents have a closing ritual consisting of journal writing and group discussions about what the day's experiences were like for them. As the young parents depart for the day, staff members offer them a "giveaway gift" (e.g., a children's book, crayons, safety plugs for electrical outlets, a baby memory book), which is especially appreciated by teen parents who are economically deprived and in need of items they can use to foster bonding with their children.[98]

According to Sue Ammen, a professor at the California School of Professional Psychology, the young parents who participated in the ATPP program experienced significant growth in empathy, more positive relationships with their children, and increased communication with their peers. However, the teenagers also experienced more alienation from their own mothers, perhaps due to tension associated with "the teen parents becoming more autonomous and responsible for their parenting role."[99] The development of such tensions underscores the importance of working with the entire family system to iron out issues that can emerge as the family adjusts to the addition of the baby to the maternal and paternal families.

Addressing Ongoing Issues with Both Extended Families

An unintended adolescent pregnancy followed by the birth of a child is a life-altering event for both the family of the young father and his partner's family. Understanding the potential roles of both families during the boy's transition to parenthood and helping both families to adjust to the changes in the family system are key aspects of the process of assisting him with the challenges of fatherhood.

Fathers, mothers, grandparents, brothers, and sisters play significant roles in shaping the paternal attitudes and behaviors of adolescent fathers.[100] It is common for the parents of an adolescent father to assist their son during negotiations with the mother's family regarding the outcome of the pregnancy and the care of the child.[101] Family members also tend to offer the young father advice about parental responsibility, encourage his support of his partner, express excitement about the arrival of the baby, and provide child care and financial assistance, and in some cases, a place for him and his partner to live after the child is born.[102] Teenage fathers receiving these various forms of support are more likely to remain involved with their child, complete school, enter the labor force, and secure employment and economic independence than young men who do not receive assistance from their families.[103]

Unfortunately, some families hinder a young man's potential to be a good father. It is common for families to have many negative reactions, such as their shock about not learning of the pregnancy until the later part of the prenatal stage and concern over whether the son would be involved in his child's life.[104] Although it is my impression from my counseling experiences with teenage fathers that most families recover from these initial troubled reactions and support their son, some families may actually discourage him from responding to fatherhood in a responsible manner if they strongly dislike his partner and her family. It is not unusual for his parents to believe that the adolescent mother wanted to get pregnant and for them to state, "She trapped my son." In these instances, the parents may give their son explicit or implicit messages that she, and not he, is responsible for the care of the baby. In other cases, young fathers from highly dysfunctional families are faced with trying to make the transition to parenthood while dealing with parents who are substance abusers, antisocial, or suffering from some form of mental illness.

Because family members can have a significant influence—good and bad—on the paternal strivings of young fathers, and recognizing that the families of teen fathers are often under considerable stress, family counseling is an essential aspect of assisting young fathers with the transition to fatherhood. Interventions designed to strengthen the quality of parent/child relationships and the connections that young men have with their families will improve their chances of overcoming the difficult circumstances associated with teenage fatherhood.[105] Boys raised by parents who exert either very low or very high control over their son's lives may be at great risk for adjustment difficulties.[106] Consequently, practitioners must help parents to utilize healthy levels of supervision and guidance in their son's life by demonstrating warmth, caring, and guidance that strikes a balance between promoting a young man's autonomy and offering him support.

For several reasons, the young father's mother is a good person to contact when the process of working with the youth's family is initiated. First, the paternal grandmother is often the person in a young man's family who is most receptive to counseling. So she can help a counselor to make inroads with the family.[107] Second, teen fathers usually identify their mothers as their primary source of support, even when both parents are present in the home.[108] Thus, the paternal grandmother can be a great ally to the counselor during the helping process with the young father. Third, the paternal grandmother may have problems that are independent of, yet exacerbated by, the crisis pregnancy. Helping her and other family members with preexisting difficulties will enable them to be more supportive of the son during his transition to fatherhood.[109]

Although the paternal grandmother is typically a key person for establishing trust with a family, counselors are advised to reach out and develop a relationship with the paternal grandfather if he is involved in his son's life. In families where the paternal grandparents have very traditional gender roles, it is a good idea to demonstrate respect by placing a phone call to the grandfather or paying him a visit and asking for his guidance as the head of the family about the young father's situation.[110]

Helping professionals must balance their work with the paternal family with outreach with his partner's family to ensure that all of the major figures in the child's life are working together to meet the needs of the child. Facilitating communication between the two families can strengthen the ties between the father and his child and increase the odds that the maternal family has access to the potentially helpful resources of the young father's family.[111] These resources, which include money, clothing, supplies, assistance with child care, guidance, and encouragement, can relive stress for the young mother and her family while yielding positive benefits for the child.[112] Keeping healthy lines of communication open between the two families also helps to ensure that that a teen father remains involved with his child and partner over time. Otherwise, conflicts between the families can go unsettled, the maternal family can shut the young man out, and that may distance himself from his partner and their child.[113]

The family of an adolescent mother goes through major changes once the young woman has her baby, and the father of the baby is in many respects an outsider who needs assistance to find his place in her partner's family:

Roles often blur when the infant is born. The teenager becomes a daughter/mother; her mother becomes a mother/grandmother. The roles of the mother and teenager expand to accommodate additional functions within the family. However, what society has not defined is the role of the baby's father, or the teenager's current partner within this family system. He usually is not living with the teenager and her baby. He is part father, part boyfriend or husband, and often developmentally an adolescent, even if his chronological age exceeds 19 years. Expectations of him vary in individual families. The mother's family will continue to function, albeit in a changed form. But the young man (boyfriend and/or father, and/or husband) is often on the outside, with no help in defining his relationship to the system.[114]

The role of the counselor then is to assist the young mother's family system to achieve a new equilibrium and to help the young father to define his place in this system. In order to do this, the counselor must reach out to the maternal family in a sensitive and considerate manner by demonstrating an understanding that this is a difficult time for the family and that the counselor is willing to assist the family with any of their needs. Making a home visit either during or shortly after this initial contact is crucial for establishing a personal connection with the family and for providing the professional with an opportunity to observe and assess the family system, especially regarding the family's readiness to support the young mother's attempts to parent her child and their perceptions about her partner and his place in their family. The counselor's first intervention with the family must be about addressing what they identify as their most urgent need, which can solidify a therapeutic bond between the counselor and the family and form the basis for an ongoing relationship that will allow the counselor to act as an intermediary between the young mother's and the young father's families.[115]

Once the counselor has established a relationship with the two families, he or she must help them to negotiate a plan of action. Some families need concrete action plans, such as formal written contracts between the two families that spell out the roles and responsibilities related to the care of the child.[116] Other families rely on informal agreements that address how financial and child-care obligations will be distributed across the two families.[117] Because formal and informal agreements create a shared responsibility for the well-being of the child, no one family is overwhelmed. Both forms of contracts also define the role boundaries between the two families so as to minimize confusion. In effect, they provide the families with a road map for how to manage the crisis of unplanned adolescent parenthood successfully.

Although contracts, whether written or unwritten, can help to prevent some intra- and interfamily conflict, tensions are inevitable. The resources and needs within and between families can change over time.[118] The adolescent parents may resent their continued dependence on their parents[119] and rebel against prior agreements. The grandparents may lose patience with the adolescent parents and take over in areas that previously had been the domain of the young parents.[120] A breakdown in the father's ability to financially support the child can strain relations between his and his partner's families.[121] Counselors must be prepared to help young fathers and their families to manage these types of ongoing difficulties.

Addressing Father-Son Wounds and Mother-Son Wounds

Adolescent fathers who have dysfunctional fathers, such as this teenager, often express a desire to not repeat the same pattern of behavior with their own children:

> My mom and my grandmother raised me. My dad? All I know is that his name was . . . , and when I was about [child's] age he left my mom. So, my mindset is that I want to be everything that he wasn't to me. Meanin' I want to be something to my son. I want to be a [cherished] memory, I don't want to be like just a name. My mom was talkin' about finding my dad, and I was like, "Well, go ahead . . . I don't care." I don't want to be like that with [child]. I want to be part of his life. I want him to say, "My dad is right there." I want to take him to ball games, I want to keep him strong, I want to be his life.[122]

The sociologist Rudy Hernandez observed a similar sentiment among the teen fathers he interviewed: "These young men seemed to present the relationship with their own father, whether bad or good, as the strongest motivating factor in their wanting to do fatherwork."[123]

The desire to be a good father is not always translated into actual good fathering behaviors. As was documented in chapter 4, a disproportional percentage of teen fathers are delinquent and somewhere between a quarter and a third of teen fathers are minimally involved with their partner, if they are involved at all, during her pregnancy. A small percentage of those who are involved are haunted by memories of abuse and neglect by their parents, and they have serious doubts about whether or not they can be good fathers due to the poor modeling of their dysfunctional parents. One burly young man named Vince had this to say to me about his dysfunctional parents:

> My dad and my mom weren't there for me. My dad took off before I could remember him. And my mom always had guys over who be beatin' on her or beatin' on me. And she'd be out at night partyin' with her friends, doin' crack and stuff when she shoulda been home takin' care of her kids. *A mother's supposed to take care of her kids, but*

not my mom! She was nothin' to us, and she didn't do nothin' for us, except bring all these jokers into our house and make the place crazy. . . . So, I ain't sure I want to know my kids 'cause I'm afraid I'll end up just like my parents, hurtin' 'em and makin' *their* lives crazy with all the shit I got into.

Young fathers like Vince need help to mourn the fact that they had dysfunctional parents, and inspiration and direction from caring adults about what it means to be a good father. There are a variety of therapeutic strategies that can be employed to help teen fathers resolve their father-son and mother-son wounds and promote their paternal strivings.[124] Specifically, counselors can help the son to:

- Acknowledge that his feelings have been hurt
- Let go of his childhood fantasies of having an ideal relationship with his dysfunctional parents
- Develop realistic expectations about what he can expect from his parents
- Become aware of and change maladaptive patterns of behavior he learned from his parents
- Forgive his parents and move on with his life
- Commit himself to becoming a good father no matter how inadequate his own parents are
- Find adult role models in the extended family (e.g., older brothers, sisters, aunts and uncles, grandmothers and grandfathers) or the community (respected teachers or coaches, Big Brothers or Mentor Fathers) who can offer their support and wisdom about being a good parent
- Experience meaning and healing through loving his own child

Couples Counseling

When mothers and fathers are equipped to handle the interpersonal stress associated with the advent of parenthood, "their children are more likely to function well socially, cognitively, and emotionally."[125] In addition, "children of parents who are able to work through and resolve conflicts are more socially competent than the children of parents who are more openly hostile" or who tend to avoid conflict altogether.[126] Thus, the provision of couples counseling, whose aim is to foster conflict-resolution skills, can promote the well-being of the children of teenage parents. Couples counseling is especially necessary with teenage mothers and fathers whose relationships are high in strife because "their children are a heightened risk for developing behavioral and emotional problems or both."[127] The provision of supportive counseling to distressed couples can help prevent a hostile disengagement among teenage parents who have decided to break up,[128] and it may be advantageous for the couple's children: "Children benefit from relationships with both parents, even if their parents are no longer romantically involved. Therefore, young parents who are not in an ongoing relationship may benefit from counseling that helps them separate their relationship with their child from their relationship with each other."[129]

One goal of couples counseling with teen parents should be helping the young mother and father to respect the important role each can play in their child's life. Skilled counselors must help each partner take ownership of the ways he or she might have alienated each other from their child. In addition, counselors should facilitate discussions between the couple "about the rights and responsibilities of both people in the child's life."[130]

Another goal of couples counseling should be to help the young parents to empathize with each other's experience. Both the young mother and the young father might have to be taught how to acknowledge each other's point of view.[131] Utilizing this approach, I have found it helpful to have each young parent take turns reflecting their partner's experience. Typically, these supportive exchanges help the couple to be more understanding of and responsive to each other's difficulties if they are linked to specific ideas about how each person can assist the other with his or her needs.

Addressing Peer Relationships

Peers play an important role in a teen father's life prior to, during, and after the pregnancy. Once the baby is born, a young father continues to need time with his friends, yet he must make the care of his child his top priority. Finding a healthy balance between fathering duties and time spent with friends is a difficult challenge. Making good choices about the friends he keeps is also important because some peers can support his adjustment to fatherhood, while others can be a negative influence. Counselors can address these issues by:

- Negotiating with family members to watch the baby so that the father has time to spend with friends
- Encouraging the father to stay away from peers who might be a bad influence and to surround himself with friends who will support his efforts to be a good father
- Reaching out to other teenage boys and girls in the community and asking them to invite the father to their social activities, assist him with his paternal responsibilities from time to time, and listen to his concerns about fatherhood[132]

Preventing Additional Unintended Pregnancies and STDs

Teenage fathers are likely to engage in high-risk sexual behavior, even after they become fathers, thereby placing them at risk to be involved in multiple unintended pregnancies and to contract sexually transmitted diseases. For example, in one investigation conducted in the state of Oregon, "the 35 young men who were adolescent fathers had a total of 45 children prior to 20 years of age,"[133] indicating that some of the men had played a role in multiple pregnancies. The majority of the forty-seven young fathers participating in an ethnographic survey administered in Philadelphia by Public/Private Ventures were at high risk for additional pregnancies and sexually transmitted diseases, including HIV. These young fathers reported that they were under great pressure from their peers to engage in unprotected sex.[134] Other investigators have observed that teen fathers tend to engage in a wide range of high-risk behaviors and associate with other boys who take sexual risks.[135]

In light of these considerations, many practitioners consider it a duty to teach teenage fathers about condom use and skills for coping with pressures to have sex. However, education about responsible sexual behavior should occur only after a strong rapport with teen fathers has been established, for it is a touchy subject with many young fathers. Ideally, the topic should be explored with groups of teen fathers who have already bonded through their participation in support-group sessions and parenting-skills classes. Within the safe confines of such groups, young fathers can discuss the pressure they experience to engage in sex and the problematic norms they might feel obliged to follow, such as the belief that it is unmanly to use a condom. Trusted group facilitators can challenge the unsafe sexual practices of participants, and group members can identify strategies they use successfully to engage in safe sexual relations. Condom use can be taught, and questions the participants have about proper condom utilization can be answered. Youth sexuality educators from Planned Parenthood are excellent authorities on proper condom use and instruction and can be consulted for such purposes.[136]

Recognizing that parent-child discussions about sex can play a crucial role in the prevention of adolescent pregnancies,[137] soliciting the support and participation of the parents of a teen father can enhance prevention efforts. The purpose of such involvement is to help the parents to "establish a moderately conservative philosophy regarding the practice of sexual behavior, establish clear rules of conduct concerning sex and drug use, and make sure that these rules are followed."[138] Parents who have difficulty developing and enforcing these types of rules require training in child management and disciplining skills and direct instruction about how to have talks with their sons about condom use. Health-care professionals can encourage parents to promote condom use by making "sure that parents have all of the information . . . they need to discuss condoms, a place to turn if they need information, and accurate information about the effectiveness and use of condoms."[139] Providing parents with brochures and communication-skills workshops about discussing condom use are some concrete ways professional can help parents with this task.[140]

For young fathers who are still enrolled in school, providing accessible, affordable, and enticing activities after school and at times when school is not in session can help young men to delay having more children.[141] Keeping young fathers engaged in recreational and after-school programs provides these youth with adult supervision and guidance, while limiting the amount of opportunities for having sex. A feature of some innovative prevention programs has been the development of creative partnerships between high schools, employers, and local colleges through which successful completion of school is linked with opportunities for work or postsecondary education. These types of programs generate a sense of hopefulness about the future and give many young men a reason to delay fathering additional children until they are older.[142]

Addressing Legal Concerns

It is very common for teenage fathers to be unaware of the legal rights and obligations associated with being the biological father of a child. Many young fathers, including some who have attended the birth of their child, know little about their options for establishing paternity.[143] Much of their confusion about legal issues is due to a lack of information and the acquisition of misinformation. This confusion is compounded by the fact that legal statutes regarding statutory rape, abortion, adoption, paternity establishment, marriage and divorce, child support, and child visitation and child custody agreements vary from state to state.[144] Consequently, teen fathers consistently express the desire to receive legal advice regarding their paternal rights and responsibilities.[145]

One way to address the legal concerns of teen fathers is to create linkages between them and legal professionals who are willing to assist young fathers with their questions.[146] Information regarding pertinent state legal regulations can be acquired free or at reduced fees at local legal-aid societies or the legal clinics of schools of law. Legal advice with teen fathers should cover the following considerations:[147]

- How statutory rape is defined and punished, and how likely local authorities are to enforce statutory rape laws
- Patient consent, parental notification, and time-limit requirements pertaining to abortion
- A father's legal right to give consent for or veto an adoption, the legal processes that are involved in arranging for an adoption, and the legal terms and conditions of various forms of adoption (e.g., open adoptions in which the biological parents maintain some sort of contact

with the child after placement for adoption versus closed adoptions in which post-adoption contact between biological parents and the child is prohibited)

- Medical tests, fees, and official procedures associated with the establishment of paternity
- Legal definitions and obligations pertaining to marriage, separation, and divorce, and whether or not the state legally recognizes common-law marriages (i.e., a relationship in which a couple lives in a nonmarital union and shares child-rearing responsibilities)
- Requirements pertaining to formal child-support obligations, the penalties for failing to make child-support payments, and the impact of child-support payments on the amount of aid that is provided to a mother who is receiving welfare
- The procedures for obtaining court-ordered child-visitation agreements, the options a father has when these agreements are violated by his child's mother, and the consequences for a father who fails to visit his child at appointment times
- The processes for obtaining child custody

Postnatal Educational, Career, and Employment Counseling

Educational and career decisions made during the prenatal phase of counseling typically represent a compromise between the teenage father's preferred plans and the rapidly emerging responsibilities of parenthood.[148] For example, a young man who had plans to receive some form of specialized training or higher education may brush them aside to take any available job in order to support his partner and child. Once earning an income, he may be lulled into a false sense of security and give up on his prior career aspirations. Other teen fathers may have remained in school but are on the verge of dropping out once the baby is born. Others have dropped out and are unemployed. Consequently, during the postnatal phase, teen fathers need help with their long-term educational, career, and employment issues.

Comprehensive educational and career counseling with teen fathers can help them to clarify their self-concepts and values, become aware of occupational options and their associated training requirements, develop effective career planning and decision-making skills, and commit to realistic educational and career plans. Also, school-based father-support programs can help young fathers to remain in school through the use of school personnel, whose role is to address a father's educational needs and to provide family-life education, and a community-resource coordinator, whose responsibility is to organize referrals to community services not available in the school.[149] Linkages with employment-placement and job-training programs can also be used to help young fathers to develop the skills they need for the job market.

Specialized services offered in the evenings and on weekends can help teen fathers who have dropped out of school to reenter educational programs.[150]

Innovative education and career programs are necessary for adolescent fathers residing in neighborhoods besieged by structural unemployment. Counselors, social workers, educators, and health-care professionals serving adolescent fathers from socioeconomically depressed areas must work together to be catalysts for creative, holistic programs that enhance the life options of economically disadvantaged adolescents, such as The Children's Aid Society's Adolescent Sexuality and Pregnancy Prevention Program, which is a long-term, community-based, multidimensional program for adolescents in the Harlem section of New York. This program was implemented at three community-center sites, and operated every afternoon and evening during the week and at two of the sites on weekends. The components of the program included family-life and sex education, academic assessment and help with homework, job club and career awareness, mental-health services, and self-esteem enhancement through the performing arts. In addition, all program participants were guaranteed admission as fully matriculated freshmen at Hunter College of the City University of New York upon completion of high school or its equivalent and the recommendation of the program director. Financial aid for college expenses also was available. The features of college admission and financial aid provided young men from the community with a realistic chance of attending college, which is a great incentive to complete school in spite of the harsh realities of being poor in an urban environment.[151]

Helping Teen Fathers Who Have Been the Victim of Child Sexual Abuse

Boys involved in a pregnancy are significantly more likely than young men who have not gotten a partner pregnant to have been the victims of some form of forced sexual contact, including being forced to have sexual intercourse against their will.[152] Therefore, asking about sexual coercion or abuse should be a routine part of any medical or psychological evaluation of teenage fathers. When a young man reveals that he has indeed been the victim of sexual abuse, a sensitive process of counseling must be initiated. If the young man is still a minor, state child-protection officials must be notified, and the boy will need extensive support while an official investigation of the abuse allegation is conducted.

We must show due concern for scarred boys who become parents, both for their sake and for the well-being of their children. Adolescent fathers who have suffered physical and sexual abuse and neglect have the potential to be impatient, impulsive, and violent. Consequently, they are at risk to use inappropriate child-rearing techniques with their own children, especially when they are under stress.[153]

Therapy with a sexually abused boy must address the impact of the abuse on his relationships, his sense of security, and his psychological well-being. Sexually abused boys typically feel damaged physically and emotionally, and they often feel that they somehow caused the abuse to happen. Abused boys desperately want counselors to hear their stories and to feel their pain.[154] They need help establishing safe boundaries with other people and learning how to trust others again:

> For teenagers who have experienced incest only, a supportive relationship with a caring adult outside the family might foster resilience and effective coping strategies. Likewise, when a teenager has been sexually abused by someone outside the family or has experienced date rape, supportive parents can lessen the distress, foster positive coping strategies and improve long-term outcomes. But when a teenager has been sexually exploited both within and outside the family, who can be trusted to help? For health care providers, developing therapeutic relationships with such teenagers can be difficult and may require persistent, respectful efforts at fostering trust.[155]

One of the goals of therapy that is unique to the psychotherapeutic process with sexually abused boys who become teen fathers is to help the young man consider any possible connections between the abuse he suffered and his role in a pregnancy. Some important questions to discuss with him are: To what extent are his sexual relationships a poor attempt to deal with a dysfunctional family? Is his role in the pregnancy an effort to reassert his sense of power in reaction to the powerlessness he felt when he was sexually abused? Could fathering a child be a way to counter fears that he might be a homosexual after having been sexually victimized by an adult man?[156] Exploring and resolving these issues as part of a comprehensive treatment process can be instrumental in helping the young man to clarify his identity, develop healthier relationships, and avoid another unintended pregnancy.

Treating Teen Fathers with Psychiatric Conditions

Recognizing that an out-of-wedlock pregnancy is a potential adverse life consequence for teenagers with a psychiatric illness, mental-health counseling is a necessity with teen fathers who suffer from depression, anxiety disorders, substance abuse, or some other type of serious psychiatric condition.[157] "Failure to address these problems when they are present may compromise both the teen father's and mother's ability to coparent effectively."[158]

Because it is beyond the scope of this book to describe the clinical treatment of these conditions, the reader is referred to several excellent handbooks from clinical psychology,[159] family therapy,[160] and psychiatry,[161] each of which contain chapters on treatment for numerous common mental-health problems of adolescents. Clinicians will find *Counseling Troubled Boys: A Guidebook for Professionals*[162] especially helpful because this book describes how counseling for child sexual abuse, depression, attention-deficit/hyperactivity disorder, aggression, and substance abuse is applied with adolescent boys.

Treating Delinquent Teen Fathers

Young fathers who engage in criminal activity and the manipulation and exploitation of others are experts at making other people hate them. Consequently, perhaps the most challenging teen fathers to help are those who have a history of antisocial behavior. There is a tendency for some mental-health professionals, who are typically successful at maintaining their professional objectivity with the people they serve, to become so frustrated and angry with delinquent teen fathers that they turn their backs on them. Nevertheless, "it must not be forgotten that delinquent youth are people who require sensitive and committed counseling in order for them to become more socialized in their relations with their women partners and their children."[163] To help this population become better fathers, practitioners must understand the clinical process of working with oppositional and antisocial youth.[164] Several issues related to that process but specific to teen fathers with criminal histories are highlighted here.

Counselors should be prepared to serve as advocates for young fathers who are returning to society from prison and who make genuine efforts to demonstrate responsible paternal behaviors. Public policy sometimes makes it nearly impossible for these young men to make the transition back to society. For example, child-support enforcement techniques allow for the accrual of child-support obligations while a young man is incarcerated and for the suspension of a driver's license if accumulated child-support debts are not repaid after release from prison.[165] Such laws make it nearly impossible for a reformed young man to get a job, become self-sufficient, and support his family.[166] Where such policies exist, counselors may have to contact local child-support enforcement officials to see if a reasonable plan for child-support payments can be negotiated.

Although public policy can impede a young father's attempts to find work after he has been released from jail or prison, it must also be emphasized that delinquent teen fathers can undermine their own adjustments to work due to their unrealistic expectations about employment and job readiness.[167] Teen fathers with long histories of antisocial behavior and incarceration are poor candidates for a smooth and successful career development, yet they tend to have grandiose appraisals of their prospects for getting a good job and financially supporting their children.[168] For example, a sixteen-year-old teen father named Frank, a high school dropout who was just placed on parole after serving nearly a year in jail for drug, burglary, and assault convictions, once boasted to me in a snarling voice that he would soon be a rock star: "I know I'm going to make it real soon. There's nobody that can play the guitar like me. . . . I've got friends who are gonna hook me up with Aerosmith's agents. I've got clubs ready to give me gigs, and everybody knows I'm awesome . . . So who needs to put up with this shit about school and jobs that don't amount to shit."

Counselors must confront teen fathers who demonstrate such deluded thinking and challenge them to replace behaviors that could undermine their success in the workforce with skills that will enhance their employ-ability. In particular, "teaching prosocial skills such as learning to cope with frustration, learning to interview, and learning to accept entry-level jobs" must be essential activities of career counseling with dysfunctional young fathers.[169]

Another post-incarceration issue with adjudicated teen fathers is that a young man's partner and her family may sever their relationship with the father while he is in prison.[170] Consequently, he could encounter great difficulty seeing his child once he is returned to society. The counselor must help the young man who faces this situation to do some serious soul searching: is he truly ready to be a responsible father? If he intends to try to reengage with his child, he must be committed to actively supporting his child and his former partner. If she and her family reject his attempts to reengage, he must be helped to understand their point of view, be patient, and demonstrate behaviors, such as regular child-support payments and consistent offers of assistance, that might change their opinion of him. If these measures fail, then he will need to consult a lawyer about applying for a visitation agreement.

An especially crucial aspect of counseling teenage fathers with a his-tory of antisocial behavior is providing carefully monitored parenting-skills training. Although it appears that teen fathers as a whole are no more likely to physically abuse their children than are adult fathers, the characteristics of some antisocial adolescent fathers and their children and environments increase the risk that child maltreatment will occur. Many of the factors asso-ciated with child maltreatment—such as being a parent at a young age, being unmarried, engaging in substance abuse, having legal problems, having a low-birth-weight, unplanned, and unwanted baby, and living in poverty, violence, and crowded conditions[171]—are typically present in subpopulations of teen fathers with histories of delinquent behavior. These fathers tend to engage in various forms of negative child-rearing practices, including the use of coercive control, which place their children at risk for developing antisocial behavior problems.[172] Consequently, intensive home-based guid-ance during parenting-skills training may be necessary in order to prevent the development of abusive child-rearing habits. Home-based instruction provides practitioners with "a more accurate and complete understanding of all the factors in the home and family that influence the quality of child-drearing" with youth who are high risk to maltreat their children.[173] Also, the "presence of a visitor in the home serves as a visible reminder to parents that excessive punishment and neglect of children is not condoned by society," which is particularly important with teen fathers from families for whom child abuse and neglect has become a pattern that has been passed from one generation to the next.[174]

In addition to addressing these issues, counselors also must confront the cavalier sexual beliefs and behaviors of some delinquent young fathers who do exploit adolescent women. The following account, told to me by a teen mother named Jennifer, soberly brings to life the painful experience of a young woman who has been hurt by a sexually callous young man:

> He did everything possible to convince me he was a great guy. He bought me gifts, wrote me poetry, took me out to dinner, and told me he loved me. And I was a damn fool because I slept with him right away and I got pregnant. Then, when he got tired of having his way with me, he stopped calling me up, and he ignored me any time I tried to see him in person. It was like I didn't exist anymore, and it didn't matter when he found out I was pregnant or after I had the baby. I was humiliated, and I still hurt whenever I think about him and how that bastard used me.

Teenage fathers who sexually exploit and then dump young women must be challenged to stop their objectification of women and to develop more sensitive, empathic ways of relating to females. They also must be taught to see the harm that their self-centeredness has caused and to understand that they have engaged in a form of sexual abuse. Cutting through their denial and coldhearted qualities can best be achieved through group work with other teen fathers who are good role models of how to be a more considerate and supportive male toward women. Contact with more socialized fathers can have the effect of challenging a young man's cavalier attitudes about women while fostering his potential to develop healthier heterosexual relations.

When an antisocial teen father does remain involved with his partner, the couple faces the risk of having significant relationship issues that could adversely impact parenting their child. Among adolescent parents, a history of paternal antisocial behavior is associated with less co-parenting and less satisfaction with the co-parenting relationship. Furthermore, antisocial teenage fathers tend to continue on a criminal path after they become parents, and their poor relationship skills lay the groundwork for relationship conflicts with their partners and dysfunctional parenting practices.[175] Thus, early intervention in the form of couples counseling, especially addressing how problems in the mother-father relationship impacts child rearing, is crucial with this subpopulation.

A final issue for counseling pertains to the naive beliefs of antisocial young fathers who convince themselves that they are stellar role models for their children. In one study, the majority of the incarcerated teen fathers believed that they could be good role models for their children and could be the type of man of whom a child could be proud.[176] These beliefs fly in the face of the histories of these young men, whose long records of criminal activity had landed them in jail and had placed them at risk to be career criminals with little potential to be either a reliably employed or admirable father. The treatment of choice for these youth is group counseling in which peers challenge each other to become true models of desirable behavior.

The Need for One-Stop Shopping

Professional helpers and volunteer mentors of teen fathers recognize that the process of helping this population is often akin to juggling two burning wands at the same time. It requires concentration, commitment, and care to help a young father to address so many needs, ranging from handling a crisis pregnancy to preparing for fatherhood, supporting his partner, parenting his child, resolving conflicts with his partner and two extended families, and making important decisions regarding school and work. Ideally, a young man can manage the transition to fatherhood better if he can find a place that provides services in one location that can assist him with each of these challenges. In chapter 6, I describe model teen-father programs and other resources that are designed to strengthen teen fathers in their role as parents.

6

Model Programs and
Useful Resources

Comprehensive Service Projects, Organizations, Web Sites, Movies, and Young-Adult Books Pertaining to Teenage Fathers

During the 1970s and through the early 1980s, it became clear that adolescent childbearing was a major social problem. Each year during that time period, about a million teenage girls got pregnant, and roughly half of those young women gave birth to a baby. The health, social service, educational, and legal systems of our country began to recognize that these young mothers and their children were at risk for a variety of social, economic, and health-related difficulties. In response to these problems, numerous multifaceted service programs for teen mothers were established to improve the life circumstances of these teenagers and their children and to reduce the number of girls having babies. Although adolescent-mother programs flourished, they did not solve the major national problems associated with adolescent pregnancy and parenthood. Furthermore, these programs did nothing to address the hardships of teen fathers, who were found to have lower income levels, less formal education, and more children over the course of their lives than their non-father peers.[1] A new approach to addressing these problems was needed.

In a historic turn of events, in 1982 the Ford Foundation funded a two-year national demonstration project known as the Teen Father Collaboration whose purpose was to encourage agencies that already work with teenage mothers and their children to extend services to teenage fathers. No project of this kind had ever been undertaken, and the geographic scope of the Collaboration was enormous. Teenage father programs were started in eight cities: Bridgeport, Connecticut; Louisville, Kentucky; Minneapolis and Saint

Paul, Minnesota; Philadelphia, Pennsylvania; Portland, Oregon; Poughkeep-
sie, New York; and San Francisco, California. Each agency from the participating cities designed and developed its own unique program. In addition,
the agencies were charged with the tasks of developing effective strategies
for reaching and helping young fathers, documenting how they developed
teen-father services, and drawing attention to the problems of adolescent
fathers in their communities. The agencies also gathered extensive information about the fathers they served.

The Teen Father Collaboration and other renowned program, such as
the Maine Young Fathers Project, Public/Private Ventures Young Unwed
Fathers Pilot Project, and the Texas Fragile Families Initiative produced a
gold mine of findings that are instructive to any professional or concerned
lay person interested in starting a local initiative to support the development of a teen-father program in his or her community. Here are some of the
lessons these projects have taught us about developing effective programs
for adolescent fathers.

Form a Service Coalition and a Board of Directors

Communities can best address the various needs of teenage fathers through
the formation of service coalitions in which professionals from different
agencies and organizations pool their resources and work collaboratively
to offer a wide range of services. For example, The Greater Bridgeport Adolescent Pregnancy Program, which was one of the sites for the Teen Father
Collaboration, was headquartered at the local YMCA, but included linkages
with other youth service organizations, such as the Bridgeport Community
Health Center and the Cardinal Sheehan Center. Through this arrangement, the Bridgeport program was able to address the social, spiritual,
and physical needs of teenage fathers from the greater Bridgeport area of
Connecticut.

The service coalition should be headed by a board of directors, which sets
policy, makes suggestions, and provides guidance for the service coalition.
Typically, the board consists of six to ten members, including residents from
the local community, professionals from local, county, state, and national
agencies serving youth, and representatives from the juvenile justice system.[2]
It is advisable to have at least one current or former teen father on the board
to offer a young father's perspective on policy matters.[3] All members of the
board should be genuinely interested in the well-being of young fathers.[4]
Preferably, the head of the board should be a "community catalyst"—that is,
a well-known and respected member of the community who has the clout
and connections to make things happen.[5] The director of the board also must
know how to deal with the public in an assertive but diplomatic manner,

particularly with citizens who believe that providing services to adolescent fathers promotes teen pregnancy. In response to such opposition, directors should be prepared to point out that the teen-parenting programs were developed only *after* premarital adolescent parenthood became a major social problem and that teen-father programs have been demonstrated to promote responsible fathering behaviors among program participants.[6]

After the board of directors has been formed, the establishment of other features and practices will help the coalition to succeed:[7]

- Experienced, hard-working, and well-connected staff
- A sense of community and strong preexisting relationships and networks within the community
- Participation and support of key organizations
- Shared leadership
- Effective interpersonal and organizational communication and decision-making
- Established conflict-management processes

Typically, local leaders, professionals, and other concerned citizens will mobilize around a coalition and promote its benefits when a program addresses the unique, urgent problems of the teens in the community.

Designate a Lead Agency and a Coordinator

Service coalitions usually designate a lead agency to conduct needs assessments and program evaluations and to function as the hub for the service coalition.[8] Ideally, the lead agency should be a setting where a multitude of services can be offered so that teen fathers can have most of their needs addressed in one location.[9] Schools and hospitals are good examples. When coalitions reach out to adolescent fathers across a vast geographic region, it may be necessary to have several lead agencies. For example, the Maine Young Fathers Project designated two service centers, one rural and one urban, as lead agencies so that adolescent fathers from different parts of the state could become participants in the program.[10]

A program coordinator works as the liaison to the many service providers making up the coalition and manages the overarching goals and activities of the program. This individual must have good people, organizational, and advocacy skills, and an understanding about the characteristics and hardships of teenage fathers. Preferably, this person should be a male who has earned the respect and trust of the local community for his commitment to helping boys and young men.[11] The coordinator of the Teen Father Collaboration offered through the Greater Bridgeport Adolescent Pregnancy Program had all of these qualifications. He was a Latino man who was considered an exemplary role model in the Bridgeport community. He had excellent street smarts and was dedicated to helping young fathers. He went out to recreational facilities, community centers, schools, and teen hangouts to promote the program. "As a result of these efforts, word of this program quickly spread throughout the streets; in fact, the program's caseload of teen fathers soon became so large that the project might have benefited from additional staffing."[12] This type of success story underscores the importance of having a respected, dynamic person as the program coordinator.

Conduct a Needs and Resources Assessment

The board of directors and the program coordinator can help to clarify the mission of their program by conducting an assessment of the needs and resources that exist in the community. This type of special assessment process typically involves completing the following tasks:[13]

- The board must designate the target community and population for the service program. For example, will the program serve the local community or a larger region? Will the program target just teenage fathers or both teenage and young-adult fathers?
- Demographic data about the target community must be collected. For example, what are the data regarding the race, ethnicity, and socioeconomic levels of the youth from the target area? Figures regarding these variables can be acquired from census data and county records and then be used to create programs that take into account the cultural diversity of the target population.
- Existing services in the target community and sources of funding must be identified.
- Teen fathers from the target community must be interviewed to establish how they learn about sources of help and which agencies and organizations they are most likely to use.

Engaging in these types of assessments provides a program with direction and clarity of purpose. For example, professionals working for the Young Unwed Fathers Pilot Project employed intake questionnaires and interviews with young fathers to develop an understanding about what the fathers deemed to be important, and how events in one domain of a young man's world could affect other spheres of his life. The information obtained from these interviews helped the project directors to realize that their program must include educational opportunities, employment and training services, fatherhood development activities, and case-management services in order for the program to appeal to the fathers who were being targeted for services. This proved to be a prudent decision. Fathers who participated in the program were surprised and grateful that someone had actually asked them about their opinions and needs. Many of these same fathers also reported that the services that were eventually provided to them helped them to remain engaged with their children even when times got very difficult for them. In short, the information that had been acquired through the assessment process helped to insure that the program was a success with the young men it was designed to serve.

Another value of conducting assessments is that their findings can inform program officials about how to vary services in statewide initiatives according to local needs. This was an important lesson arising from the Texas Fragile Families Initiative (TFF), which had numerous service sites throughout Texas. Based on its assessment of the different communities participating in the project, TFF officials determined that professionals working in smaller rural communities would have to include services that address the high unemployment rates and transportation issues experienced by the young fathers residing in those areas. Program administrators also ascertained from their assessments that across settings, programs targeting fathers who are still teenagers would be best served through school-based services, while older fathers would be more appropriately helped though community-based health clinics and employment service centers. In addition, services had to be adjusted for the various cultural populations in different parts of the state. For example, program staff working in El Paso and Laredo developed culturally sensitive practices for the high concentration of Latino males residing in those cities, while practitioners in Dallas and Houston had to employ strategies that were responsive to the needs and traditions of larger numbers of African-American fathers.[14] Making these adjustments based on the demographic data and resource information collected through assessment enabled the TFF to be one of the most successful statewide initiatives ever directed at young low-income fathers.

Develop an Implementation Plan

As personnel move closer to implementing a program for teen fathers, they think about their objectives and how they are going to achieve them. Some key questions to consider during this stage are: How we will know when we have achieved our goals? What is our timeline for hiring staff and opening our doors to young fathers? What will be the role of each agency in serving young fathers? How often will we offer in-service training and special meetings for our staff to help them feel competent in working with young fathers?

A large planning group, consisting of representatives from numerous government and private organizations, addressed these types of questions while developing an implementation plan for the Maine Young Fathers Project. For example, linkage agreements, spelling out the types of each service that participating agencies would provide, were developed. Procedures for making referrals between agencies were put into place. A goal-attainment scale was used "to assess client needs, to set goals collaboratively with the client, to identity sources to be utilized, and to measure client progress."[15] And special in-service seminars, teaching personnel about strategies for working with young fathers, paternity rights and responsibilities, male sexuality, and domestic violence, were provided. As a result of this planning, the project was later implemented with a clear idea about how staff should proceed in their work with teenage and young-adult fathers.

Conduct and Monitor the Implementation Process

During the implementation phase, the program is launched and all of the prior plans are put into action. In addition, the program coordinator schedules meetings periodically to assess the ongoing implementation of the program. At these meetings, the coordinator should foster communication between representatives from coalition agencies to discuss program successes and failures and to generate potential solutions to any difficulties that are related to carrying out the objectives of the implementation plan. During these interchanges, the coordinator can determine if the program is achieving its objectives and whether or not a revision of the original implementation plan is necessary by asking the following key questions:[16]

- Are appropriate personnel, equipment, and financial resources available in the right quantity, in the right place, and at the right time to meet program needs? If not, what barriers are preventing these activities from taking place?
- Are expected "products" of the program actually being provided? Is the program providing the expected services, and reaching the target population?
- What key ingredients contribute to the results being achieved?
- Are the activities being completed on time? Is the time line adequate to reach the established objectives?

Responses to these questions can determine what changes are needed while the program is still in progress. For example, initially the Maine Young Fathers Project consisted of three service sites. However, during the implementation phase, it was discovered that one of the sites, a rural health center located in the easternmost tip of Maine, was unsuccessful in recruiting young fathers. Consequently, this site was dropped from the program and all subsequent resources and outreach and service efforts were concentrated on the two remaining sites. On the basis of this reallocation, a more focused and informative analysis of successful work with young fathers was possible.[17] Careful monitoring of the Texas Fragile Families Initiative also led to important programmatic changes during the implementation phase. Based on numerous meetings between state-level and local coordinators, it was learned that some sites required additional technical assistance to learn how to record their professional activities with young fathers more accurately and efficiently. Also, it was determined that some sites would have to expand their hours of operation from the daytime to include evening and weekend hours in order to make their services available to more fathers.[18]

Evaluate the Effects of the Interventions

A common problem experienced by administrators of teen-father service programs is that many of the practitioners working with young fathers are not inspired to collect information that is necessary for an analysis of program effectiveness. Many social-service workers believe that serving people, rather than recording data, is the real work of social services. Consequently, evaluation is much lower on their list of priorities.[19] Nevertheless, programs that do not demonstrate some type of positive impact with teen fathers run the risk of losing community, administrative, or funding support, which could result in program termination.[20] Consequently, evaluating the impact of teen-father programs is crucial for their survival.

At a minimum, programs serving youth should collect data regarding the number of hours of service that have been provided, the number of youth that have been served, and customer satisfaction regarding services received.[21] In addition, with teen-father programs, there should be an evaluation of the following outcomes:[22]

1. *Legal aspects of fatherhood.* How many participants establish paternity and provide child support? Several forms of child support should be measured, including court-ordered child-support payment, voluntary financial support, and providing materials such as diapers, clothes, and furniture.

2. *Self-sufficiency.* What are the rates of the following: job acquisition; reductions in a father's age-grade discrepancies; school reenrollment; diploma acquisition; participation in the Special Supplemental Nutrition Program for Women, Infants and Children (WIC), Children's Health Insurance Program (CHIPS), and Medicaid; child immunizations; and changes in household income?

3. *Effective parenting skills.* How much time does each father spend with his child? What does he know about child development? How competent

is he with his parenting skills? Has he served as a coaching partner in Lamaze classes? How often does he join his partner during her prenatal health-care appointments?

4. *Behavioral issues.* Are there reductions in subsequent pregnancies, STDs, violence, substance abuse, and mental health conditions such as depression?

Although it is beyond the scope of this book to provide a detailed technical description of conducting an outcome assessment for a teen-father program, there are excellent resources interested readers can consult on the subject. *The Sourcebook of Comparison Data for Evaluating Adolescent Pregnancy and Parenting Programs*[23] contains thorough coverage of the subject of evaluating adolescent pregnancy and parenting programs, and numerous publications on the subject are cited in *A Basic Bibliography on Adolescent Sexuality, Pregnancy Prevention and Care Programs and Program Evaluation.*[24] Four other publications are superb final reports describing the program development, implementation, and evaluation stages of multifaceted programs serving adolescent and young-adult fathers: *The Teen Parent Collaboration: Reaching and Serving the Teenage Father;*[25] *If the Shoes Fit: Final Report and Program Implementation Guide of the Maine Young Fathers Project;*[26] *Young Unwed Fathers: Report from the Field;*[27] and the *TFF Final Evaluation Report.*[28]

Characteristics of Successful Programs

The professionals who worked on the Teen Father Collaboration, the Maine Young Fathers Project, the Young Unwed Fathers Pilot Project, and the Texas Fragile Families Initiative were deeply interested in figuring out a way to connect with populations of young men who had a history of being difficult to engage in service programs. One of the ways they approached this challenge was to carefully examine how the construction of fatherhood programs affected the participation of these hard-to-reach youths. As these professionals went out into their surrounding communities, interviewed adolescent boys and young adult men, and started offering services, they began to understand better what drove these men away from service providers and what drew these men into social-service, mental health, and medical facilities.

Many programs for teenage fathers failed to attract and retain participants because they offered only a single service, such parenting-skills training, or they attempted to do too much in a short period of time ranging from a month to six weeks. They were quick fixes that failed to comprehend the many practical needs of adolescent fathers, such as the necessity of finding a decent job, and their many personal difficulties, such as conflicts with their partners and problems with the legal system.[29] The young men these programs were designed to serve sensed the inadequacies of these programs, so they stayed away from them, complaining that the programs lacked either a service they desperately wanted or a personal touch and a steady mentor to whom the young men could turn as they tried to cope with the many demands placed on their lives.[30]

The overarching lesson from these experiences was clear: if programs do not provide the full range of services addressing the variety of needs of young fathers, "clients will either leave in frustration or seek help elsewhere."[31] Learning from prior failures, the designers of model adolescent-father programs recognized that they had to make some radical changes in both the design and the delivery of their programs. First, rather than offering services that appealed to adolescent mothers, they decided to include a wide array of services that teenage fathers have deemed to be important, including preparation for fatherhood, couples and family counseling, peer support groups, mentoring from adults, educational and career counseling, educational instruction and GED classes, computer training, job training and placement, child-care services, health care, education about HIV/AIDS and other sexually transmitted diseases, sex and family life education, instruction about contraceptives (especially condom use), substance-abuse and mental health counseling, crisis intervention services, and legal counsel regarding paternity, child support, and child custody matters.[32] Second, they secured sufficient funding to keep their young-father programs in place for at least a couple of years, which would allow for continuity of service to fathers. Third, they staffed their programs with caring case managers who would be an anchor for teen fathers during the transition to adulthood.

These features proved to be the vital ingredients of successful programs. In addition to seeing the young men in their offices, the case managers visited the young men in their homes and met them in other locations, such as recreation centers. Through these varied contacts made over a period of time, the young fathers began to trust the case managers and relied on their assistance to make sense of and navigate the intimidating and confusing bureaucracies of the health, social-service, educational, employment, and legal systems to which the teen-father programs were linked.[33]

Flexibility and adjusting programs to fit the needs of particular fathers are other factors that can contribute to program successes. For example, boys who become fathers between the ages of twelve and fourteen, though rare, are still children physically, psychologically, and socially. "Emotionally they are still dependent on their families and other adults,"[34] and they are grossly unprepared for parenthood. Consequently, young fathers and their partners from this age group are too young to take on the responsibilities of raising a child, even though they might assist with providing child care for their babies as would an older child caring for a sibling under the supervision of his or her parents. Undoubtedly, boys and girls in this age group who become parents will need the direct, ongoing, and significant assistance of both families emotionally and financially if they opt to keep the baby. The provision of school-based or community-based child-care services is crucial so that they can continue with their educations, and life-skills training and counseling is required to help them succeed with the challenges of adolescence and later with their transition from adolescence to adulthood.[35] By comparison, "Middle adolescent mothers and fathers [age 15–18 years] have the capacity to plan and make decisions for their lives if they are given viable choices. They should have some capacity for empathy and insight, and can make very good parents, given proper support. School-based programs, such as sex education, parenting classes, child development, and family services have been effective for this age group."[36]

The life experiences of late adolescent mothers and fathers age eighteen and nineteen is much different from those of young teens.[37] Teen fathers in this age group who have completed high school fare well when the family supports their efforts to learn parenting skills and provide financial assistance as needed, and when service programs help them with job training and placement. Teen fathers who never completed high school also require GED classes so that they are better prepared for higher education and the world of work.[38]

One of the tricky challenges with older teenage fathers is knowing how to respond to their employment needs. Case managers from the Texas Fragile Family Initiative (TFF) reported that job training and placement was a top service requested by the older fathers the TFF served. Accordingly, TFF professionals were quick to respond to this demand by trying to address the employment difficulties of their clients. However, TFF practitioners also found that some fathers would leave a program immediately after securing a job if they had not been engaged more fully in other services.[39] Thus, skilled case managers must ascertain and respond to other needs a young man has, such as helping him to resolve conflicts with his partner and learning effective parenting skills, while marshalling job-placement services for his benefit.

Across all these age groups, programs are more likely to be effective if there is a focus on promoting connections between young men and their families, schools, and communities. These types of ties can play a key role in preventing additional high-risk sexual behavior among boys who have become fathers.[40] Recognizing the significance of these connections, successful programs try to strengthen the bonds that young fathers have with their families through providing family counseling, parenting-skills training, and support groups for grandparents. In addition, these programs have either in-house educational services or linkages with existing GED programs staffed by caring teachers and counselors who help young fathers to further their educations and address their career needs. Successful programs also utilize trustworthy mentors from nearby neighborhoods and provide recreational programs and support groups to help adolescent fathers feel like they are members of a caring community.

Creating supportive relationships between adolescent fathers and their families, educational personnel, and people in the community was a crucial feature of the Young Unwed Fathers Pilot Project, which achieved many positive outcomes, including an increased number of fathers seeing their child on a daily basis, earning their diplomas or GEDs, obtaining jobs, declaring paternity, paying child support, and demonstrating knowledge about child-support laws.[41] Testimonies from fathers who participated in the program reported that it helped them to develop the sense that the program staff really cared about them and that maybe the system was not out to "get them" after all. Sensing that people wanted them to succeed helped many of the fathers change their attitudes about fatherhood, child support, education, "the system," and work, as illustrated by this young father's statement:

> Before, like I always said I wasn't gonna cooperate with child support. . . . But now as long as I still get the opportunity like [this program for young fathers] and they give me an opportunity to finish my education . . . then I'll cooperate. That's why I like this program so much, you know, that's why I'm out here every day just about and doin' what I'm supposed to do. . . . The education is gonna pay me back in the long run. . . . It'll help me get a job to keep the man off my back, and still have money left over to support my needs.[42]

Promoting the kinds of connections that can enhance a young man's life can be difficult due to the financial, transportation, and social barriers that dissuade some youth from participating in service programs for adolescents.[43] To overcome these roadblocks, professionals targeting boys from impoverished communities may have to offer them free transportation[44] and financial incentives for their participation in a program.[45] One case manager in the Maine Young Fathers Project reported that she offered constant encouragement to the young fathers she served as a way to keep them involved in the program. Specifically, she talked with the fathers on a regular basis by either meeting with them face to face or calling on the phone once a week. She also "spent a lot of time transporting clients to appointments (although she did set reasonable limits),"[46] and she organized pizza parties and swimming parties for the young men. Case managers from the Texas Fragile Families Initiative found that offering even small yet tangible gifts, such as a package of diapers, reduced the pessimism some young men had toward social-service agencies and inspired them to have more contact with their case workers.[47] Recognizing the poor economic circumstances of teen fathers in Los Angeles, professionals from a community-based project in the Los Angeles area paid teen fathers who participated in their program $15 to $35 for each questionnaire they completed and $15 for each HIV prevention class they attended.[48] In response to the fluctuating work schedules of the fathers and the difficulties some had with transportation, sessions were held in the participants' homes and in local venues close to the father's residences (e.g., in nearby clinics and libraries).[49] These types of special accommodations can make a young man's participation in a program possible.

Remain Sensitive to the Culturally Based Concerns and Needs of the Community

A vital consideration for all teen-father initiatives, from the early days of developing a program through the final days of its implementation and evaluation, is to remain sensitive to the culturally-based concerns and needs of the community, which are largely determined by the socioeconomic, racial, ethnic, and religious backgrounds of the people in the area. A sample of these considerations is provided here to illustrate the process of devising programs in a culturally sensitive manner.

Although it is true that non-Hispanic white teens have the lowest teen pregnancy rate among the major racial and ethnic groups in the United States, white teenagers account for approximately one-half of all teen pregnancies nationwide.[50] This fact is often unknown if not denied by many white adults who are under the impression that teenage pregnancy is a phenomenon that exists only in minority neighborhoods. Knowing how to deal with this misconception in a sensitive manner represents one of the biggest hurdles that must be cleared during the development of teen-father programs in white communities. For example, the coordinator of a teen-parent program in New Haven, Connecticut, reported on a national television news show that white parents in her community often react to proposals for teen-parenting programs with shock and the claim, "This doesn't happen in *our* community." She went on to explain that effective program development in the presence of such reactions requires providing accurate information about local teen pregnancy rates, the sexual attitudes of area teenagers, and the pressures and problems experienced by white teenagers who engage in high-risk sexual behaviors.[51] It is prudent for professionals in similar situations to react in an empathic manner with surprised parents who are alarmed by the news that their teenagers are at greater risk than they had ever imagined.

Because the teen pregnancy rates are much higher in African-American and Latino youth, there is a greater recognition of the teen pregnancy problem in African-American and Latino communities, but many of the concerns and needs of the people in these communities differs from those in white communities. For example, a major source of tension that can lead to opposition to teen-father programs is the historical maltreatment of African Americans and Latinos by the health, mental health, educational, and legal systems in the United States. As a result of this painful history, many African Americans and Latinos are suspicious of professionals employed in these systems, and some even believe that these professionals are agents of a plot to commit genocide against their people, especially minority boys.[52] These fears sometimes surface when new programs are proposed for teen fathers, and the best way to prevent their emergence is to do some careful and culturally sensitive planning with leaders in the community throughout the entire life of a program. For instance, in African-American communities, enlisting the input of respected African-American leaders and clergy from the African American Church will earn trust for the program while helping to insure that any programs developed for African-American teen fathers are in touch with the cultural experiences of these youth. In Latino communities, similar measures will be successful with the involvement of the Catholic Church, and efforts to address immigration and illegal-alien issues will also be necessary since the latter concerns can be barriers to service utilization for young fathers who fear deportation or who have acculturation and language challenges.

These examples are just a few of the many cultural considerations pertaining to sensitive program development. For a more exhaustive discussion of these issues, the reader is referred to *Multicultural Counseling with Teenage Fathers: A Practical Guide*.[53]

Model Programs for Teenage and Young-Adult Fathers

Most programs serving young fathers have targeted males who range in age from their early or middle teens to their middle twenties. Some of the programs have been for fathers only, and others have served adolescent mothers and fathers. In this section, these programs are described and directions on how to learn more about them are provided.

Pioneering Teen-Father Programs

In response to the historical neglect of teenage and young-adult fathers, several pioneering teen-fathers programs were developed and delivered during the 1980s, 1990s, and early 2000s. These research and pilot projects yielded important information regarding the process of recruiting and serving teen fathers successfully, so they became models for many current

programs serving teen fathers. Consequently, even though they are no longer in operation, they are described here in chronological order so that current practitioners can take advantage of the lessons these programs have
taught us about effective outreach with adolescent fathers.

TEEN FATHER COLLABORATION. The Teen Father Collaboration was a
two-year groundbreaking national demonstration project that served 395
adolescent fathers at eight settings throughout the United States. Launched
in 1983, the program offered a variety of services, including counseling,
educational assistance, and job training with the goal of helping teen and
young-adult fathers to contribute to the social, emotional, and economic
well-being of their children.[54]

The Teen Father Collaboration was a major success and its methods for
working with young fathers have become the standard of practice for many
teen-father programs across the country. By the end of the project, 56 previously unemployed participants had taken part-time jobs, and 92 participants
had found full-time employment. Nearly one-half of the non-graduates
who were not enrolled in high school when they entered the program had
returned to school, had obtained their GEDs, or had enrolled in GED classes.
An aggressive approach to recruitment and a good knowledge of the community by the practitioners who worked with the young fathers were identified as chief factors in producing these encouraging outcomes. Men in their
twenties or thirties from the same ethnic and cultural background as the
teenage clients usually succeeded best as counselors.[55]

Another important lesson from the Teen Father Collaboration was that
ambivalence on the part of a cooperating agency was probably the most
serious hindrance to project efforts. Where top-level administrative support
was lacking, a program was largely ineffectual. Nonetheless, the project may
also have helped to erase the stereotype that all teenage fathers neglect their
parental responsibilities because it demonstrated that a substantial number
of these young men want help with their fatherhood duties.[56] An extensive
description of this landmark initiative is reported in *The Teen Parent Collaboration: Reaching and Serving the Teenage Father.*[57]

MAXIMIZING A LIFE EXPERIENCE. The Maximizing a Life Experience (MALE)
support group served eight unwed teen fathers ranging in age from fifteen to
eighteen years. The group met for eight weekly one-hour sessions in a suburban high school and took a three-hour field trip to a Planned Parenthood
center. The participants watched presentations and movies, read materials,
and had discussions. Topics covered through these activities included their
reactions to the pregnancy and fatherhood, their legal rights and responsibilities, and reproductive health and contraceptive use.[58]

The boys from the MALE group liked the program very much, especially its supportive atmosphere and the opportunities it gave them to discuss their situations with others who had similar problems. Most of them had not been aware that they shared the unwed-father role before joining the group. The most common program change suggested by the boys was to have longer and more frequent sessions.[59]

The participants also reported that the MALE group prompted them to make several changes in their attitudes and behaviors. By the end of the program, seven of the boys stated that they now considered the possibility of pregnancy before having sexual relations, and that they would consider abortion as an option if they were to be involved in a pregnancy again. All eight group members agreed that the man should share contraceptive responsibility, compared with four at the start of the program; and seven members reported that they now used contraceptives consistently, compared with three at the program inception. One year after the completing of the program, four of the boys were in college or technical school, two were in the military, and two were still in high school. None were married or had a second child, and all were continuing to contribute toward the support of their child.[60]

Although much smaller in scale than the Teen Father Collaboration, the MALE program was significant because it was one of the first published accounts of a school-based support group for teen fathers.   The full report about the MALE program was published in *The School Counselor*,[61] a professional journal available in most college and university libraries.

MAINE YOUNG FATHERS PROJECT. The Maine Young Fathers Project was a statewide service program that assisted 53 teen and young-adult fathers in Maine. The project was administered in three locations and offered case management and linkages with a variety of agencies where the fathers received help to develop their parent skills and self-sufficiency, producing numerous positive results: increased employment rates; increased use of resources for food, clothing, and transportation; more frequent use of wellness and sick-care services for both the father and his child; heightened participation in parenting-skills training; more responsible use of birth control; increased frequency of interactions between the father and his child; more fathers establishing paternity; greater use of a support system; improved interpersonal relationships; increased utilization of public aid; greater implementation of plans to manage financial affairs; and increased financial support of the child.[62] A gold mine of information related to the process of creating, implementing, and evaluating the program is provided in *If the Shoes Fit: Final Report and Program Implementation Guide of the Maine Young Fathers Project*.[63]

PUBLIC/PRIVATE VENTURES YOUNG UNWED FATHERS PILOT PROJECT. The Young Unwed Fathers Pilot Project served 155 teenage and young-adult fathers at six sites throughout the United States. The project chronicled the difficult life circumstances experienced by most of the fathers, including high unemployment, crime, school drop-out, and drug-use. The program emphasized teaching the fathers life and employment skills, provided case-management and support-group services, and promoted the fathers' understanding and responsiveness to child-support duties. The participants demonstrated increased rates of: school and GED enrollment; participation in job-readiness training and parenting-skills classes; employment, wages, and benefits earned; knowledge regarding child-support laws, legal rights, and paternal responsibilities; legal establishment of paternity and child-support payments; and positive attitudes toward the child-support system.[64] *Young Unwed Fathers: Report from the Field,* the major publication pertaining to this project, is a rich source of information about teen fathers and how to help them.[65]

MAZZA PROJECT. In 2002 an investigator named Carl Mazza published an article about a special service initiative for sixty urban African-American teen fathers age sixteen to eighteen. Because the location of the study was not indicated and there was no name given for the program, it is referred to here as the Mazza Project.

Mazza was interested in seeing if comprehensive service programs were superior to simple service programs providing only one form of assistance to teen fathers. So he designed a study in which one group of fathers would receive multifaceted services, while another group were provided parenting-skills training. The comprehensive program consisted of weekly individual counseling, biweekly group counseling, educational and vocational referrals and placement, medical care and referrals, housing and legal advocacy, cultural and recreational activities, and parenting-skills training. Fathers in the second group received only group parenting-skills training once a week.[66]

The results of Mazza's study were striking. Over the course of the investigation, boys in the comprehensive program far exceeded boys from the parenting-skills group in gains they made in a number of important achievements and behaviors. Relative to the fathers in the parenting-skills group, the boys in the comprehensive program made significantly greater gains in employment rates, short-term and long-term career planning, feeling positive about their current and future relationships with their children, condom use during sex, seeing themselves as being a responsible man, having close friends, and being willing to consult with a social worker about a personal problem. A major finding of this study was that the fathers from the parenting-skills training group remained unchanged for most of the outcome variables and declined on some of them. Overall, the results of this study demonstrated the powerful benefits of a comprehensive service program, while indicating that "programs for young fathers that focus only on teaching parenting skills are ineffective."[67] Mazza's report was published and can be found in the journal *Adolescence*.[68]

FATHERS FOREVER PROGRAM (FFP). Located in Buffalo, New York, FFP was an educational, employment, and psychosocial support program for young men age sixteen to twenty-one who were either expectant fathers or already had a child and who met federal guidelines for poverty. FFP provided GED and college-preparation classes, a weekly support group, life-skills training, parent education, job-skill training, paid internships, and informal counseling. Young men who completed the FFP were much more likely than those who dropped out of the program to receive their GED and be placed in an internship, an employment-training service, or a job. A complete description of the program is in the journal *Families in Society: The Journal of Contemporary Human Services*.[69]

TEXAS FRAGILE FAMILIES INITIATIVE (TFF). Recognizing that young low-income fathers are an integral part of families that can be considered to be fragile due to the many hardships these families experience, the Texas Fragile Families Initiative was launched to "facilitate the development of social services for young, low-income fathers as they support the emotional, physical, and financial needs of their children."[70] This project, which was delivered in eleven communities throughout Texas, served over a thousand never-married young men, about a third of whom were eighteen years old or younger. Comprehensive services were offered in a variety of school- and community-based settings. The *TFF Final Evaluation Report* is filled with data regarding the characteristics of young, unmarried fathers who are poor, the barriers that impede the lives of these young men, and recommendations pertaining to practice, program development, evaluation, funding, and policy.[71] TFF has also published a press release that contains the names, addresses, and phone numbers for the program sites that were a part of the initiative,[72] which is valuable contact information for people who might want to talk with professionals that have developed and delivered services for teen fathers.

Current Father-Only Programs

Professionals developing programs for teenage fathers who have an understanding of these historically important programs might also be interested in learning about how existing programs serve this population. Consequently, in this section current programs designed exclusively for young fathers are described and contact information is provided.

As a preliminary note, I must emphasize that it is very difficult to identify a comprehensive list of current teen-father programs. Although numerous programs for teen fathers are listed in the Web sites for various agencies and organizations, my research on these programs revealed that the majority of them were either no longer in operation or they rarely actually served fathers. For the programs described in this section, I have verified that the programs are active and actually serving teen fathers in a systematic, ongoing manner at the time this chapter was written.

CHILDREN'S TRUST FUND (CTF). CTF is an umbrella organization created in 1988 by state law in Massachusetts as a public-private venture to prevent child abuse and neglect by supporting parents and strengthening families. CTF funds, evaluates, and promotes the work of over a hundred agencies that serve parents and children, including many agencies that offer services to teen mothers and fathers. For example, Healthy Families is a special program delivered throughout Massachusetts for first-time mothers and fathers who are twenty years old or younger. Trained professional make visits to the homes of young parents and assist the parents in creating a stable home environment and developing effective parenting skills. Healthy Families also sponsors mom-and-dad support groups, child-development classes, and child playgroups. Another noteworthy program of CTF is the CTF Fatherhood Initiative, which is a statewide program whose aim is to infuse services for fathers in CTF-sponsored settings. One activity of the Fatherhood Initiative is the MELD Young Dads support groups, which offer supportive counseling, parent education, GED classes, and employment services to teenage and young-adult fathers. To learn more about the dozens of services coordinated by CTF, contact:

> The Children's Trust Fund
> 294 Washington St.
> Suite 640
> Boston, MA 02108
> (617) 727–8957
> http://www.mctf.org/index.aspx

FATHERS COUNT PROGRAM (FC). FC is one of numerous programs administered by Inwood House for at-risk youth in New York City. FC is designed to inspire young fathers age fourteen to twenty-one to accept their paternal responsibilities and to become role models for their children. Senior young fathers from the program mentor new adolescent dads in a safe environment in which health and supportive peer norms are fostered. The program provides parenting and family-planning classes, educational and vocational referral and placement, recreational activities, and counseling. The program serves approximately forty young fathers each year, most of whom are African-American and Latino youths. For more information contact:

Inwood House
320 East 82nd St.
New York, NY 10028
(212) 861–4400
http://www.inwoodhouse.com/contact.html

FATHER SUPPORT SERVICES OF CATHOLIC CHARITIES NORTH, LYNN, MASSACHUSETTS. Catholic Charities North of Lynn, Massachusetts takes a positive approach to helping teen fathers. The organization runs eight- to twelve-week groups for young fathers in community, hospital, and prison settings. The educational support groups emphasize five principles of responsible fatherhood: giving affection; demonstrating respect to the child's mother; offering gentle guidance; providing financial support to the child as well as the mother; and refraining from illegal activity and drug and alcohol abuse. In addition to fostering good parenting skills, Father Support Services also assists teenage and young-adult fathers in completing school and finding jobs. Annual reunions are held with former and current members of the groups, who enjoy picnics and recreational activities with their families and children. Father Support Services also plays a role in the Alliance on Teen Pregnancy, which sponsors an annual conference on fatherhood. More information about the innovative work of Father Support Services can be obtained at:

Father Support Services
55 Lynn Shore Drive
Lynn, MA 01902
(781) 593–2312
http://www.ccab.org/fathers_services.htm

PROJECT DADS. The purpose of Project Dads, a service of the Children's Aid Society of Birmingham, Alabama, is to help teen fathers become more responsible and effective parents through providing comprehensive out-reach, adult male mentoring, intensive case management, and peer support. Peer-support groups for the fathers emphasize a variety of topics, including relationship and life skills, infant care, family planning, safe sex, and career counseling. These services are free and confidential and open to fathers who are under twenty-one. For an in-depth description of this program contact:

Project Dads
Children's Aid Society of Birmingham
181 West Valley Ave., Suite 300
Homewood, AL 35209
(205) 251–7148
http://www.childrensaid.org/projectdads.html

ROCHESTER FATHERHOOD RESOURCE INITIATIVE (RFRI). RFRI is a community-based organization that provides a host of services designed to help fathers, including case management, court advocacy and legal assistance, employment and educational services, parenting, relationship and anger-management skills training, and HIV/AIDS education workshops. RFRI coordinates a weekly support group for teen and young-adult fathers through which these young men are linked to other fathers and the various service wings of RFRI. This organization is a leader in developing methods for engaging hard-to-reach fathers and helping them to become more involved in their families. For information contact:

Rochester Fatherhood Resource Initiative
775 South Plymouth Ave.
Rochester, NY 14608
(585) 235–3160
http://www.rfriweb.org/index.html

STEP-UP PROGRAM. STEP-UP (Skills, Training, Education, Employment Program for Unemployed Male Parents) is a special program for teen fathers that was initiated in Phoenix in 1990. The program emphasizes self-sufficiency and a father's responsibility to parent and provide financial support for his child. In September 1994 the U.S. Department of Health and Human Services selected STEP-UP to be one of four national programs to be replicated. Contact information for the program is:

STEP-UP Young Fathers
Young Families CAN
Travis L. Williams Family Services Center
4732 S. Central Ave.
Phoenix, AZ 85040
(602) 495–7522
http://phoenix.gov/YOUTH/tparents.html

UNION INDUSTRIAL HOME (UIH). UIH has been a leader in providing services for fathers of all ages in the greater Trenton, New Jersey, area since the early 1990s. The UIH Operation Fatherhood initiative assists unemployed and underemployed non-custodial fathers of children receiving public assistance by providing career assessments, job-skills training, job placement, and computer-skills instruction. The UIH Father Center offers parent education, job-search information, and interactive events such as storytelling and music programs involving fathers and their children. Also, through its membership in the Trenton Men's Collaborative, UIH staff assist fathers in linking up with over two dozen other agencies that provide a wide range of services such as substance-abuse counseling and housing assistance. For more information contact:

> Union Industrial Home
> 864 Bellevue Ave.
> Trenton, New Jersey 08618
> (609) 695–1492
> www.uih.org

VENTURA COUNTY ADOLESCENT FAMILY LIFE/TEEN FATHERS PROGRAM. A division of the Health Care Agency of Ventura County, California, the Adolescent Family Life (AFL) Program is dedicated to fostering the optimal development of teenagers. AFL administers the Teen Fathers Program, which is based on the assumption that many teenage boys and young men who become fathers have tremendous potential to be good parents but often lack the information and resources to become fully functioning fathers. Consequently, the program offers support to fathers age twenty-five and younger through providing parent education, employment services, relationship and substance-abuse counseling, and legal information about paternal rights and responsibilities. For more information contact:

> Adolescent Family Life/Teen Fathers Program
> 2500 South C St., Suite E
> Oxnard, CA 93033
> Telephone: (805) 385–9131
> Fax: (805) 385–9134
> http://www.vchca.org/ph/nursing/teendads.htm

YOUNG FATHERS PROGRAM (YFP). YFP is a multifaceted service program for fathers age fourteen to twenty-six in Denver, Colorado, that was formed through a cooperative arrangement between Parent Pathways, an organization whose mission is "to help teen parents raise healthy families," and the Denver

Public Schools. YFP is one of many service projects for teen parents administered by Parent Pathways, and it is based at the Florence Crittenton School, which has served unwed mothers since the 1920s. The YFP coordinator does extensive outreach with young fathers in the Denver schools and community. Male-friendly outreach and rapport-building activities include providing free meals, good-natured "trash talking," and periodic trips to wilderness areas. Support groups for teenage and young-adult fathers are organized at local schools, community centers, and the Florence Crittenton School.

A guiding assumption of YFP is that many young men would like to be responsible fathers but they lack parenting information and skills. Consequently, there is a strong emphasis on teaching the fathers hands-on parenting skills, such as how to feed, diaper, and bathe babies. Understanding the perspective of teen moms is promoted through an activity in which the fathers wear an "empathy belt," which is a weighted, artificial belly that simulates the experience of carrying the extra weight associated with a pregnancy. Other services include case management, educational and career planning, guidance about paternity establishment and child-support orders, and job-training referrals. More extensive information about YFP can be acquired at:

Young Fathers Program of Parent Pathways
Florence Crittenton School
96 S. Zuni St.
Denver, Colorado 80223
(303) 733–7686
e-mail: info@parentpathways.org
http://www.parentpathways.org/youngfathers.html

YOUNG MEN IN TRANSITION PROGRAM (YMTP). YMTP is a special service for teen fathers in the greater St. Paul/Minneapolis metropolitan area of Minnesota. YMTP sponsors school-based, teen-father support groups serving between sixty and one hundred young fathers a year. Parent education, mentorship, and one-on-one counseling are key components of the program. YMTP is one of the few teen father programs that has been in existence for over ten years, and it has developed a strong tradition of trust with young men in its service area. Pertinent information can be found at:

Young Men in Transition Program
Catholic Charities/Seton Service
1276 University Ave. W.
St Paul, MN 55104–4101
(651) 641–1180
http://www.ccspm.org/services/dadsConnection.html

Programs for Teen Mothers and Teen Fathers

Some agencies addressing the needs of youth have done a fine job serving both teen mothers and teen fathers. A description of several of these programs follows.

ATTACHMENT TEEN PARENTING PROGRAM (ATPP). The ATPP was a ten-week parenting program for teen parents and their babies age one month to two years. Although most of the participants of the program were adolescent mothers, ATPP also served some teenage fathers. ATPP provided young parents with coeducational parent education within a supportive group format. In particular, the parents were taught structuring (helping one's baby to feel safe), challenging (stimulating the baby's learning in developmentally appropriate ways), enjoying (having fun with one's child), and nurturing (holding, touching, feeding, and comforting one's baby in a loving manner) skills; then they were taught how to apply the skills with their own baby. Participants also engaged in support-group discussions about their experiences as parents.

An in-depth description of this program is provided in the book *Short-Term Play Therapy for Children*.[73]

FAMILY SPIRIT PROGRAM (FSP). The Family Spirit Program is an exemplary program designed to serve pregnant and parenting Native American teenagers in a culturally sensitive manner. Targeting adolescents from Navajo and Apache reservations in the southwestern United States, FSP provides educational services, access to community resources, and personal counseling. Using a home-visiting model, outreach workers meet with teen parents, either as couples or individually, to teach parenting, life, and self-help skills. FSP counselors are members of the Native American community who help the young parents to become competent parents while accessing education, legal assistance, mental health care, employment services, substance-abuse counseling, and medical care for their baby. FSP researchers evaluate the effectiveness of the program with the goal of reporting successful features of the program to other communities interested in replicating the FSP model. FSP has been implemented at several reservations, and it is administered by Johns Hopkins University. For more information contact:

The Family Spirit Project
Johns Hopkins Center for American Indian Health
621 N. Washington St.
Baltimore, MD 21205
(410) 955–6931
http://www.jhsph.edu/caih/Service_Projects/Family_Spirit_Project.html

PENNSYLVANIA DEPARTMENT OF EDUCATION TEEN PARENT PROGRAMS. The Pennsylvania Department of Education administers two programs, the Pregnant and Parenting Teen Program (PPT) and the Education Leading to Employment and Career Training Program (ELECT), which serve thousands of students at 43 PPT sites and 27 ELECT sites throughout Pennsylvania. The purpose of these programs "is to help teen parents stay in school, obtain a high school diploma or GED, have healthy babies, become capable parents, and prepare to become self-sufficient adults."[74] According to the Web site for the program: "All ELECT and PPT programs are located in public local schools and provide teens with: pregnancy prevention information, individual and group counseling, day care and transportation help, health and nutrition instruction, and parent and child development education. The projects also work extensively with local community organizations to coordinate services and insure that teens and their children know where to turn after graduation."[75]

Pennsylvania also operates the Safe Haven service, which is a toll-free (1–866–921-SAFE) crisis line that students can call for assistance about pregnancy resolution options. This service is specifically designed to prevent desperate expectant parents from abandoning their babies. Expectant teens can call the number and receive information about hospitals that will allow the teens to drop off their babies anonymously without any fear of criminal charges being filed. For more information about PPT, ELECT, and Safe Haven, contact:

Teen Parent State Coordinator
Pennsylvania Department of Education
333 Market St.
Harrisburg, PA 17126
(717) 346–9366 or (717) 783–6788
http://www.pde.state.pa.us/svcs_students/cwp/view.asp?a=175&Q=48
401&svcs_studentsNav= percent7C

PORTLAND PUBLIC SCHOOLS TEEN PARENT SERVICES. The Portland Public Schools Teen Parent Services is a special service program for pregnant and parenting teens in several traditional high schools, magnet schools, and alternative schools in the Portland Public School System. The program coordinates support groups, crisis counseling, parent education, case management, free transportation and child care, and maternity and paternity leaves for pregnant and parenting teens. The program has a cooperative arrangement with the Portland State University Center for Healthy and Inclusive Parenting, which provides special consultation and support groups for young dads. To learn more about these services, contact:

Portland Public Schools Teen Parent Services
4039 N.E. Alberta Ct.
Portland, OR 97211
(503) 916–5260
http://159.191.14.143/.docs/_sid/aba96092285ac7dd660c952dae8b075e/
pg/10050

TEEN AND YOUNG PARENT PROGRAM. A service of the University of Maine Cooperative Extension, the Teen and Young Parent Program links teen mothers and fathers with caring adult mentors who provide friendship and support to the young parents during the prenatal and postnatal period. Professionals conduct parent-education sessions with the young parents in their homes, and the program organizes monthly group activities, such as open swimming periods at the local Y and potluck dinners for the parents. The program publishes a newsletter, *Father Time,* which features topics of interest to young fathers. Program information is available at:

Teen and Young Parent Program
P.O. Box 805
231 B Park St.
Rockland, ME 04841
(207) 594–0975
http://www.umaine.edu/ceskl/T&YPP.htm

TEEN PARENTING PROGRAMS IN NEW MEXICO. New Mexico has dozens of programs that serve parenting and pregnant teens throughout the state, many of which serve teen fathers in some capacity. For example, between 1997 and 2000, 42 of 53 existing teen-parent programs targeted adolescent fathers. A total of 276 young fathers had been served during the time period, representing 9 percent of the 3,194 teenagers served. Teen fathers who had received some type of service had consistently improved their educational levels and employment rates.[76] The names of the programs serving teen fathers in New Mexico, which are too numerous to reproduce here, are listed in a special article on the subject published in the journal *Adolescence.*[77]

TEEN PREGNANCY/PARENTING PROGRAM. The highly innovative Teen Pregnancy/Parenting Program, also referred to as TP3, is administered by the Day Care and Child Development Council of Tompkins County in Ithaca, New York. TP3 serves pregnant and parenting young men and women up to age twenty-one who are residents of Tompkins County. Each participant is assigned a case manager who links the parent up with health care for the parent and his or her child, food, clothing, shelter, education, and job training.

Effective parenting is fostered through education on prenatal and childbirth issues, child-development seminars, parenting discussion groups, one-on-one counseling, and adult mentoring. Some of the teen and young-adult parents do panel presentations on the realities and hardships of early parenthood at local middle schools and high schools. An especially laudatory achievement of TP3 is its poster series, "The Importance of Being There," which features three posters depicting photos of young fathers engaged in nurturing activities with their sons. Additional information about TP3 can be obtained at:

Day Care & Child Development Council of Tompkins County, Inc.
609 West Clinton St.
Ithaca, New York 14850
(607) 273–1055
e-mail: daycare@daycarecouncil.org
http://www.daycarecouncil.org/tp3.htm

TEENAGE PREGNANCY AND PARENTING PROJECT (TAPP). The TAPP program is a comprehensive case management service for pregnant and parenting teens in the San Francisco area. The primary objectives of this program are to promote responsible parenthood and to reduce the number of second births to teen parents. With young fathers, there is an emphasis on promoting the well-being of the baby and on helping adolescent fathers to complete school. TAPP also provides parenting education, child-care support services, nutrition and health education, job readiness, mental health programs, relationship-violence prevention, and academic counseling. All services are free. More detailed information regarding TAPP can be acquired by contacting:

The Family Service Agency of San Francisco
2730 Bryant St., 2nd Floor
San Francisco, CA 94110
(415) 695–8300
http://www.fsasf.org/programs/children_youth_family.
html?PHPSESSID=9e41cfcd21bcf49977ab94726705bab3

UCLA/BIENVENIDOS FAMILY SERVICES NATIONAL LATINO FATHERHOOD AND FAMILY INSTITUTE HIV PREVENTION PROGRAM (UB). The UB program is a community-based HIV prevention research project for teen mothers and fathers.[78] A team of academicians from the UCLA School of Nursing and the Bienvenidos Family Services National Latino Fatherhood and Family Institute HIV Prevention Program, a community-based organization, developed the UB program with consultation provided by a community advising board. HIV awareness, understanding HIV infection, attitudes and beliefs about HIV and safer sex, condom-use skills, refusal skills, conflict-negotiation skills, and contraception and disease prevention were taught to teen mothers and teen fathers in a twelve-hour curriculum spread out over six sessions. Male and female professionals from the Bienvenidos program and UCLA facilitated the sessions. Preliminary results pertaining to the outcomes of the UB program indicated that the participants demonstrated an overall steady decline in unprotected sex from the start of the program through a six-month follow-up evaluation. Another admirable feature of the program is that it incorporated culturally sensitive approaches to program development and instruction, which earned the UB professionals the trust and respect of the community.[79]

Useful Organizations and Web Sites

The organizations and Web sites described in this section are dedicated to helping boys, men, and families. Although most of them do not have specific initiatives targeting teenage fathers, they do offer services and resources that can be helpful to practitioners who work with boys facing fatherhood challenges. The list of organizations provided here is representative, rather than exhaustive, of youth- and father-oriented entities. For a more comprehensive list of special fatherhood initiatives, contact the Quality Improvement Center on Non-Resident Fathers and the Child Welfare System.[80]

100 BLACK MEN OF AMERICA. This organization is dedicated to improving the quality of life and enhancing the educational and economic opportunities of all African Americans. It also sponsors numerous mentoring programs for African-American boys, the details about which can be obtained at:

> 100 Black Men of America
> 141 Auburn Ave.
> Atlanta, GA 30303
> (404) 688–5100
> (800) 598–3411
> www.100blackmen.org

CENTER FOR SUCCESSFUL FATHERING (CSF). CSF offers numerous seminars and resources to promote father's involvement with their children. For example, the Accepting the Challenges of Fatherhood Curriculum is designed for use with groups of fathers. It explores the roles of fathers in child development and the consequences of father absence. Special modules are focused on fathering skills and the role of mothers in supporting father's involvement with their children. This curriculum has been adopted for use with teen fathers. For more information, contact:

Center for Successful Fathering
13740 Research Blvd, Suite B-4
Austin, TX 78750
(800) 537–0853
(512) 335–8106
e-mail: info@fathering.org
http://www.fathering.org/Default.asp

FATHERHOOD PROJECT. Administered through the Families and Work Institute, "The Fatherhood Project® is a national research and education project that is examining the future of fatherhood and developing ways to support men's involvement in child rearing. Its books, films, consultation, seminars, and training all present practical strategies to support fathers and mothers in their parenting roles. The Fatherhood Project® is the longest-running national initiative on fatherhood—founded in 1981 at the Bank Street College of Education in New York City by Dr. James A. Levine, and relocated in 1989 to the Families and Work Institute."[81] Pertinent information about this organization can be obtained at:

Families and Work Institute
267 Fifth Ave., Floor 2
New York, NY 10016
(212) 465–2044
http://www.familiesandwork.org/index.html

INDIANA FATHERS AND FAMILIES. The Indiana Social Services Administration has been a leader in funding numerous programs throughout Indiana whose mission is to increase the emotional and financial involvement of fathers in the lives of their children. This special initiative, known as Indiana Fathers and Families, supports a wide range of holistic, supportive services and training, including shelter, education, employment, parenting skills, co-parenting communication, active involvement in children's lives, and medical and mental health for fathers, including teenage fathers. For more information, see:

Indiana Fathers & Families
DCS/Child Support Bureau
402 W. Washington St., Room W360
Indianapolis, IN 46204
http://www.in.gov/dcs/fathers

NATIONAL BLACK CHILD DEVELOPMENT INSTITUTE (NBCDI). NBCDI is a nonprofit organization that has provided and supported programs, workshops, and resources for African-American children, their parents, and their communities since 1970.

> National Black Child Development Institute
> 1101 15th Street, NW
> Suite 900
> Washington DC 20005
> (202) 833–2220
> e-mail: moreinfo@nbcdi.org
> http://www.nbcdi.org

NATIONAL CENTER FOR FATHERING (NCF). NCF and its Web site, www. fathers.com, contains numerous tips for dads, information about national fatherhood initiatives, training programs for fathers, and research findings on fathers and trends in fathering behaviors. NCF supports special father programs, such as the Urban Father/Child Project, whose purpose is to increase the well-being of disadvantaged inner-city children through outreach with fathers in urban areas. Fathers.com has numerous links to other Web sites featuring information about fathers' legal concerns and rights. NCF can be accessed through the following:

> The National Center for Fathering
> P.O. Box 413888
> Kansas City, MO 64141
> (800) 593-DADS
> (913) 384–4661
> e-mail: dads@fathers.com
> http://www.fathers.com

NATIONAL CENTER ON FATHERS AND FAMILIES (NCOFF). Based at the Graduate School of Education of the University of Pennsylvania, NCOFF is a research, policy, and resource center pertaining to fatherhood. The NCOFF Web site has links to numerous free databases on fatherhood publications, organizations serving fathers, and special forums pertaining to research, policy, and practice regarding fatherhood. The contact information for NCOFF is:

> National Center on Fathers and Families
> University of Pennsylvania
> 3440 Market St., Suite 450
> Philadelphia, PA 19104–3325
> (215) 573–5500
> http://www.ncoff.gse.upenn.edu

NATIONAL FATHERHOOD INITIATIVE (NFI). NFI was formed in 1994 to "stimulate a broad-based social movement to combat father absence and promote responsible fatherhood."[82] "NFI's mission is to improve the well being of children by increasing the proportion of children growing up with involved, responsible, and committed fathers."[83] NFI organizes public awareness campaigns, develops curricula, provides training, and disseminates research findings pertaining to fatherhood. Many of its resources are excellent tools for working with teen fathers. For example, NFI recently produced an interactive CD-ROM, *Boyz 2 Dads*, that simulates a young man who faces crucial decision-points related to sexual activity and fatherhood. *Boyz 2 Dads* includes a discussion guide that parents and other concerned adults can use with a young man to help him discuss numerous topics as he moves through *Boyz 2 Dads*. The topics include pressure to have sex, the implications of becoming a father at an early age, what it means to be a caring father, and the qualities of effective communication. Thus, *Boyz 2 Dads* can be an effective tool in helping teen fathers to avoid a second unplanned pregnancy, or it can be used with non-fathers to prevent early paternity. *Boyz 2 Dads* can be coupled with other resources available from NFI, such as *24/7 Dad* (a fathering skills program) and *Doctor Dad* (featuring how fathers can attend to the basic health-care needs of their children), to assist teen fathers with their parenting skills and responsibilities.

NFI also is an excellent resource for professionals and community leaders who want to work with fathers. NFI offers workshops specializing in the development, marketing, and implementation of father service programs, including highly specialized programs for particular populations of fathers. For example, *Inside-Out Dad* is a prepackaged curriculum that practitioners can use to prepare incarcerated fathers to maintain bonds with their children during periods of imprisonment and to enhance child-father relationships during reentry into society. NFI also has several sophisticated publications on fatherhood for professionals, such as *Father Facts*, which documents the harmful toll of father absence and the enriching benefits of father presence on children and society. For information about the many valuable resources on fatherhood from NFI, contact:

National Fatherhood Initiative
101 Lake Forest Blvd., Suite 360
Gaithersburg, MD 20878
(301) 948–0599
http://www.fatherhood.org

NATIONAL LATINO FATHERHOOD AND FAMILY INSTITUTE. Building upon familiar cultural traditions, The National Latino Fatherhood and Family Institute "helps fathers of all ages develop strong, active roles in the lives of their children, while concurrently addressing the very painful aspects of child abuse, domestic violence, gang violence, school failure, illiteracy, teen pregnancy and other related issues."[84]

NLFFI sponsors many father-support initiatives, including the Con Los Padres Program, whose purpose is to help young fathers to become competent parents by teaching them about their child's development and their paternal rights and responsibilities. NLFFI also provides many publications targeting young Latinos, including a bilingual brochure on teen pregnancy that emphasizes both the blessings and the burdens associated with early fatherhood. For more information contact:

NLFFI
5252 E. Beverly Blvd.
East Los Angeles, CA 90022
(323) 728–7770
www.nlffi.org

NATIONAL ORGANIZATION OF CONCERNED BLACK MEN (CBM). Since 1975, CBM has sponsored numerous out-of-school enrichment and prevention programs for African-American children. For example, the CBM Peer Education and Reproductive Counseling For Young Men Project (PERCY) is designed to foster male sexual responsibility, strengthen hope about the future, and link young males with caring adult mentors. This and other CBM programs are described at:

Concerned Black Men National Office
The Thurgood Marshall Center
1816 12th Street, NW
Washington DC 20009
(202) 783–6119
(888) 395–7816
e-mail: info@cbmnational.org
http://cbmnational.org/index.htm

NATIONAL URBAN LEAGUE. Since 1910 the National Urban League has been dedicated to empowering African Americans, including many special initiatives targeting youth. For example, the NULITES Program (National Urban League Incentives to Excel & Succeed) "encourages youth to become leaders, embraces positive aspects of youth culture and cultivates leadership skills by appointing youth mentors who organize and execute activities under adult supervision."[85] For a description of these and other National Urban League programs, contact:

The National Urban League
120 Wall St., 8th Floor
New York, NY 10005
(212) 558–5300
http://www.nul.org

NATIONAL PRACTITIONERS NETWORK FOR FATHERS AND FAMILIES, INC.
(NPNFF). An excellent source of resources for professionals whose work
involves helping fathers, NPNFF is a national organization

> whose mission is to build the profession of practitioners working
> to increase the responsible involvement of fathers in the lives of
> their children. NPNFF's programs and services are designed to foster
> communication, promote professionalism, and enhance collabora-
> tion among individuals working with fathers and fragile families.
> NPNFF seeks to strengthen practitioners in their day-to-day work
> with fathers and fragile families. Through publications, conferences,
> training events, technical assistance, advocacy, collaboration with
> other fathers and families organizations, and networking opportuni-
> ties, NPNFF, as a national membership organization, represents the
> perspective of the fatherhood and fragile families program practitio-
> ners sector on public policy issues. Through participation in national
> advocacy coalitions and collaborative efforts, NPNFF ensures that the
> voice of the individuals who work with fathers in local programs will
> be heard as national policy decisions are made.[86]

Professionals who join NPNFF have access to numerous publications,
such as *The Practitioner, Member Service Memo,* and *Public Policy Report.* Collectively, these publications provide members with information regarding
effective programs for promoting father involvement in families, federal legislation and policy issues pertaining to fatherhood, funding sources, upcom-
ing conferences, training opportunities, and job openings. Membership also
includes discounts on purchasing several fatherhood curricula. NPNFF can
be reached at:

The National Practitioners Network for Fathers and Families
1003 K Street NW, Suite 565
Washington DC 20001
(800) 34N-PNFF
(202) 737–6680
e-mail: info@NPNFF.org
http://www.npnff.org

PLANNED PARENTHOOD. Planned Parenthood is a national organization dedicated to the provision of reproductive health care and education. The Planned Parenthood Web site has a special link, "Men's Health," which features numerous topics that would of interest to adolescent males, including "A Young Man's Guide to Sexuality," "Are You Safe in Your Relationship?" and "How to Be a Good Parent." Planned Parenthood operates reproductive health clinics throughout the United States, and the organization is a leader in providing high-quality information on teen health, pregnancy, and child-bearing among U.S. teens, and facts for teens about sex, STDs, and safe sex. For more information, contact:

Planned Parenthood Federation of America
434 West 33rd St.
New York, NY 10001
(212) 541–7800
fax: (212) 245–1845
e-mail: communications@ppfa.org
http://www.plannedparenthood.org/pp2/portal

SIECUS. SIECUS—The Sexual Information and Education Council of the United States—is an organization dedicated to providing accurate information and comprehensive education about sexuality and sexual-health services. Professionals, parents, and other concerned adults can contact SIECUS for up-to-date, scientifically based information about adolescent sexuality, contraception use, and preventing STDs and pregnancy among teenagers, including numerous publications available in both English and Spanish:

SIECUS NY Office
130 West 42nd St., Suite 350
New York, NY 10036–7802
(212) 819–9770
fax: (212) 819–9776

SIECUS DC Office
1706 R Street, NW
Washington DC 20009
(202) 265–2405
fax: (202) 462–2340
e-mail: siecus@siecus.org
http://www.siecus.org

WEB SITES WITH INFORMATION FOR TEEN FATHERS. *About.com*. About.com is a hub of links to sites that provide information and solutions to many common problems. About.com has three links that can be of great assistance to teen fathers. The first is Teen Fatherhood FAQ, which is located at http://teenadvice.about.com/od/teenfathers/a/teenfathersFAQ.htm. Young fathers who are seeking sound information on paternal rights and responsibility, paternity testing, marriage, and adoption will find this site useful.

A second link within the About.com domain is Single Dads, which provides information on a wide range of subjects pertaining to single fathers, including fatherhood, parenting, child development, and child support and visitation. Single Dads can be accessed at http://singleparents.about.com/od/singledads.

The third link via About.com is Teenage Single Parents, which is located at http://singleparents.about.com/od/teensingleparent. Through this site, a person can acquire plenty of practical information regarding issues that are of concern to single teenage parents, such as getting help from the government or health insurance for a child, addressing divorce and separation, and handling the challenges of single parenthood.

YPPO.com. The Young Positive Parenting Organization (YPPO) is a Web-based source of support and information for teen parents. "Dads," one of the links on the YPPO homepage, contains twenty accounts written by teenage fathers about their experiences, a message board, and an e-mail list for discussion purposes. Through the latter two features, teen fathers can contact each other for advice and support.

Documentaries and Docudramas about Teen Fathers

Numerous visual media about teenage fathers have been produced. Unfortunately, most of these productions are in an outdated format or they are poorly made docudramas that are neither engaging nor realistic. The following videos are documentaries that I have personally reviewed and that provide a gripping account of parenthood from a young father's perspective. They can be used as a stimulus with teen fathers to discuss their own experiences or with other audiences to education them about teenage fatherhood.

Fathers Too Soon? Although this video was produced in 1987, a long time ago, and it is only approximately nine minutes long, it remains one of the most powerful documentaries on teen fathers I have ever seen. The documentary features a handful of teen fathers from different races talking about their reactions to learning that their girlfriend was pregnant, supporting her during the pregnancy, adjusting to being a father, and sharing their hopes for the future. This video is very moving because it captures the full range of emotions expressed by the young men regarding the stress and joys they experience about fatherhood and the impact it has had on their lives. It can be ordered by contacting:

Planned Parenthood Association of Cincinnati, Inc.
2314 Auburn Ave.
Cincinnati, OH 45219
(513) 721–7635
e-mail: info@ppwo.org
http://www.plannedparenthood.org/pp2/cinti

Fathers Too Soon. Bearing the same title as the Planned Parenthood video minus the question mark, *Fathers Too Soon* is a joint production of the Channel One Network and the National Campaign to Prevent Teen Pregnancy. This video is designed to prevent teenage fatherhood by promoting awareness of the consequences of becoming an adolescent father. Both the video and the accompanying discussion guide address the impact of parenthood on a young man's relationships, his education and career, and his financial circumstances. The video can be ordered at:

National Campaign To Prevent Teen Pregnancy
1776 Massachusetts Ave., NW
Suite 200
Washington DC 20036
(202) 478–8500
http://www.teenpregnancy.org/resources/reading/audiovisual.asp

Teen Dads: The Forgotten Half. This documentary features several teenage fathers from the Baltimore, Maryland, area. The film emphasizes each father's reaction to the pregnancy and their degree of paternal responsibility, which range from those who are fully committed to those who abandon their partner and child. The film stresses that few teen fathers get married and that most young fathers struggle with pressures to have sex, peer messages about being macho, the needs of adolescent fathers, and the impact of a father's level of responsibility on his partner and his child. Copies can be obtained at:

Films for the Humanities and Sciences
P.O. Box 2053
Princeton, NJ 08543–2053
(800) 257–5126
www.films.com

Teen Dad's Point of View. Available in both DVD and VHS format, this film features a group of teen fathers talking about their relationships with their partners and their babies. A major strength of this documentary is that it demonstrates that teen fathers vary greatly in terms of their character. The fathers range from those who express an intense devotion to their child and who seem to have a clear direction in their lives, to others who seem to be unstable and in trouble with the law. The film is available from:

Cambridge Educational
P.O. Box 2053
Princeton, NJ 08543–2053
(800) 257–5126
e-mail: custoserv@filmsmediagroup.com
http://www.cambridgeeducational.com/ContactUs.aspx

Young Men as Fathers: For Teens and Young Men. Produced by Life Media Services for Kids Safety America, *Young Men as Fathers* portrays a group of teenage boys from different racial and ethnic backgrounds talking about how they learned their girlfriend was pregnant, their fears and reactions to the pregnancy, and the impact of the pregnancy on their relationships with their friends and families. Several types of young men are profiled, including those who are very caring for their children as well as others who are aloof and neglectful of their paternal responsibilities. The movie is an excellent educational resource because it shows real teenage fathers and it includes numerous questions that appear throughout the film for discussion purposes. To order, contact:

Films for the Humanities and Sciences
P.O. Box 2053
Princeton, NJ 08543–2053
(800) 257–5126
www.films.com

Young Adult Books about Teenage Fatherhood

Although an Internet search of books for young readers on teenage fathers will yield many book titles on the subject, most are out of print and no longer available for purchase. The books described in this section have been verified to be either still in print or are out of print but available through remainder sales or specialty book companies. They can be ordered directly from the publisher or through a book distributor such as Amazon.com. The books listed here are for young-adult readers only, and can be used with teen fathers themselves or in discussions groups with teenagers as tools to foster thinking about adolescent fatherhood. I have not included scholarly books on the subject, since those have been cited throughout the book in earlier chapters. I also have omitted simplistic youth books on teenage fatherhood that take a pejorative view of adolescent fathers, fail to address the challenges young fathers face in a realistic manner, or lack any information about coping with early paternity.

Reality Check: Teenage Fathers Speak Out (revised edition) by Margi Trapani.[87] Five teenage fathers describe the hardships of parenthood and the love they have for their children. Several topics are especially emphasized, including the limited free time associated with being a father, financial pressures, and the young men's commitment to remaining good fathers. The book is published by the Rosen Publishing Group and can be ordered at http://www.rosenpublishing.com/showtitle.cfm?id=PK000000994.

Teen Dads: Rights, Responsibilities, and Joys by Jeanne Warren Lindsay.[88] This excellent book provides information to help expectant teen fathers to assist their partners with the pregnancy-resolution process, prenatal care, labor, and delivery. It also provides teen fathers with advice about caring for their child from infancy through toddlerhood and maintaining a healthy relationship with their partner. In addition, it challenges young fathers to accept their paternal responsibilities and to plan for their futures in a constructive manner. Available from Morning Glory Press at: http://www.morningglorypress.com/catalog.

Teenage Fathers by Karen Gravelle and Leslie Peterson.[89] This powerful book is filled with the real-life stories of thirteen teenage fathers and their varied reactions to parenthood, which range from boys who abandoned their children by age nineteen to those who continued to maintain all of their parental responsibilities. Originally published in 1992 by Silver Burdett Press, this book is now available only at Backinprint.com at the following URL: http://corppub.iuniverse.com/marketplace/backinprint/0595152708.html.

7

Policy Considerations

What America Must Do to Prevent Early Fatherhood and Help Teenage Boys Who Are Fathers

Institutional and public policies play a large role in determining the types of services that are offered and who is going to receive them. A surprisingly high number of adolescent fathers grasp this reality in spite of their seemingly unsophisticated ways, and they have many strong opinions about how their lives are affected by the policies and practices pertaining to service provision that have been established in our nation. On the whole, boys who become fathers at an early age are skeptical that the people who are in positions of power and set policy really care about or understand what it is like to be a father during one's teenage years. Although a minority of adolescent fathers have faith that our nation is guided by a fair and just system, many others feel rejected by society and express pessimistic attitudes that range from a lack of confidence in policy makers to the bitter conviction that the system is out to get them.[1] Impoverished teen fathers especially believe that our government and the professionals who work in hospitals, family-planning clinics, social-service agencies, and the legal system are hostile toward them.[2]

The perceptions and complaints of teenage fathers about institutional and government policies, though at times exaggerated, are not unfounded. Historically, both institutional and public policies have not been father-friendly. Longstanding traditions in child and family services and policies pertaining to paternity establishment, child support, child custody, child visitation, welfare, and statutory rape have included adversarial features toward boys and men that offset many of their positive components. In addition, public policy has not adequately addressed the complicated needs of young fathers from disadvantaged environments, nor has it fostered a sensible and effective approach to preventing STDs and premarital pregnancies and childbirth among our nation's teenagers, or a consistent policy regarding confidentiality for reproductive-health services. And the policies of educational systems regarding school-based services for teenage parents have been woefully neglectful of teenage fathers. Therefore, a critical examination of many of our nation's policies is warranted.

Child and Family Services Policies and Practices and Their Impact on Fathers

Until recently, helping professionals did not take the father's role seriously, and the services they offered were not geared to accommodate fathers. Furthermore, in some agencies charged with serving children and families, the organizational structure, background of employees, and nature of the services offered have reflected a pattern of discrimination against fathers:[3]

- Child-welfare workers tend to view mothers and children as their primary clients, while adhering to the stereotype that fathers are problematic and hard to reach. Professionals who operate according to these beliefs are unlikely to reach out to fathers, and they are likely to alienate men from participating in social services.
- The working hours of most public agencies do not include evening or weekend hours. This schedule prevents fathers who work during the day from being able to make appointments with child-welfare workers.
- Child welfare is primarily a female profession. Women have been reluctant and at times incapable of doing the kind of outreach that is necessary to connect with fathers, such as meeting with young men in their neighborhoods in pool halls, recreation centers, and other places where they like to hang out.
- Most social-welfare workers have white European backgrounds, but their clients are often ethnic minorities. This mismatch of cultures can be the cause of feelings of strangeness between helpers and the receivers of service.[4]

All of these barriers to effective service provision with fathers have been found in programs designed to assist teenage fathers, and they have persisted over time. In the mid-1980s the coordinators of the groundbreaking Teen Father Collaboration documented that these types of policies and practices in child-welfare agencies consistently deterred fathers from being helped effectively.[5] The same types of problems were reported again in 1994 by program officials from the Young Unwed Fathers Pilot Project,[6] and once again in 2004 by the project administrators of the Texas Fragile Families Initiative.[7] Clearly, changes in agency policies and practices pertaining to fathers must be made in order to establish an ongoing tradition of father-friendly service.

As a first step to becoming more father-oriented, administrators may have to assess their agency's commitment to serving fathers. This assessment process should include taking stock of the attitudes of staff members about teenage fathers:

> Program coordinators need to talk with fatherhood staff about their own preconceived notions, past experiences, and assumptions about fathers and fatherhood. All staff members need to recognize the prejudices they may subtly communicate to their clients. This is important not just with new staff, but also with more experienced staff members who may suffer from emotional fatigue or cynicism. The constant struggle and challenges and few resources can be draining and have a huge impact on staff morale and attitude.[8]

In order to address these issues, administrators should provide their staff with ongoing training and support, including open forums during which case managers have frank discussions with their fellow workers and supervisors about their fears, frustrations, shifting attitudes, and successes pertaining to their work with young fathers.[9] During these discussions, supervisors can boost the morale of overworked case managers by empathizing with their difficulties, offering them encouragement, and expressing appreciation for their efforts. It is also advisable to have open and honest discussions about the mission of an agency. Because many workers may consider helping women and children to be their top priority, supervisors might want to point out that helping fathers can also help mothers and their children through the economic and social benefits that are associated with healthy father-family relations, and that "inadvertent or conscious discrimination against either parent can result in poorer service to children."[10]

Taking supportive action to address anti-father biases must be accompanied by changes in staffing and operating policies and practices. Organizations that have an abundance of female case workers may have to recruit more male case managers who are comfortable with and skilled at working with male youth, while assisting female professionals with their questions and concerns about engaging and working with hard-to-reach adolescent fathers.[11] Fatherhood-oriented staff must be fully integrated into child and parent agencies and not be seen as simple add-ons to an organization.[12] Flexible hours of operation, including drop-in times and evening and weekend office hours, should be instituted.[13] In order to achieve this flexibility and a smooth coordination of services, full-time rather than part-time case managers dealing with fathers should be hired.[14] Finally, education about the particular cultural backgrounds of fathers from target communities must be provided in order to foster greater awareness and sensitivity about the unique cultural perspectives of these young men.[15]

Public Policy and the Role of Fathers in Families

The degree to which agencies can institute these types of changes will depend greatly on how funding is allocated through public policy. Historically, public policy in the United States has placed little emphasis on the role of fathers in families. Instead, policies related to families have been concerned primarily with helping women and children, which resulted in most social-service programs being women- and child-oriented.[16] This fact was not lost on one young father who wanted help, looked for a father program, and found none until a special project for adolescent and young-adult fathers was finally initiated in his neighborhood:

> Until this young father's program came along there was nothing for us, just a lot of counseling and help for women. Men are left on their own to deal with it and like if your girlfriend or your wife is pregnant, sometimes men be goin' through some depression, you know, you be thinking about certain things and you ain't got nobody to talk to. But if a lady's goin' through that, she got all kinds of pregnant women groups to go to and they can help and stuff like that. But for a man, you ain't really got nobody. You all alone by yourself unless you find a group like we got now through this young father's program.[17]

Through the early 1990s, with few exceptions, policies pertaining to fathers were focused on the responsibilities of men for the economic support of women and children.[18] However, public policy began to demonstrate an expanded view of the father role during the Clinton administration. In a June 1995 memo, President Bill Clinton ordered all branches of the federal government to ensure that federal services and programs pertaining to families support men in their role as fathers. This memo marked the beginning of what has become known as the Federal Fatherhood Initiative, a government-wide effort to strengthen the role of fathers in families.[19]

The Federal Fatherhood Initiative attempted to raise awareness about the problems of children who are raised in father-absent homes, support research investigating the role of fathers in their families and the impact of fathering on child well-being, and sponsor services that would assist men to promote their child's health and development. Special funds from the annual budget were earmarked for the development of father services, and agencies throughout the federal government began to introduce new program ideas whose purpose was to promote the economic self-sufficiency and parenting competencies of fathers.[20]

The goal of fostering father involvement in families continued with the Bush administration. In 2001 President George W. Bush identified strengthening families as the twelfth priority of his administration. Related to this objective, the Bush administration expressed concern for "the dramatic increase in the number of children living without fathers," estimating that "60 percent of children born in the 1990s will spend a significant portion of their childhood in a home without a father."[21] The administration also reported that father absence is linked to poverty and antisocial behavior, while the presence of two committed, involved parents is associated with "better school performance, reduced substance abuse, less crime and delinquency, fewer emotional and other behavioral problems, less risk of abuse and neglect, and lower risk of teen suicide."[22] Thus, preventing father absence and promoting the involvement of a loving father and mother in the lives of children became important components of the Bush administration's strategy for strengthening families.

In *A Blueprint for New Beginnings: A Responsible Budget for America's Priorities,* the Bush administration declared, "There is simply no substitute for the love, involvement, and commitment of a responsible father,"[23] and proposed allocating $315 million over a five-year period (2002–2006) for the Promoting Responsible Fatherhood Initiative. This initiative emphasized balancing policy that provides child-support enforcement with strategies that promote paternal emotional commitments by:

- Improving the job skills of low-income fathers
- Promoting marriage among parents
- Helping low-income fathers establish positive relations with their children and their children's mothers
- Enlisting the assistance of faith-based and community groups that are close and responsive to the needs of fathers and families

Since the publication of *A Blueprint for New Beginnings,* Congress and the Bush administration have supported the creation of numerous resources and programs pertaining to underserved populations of fathers.[24] The study of these populations has fostered an increased awareness about the needs of adolescent fathers. For example, it is now possible to find the subject of teenage fathers in numerous reports regarding fatherhood that are published by the Department of Health and Human Services. In addition, a small number of father service programs are now expanding their missions to help hard-to-reach adolescent and young-adult fathers. Thus, although most of the language in official government policies pertaining to fatherhood is general and not specifically focused on teenage fathers, the increased emphasis on serving fathers has had a positive spillover effect on boys who become parents. Public policy should continue to strengthen the role of fathers in families, and specific language regarding the needs of adolescent fathers and the mission of serving them should be infused into future policies pertaining to fatherhood initiatives.

Policies Pertaining to Paternity Establishment, Child-Support Enforcement, Ex-Convict Teen Fathers, Legal Services, Custody Decisions, and Visitation

Approximately 80 percent of teenage fathers are not married to the mothers of their children,[25] and over half of these young men do not live with their child.[26] In order to have their rights regarding child support, child custody, and child visitation recognized by the legal system, it is crucial that adolescent fathers establish paternity. Yet a surprisingly high percentage of teenage fathers—probably at least 30 percent—do not take the legal steps to declare their paternity[27] either due to their naïveté about their legal rights and responsibilities or because of their deep mistrust of the legal system.

On the whole, adolescent fathers are unaware of the many benefits that are associated with establishing paternity. The legal declaration of paternity can help a father to maintain an open relationship with his child, and it can ensure that his child receives the same rights as other children, including "inheritance rights, access to the father's medical and life insurance benefits and to Social Security and veterans' benefits."[28] Moreover, "It also may be important for the child's health for doctors to know the father's medical history, especially if there is a history of medical conditions in the father's family."[29] In addition, through the establishment of paternity, a father can have a legal say in matters pertaining to custody and visitation with his child, and his child-support obligations will be clarified so that he knows exactly how much financial support he is legally required to provide for his child's well-being. Because they are uninformed about these benefits, many teen fathers fail to establish paternity.

Other teenage fathers, especially those who are poor, are notoriously suspicious of the child-support system, so they resist declaring their paternity legally. Many of their attitudes about child support reflect the mind-set of disenfranchised people who believe that the system is unfair and out to get them.[30] Some of the teenage boys participating in the Public/Private Ventures Young Unwed Fathers Pilot Project expressed fear that the money they pay for child support would go into the hands of the rich. They also believed that the system was coercive and rigid because it did not recognize informal contributions that the fathers had made to their partners and their families, such as providing diapers, baby formula, and transportation. The fathers were convinced that the system was designed to keep them from ever being able to get ahead financially, noting that the money they contribute to child support is used to offset the cost of welfare benefits paid to the mothers of their child. On the basis of these beliefs, some of the fathers actually reduced their efforts to seek formal employment and they increased their attempts to find work that paid them under the table. They and their partners also conspired to hide the father's identity from officials.[31]

Child-Support Enforcement

Understanding the roots of this mistrust requires an examination of child-support enforcement policies in the United States. In 1975 the federal government instituted the Child Support Enforcement Program (CSE) through the passage of Title IV-D of the Social Security Act. The purpose of CSE is to establish and enforce child support for children raised in single-parent households, and its policies "are meant to provide economic security for children and custodial parents, to prevent single-parent families from entering the welfare system, to help families leave that system quickly, and to reduce welfare spending."[32] Administering the program is shared: "States take the primary responsibility for administering the CSE program, although the federal government shares the administrative costs, monitors, evaluates, and provides technical assistance, and, under certain conditions, directly assists in locating absent parents and obtaining support."[33]

Once paternity is established, the amount of the child-support award is determined by the CSE system, and a father is expected to pay it. Together, the federal and state governments make a concerted effort to make sure that non-custodial fathers meet their child-support obligations. The CSE program has numerous tools that can be used to collect payments from young fathers with child-support orders, including the following: "Automatic wage withholding, delinquency notices, regular billings, liens on personal and real property, reporting of arrearage to credit bureaus, seizure and sale of property, garnishment of wages, federal and state tax garnishment, the interception of unemployment benefits, civil or criminal contempt-of-court charges for nonsupport, and incarceration."[34]

Unfortunately, "there is no body of state law that suggests that very young fathers should be held to a different standard due to their age."[35] Consequently, even though a youth may be enrolled in school as a full-time student or unemployed or under-employed, he may be required to make child-support payments. For many teenager fathers who reside in separate households from their children, even a token child-support obligation can be a major financial burden. About half of these fathers live in poor households at the time their first child is born. Also, these young men earn incomes that are on average about 71 percent of the poverty threshold for a family of three. Collecting even modest percentages of the gross income of these young men for child support will push many of them into deeper poverty. "Thus, because of the low economic resources of the households of many absent teenage fathers, rigorous CSE enforcement may result in merely shifting poverty, along with its societal burdens, from one household to another."[36]

When the financial circumstances of low-income adolescent fathers are fully considered, it is easy to see that providing child support is nearly impossible for some of them. The majority of the young men who had participated in the Texas Fragile Families Initiative (TFF) reported that their incomes did not meet their needs "very well" or "at all."[37] Furthermore:

> Estimates of the amount it would take for a single adult to live in an average TFF community like Waco, Texas, suggest that even a wage of $7.50 per hour would barely allow for a single adult to meet expenses like housing, transportation, and other basic needs, let alone allow him to contribute meaningful support to his family. In addition, 50 percent of fathers who worked reported that their employers failed to offer benefits such as vacation or sick leave. When one takes into account the minimum child support order of $160 in child support per month, it is not surprising that fathers in fragile families are increasingly labeled "deadbroke" instead of "deadbeat."[38]

The traditional policy of pursuing young fathers from fragile families to provide child support for their children must be reevaluated and modified because "fathers who cannot pay child support accumulate debts that can lead them to evade the system and its penalties altogether—and further limit their contact with their children."[39] Consequently, the child-support system has not helped low-income, non-custodial adolescent fathers to fulfill their parenting roles.[40]

Another problem with many current child-support policies is that they allow states the option of making the young father's parents responsible for child-support payments if the father is a minor and living with them. Policies such as this may lead parents to push young fathers out of the home.[41] Considering that teen fathers need the support of their parents during the transition to fatherhood and that they tend to come from communities with high unemployment rates, these policies could prompt young fathers to consider illegal activities as a way to earn a living, while undermining the chances that they will be positively involved in their children's lives.

Clearly, our nation must find a way to help economically disadvantaged fathers to support their children financially while fostering their involvement with their children. Therefore, efforts to ensure that fathers meet their financial obligations must be balanced by the recognition that many teenage fathers have very limited incomes and earning opportunities and that "fathers also make important contributions through support, childcare, and socialization."[42] Thus, child-enforcement officials are urged to develop programs that broaden their interpretation of child support by reducing financial support requirements for impoverished teenage fathers who demonstrate other committed forms of support for their children and partners:

> For example, the Teen Alternative Parenting Program (TAPP) in Marion County, Indiana, allows young fathers to use in-kind credits for the payment of child support. Each father signs one or more ninety-day contracts in which a certain amount of child support will be considered "paid" if the youth completes a week of school without any unexcused absences, attends parenting classes, babysits his child, and/or attends GED, vocational education, or training classes. The emphasis on childcare and developing good parenting skills in TAPP explicitly acknowledges that fathers, even young absent fathers, can contribute in many ways to the development of their children.[43]

Another innovative and constructive modification to child-support policies is linking child-support enforcement with employment assistance for low-income non-custodial fathers. The Parents' Fair Share Program (PFS), which "provided employment and training services, peer support groups, voluntary mediation between parents, and modified child support enforcement,"[44] is considered an exemplary alternative to the traditional child-support enforcement model. Between 1994 and 1996 more than 5,500 fathers were assigned to either a traditional child-support enforcement program or the PFS. PFS participants experienced increased employment and income, and more active parenting. Compared to the men assigned to the traditional program, the PFS fathers also paid more child support.[45]

One of the most successful nontraditional child-support programs is Project Bootstrap, which was operated at several of the sites participating in the Texas Fragile Families Initiative (TFF). A central feature of Project Bootstrap was the augmentation of traditional child-support practices with workforce and life-skills training services. Young men who enrolled in the project were required to establish paternity, pay child support, and participate in TFF responsible-fatherhood activities. In exchange, these fathers received a stipend of $1,325, workforce services, and educational and life-skills training. Compared to non-Bootstrap fathers, the participants were five times more likely to establish a child-support order, twice as likely to enroll in GED classes, and three times as likely to receive on-the-job training.[46] Thus, Bootstrap fathers were more likely to meet their legal responsibilities as fathers, while moving toward greater self-sufficiency.

The benefits produced by TAPP, PFS, and Project Bootstrap demonstrate that using discretion with child-support decisions pertaining to low-income adolescent fathers is prudent. Although it makes sense to apply enforcement techniques with teen fathers who have the ability to pay child support but refuse to do so, flexible alternatives are necessary with young men who cannot afford to support themselves and their families.[47] Based on the success of these programs, proponents of CSE reform have urged that these approaches to child-support enforcement be replicated at the national level.[48] Features of future programs should include longer-term services to produce even higher employment rates, participation of custodial mothers, providing legal services to address visitation disputes, and mandating fathers' participation in employment-related activities to increase child-support payments.[49] Legislators should explicitly make low-income non-custodial fathers a targeted priority for state-funded workforce-development services in order to help these men to become more self-sufficient and capable of meeting their child-support obligations.[50] In addition, allowing the informal support contributions of fathers to offset arrearages or to be used in lieu of part of their current child-support payments will motivate more young fathers to participate in the child-support system.[51]

Incarcerated Teen Fathers

Policy makers are also encouraged to give careful consideration to some special issues pertaining to child-support enforcement with teen fathers who are incarcerated. Young fathers released from prison systems face numerous barriers to providing child support:

> Historically, businesses are reluctant to hire convicted felons. Many job application questions are now structured to elicit information concerning any legal system encounter even if an offense is minor or a conviction overturned. To omit such data is grounds for immediate termination. Post-incarcerated males may be functionally illiterate or lack prerequisite job readiness skills to successfully maintain employment. To complicate matters, while incarcerated, these fathers may have continued to accrue sizable financial child support obligations and back payments. In some states such as Texas, outstanding child support payments still accumulate during prison confinement. Upon release, until his child support financial obligations are met, the father cannot qualify for a driver's license, limiting employment opportunities. Such constraints may force males to turn to more lucrative but illegal means to address this debt.[52]

These comments illustrate that teen fathers reentering society after incarceration are sometimes placed between a rock and a hard place when it comes to child-support issues. To ease the financial burden these young men face upon reentry into society, child-support obligations should be frozen (or reduced to cover only those nominal wages earned in prison) while a young man is incarcerated.[53] Young men who want to demonstrate responsible fatherhood after their release from jail may have the greatest need for assistance with paternity matters, including child support.[54] Specifically, adolescent fathers with a history of incarceration need intensive, structured services that are focused on immediate employment after exiting custody, as well as other forms of support including alcohol and drug treatment, support groups for children of alcoholics, parent education, gang interventions, and long-term career education and counseling. Ideally, these services should "be put in place while the youth is still in the correctional facility, be built upon as the youth exists into the community, and be extended over time as needed."[55] Providing these services has been shown to reduce the recidivism rate of adolescents with a history of fatherhood and delinquency.[56] These services are also likely to increase the odds that young fathers will pay child support and be more effective fathers once they are returned to society.

It must be acknowledged that one of the reasons some men end up in prison is because they don't care about their families and are not concerned at all about their child-support obligations. So child-support enforcement officials must find a balance between assuring that delinquent fathers fulfill their child-support obligations while not making it impossible for those who want to fulfill these duties to do so. These considerations point toward the creation of flexible child-support policies that leave room for considering a father's individual history and creating payment plans that will enhance his chances of fulfilling his child-support responsibilities. For example, it is reasonable to issue driver's licenses to young ex-cons who demonstrate ongoing efforts to obtain employment and make child-support payments. It is also reasonable to slap penalties, such as a return to jail, on fathers who make no attempts to establish self-sufficiency and provide child support. It is also sensible to recommend that young fathers who have demonstrated a good adjustment while in prison be enrolled in programs like TAPP and PFS after they are returned to society.

Legal Services for Teen Fathers

Both law-abiding adolescent fathers and young men with criminal histories may need legal assistance with paternity-related matters. Although it is common for unwed adolescent parents to reach informal agreements regarding paternity, child custody, child support, and visitation—which are often unstated but implicitly understood and dictated by folk customs honored in the community[57]—sometimes adolescent fathers must take legal action when they have irreconcilable conflicts over these issues with their partner and her family. For example, a young man may want to contest a charge that he is a child's father, or he may desire to file a petition to establish paternity with a baby he believes he has fathered. In other situations, he might want to fight for custody of his child when the mother is unfit to be a parent, or he may want to formalize a visitation agreement when his partner and her family deny him access to his child.[58] However, most teenage fathers cannot afford a lawyer to act on their behalf regarding their legal disputes, and although the courts in some states will appoint a lawyer or legal guardian to represent a father who is under the age of eighteen, historically the availability of legal-aid services to teenagers has been extremely limited.[59] Thus, the right of teenage fathers to "court-appointed counsel is far from settled as a national issue."[60]

In light of this state of affairs, public policy must support the expansion of legal services for unwed adolescent fathers who are indigent. These young men need competent legal advice regarding paternity matters, and their legal rights must be protected by our nation's court system. For example: "When a paternity case is adjudicated for an absent father who is a teenager, local jurisdictions must make the putative father aware of the implications of paternity establishment, his right to contest the paternity, and his right, if it exists, to a guardian *ad litem* or court-appointed counsel. When the defendant has a right to a guardian *ad litem* or court-appointed legal counsel, that right must be safeguarded."[61]

Custody Decisions

The legal system also must reexamine the longstanding practice of automatically awarding custody of a child to his or her mother. In the vast majority of cases involving a teen father and his partner, the mother has custody of the child, and both parties accept this arrangement because either the couple is comfortable with traditional gender role expectations dictating that a mother takes on infant child-care duties or because a young man may want custody but he is unaware of or intimidated by the legal process of petitioning for custody.[62] Nevertheless, some fathers do fight for custody of their child, and those who do go up against a long history of child-custody decisions that favor mothers.

From the colonial period through the 1800s, "fathers were considered the head of their households and thus the proprietors of all property and individuals in the household."[63] However, over the last century fathers' rights as the owners of wives and children were gradually eliminated by judicial decisions and policies emphasizing the preeminent role of the mother in child well-being. "It was argued that young children need the tender care of their mothers, and hence that they should be placed in the custody of their mothers rather than their fathers in case of divorce. Only recently has this 'tender years doctrine' been challenged successfully in courts."[64] In the vast majority of cases, however, judicial decisions have followed the dictates of the "tender years doctrine" by awarding custody of children to mothers.[65] Thus, in cases of divorce or separation, fathers of all ages are unlikely to be awarded child custody.

It is not surprising that very few adolescent fathers have custody of their children. Most young fathers are not married, and their children tend to reside with the child's mother, who typically lives with her family.[66] Although young fathers usually accept the mother's custody of the child, about one in five experience custody conflicts,[67] and some of these disputes result in bitter custody battles. In my experiences counseling young men involved in these battles, the courts have consistently continued the practice of awarding custody to the adolescent mother. In cases where the adolescent mother and her family can provide the baby with the type of consistency of care that is crucial for a child's healthy development, the awarding of custody to the mother is a reasonable practice. Nevertheless, giving custody of a baby to an adolescent mother should not be axiomatic, for there are circumstances in which it might be prudent to award custody of the child to a teenage father. For example, if a young mother is unstable and her family is not capable of providing her with the type of structure and guidance that could help her to become an effective mother, the father and his kinship network might be a more desirable alternative. Nevertheless, the implicit maternal preference regarding child-custody decisions by judges could undermine awarding custody to an adolescent father, even when he might be a more suitable parent to raise the child.

Ross Thompson, a professor of psychology at the University of California, Davis, has urged judges to consider evidence from research in child development as a basis for making custody decisions that are in the best interest of the child. This research has verified that fathers can be a significant figure in an infant's life from a very early age, and that they "can be adequate and competent in the primary caretaking role" if they choose to be.[68] Because children of divorce tend to fare better with the same-sex parent, "the child's gender should be considered in determining a custody award."[69] However, maintaining consistency of caretaking responsibilities is extremely important with infants and toddlers. If an infant or toddler is currently receiving high-quality care in an environment that fosters the child's well-being, he or she is likely to experience a significant degree of stress if custody is switched during this critical stage of development. Other evidence shows that "children's initial postdivorce adjustment is predictive of their long-term coping with changed family conditions."[70] Consequently, when custody decisions are being made in the aftermath of a recent divorce or separation, it is advisable to give greater weight to factors that might promote the child's adjustment to the divorce. Finally, although some couples might prefer a joint-custody decision, judges are encouraged to remember that joint custody is not a panacea. In order to protect the child's best interests, joint custody should be awarded only when certain vital questions have been answered:

- Can both parents establish the kind of cooperative arrangement necessary to make joint decisions concerning the child's present and future welfare?
- Will the child be protected from loyalty conflicts and other stresses that may be engendered by continuing disputes between the mother and father?
- If the child alternates between two home environments, how can consistency in basic caretaking activities be maintained?[71]

Visitation Issues

Although these recommendations regarding child custody are reasonable, it is highly doubtful that judges will make dramatic changes in child-custody decisions in the near future. Consequently, considering that most teenage fathers are not married to their partners, non-custodial fatherhood will remain a fact of life for these young men, and they are likely to continue to have many problems regarding visitation issues. As was described in chapter 3, blocked visitation is a chronic source of stress for adolescent fathers, and as the following account illustrates, tension regarding visitation is often tied to a father's success to meeting his child-support obligations, whether they are formal or informal:

> I was working for a while doin' carpentry and crap like that and givin' her money and stuff, until the guy who hired me had to take in his nephew and then he got my job. Then I was cut out from havin' any money to give my baby's momma, and before you knew it, she was pressurin' me and tellin' me that if I didn't come up with some cash, she was gonna cut me off from seein' my baby. And that's exactly what she did. I'd go over there and her momma would say to me, "What you doin' comin' 'round here when you ain't got no money to give us?!"—treating me like I was some kinda crook or freeloader. And damn, there were times I wanted to hit that old hag but I had to hold back because then I'd be in worse trouble than I'm in now.

From the perspectives of young fathers, the legal system does little to help them with their problems regarding visitation. One of the consistent perceptions of adolescent fathers is that judges have strong biases that favor mothers and that the rights of fathers are ignored. Many teen fathers who cannot afford a private attorney to help them resolve visitation disputes become hopeless about ever having access to their child, give up on their attempts to assert their rights, and gradually distance themselves from their child. These are tragic outcomes that must be prevented if our society is to truly embrace the ideal that fathers can and should play a meaningful role in their child's life. Consequently, public policy should support special provisions for legal aid that is tied to promoting healthy father involvement in families. Adolescent fathers should be a targeted population of such measures, with a particular emphasis on addressing their visitation concerns.

Welfare Policies

Historically, our nation has embraced the belief that "women and children are entitled to support by men, and that when men fail (for whatever reason) to provide support, the state accepts responsibility in their stead."[72] Consequently, welfare policies have been designed, in theory, to address the financial needs of mothers and their children.

There are strong links between welfare use and adolescent parenthood. Teenagers who reside in communities with high rates of poverty and welfare dependency are at higher risk to become adolescent parents. Also, a substantial number of teenage parents are unmarried, they spend extended periods of time on welfare, and they receive a disproportional amount of welfare funding over the course of their lives.[73] Consequently, public-policy debates regarding welfare issues typically include discussions about the problem of teenagers having and raising children out of wedlock.

During the 1990s, both Congress and the Clinton administration expressed concern that the welfare system in place at the time fostered family reliance on public assistance. There was also alarm among government officials and the public about the high rate of nonmarital and adolescent childbearing. The intersection of these issues galvanized support for the passage of a welfare reform bill known as the Personal Responsibility and Work Opportunity Reconciliation Act of 1996 (PRWORA), which emphasized making government assistance for the needy a transition to work.[74]

PRWORA replaced the prior welfare program, known as Aid to Families with Dependent Children (AFDC), with Temporary Assistance for Needy Families (TANF).[75] PRWORA required TANF recipients to work or look for work in order to receive government assistance, and it placed a five-year limit on the provision of welfare to those recipients. The bill included comprehensive child-support enforcement, featuring systems to track parents who are delinquent in their child-support payments, procedures for streamlining the process for establishing paternity, and tough new penalties for parents who owe child support. Special teen-parent components of the legislation required unmarried minor parents receiving welfare to live with a responsible adult or in an adult-supervised setting, and to participate in education and training activities. PRWORA also set aside mandatory funds for abstinence-only education as a teen pregnancy prevention strategy.[76] In 2005, PRWORA was reauthorized through the passage of The Deficit Reduction Act of 2005, which continued many of the provisions of the 1996 act while adding new initiatives, such as funding to promote father involvement, healthy marriages, and two-parent families.[77]

The architects of PRWORA believed that allowing only time-limited opportunities to raise children at home with government support would eliminate from welfare the monetary incentives for pregnancy, while pushing welfare recipients toward employment and marriage. It was also hoped that requirements for education or work were necessary incentives to help young mothers to complete their education and obtain employment.[78] These reforms were "intended to promote self-sufficiency, enhance healthy parental functioning, and reduce repeat pregnancies."[79]

Proponents of PRWORA have argued that the program has been a success because it helped to reduce the number of people on the welfare rolls. According to the United States Department of Health and Human Services, "Between PRWORA's enactment in August 1996 and March 2006, TANF caseloads for families declined 59 percent, from 4,408,508 to 1,814,040. This is the largest welfare caseload decline in history and the lowest percentage of the population on welfare since 1969."[80] PRWORA supporters have also asserted that the implementation of the bill helped to reduce the overall poverty rate during the 1990s.[81]

However, critics of PRWORA charged that the reduction in welfare dependency and modest drop in poverty was largely the result of a booming economy of the late 1990s and early 2000s and not PRWORA, and they voiced concern that participants of TANF are not sufficiently trained to succeed in the marketplace, which places many of them at risk to sink deeper into poverty,[82] especially recipients who are non-English-speaking immigrants.[83] Indeed, the positive developments of moving a significant number of people off welfare "shroud many disturbing realities for millions of current and former welfare recipients."[84] Most former welfare recipients are not working full-time or full-year, and those who are employed tend to earn between $6.00 and $8.00 per hour, which is "a wage insufficient to enable them to provide for their families."[85] In several states, such as Maryland, South Carolina, and Washington, over half of former TANF recipients are working but earning a wage that keeps them well below the poverty line. Many adults who moved from welfare to work neither receive nor can afford health care, and 28 percent are unable to pay their housing and utility bills.[86]

It is likely that PRWORA affects different sets of mothers in different ways: "For example, for young mothers with high school degrees and work experience, the benefit changes and time limits may provide the needed incentive to obtain and maintain stable employment. Mothers with low education skills and poor functioning or with other family problems such as a disabled child may have great difficulty maintaining stable employment and thus may suffer a substantial loss in income."[87]

There is other disturbing evidence regarding the impact of the welfare-to-work movement on the adolescent children of parents receiving welfare. In an experimental analysis comparing the effects of traditional welfare and the welfare-to-work programs on adolescent adjustment, adolescents whose parents had been enrolled in welfare-to-work programs were more likely than youth from families receiving traditional support to demonstrate lower academic achievement and an increased likelihood of arrests, convictions, and other involvement with the police. The youths from the welfare-to-work families were also more likely to show an increase in smoking, drinking, drug use, and behavior problems at school. The investigators of this study could not be certain as to why the welfare-to-work programs were having negative effects on the adolescents: "But they hypothesized that parents in the programs might have less time and energy to monitor their adolescents' behavior once they were employed; that under the stress of working, they might adopt harsher parenting styles; or that the adolescents' assuming more responsibilities at home when parents got jobs was creating too great a burden."[88]

It is also possible that PRWORA affects various groups of adolescent fathers and their families in different ways. The father provisions of this law were designed to increase paternity establishment, paternal monetary contributions, and father-child interactions, all of which can have both direct and indirect benefits for the children of teen fathers who are not married to the child's mother. However, promoting the presence of dysfunctional young fathers, such as those who have histories of serious drug abuse and antisocial behavior, could have a detrimental impact on some mothers and their children. Furthermore, increased demand for fathers' contributions could decrease overall paternal financial support by interfering with informal child-support agreements that have been established between fathers and their partners.[89] Most states take the majority of official child-support payments to offset welfare costs. Consequently, even though mothers receiving TANF benefits are required to cooperate with state officials in locating fathers and establishing paternity, many young parents collude to hide the identity of the father so that he can secretly provide informal financial support while the family continues to receive welfare assistance.[90]

Another potential problem with the PRWORA policies pertains to the co-residency requirement. Research has demonstrated that three-generational households consisting of grandmothers, older teenage mothers (eighteen or nineteen years old), and their children tend to be characterized by poor parenting practices by both the young mothers and the grandmothers, but better parenting when older teen mothers and their children live apart from grandmothers but continue to receive guidance and support from the grandmothers. In addition, for poor families, co-residing can strain grandmothers whose emotional and financial resources become spread across three generations within one household. Consequently, the forced co-residency component of PRWORA "may increase tensions between some mothers and grandmothers and lead to poorer parenting, especially for older teenagers."[91]

A major concern regarding PRWORA pertains to the provisions for funding abstinence-only education as a teen pregnancy prevention strategy. Teaching abstinence is only effective as a pregnancy reduction tactic if it is paired with information and access to contraceptives for older teenagers. Thus, communities that employ abstinence education as their only approach to pregnancy prevention are likely to deprive sexually active teenagers of important methods for preventing STDs and unplanned pregnancies.

Based on these issues, several changes regarding PRWORA polices are recommended:

- The federal government must provide a wider safety net for young parents who have difficulty becoming financially self-sufficient within the five-year time limit for TANF assistance.[92]
- "Pass-through" policies, which permit "formal child support by low-income fathers to 'pass through' to their families instead of being collected by the state to recoup the costs of public assistance paid to the custodial mother,"[93] should be enacted. The implementation of pass-through policies will likely increase the number of teen fathers declaring paternity and participating in the child-support system, while fostering a standard of living that will allow low-income families headed by teen parents to meet their basic needs.
- State governments should consider "matching support payments made by low-income fathers, gradually phasing out these funds at higher levels of income."[94]
- Marriage promotion between young parents must be limited to couples who can either demonstrate or develop the requisite skills for sustaining a supportive marriage, while highly dysfunctional couples are probably better off living apart.
- The requirement that unmarried parents reside with a responsible adult makes sense for young adolescent parents, but the application of this policy with older teen parents should be reexamined.[95]
- Further study of the detrimental impact of welfare-to-work on the adolescent children of TANF is needed to determine what additional

support TANF families with teenagers need to help those youths to fare better.

- Pregnancy prevention programs that include teaching abstinence with preteens and contraceptive use with teenagers should be eligible for federal funding through PRWORA.

Policies Regarding Statutory Rape

A young man who is at least eighteen years old can be charged with statutory rape if he has sex with a girl who is under the age of consent to engage in sexual relations with an adult. Statutory rape laws were originally developed to protect young unwed girls from men who might exploit and impregnate them and not take responsibility by marrying them.[96] These laws were also designed to discourage adults from transmitting sexual diseases to youngsters who do not understand STDs. Such youngsters "lack the knowledge of and access to reliable methods of contraception."[97] Because adult men often have sex with young girls and are responsible for a surprisingly high percentage of the births to girls who are fifteen years old or younger, particularly in certain states such as California, the issue of statutory rape is central to discussions of teenage pregnancy and parenthood.[98]

Due to the great number of statutory rape laws, which vary from state to state, and the many ways in which statutory rape is defined, there is massive confusion regarding the circumstances that can place a young man at risk to be charged with a sex crime. As a result, many young adult men who are eighteen or nineteen years old, including numerous teenage fathers in that age group, worry that they could face statutory rape charges if their sexual relationship with a girl who is officially a minor were revealed to the authorities. The fear that social-service and health-care professionals might turn them in to the authorities for suspicion of statutory rape deters many young men from participating in programs for adolescent fathers and going to family planning clinics.[99] This concern is so great in some traditional Latino communities, where relationships between younger females and adult males are culturally sanctioned, that it causes a considerable number of young Latino fathers to carefully limit their contact with their partners and children.[100]

Although some prosecutors are reluctant to file statutory rape charges when they sense a couple share an ongoing, non-exploitive relationship, other prosecutors adhere to a rigid application of laws defining statutory rape offenses. These variations in practice reflect a controversy associated with different points of view pertaining to the age-of-consent provisions that are central components of statutory rape laws. The rationale for age-of-consent doctrines is that although a minor may be biologically mature enough to desire and engage in sexual intercourse, he or she many lack the capacity to make mature and rational decisions regarding sex and may be vulnerable to the manipulation and deceit of a much older person.[101] However, the age at which a boy or girl reaches the maturity to make informed sexual decisions is open to great debate: "This is perhaps one of the major points of contention in statutory rape controversies; even a young teenager might possess enough social sense to make informed and mature decisions about sex, and, conversely, some people well above any agreed-upon age of consent might never develop the ability to make mature choices about sex, as even many mentally healthy individuals remain naive and easily manipulated throughout their lives. Any agreed-upon age of consent, therefore, is more or less arbitrary."[102]

Thus, it is clear that sex between young adult men and younger women is exploitive in some situations but not in others. Yet, in some jurisdictions, all cases of sex between an adult man and a girl who is a minor are handled in the same way, regardless of the degree of sexual coercion or lack thereof that was involved.

The participants of a special conference regarding school-based and school-linked services for pregnant and parenting teens, which was sponsored by the National Institute on Early Childhood Development, discussed some of the problems associated with current laws pertaining to statutory rape. The participants noted that the threat of prosecution remains high for young adult males who father a child with an adolescent girl because some state laws, such as those in California, dictate that statutory rape cases must be reported as child abuse. The participants raised serious concerns about the counterproductive results of these laws because they give educators, health-care professionals, and caseworkers who are aware of the age differences between teenage girls and their partners no discretion about how to respond when such couples have sexual relations. The participants were also troubled that "reporting requirements like California's could undermine efforts to strengthen the involvement of fathers in teen parent families."[103]

In response to this problem, the conference participants encouraged states to develop guidelines on statutory rape that distinguish cases involving predatory rape versus those that involve a sexual relationship between two individuals who are in a non-exploitive relationship.[104] In the latter cases, there should be no burden to report a couple to officials for statutory rape charges. Eliminating counterproductive reporting mandates will help ease the wariness of many young-adult fathers about being involved in their families and seeking and utilizing much-needed services. Freeing professionals to focus on serving these young men, rather than reporting them, will enhance the efforts of these professionals to assist many more teenage fathers with their paternal concerns and responsibilities. In those cases in which there is any evidence indicating that an adult male has acted in a sexually coercive, exploitive, or predatory manner with a young girl, mandated reporting of abuse should be required so that the best interests and well-being of the youth are safeguarded.

Policies to Promote Positive Youth Development and Connections in Disadvantaged Communities

America's Promise Alliance, an organization dedicated to the well-being of children and youth, reported that certain life circumstances, including the influence of caring adults, safe places to live and study, a healthy early development, an effective education, and opportunities to help others, are crucial for the future success and adjustment of children and adolescents. The Alliance concluded that children who enjoy the sustained and cumulative benefit of having at least four of these five advantages present in the various contexts of their lives "are much more likely to be academically successful, civically engaged and socially competent, regardless of their race or family income."[105] However, more than 10 million American youth—about one out of every five children—are receiving none or only one of these crucial advantages, putting them in a state of tremendous disadvantage. "Children from low-income backgrounds are much less likely to enjoy these resources that are those from more affluent families," and "African American and Hispanic children are half as likely as Whites to receive them."[106]

One of the outcomes linked to children who face such disadvantages is adolescent parenthood. The teenage birth rate in the poorest counties and metropolitan areas in the United States is higher—typically at least twice as high—than in more affluent areas.[107] Recognizing that problems in poor neighborhoods, such as high concentrations of unemployment, crime, and idle youth, are linked to earlier initiation of sexual intercourse and teenage parenthood, "an exclusive focus on behavior and personal responsibility will have a limited effect on sexual initiation unless contextual influences at the neighborhood level are addressed."[108] Furthermore, reduction of early parenthood, by itself, will not eliminate the powerful effects of growing up in poverty and disadvantage.[109]

Many adolescent fathers are all too familiar with the terrible disadvantages of growing up in multi-problem communities. One young father, who was raised in a neighborhood besieged by poverty, substance abuse, and violence, had this to say about the terrible conditions and scary hazards in his day-to-day experiences:

> My neighborhood's pretty bad. . . . Because by them tearing down a lot
> of houses, they just leave it with empty lots, and those houses that's
> still standin' . . . if they're not crack houses, they have speakeasies

where they sell wine and liquor for a dollar. And the majority, everybody around there they just either on dope or they sell dope or they
alcoholic or they sell alcohol. And the corner store, like the can goods
been in there about 15 years. . . . Some of the corner stores sell drugs,
buy food stamps from the poor people, you know, the one that's on
drugs, [who] instead of them usin' 'em to buy food for the kids, they
sell 'em for dope. . . . My alarm clock is a shotgun, you know. . . . So,
it's pretty bad. . . . I thank God every day that I make it to my destina-
tion and make it back.[110]

Public policy must address the types of difficult life circumstances
reported by this father, which place too many of our nation's children at risk
for early parenthood.[111] Specifically, policy must support sustained, programmatic efforts to reduce the concentration of poverty and provide positive
adult role models in highly disadvantaged communities.[112] In addition, policy
must support providing interventions that "improve important parenting
skills (e.g., monitoring and communication) or increase young people's
commitment to school. Such interventions should be carried out early—that
is, with children who have not reached adolescence."[113] Also, more funding
should be provided for programs that involve youth in community service
before grades five and six because research has demonstrated that com-
munity-service programs reduce sexual activity among elementary school
students.[114] Other research findings show that strong connections with one's
family and school can inoculate some youth from engaging in high-risk
behaviors, including risky sex. Therefore, programs that attempt to link
males to positive influences, whether at the family, school, or community-
program level, should begin as early as possible.[115]

One of the glaring problems in disadvantaged communities is the lack of
high-quality educational and recreational activities and employment opportunities, which leaves many poor teenagers, such as this young father, with
few positive outlets in life:

They ain't got no recreation centers, pools and all that kind of stuff. . . .
And what they got in my neighborhood is so little that it always be
too many people . . . hundreds of people at one little activity. . . . And
there ain't be no jobs for the young people . . . old people neither. . . .
I mean if people can't do nothing with theirselves, their time . . . they
ain't got no inspiration, I mean they ain't inspired to do nothing. . . .
So most of us end up in situations where we in trouble . . . with the
law, layin' up and havin' kids cuz there's nothin' else to do.[116]

More funding must be provided for initiatives that help communities to
organize themselves around children's needs so that adolescent fathers like

this one have a sense of direction and purpose to their lives. Specifically, funding initiatives should target programs in low-income communities that maximize school achievement and recreation programs where at-risk youth have multiple opportunities for receiving support and guidance from caring adult mentors.[117] In addition, federal workforce development policies should include guidelines specifically pertaining to the employment needs of young fathers from low-income areas.[118]

Boys who live in poor, multi-problem neighborhoods, come from single-parent families, have strained family relations and academic difficulties, and associate with delinquent peers and engage in antisocial behavior are at the highest risk to become teenage fathers. Youth who show this particular cluster of characteristics should be a top priority of public policy. These youth require highly specialized programs that are designed to teach them basic life skills, address negative peer influences, promote school success, and direct them to alternatives to early parenthood.[119]

Several innovative programs have been designed to prevent teenage pregnancy and parenthood and many of the other problems rampant in disadvantaged communities though the application of the positive youth-development model, which focuses on promoting positive qualities in children while addressing their many needs in a holistic manner.[120] A central feature of the approach is the formation of neighborhood partnerships that involve a coalition of professional agencies and health-care centers with educational systems and the business sector to improve the well-being and life options of children and adolescents in low-income areas.[121] Some of these programs, such as the Kansas School/Community Sexual Risk Reduction Replication Initiative and the Children's Aid Society–Carrera Program, are especially designed to prevent first-time pregnancies, while others, such as the Mazza Project, help young men who are already fathers to improve their fathering behaviors, life circumstances, and skills while avoiding involvement in any additional unplanned pregnancies.

The Kansas Initiative targeted youths in three low-income areas of Kansas that had high teen pregnancy rates, and it featured after-school and summer activities, peer-support groups, sexuality education in the community for youth and parents, mentoring, tutoring, peer leadership training, and media attention to the problems and solutions associated with adolescent pregnancy.[122] The Children's Aid/Carrera project served high-risk adolescents in the Harlem section of New York City by offering employment services, academic assistance, comprehensive family life and sexuality education, arts and athletic activities, and dental, mental health and medical services, including STD testing and contraceptives.[123] Both programs have shown promising results in reducing high-risk sexual behavior and expanding the life options of disadvantaged youth.

The Mazza Project assisted thirty young fathers from the inner city who had struggled with high rates of unemployment, no clear career plans, few friends and confidants, and inconsistent contraceptive use. The project helped the majority of these adolescent fathers to gain employment, develop career plans, improve their relationships with their children, widen their support networks, and use condoms more consistently during sexual intercourse.[124] Public policy should support the replication of these model programs because all three promoted the positive development of adolescents in spite of the many problems that existed in the youths' family, school, and community.

Policies to Prevent STDs and Premarital Pregnancy and Childbirth among America's Teenagers

Public policy to address the needs of adolescents from disadvantaged communities must be paired with a more concerted national drive to prevent STD infection and reduce the number of unwed American teenagers who get pregnant and become parents. Policy makers must reconsider our preferred methods of preparing children for sex in spite of the fact that the teen pregnancy rate in the United States recently dropped to an all-time low. Dramatic changes in policy are necessary because the higher rates of teen pregnancy, adolescent births, and STDs and the lower levels of contraceptive use among teenagers in the United States compared with teenagers in other developed countries suggest that there is substantial room for improvement in our nation's efforts to prevent high-risk sexual behavior by adolescents.[125]

The teen pregnancy rate in the United States is still considerably higher than in many other developed nations, including Great Britain, France, Canada, Sweden, and the Netherlands.[126] Major differences between the United States and these other Western countries in preventing teen pregnancy have been attributed to variations in public policy. While the federal government of the United States has gradually swung in the direction of supporting an approach to pregnancy prevention that is based largely on teaching sexual abstinence to minors, other Western nations have endorsed policies that generally support easy youth access to contraceptives and systematic instruction about contraceptive use in schools and other institutions and through media campaigns.[127] In order to bring our teen pregnancy rate in line with that of other nations that have more successful campaigns to prevent adolescent childbearing, some important policy revisions must occur.

What form should these policy changes take? Extreme approaches to pregnancy prevention, which solely emphasize either abstinence or safe sex and condom use, would be a big mistake. Instead, balanced approaches to pregnancy prevention, which combine abstinence education with education about safe sex tailored to the needs of particular populations of youth, should begin with children in elementary school, probably before the fifth grade, particularly in communities where there is a high rate of sexual activity among younger teenagers.[128] Abstinence-based messages about sexual behavior may be effective for children who do not see themselves as ready for sex.[129] With these youth, it can be especially helpful to promote the continuation of abstinence through the development of peer support groups and parent-child communication that reinforce the choice to delay first intercourse. At the same time, health-care and mental-health professionals must bear in mind that about one-fifth of all youth and even higher percentages of urban youth report having their first experience with sexual intercourse prior to age fifteen. These youth and those who anticipate that they will have sex in the near future need education about the potential consequences of having sex, peer pressure, and skills in safe-sex negotiation and condom use.[130] Youth who have multiple sexual partners will need intensive guidance about the dangers associated with sexual risk-taking, while "adolescents who have sex in the context of a committed relationship may respond best to interventions that address relationship issues such as trust and commitment, or that involve their partner."[131]

There is extensive research evidence demonstrating that successful programs employ this balanced approach to prevention that combines sexual health information about abstinence with contraceptive or reproductive-health services. This research verifies that combined approaches, which are sometimes referred to as the "abstinence plus" model,[132] have been shown to produce:

- Significant delay in the timing of first intercourse
- Reductions in sexual risk-taking behaviors, including increased use of condoms and other forms of contraception, and in the number of sexual partners, frequency of sex, and incidence of unprotected sex
- Significant declines in teen pregnancy, births, HIV, and other STDs[133]

Numerous prevention programs employing a balanced approach to prevention have been implemented. For example, the Family Planning Council of Philadelphia has developed the Health Resources Center program, which is a highly successful school-based balanced service emphasizing both abstinence and safe-sex practices. "Students are informed that abstinence is the only sure way to prevent pregnancy and infections, yet those who choose to be sexually involved can receive free condoms or tests for STDs and pregnancy during regular school hours."[134] A similar model has been adopted in Georgia, which began using TANF funds in 1997 "to support a new youth development program that both seeks to encourage teenagers to delay initiation of sexual intercourse and provides family planning service to adolescents who are sexually active or already have a child."[135] Nineteen other school- and community-based programs, the majority of which employ this balanced approach to prevention, are described in detail in a special publication available online from Advocates for Youth, an organization dedicated to helping youth to make informed and responsible decisions about their reproductive and sexual health.[136]

In spite of the many positive outcomes produced by these and other abstinence-plus programs, there has been a strong movement to replace comprehensive sex education programs with abstinence-only education. Abstinence-only proponents have contended that most sex educators do not include instruction on abstinence and that "sex education programs condone homosexuality, teach students how to have sex and undermine parental authority."[137] In a campaign to address these alleged transgressions, abstinence-only advocates have lobbied successfully for changes in policy pertaining to sex education at the federal, state, and local levels. The Bush administration has decided to support abstinence-only education as the primary vehicle for the prevention of sex-related problems in American youth, and numerous communities throughout the country have embraced this policy. Only nineteen states require that high school sex-education courses cover contraception, and approximately one-third of U.S. school districts "forbids dissemination of any positive information about contraception, regardless of whether their students are sexually active or at risk of pregnancy or disease."[138] In these school districts, students must be taught that abstinence is the only acceptable option outside of marriage.[139]

Many of the charges asserted by abstinence-only proponents are unfounded, and there is no sound scientific evidence supporting the utility of abstinence-only education. For example, contrary to the claim that sex educators skip abstinence education, research has documented that at least 78 percent and possibly as many as 90 percent of sex-education teachers cover abstinence in their curriculums.[140] Other research completed in the United States and several other Western nations shows that teaching about contraceptives and making condoms available in schools does not promote teenage sexual behavior.[141] Furthermore, in a critical review of the existing research on abstinence-only programs, the National Campaign to Prevent Teen Pregnancy's Effective Programs and Research Task Force concluded: "There do not currently exist any abstinence-only programs with strong evidence that they either delay sex or reduce teen pregnancy."[142] Consequently, emphasizing abstinence-only education as the principle means for preventing pregnancies and STDs in teenagers is misguided.

This is not to say that abstinence education should be abandoned. There are many good reasons to teach abstinence to children. Abstinence is the first and best choice for preventing STD infection and unplanned pregnancies. Abstinence is also a healthy strategy for children and adolescents who are not emotionally prepared to engage in sexual relations.[143] Consequently, "we must indicate at every opportunity that the consequences of immature sexual behavior are severe, emotionally and physically."[144] However, "adolescents have been experimenting with sex from time immemorial and will continue to do so."[145] Depriving youngsters who are already sexually active of tools they can use to engage in safe sex is a violation of their basic rights to protect their reproductive health.[146] Moreover, the widespread adoption of an abstinence-only model of sex education is likely to derail our nation from its recent progress in its campaign to prevent teen pregnancy and to curtail adolescent STDs. Instead of moving away from abstinence-plus programs, which have been proven to be effective, the focus of public policy should be on enhancing certain components of comprehensive sexual education programs through the adoption of the following guidelines:[147]

Programs should begin earlier and target younger adolescents. Traditionally, sexual-health programs have targeted older teens. However, adolescents who experience early puberty are at increased risk for early sexual activity. Developmentally appropriate sex education and counseling programs for younger teens are required.

New program models for minority teenagers need to be developed. African-American youth have an earlier onset of sexual activity and Latino youth use contraceptives at relatively low levels compared to other racial and ethnic groups. Culturally sensitive programs are needed to reduce the risk among African-American and Latino youth.

Risk-reduction programs need to be systematically linked to other youth programs that directly address socioeconomic disadvantage. There is a heightened risk among impoverished youth. Reproductive-health, social-service, and educational professionals must form coalitions that improve the life circumstances of youth by providing holistic programs that include career and academic counseling, mentoring, and sex education.

Programs need to understand that many youth lack the skills to practice safe sex. Programs must teach a variety of behavior skills that will help youth to use condoms effectively, to negotiate with partners about safe sex, and to refuse sex when it is not desired.

Programs need to effectively address the influence of peer groups, social norms, and pressure to have sex. Educational and support groups with norms reinforcing risk-reduction behaviors can be a powerful antidote to competing pressures to have sex.

Programs should not assume that sexual behavior is volitional. Health-care and counseling professionals must develop protocols for asking sexually active youth about whether their sexual encounters have been voluntary, and they should refer adolescent boys and girls who have experienced coerced sex for specialized counseling designed to address the mental-health needs of these youth.

Programs should not assume that sexual activity among teenagers is limited to vaginal sex. American adolescents engage in many forms of sexual activity, not just intercourse. Consequently, education about safe sex must include instruction about sexually transmitted diseases that can be contracted though oral and anal sex.

Programs cannot assume that teenagers are un-ambivalent about preventing pregnancy. Values-clarification exercises and education about the realities of being a parent while a teenager are needed for youth who are either ambivalent or supportive of out-of-wedlock childbearing.

Programs must do a better job of structuring services for males. Historically, the majority of pregnancy-prevention programs were designed for young women. In the future, programs must be developed with services and approaches that appeal to young men so that they too can be more knowledgeable about delaying sexual activity and engaging in safe sex.

Programs must reflect a better understanding and responsiveness to males who initiate sex at a very early age. There is a particular lack of knowledge about subpopulations of boys who start having sex at a very early age. Interventions that address forced sex and the pressure older boys place on younger boys to become sexually active are needed.

Programs must replace the one- or two-time-visit tradition with longer-term treatment options. Youths who use adolescent-health, school-health, and family-planning clinics tend to make an initial visit and one follow-up appointment to address their reproductive-health concerns. The complex realities of adolescent sexuality, however, demand that more-sustained education and treatment be provided, perhaps in the form of waiting-room advice from health educators, discussion groups with other teenagers, and follow-up phone calls and e-mail contacts.

The challenge of better serving the needs of young men is an issue that warrants additional consideration. Targeting high-risk adolescent males is necessary to reduce the unintended consequences of adolescent pregnancy.[148]

Although family-planning clinics in the United States have made increased efforts to serve teenage boys and men, there are still some agencies that do not serve male clients.[149] Males who do receive services are relatively few in number due to a number of barriers that deter many boys and men from seeking information, counseling, and treatment at reproductive-health centers. These barriers include "funding constraints, men's unawareness of services, and perceptions that clinics are the domains of women."[150] Nevertheless, these barriers can be reduced when the administrators and staff of reproductive-health clinics commit themselves to institutional policies that emphasize reaching out to and serving boys and men and making the service environment more geared toward males.

For example, in 2000 the New Generation Health Center (NGHC) in San Francisco "initiated a male involvement program that was designed to expand its capacity to involve adolescent males in reproductive-health activities and to increase direct services provided to adolescent and young adult males, including individualized counseling, physical examinations, condom provision, and STD testing."[151] NGHC operated special male clinics offered one-half day each week. The clinic was staffed by four rotating adolescent-medicine fellows, a family nurse-practitioner, a clinic assistant, two health educators, and peer educators. "Male-friendly posters, educational materials and recreational games were added to the waiting room" in an attempt to make the clinic a comfortable environment for male clients.[152] Special outreach initiatives targeted two local high schools and the community near the clinic. Collectively, these features increased the capacity of the clinic to serve males: "In the first year of the male clinic, the number of adolescent and adult male clients served at the facility increased by 192 percent and 119 percent, respectively, over the previous year."[153] In addition, the expansion of services to male clients did not appear to affect the level of satisfaction among female clients, which remained high.

For the past several years, the federal government has recognized the importance of considering the role of adolescent males in pregnancy prevention, and it has produced two publications on the subject, *2002 National Directory–A Resource Guide to Male Reproductive Health Programs* and *Male Involvement Projects–Prevention Services*. Both are available through the Publications Access Area of the Office of Population Affairs Clearinghouse.[154]

Another direction of public policy should be the support of programs that recognize the important role parents can play in preventing unintended pregnancies. Comprehensive sex education targeting adolescents must be augmented by services for parents that teach them accurate information about STDs and contraception and skills for discussing sensitive sexual topics with their children. These programs should also help parents to establish and enforce clear rules regarding sexual behavior.[155]

Confidentiality and Parent-Involvement Policies Pertaining to Contraceptive, STD, and Abortion Services

The extent to which parents should be involved in their children's access to education and services regarding STDs, contraceptives, and abortion is a highly complicated and controversial issue that has been the focus of widespread political and public policy debate in the United States. It is also a highly confusing matter because states vary widely with regard to requirements pertaining to parental notification of minors' use of reproductive-health services. Although no federal law guarantees adolescents the universal right to confidential reproductive-health education and treatment, all states allow minors to have access to confidential reproductive-health services to some extent.[156] But the range of services available to minors without their parental involvement varies widely from state to state. As of November 2006, thirty-four states required some type of parental involvement, consisting of consent or notification, in a minor's decision to have an abortion. In two states, Oklahoma and Utah, both parental notification and approval are required before a young woman can have an abortion.[157] In other states, however, adolescent boys and girls have access to a variety of confidential services. For example, in New Jersey minors have the right to consent on their own to contraceptive counseling and services, abortion, medical care related to pregnancy, and testing and treatment for STDs or treatment for sexual assault.[158]

Advocates of parental-notification laws "contend that government policies giving minors the right to consent to sexual health services without their parents' knowledge undermine parental authority and family values and are tantamount to condoning early sexual activity."[159] The United States Conference of Catholic Bishops (USCCB), a staunch proponent of parental involvement, has argued that parents are a child's most reliable and trusted source of information about sex and birth control, and that parents have the rightful role to be the primary educator of their children. Consequently, the USCCB has declared, "Government agencies or counselors cannot replace and should not interfere with the rights and responsibilities of loving parents, particularly in sensitive matters dealing with human sexuality and the transmission of human life."[160] Similarly, leaders of Concerned Women for America have taken the stand that parents should be "the main providers of information about sex to kids," that parent-child discussions about sex are the best deterrent to teenage pregnancy, and that government interference in parent-child communications about sexual issues, contraceptives, and abortion will result in greater teenage sexual activity.[161] With regard to the issue of parental involvement and abortion, the National Right to Life Committee (NRLC) has warned that parental notification is necessary to protect a pregnant minor who might be pressured by an older boyfriend or one of his family members to have an abortion against her will. In addition, the NRLC has affirmed that parents have a right to notification because they are financially responsible for any complications resulting from an abortion to a minor. Furthermore, the NRLC contends that notification and consent laws allow parents to discuss the possible emotional, physical, and spiritual consequences of abortion with their daughters.[162]

Some of these justifications for parental notification reflect valid concerns, but others are either overstated or contradicted by evidence from research on teen sexual behavior. Among the valid concerns are the potentially constructive role that competent parents can play in abortion decisions and the responsibilities parents must bear if their daughter has complications arising from an abortion. Research shows that mothers, in particular, tend to be a vital confident when a daughter is considering an abortion[163] and that most parents support parental notification when a minor is considering an abortion.[164] Parents can provide vital information regarding the medical history of a girl preparing for an abortion, such as any allergies she might have to medications.[165] Thus, the input of a concerned parent during an abortion procedure can prevent risks and complications for pregnant teens. There has also been an extreme case in which a twelve-year-old girl was impregnated by an eighteen-year-old man and taken across state lines by the man's mother for an abortion without the consent of the girl's parents, which raises serious questions about the vulnerability of very young girls whose parents are not involved in abortion decisions.[166] Thus, promoting the involvement of competent parents in the abortion process is a goal that warrants serious consideration.

However, although supportive parent-child communications, particularly with caring parents who convey accurate information about the consequences of sexual activity and options for preventing STDs and pregnancy, can have a positive impact on the sexual decisions of some adolescents, overall such communications have not been associated with an increased likelihood that sexually active teenagers will consistently use effective contraceptive measures.[167] Also, providing information about contraceptives by nonparents does not increase rates of teen sexual activity,[168] and it may even reduce the likelihood of adolescents engaging in sexual intercourse.[169] There is also compelling evidence debunking the myth that contraceptive services promotes teen pregnancy: Teenagers in Great Britain, Canada, France, and Sweden have greater access to contraceptives than do American youth, yet the U.S. adolescent pregnancy rate far exceeds the rates in these countries.[170]

Parental-notification policies have been opposed by several organizations, including the American Medical Association, the American College of

Obstetricians and Gynecologists, and the Society for Adolescent Medicine, which "have issued statements asserting that confidential reproductive-health service should be available to minors."[171] Several rationales for this position have been provided. Many health-care professionals "believe that teenagers might avoid seeking contraceptive and STD services if they were forced to involve their parents."[172] In some cases, pregnant teenagers who consulted their parents about abortion "under compulsion of the law and against their better judgment" have been "kicked out of their homes, beaten, and prevented from having an abortion."[173] Consequently, it is feared that pregnant adolescents who feel that they cannot confide in their parents might seek illegal abortions, which are dangerous to their health.[174] The procedures involved in contacting and involving parents could result in critical delays in adolescents' receiving treatment for STDs or having abortions, which increases the odds that youngsters seeking such services will experience medical complications.[175]

There is a substantial body of research demonstrating that mandatory parental notification for contraceptives would drastically decrease the use of sexual health-care services by teenagers, which would result in the spread of STDs and increased numbers of adolescent pregnancies and births to teens. Part of the reduction in service utilization would be linked to a loss of trust in health-care professionals: High school students report that they are more willing to talk about their sexual activities, ask questions about contraceptives, and seek health care for sensitive sexual concerns from physicians who assure confidentiality than from doctors who give no such assurances. They are also more likely to say they would return to a physician who gave them unconditional assurances of confidentiality than to one who mentioned exceptions.[176] Troubling percentages of adolescent clients who normally use family-planning clinics would likely make undesirable changes in their behavior if parental notification were required: 15 percent–33 percent would stop using clinic services altogether. Among these teens, there would likely be an increased use of nonmedical forms of contraception, including the hazardous practice of withdrawal, an increased proportion of teens having unprotected sex, and decreased use of STD and pregnancy testing.[177]

Parental-notification laws pertaining to contraceptives would also likely create substantial health and economic costs. One investigator estimated that a state parental-notification law in Texas would cause more than a third of the state's teenage clients of family-planning clinics to forego reproductive-health care, which would result in 5,372 more births, 1,654 more abortions, 2,243 additional cases of chlamydia, 521 new cases of gonorrhea, and 501 additional cases of pelvic inflammatory disease each year that the law was in effect. In addition, the law would cost nearly $44 million in new expenses for the state annually.[178]

What is often ignored in these arguments regarding the pros and cons of parent notification are the opinions and needs of adolescent fathers related to reproductive-health issues. Boys who become fathers have many questions about sex and contraceptives in spite of the fact that they are sexually experienced. A common need expressed by adolescent fathers is for confidential information, testing, and health care for HIV and other sexually transmitted diseases.[179] They also tend to want confidential education about contraceptives.[180]

In summary, parents have a legitimate interest in the sexual behaviors of their children, and the input of concerned, competent, and supportive parents regarding sexual practices and abortions among minors can help to prevent negative outcomes, all of which are reasons to involve parents in the reproductive-health activities of their children. Nevertheless, "few adolescents would abstain from sex in response to mandated involvement," and parental-notification laws would produce numerous adverse outcomes, including reduced trust of physicians, increased rates of unprotected sex, unreliable contraceptive practices, and reduced STD awareness and testing. These changes in the behaviors of young people would result in rises in STDs, pregnancies, and births, which would pose a significant economic burden on the public. In addition, parental notification would be contrary to the expressed desires of adolescent fathers regarding their reproductive-health preferences.

Consequently, it appears that the best policy direction would be for protection-of-confidentiality practices that are linked with concerted efforts to promote parent-child discussions about sexual matters. A model for this type of policy already exists with Title X services. Title X of the Public Health Service Act is "the only federal program dedicated to providing family planning services to low-income women and teenagers."[181] Title X clinics are mandated to provide confidential services to all clients, regardless of age, but they are also mandated "to encourage adolescents to include their parents in their contraceptive decisions."[182] This balanced approach should be the norm for policies regarding contraceptive, STD, and abortion services for minors. Specifically, reproductive-health professionals should be allowed to assure minors of confidentiality, but they should also be required to engage an adolescent boy or girl in personal counseling whose purpose is to encourage the youth to consider having conversations with his or her parents about sexual matters. In addition, public funding should be earmarked for programs that provide parents with medically accurate information about contraceptives and teach them strategies for overcoming their discomfort about discussing sexual subjects with their children.[183]

It appears that many teenagers using clinic-based family-planning services already inform their parents about their clinic visits, ranging from 41 percent after their first visit to 72 percent after their subsequent visits.[184] Encouraging youth to discuss sexual matters with their parents is likely to increase the percentages of boys and girls who inform their parents of their sexual intentions and actions, which would increase the number of youngsters who can enlist the guidance of their parents. The decisions of those who refrain from involving their parents should be respected and kept in confidence so that teenagers who cannot confide in their parents are assured that they can put their trust in the expertise of professionals whose ethical standards demand that they promote the well-being of their clients.

Policies Regarding Educational Services for Teenage Fathers

One of the most consistent and sad facts about teenage fathers is that a high percentage of them do not complete high school. Over 50 percent of the hundreds of adolescent fathers who participated in the Texas Fragile Families Initiative (TFF),[185] the Teen Father Collaboration,[186] and the Maine Young Fathers Project were high school dropouts.[187] The dropout rate for the young men involved in the Public/Private Ventures Young Unwed Fathers Pilot Project (PPV) was even higher; approximately three-quarters of these fathers had failed to graduate from high school.[188]

The educational deficiencies of teenage fathers indirectly affect their involvement with their children. The lack of a basic education can severely limit a young man's career options, and the resulting employment difficulties can adversely impact his ability to support a family, which can create serious tensions between him and the mother of his child. These conflicts may result in him being denied access to his child by the mother and her family. If he has legally established paternity, his financial difficulties associated with substandard educational qualifications might also make it difficult for him to pay child support, which could result in his being assessed for arrearages. Thus, obtaining a GED and preferably some form of higher education or special marketable skill is one of the greatest needs of young fathers who have dropped out of school. Also, for fathers who are still in school, dropout prevention is crucial.[189]

Adolescent fathers who have dropped out of school tend to consider securing a job to be an immediate priority and completing a GED to be a longer-term goal. Once expectant teenage fathers have a child, they often lose sight of this goal as they become preoccupied with the responsibilities of fatherhood and the other pressing issues in their lives. Consequently, many need some type of special assistance or incentive to resume their educations. The TFF addressed this need by offering fathers enrolled in the Project Bootstrap program stipends that could be used as incentives to attend GED classes or to complete portions of the GED exam.[190] Financial incentives were

also made available to young fathers associated with one of the sites participating in the PPV.[191] These financial incentives were considered to be a key
factor in the decision made by many of the TFF and PPV fathers to complete
their GED,[192] as was verified by this young man from the PPV program:

> I was looking for a job and I went to Manpower and one of the guys
> in there . . . saw that my girlfriend was pregnant and he said . . . hey
> man, there's this neat program and he was just telling me all about it.
> It kind of sounded too good to be true when he was telling me . . . they
> pay for your school, they give you money to go . . . you have books. You
> can pick whatever you want as a career and they pay for it. . . . I was
> thinking . . . you just can't pass up something like that. And so . . . he
> told me to come back tomorrow and I was there. I wanted to do it.[193]

This testimony is persuasive evidence that helping adolescent fathers
who are school dropouts to obtain their GEDs is a worthy feature for future
policy initiatives designed to foster father involvement in families. These
initiatives should include funding for financial incentives that will help low-
income fathers to enroll and persist with their GED studies.

Youthful fathers who are still enrolled in school also need special assistance to complete their educations. One would expect that this assistance is
readily available considering that there are numerous school-based teenage
parenting programs and that public schools are prohibited by federal law
from engaging in discrimination based on sex.[194] However, although there
are numerous school-based services for pregnant teens and teen mothers, historically relatively few adolescent parenting programs operating in
school systems have either included or reached out to student fathers.[195] This
neglect is due in part to the failure of school counselors to comprehend the
service needs of this population.[196]

In spite of this neglect, helping adolescent fathers to achieve a strong
educational foundation remains one of the most important contributions
schools can make to counter the negative consequences of adolescent parenthood for young fathers.[197] Schools are a logical choice and a cost-effective
setting for fatherhood programs because:[198]

- Younger, in-school fathers are less likely to face serious substance-abuse
  issues or have extensive criminal backgrounds.
- A young age is significantly related to the likelihood that a father is still
  involved with his family and willing to seek out assistance with parenting skills.
- Focusing on younger fathers appears to help reduce repeat teenage births.
- School-based programs boost high-school graduation rates and thereby
  reduce barriers to employment.

- School-based programs offer support that make them one of the most effective programs at recruiting and retaining fathers.

For these reasons, public policy should support the creation of school-based teen-father programs where none exist and the expansion of programs that are currently operating. Several recommendations resulting from the Texas Fragile Families Initiative represent specific innovations that policy makers should consider:[199]

- Develop courses that cover topics like relationship skills and marriage, and offer these courses for credit to student fathers as an incentive for fathers to remain in school and as a mechanism to provide program staff with daily contact with fathers.
- Build father-centered program services into existing parenting or life-skills classes.
- Offer and facilitate support groups for in-school dads during lunch, free periods, or after school.
- Engage young fathers as presenters in pregnancy-prevention services targeting other students. Through these presentations, young dads can share their experiences and provide other students with insights into the struggles of teenage fathers.
- Recruit older, out-of-school fathers to serve as mentors to fathers still enrolled in school.

Conclusion

For too long, our culture has treated boys who become fathers during their teenage years as detached misfits who are the architects of many of our nation's problems, rather than seeing these youth for who they really are: young men trying to navigate a complex array of difficult life circumstances that place them at a tremendous disadvantage in life. As a society, we must carefully rethink our assumptions about adolescent fathers and provide these young men with opportunities "to learn about themselves, to discover their strengths, to realize their importance, and to confront their weaknesses."[200] Most of all, we must enhance their life options in order to help them be supportive of their partners and know and love their child.

Caring adults from all walks of life who are aware of the hardships associated with adolescent paternity must educate the rest of the world about the stresses and changes a young man goes through when he becomes a father while he is, in so many respects, ill-prepared to be a parent. We must convince our nation's leaders and the professionals who staff our country's agencies, schools, and clinics that youthful dads have a variety of complicated needs, and that these young men can be inspired to be successful parents and productive citizens as long as we convey to them that they are welcomed and valued members of society. If we meet these worthy challenges, then we will have taken a huge leap toward a future in which the children of teenage fathers will be heard to say, "My father was everything a man could be to his child, and I love him for it."

NOTES

CHAPTER 1   THE LOOMING CRISIS AMERICA MUST CONFRONT

1. Ventura, S. J., Mosher, W. D., Curtin, S. C., Abma, J. C., & Henshaw, S. (1999). Highlights of trends in pregnancies and pregnancy rates by outcome: Estimates for the United States, 1976–96. *National Vital Statistics Reports, 47*(29). Hyattsville, MD: National Center for Health Statistics. Retrieved September 4, 2007, from http://www.eric.ed.gov:80/ERICWebPortal/custom/portlets/recordDetails/detailmini.jsp?_nfpb=true&_&ERICExtSearch_SearchValue_0=ED437476&ERICExtSearch_SearchType_0=eric_accno&accno=ED437476

2. Darroch, J. E., Singh, S., Frost, J. J., & the Study Team. (2001). Differences in teenage pregnancy rates among five developed countries: The roles of sexual activity and contraceptive use. *Family Planning Perspectives, 33*(6), 244–250, 281.

3. Ventura, S. J., Abma, J. C., Mosher, W. D., & Henshaw, S. K. (2005). *Recent trends in teenage pregnancy in the United States, 1990–2002.* Hyattsville, MD: National Center for Health Statistics. Retrieved September 9, 2007, from http://www.cdc.gov/nchs/products/pubs/pubd/hestats/teenpreg1990–2002/teenpreg1990–2002.htm

4. National Center for Health Statistics. (2004). *NCHS data on teenage pregnancy.* Retrieved September 4, 2007, from http://www.cdc.gov/nchs/data/factsheets/teenpreg.pdf; see also Ventura, S. J., Abma, J. C., Mosher, W. D., & Henshaw, S. (2004). Estimated pregnancy rates for the United States, 1990–2000: An update. *National Vital Statistics Reports, 52*(23). Hyattsville, MD: National Center for Health Statistics. Retrieved September 4, 2007, from www.cdc.gov/nchs/data/nvsr/nvsr52/nvsr52_23.pdf

5. The National Campaign to Prevent Teen Pregnancy. (2004). *The relationship between teenage motherhood and marriage.* Retrieved January 12, 2006, from www.teenpregnancy.org/works/sciencesays.asp

6. Landry, D. J., & Forest, J. D. (1995). How old are U.S. fathers? *Family Planning Perspectives, 27,* 159–161; see also Males, M., & Chew, K. S. (1996). The ages of fathers in California adolescent births. *American Journal of Public Health, 86* (4), 565–568.

7. Martin J. A., Hamilton B. E., Sutton P. D., Ventura S. J., Menacker, F., & Munson M. L. (2003). Births: Final data for 2002. *National Vital Statistics Reports, 52*(10). Hyattsville, MD: National Center for Health Statistics; see also Martin J. A., Hamilton B. E., Sutton P. D., Ventura S. J., Menacker, F., & Munson M. L. (2005). Births:

Final data for 2003. *National Vital Statistics Reports, 54*(2). Hyattsville, MD: National Center for Health Statistics; U.S. Census Bureau (2000). *Projections of the total resident population by 5-year age groups, and sex with special age categories: Middle Series, 1999 to 2000.* Retrieved September 4, 2007, from http://www.census.gov/popest/ estimates.php; U.S. Census Bureau (2004). *Annual estimates of the population by sex and five-year age groups for the United States: April 1, 2000 to July 1, 2003.* Retrieved September 4, 2007, from http://www.census.gov/popest/estimates.php

8. Tauber, M., Fields-Meyer, T., & Smith, K. (2005, January 31). Special report: Young teens and sex. *People Magazine,* 86–96.

9. Darroch, J. E., Singh, S., Frost, J. J., & the Study Team. (2001). Differences in teenage pregnancy rates among five developed countries: The roles of sexual activity and contraceptive use. *Family Planning Perspectives, 33*(6), 244–250, 281.

10. Singh, S., & Darroch, J. E. (2000). Adolescent pregnancy and childbearing: Levels and trends in developed countries. *Family Planning Perspectives, 32,* 14–23.

11. Benson, P. L., Scales, P. C., Leffert, N., & Roehlkepartain, E. C. (1999). *A fragile foundation: The state of developmental assets among American youth.* Minneapolis: Search Foundation.

12. Pears, K. C., Pierce, S. L., Kim, H. K., Capaldi, D. M. & Owen, L. D. (2005). The timing of entry into fatherhood in young, at-risk men (p. 443). *Journal of Marriage and Family, 67,* 429–447; see also Spingarn, M. D., & DuRant, R. H. (1996). Male adolescents involved in pregnancy: Associated health risk and problem behaviors (p. 262). *Pediatrics, 98*(2), 262–268; Thornberry, T. P., Wei, E. H., Stouthamer-Loeber, M., & Van Dyke, J. (2000). Teenage fatherhood and delinquent behavior. *Juvenile Justice Bulletin,* January 2000. Available online at http://www.ncjrs.org/html/ojjdp/ jjbul2000_1/contents.html

13. Hernandez, R. (2002). *Fatherwork in the crossfire: Chicano teen fathers struggling to take care of business.* (Report No. JSRI-WP-58). East Lansing, MI: Michigan State University, Julian Samora Research Institute. (ERIC Document Reproduction Services No. ED 471 926); see also Johnson, L. B., & Staples, R. (2005). *Black families at the crossroads: Challenges and prospects* (Rev. ed.). San Francisco: Jossey-Bass.

14. The National Campaign to Prevent Teen Pregnancy. (2006, October). *Teen sexual activity, pregnancy and childbearing among non-Hispanic White teens.* Retrieved September 17, 2007, from http://www.teenpregnancy.org/resources/reading/fact_ sheets/default.asp; see also The National Campaign to Prevent Teen Pregnancy. (2006, October). *Teen sexual activity, pregnancy and childbearing among Black teens.* Retrieved September 17, 2007, from http://www.teenpregnancy.org/resources/reading/fact_sheets/default.asp; The National Campaign to Prevent Teen Pregnancy. (2006, October). *Teen sexual activity, pregnancy and childbearing among Latinos in the United States.* Retrieved September 17, 2007, from http://www.teenpregnancy. org/resources/reading/fact_sheets/default.asp

15. Hoffman, S. D. (1998). Teenage childbearing is not so bad after all . . . or is it? A review of the literature. *Family Planning Perspectives, 30,* 236–239, 243; see also Kiselica, M. S. & Pfaller, J. (1993). Helping teenage parents: The independent and collaborative roles of school counselors and counselor educators. *Journal of Counseling and Development, 72,* 42–48; Thornberry, T. P., Smith, C. A., & Howard, G. J. (1997). Risk factors for teenage fatherhood. *Journal of Marriage and the Family, 59,* 505–522.

16. Kiselica, M. S. (1995). *Multicultural counseling with teenage fathers: A practical guide.* Thousand Oaks, CA: Sage.

17. Achatz, M., & MacAllum, C. A. (1994). *Young unwed fathers: Report from the field* (p. 23). Philadelphia: Public/Private Ventures; see also Barret, R., L., & Robinson, B. E. (1982). A descriptive study of teenage expectant fathers. *Family Relations, 31,* 349–352; Brown, S. (1990). *If the shoes fit: Final report and program implementation guide of the Maine Young Fathers Project.* Portland, ME: Human Services Development Institute, University of Southern Maine; Fry, P. S., & Trifiletti, R. J. (1983). Teenage fathers: An exploratory study of their developmental needs and anxieties and the implications for clinical-social intervention services. *Journal of Psychiatric Treatment and Evaluation, 5,* 219–227; Furstenberg, F. F. (1976). *Unplanned parenthood: The social consequences of teenage childbearing.* New York: The Free Press; Hardy, J. B., & Zabin, L. S. (1991). *Adolescent pregnancy in an urban environment: Issues, programs and evaluation.* Washington DC: Urban Institute Press; Klerman, L. V., & Jekel, J. F. (1973). *School-age mothers: Problems, programs and policy.* Hamden, CT: Shoe String Press; Lerman, R. (1993). A national profile of young unwed fathers. In R. Lerman & T. Ooms (Eds.), *Young unwed fathers: Changing roles and emerging policies* (pp. 27–51). Philadelphia: Temple University Press; Lorenzi, M. E., Klerman, L. U., & Jekel, J. F. (1977). School-age parents: How permanent a relationship? *Adolescence, 12,* 13–22; Panzarine, S., & Elster, A. B. (1983). Coping in a group of expectant adolescent fathers: An exploratory study. *Journal of Adolescent Health Care, 4,* 117–120; Redmond, M. A. (1985). Attitudes of adolescent males toward adolescent pregnancy and fatherhood. *Family Relations, 34,* 337–342; Rivara, F. P., Sweeney, P. J., & Henderson, B. F. (1986). Black teenage fathers: What happens after the child is born? *Pediatrics, 78,* 151–158; Romo. C., Belleamy, J., & Coleman, M. T. (2004). *TFF final evaluation report.* Austin, TX: Texas Fragile Families Initiative; Salguero, C. (1984). The role of ethnic factors in adolescent pregnancy and motherhood. In M. Sugar (Ed.), *Adolescent parenthood* (pp. 75–98). New York: SP Medical and Scientific Books; Sullivan, M. L. (1985); *Teen fathers in the inner city: An exploratory ethnographic study.* (Report No. UD 024 536). New York: Vera Institute of Justice. (ERIC Document Reproduction Service No. ED 264 316); Vaz, R., Smolen, P., & Miller, C. (1983). Adolescent pregnancy: Involvement of the male partner. *Journal of Adolescent Health Care, 4,* 246–250; Westney, O. E., Cole, O. J., & Munford, T. L. (1986). Adolescent unwed prospective fathers: Readiness for fatherhood and behaviors toward the mother and the expected infant. *Adolescence, 21,* 901–911; Williams, C. W. (1991). *Black teenage mothers: Pregnancy and child rearing from their perspective.* Lexington, MA: Lexington Books.

18. Cutrona, C. E., Hessling, R. M., Bacon, P. L., & Russell, D. W. (1998). Predictors and correlates of continuing involvement with the baby's father among adolescent mothers. *Journal of Family Psychology, 12,* 369–387; see also Fagot, B. I., Pears, K. C., Capaldi, D. M., Crosby, L., & Leve, C. S. (1998). Becoming an adolescent father: Precursors and parenting. *Developmental Psychology, 34*(6), 1209–1219; Furstenberg, F. F., Brooks-Gunn, J., & Morgan, S. P. (1987). *Adolescent mothers in later life.* New York: Cambridge University Press; Gershenson, H. P. (1983). Redefining fatherhood in families with White adolescent mothers. *Journal of Marriage and the Family, 45,* 591–599; Hardy, J. B., & Zabin, L. S. (1991). *Adolescent pregnancy in an urban environment: Issues, programs and evaluation.* Washington DC: Urban Institute Press; Lerman, R. (1993). A national profile of young unwed fathers. In R. Lerman & T. Ooms (Eds.), *Young unwed fathers: Changing roles and emerging policies* (pp. 27–51). Philadelphia: Temple University Press; Lorenzi, M. E., Klerman, L. U., & Jekel, J. F. (1977). School-age parents: How permanent a relationship?

Adolescence, 12, 13–22; Rivara, F. P., Sweeney, P. J., & Henderson, B. F. (1986). Black teenage fathers: What happens after the child is born? *Pediatrics, 78,* 151–158; Robinson, B. (1988). *Teenage fathers.* Lexington, MA: Lexington Books; Salguero, C. (1984). The role of ethnic factors in adolescent pregnancy and motherhood. In M. Sugar (Ed.), *Adolescent parenthood* (pp. 75–98). New York: SP Medical and Scientific Books.

19. Kiselica, M. S., Stroud, J. C., Stroud, J. E., & Rotzien, A. (1992). Counseling the forgotten client: The teen father. *Journal of Mental Health Counseling, 14,* 338–350.

20. Achatz, M., & MacAllum, C. A. (1994). *Young unwed fathers: Report from the field* (p. 23). Philadelphia: Public/Private Ventures; see also Kost, K. A. (1997). The effects of support on the economic well-being of young fathers. *Families in Society, 78,* 370–382; Vera Institute of Justice. (1990). *The male role in teenage pregnancy and parenting: New directions of public policy.* New York: Author.

21. Marsiglio, W. (1986). Teenage fatherhood: High school completion and educational attainment. In A. B. Elster & M. E. Lamb (Eds.), *Adolescent fatherhood* (pp. 67–88). Hillsdale, NJ: Erlbaum; see also Marsiglio, W. (1987). Adolescent fathers in the United States: Their initial living arrangements, marital experience and educational outcomes. *Family Planning Perspectives, 19,* 240–251; Pirog-Good, M. A. (1996). The educational and labor market outcomes of adolescent fathers. *Youth & Society, 28*(2), 236–262.

22. Achatz, M., & MacAllum, C. A. (1994). *Young unwed fathers: Report from the field* (p. 23). Philadelphia: Public/Private Ventures; see also Furstenberg, F. F., Brooks-Gunn, J., & Morgan, S. P. (1987). *Adolescent mothers in later life.* New York: Cambridge University Press; Kiselica, M. S., & Murphy, D. K. (1994). Developmental career counseling with teenage parents. *Career Development Quarterly, 42,* 238–244; Pirog-Good, M. A. (1996). The educational and labor market outcomes of adolescent fathers. *Youth & Society, 28*(2), 236–262; Sullivan, M. L. (1985). *Teen fathers in the inner city: An exploratory ethnographic study.* (Report No. UD 024 536). New York: Vera Institute of Justice. (ERIC Document Reproduction Service No. ED 264 316)

23. Kiselica, M. S. (1995). *Multicultural counseling with teenage fathers: A practical guide.* Thousand Oaks, CA: Sage.

24. Ibid.

25. Robinson, B. (1988). *Teenage fathers* (p. 39). Lexington, MA: Lexington Books.

26. Hendricks, L. E. (1980). Unwed adolescent fathers: Problems they face and their sources of social support. *Adolescence, 15,* 861–869; see also Hendricks, L. E. (1980). Unmarried Black adolescent fathers' attitudes toward abortion, contraception, and sexuality: A preliminary report. *Journal of Adolescent Health Care, 2,* 199–203; Hendricks, L. E. (1983). Suggestions for reaching unmarried Black adolescent fathers. *Child Welfare, 62,* 141–146; Hendricks, L. E. (1988). Outreach with teenage fathers: A preliminary report on three ethnic groups. *Adolescence, 23,* 711–720; Hendricks, L. E., Howard, C. S., & Caesar, P. P. (1981). Black unwed adolescent fathers: A comparative study of their problems and help-seeking behavior. *Journal of the National Medical Association, 73,* 863–868; Hendricks, L. E., & Montgomery, T. (1983). A limited population of unmarried Black adolescent fathers: A preliminary report on their view on fatherhood and the relationship with the mother of their children. *Adolescence, 18,* 201–210; Hendricks, L. E., Montgomery, T., & Fullilove, R. E. (1984). Educational achievement and locus of control among Black adolescent fathers. *Journal of Negro*

Education, 53, 182–188; Hendricks, L. E., & and Solomon, A. M. (1987). Reaching Black adolescent parents through nontraditional techniques. *Child and Youth Services*, 9, 111–124.

27. Hendricks, L. E. (1988). Outreach with teenage fathers: A preliminary report on three ethnic groups. *Adolescence*, 23, 711–720.

28. Children's Defense Fund. (1986). *Adolescent pregnancy: What the states are saying.* Washington DC: Author; see also Kiselica, M. S. (1992, August). *Are we giving teenage fathers a mixed message?* In L. Silverstein (Chair), *Transforming fatherhood in a patriarchical society.* Symposium conducted at the Annual Convention of the American Psychological Association, Washington DC; Kiselica, M. S. (1998, March). *School-based services for teenage parents: Results of a state survey.* Paper presented at the World Conference of the American Counseling Association, Indianapolis, IN; Kiselica, M. S., & Sturmer, P. (1993). Is society giving teenage fathers a mixed message? *Youth and Society*, 24, 487–501; Kiselica, M. S., & Sturmer, P. (1995, August). *Outreach services for teenage parents: Has gender equity been realized?* Paper presented at the Annual Convention of the American Psychological Association, New York; Sample, J. (1997). *Engendering fatherhood: Provision of services and professional attitudes toward young fathers.* Unpublished master's thesis, Oklahoma State University, Stillwater, OK; Smollar, J., & Ooms, T. (1987). *Young unwed fathers: Research review, policy dilemmas, and options: Summary report.* Washington DC: Department of Health and Human Services; U.S. Congress. (1986). *Teen pregnancy: What is being done? A report of the select committee on children, youth, and families.* (December, 1985). Washington DC: U. S. Government Printing Office.

29. Robinson, B. (1988). *Teenage fathers.* Lexington, MA: Lexington Books; see also Kiselica, M. S., & Sturmer, P. (1993). Is society giving teenage fathers a mixed message? *Youth and Society*, 24, 487–501.

30. Kiselica, M. S., Gorczynski, J., & Capps, S. (1998). Teen mothers and fathers: School counselor perceptions of service needs. *Professional School Counseling*, 2, 146–152; see also Smith, L. A. (1989). *Window on opportunities: An exploration in program development for Black adolescent fathers.* Unpublished doctoral dissertation, The City University of New York.

31. Kiselica, M. S. (1999). Avoiding simplistic stereotypes about boys and men and the challenge of thinking complexly: A call to the profession and a farewell address to SPSMM. *SPSMM Bulletin*, 4(4), 1–2, 16.

32. Hendricks, L. E. (1988). Outreach with teenage fathers: A preliminary report on three ethnic groups. *Adolescence*, 23, 711–720.

33. Kiselica, M. S. (1995). *Multicultural counseling with teenage fathers: A practical guide.* Thousand Oaks, CA: Sage.

34. Kiselica, M. S. (2001). A male-friendly therapeutic process with school-age boys. In G. R. Brooks and G. Good (Eds.), *The handbook of counseling and psychotherapy with men: A guide to settings and approaches* (Vol. I) (pp. 43–58). San Francisco: Jossey-Bass.

35. Kiselica, M. S. (1995). *Multicultural counseling with teenage fathers: A practical guide.* Thousand Oaks, CA: Sage.

36. Ibid.

37. Kiselica, M. S. (2001). A male-friendly therapeutic process with school-age boys. In G. R. Brooks and G. Good (Eds.), *The handbook of counseling and psychotherapy*

with men: A guide to settings and approaches. (Vol. I) (pp. 43–58). San Francisco: Jossey-Bass.

38. Kiselica, M. S. (1996). Parenting skills training with teenage fathers. In M. P. Andronico (Ed.), *Men in groups: Insights, interventions, and psychoeducational work* (pp. 283–300). Washington DC: American Psychological Association; Kiselica, M. S., Rotzien, A., & Doms, J. (1994). Preparing teenage fathers for parenthood: A group psychoeducational approach. *Journal for Specialists in Group Work, 19,* 83–94.

39. Kiselica, M. S. (1995). Healing father-son wounds with adolescent fathers. *The Psychotherapy Bulletin, 31,* 66–69.

CHAPTER 2   THE SEXUAL WORLDS OF AMERICAN TEENAGERS

1. National Adoption Information Clearinghouse. (2005). *Voluntary relinquishment for adoption: Numbers and trends.* Retrieved January 12, 2006, from http://naic.acf.hhs.gov/pubs/s_place.cfm

2. Bachu, A. (1999). Trends in premarital childbearing: 1930 to 1994. *Current Population Reports,* 23–197. Washington DC: U.S. Census Bureau; see also The National Campaign to Prevent Teen Pregnancy. (2004). *The relationship between teenage motherhood and marriage.* Retrieved January 12, 2006, from www.teenpregnancy.org/works/sciencesays.asp

3. Henshaw, S. K. (2004). *U.S. teenage pregnancy statistics with comparative statistics for women aged 20–24.* New York: The Alan Guttmacher Institute; see also The National Campaign to Prevent Teen Pregnancy. (undated). *Teen birth rates in the United States, 1940–2004.* Retrieved August 1, 2006 from http://www.teenpregnancy.org/resources/reading/fact_sheets/default.asp; The National Campaign To Prevent Teen Pregnancy. (2003). *Science Says: The sexual attitudes and behavior of male teens.* Retrieved January 12, 2006 from www.teenpregnancy.org/works/sciencesays.asp

4. Martin J. A., Hamilton B. E., Sutton P. D., Ventura S. J., Menacker, F., & Munson, M. L. (2003). Births: Final data for 2002. *National Vital Statistics Reports, 52*(10). Hyattsville, MD: National Center for Health Statistics; see also Martin J. A., Hamilton B. E., Sutton P. D., Ventura S. J., Menacker, F, & Munson, M. L. (2005). Births: Final data for 2003. *National Vital Statistics Reports, 54*(2). Hyattsville, MD: National Center for Health Statistics; U.S. Census Bureau. (2000). *Projections of the total resident population by 5-year age groups, and sex with special age categories: Middle Series, 1999 to 2000.* Retrieved January 12, 2006, from http://www.census.gov/popest/estimates.php; U.S. Census Bureau. (2004). *Annual estimates of the population by sex and five-year age groups for the United States: April 1, 2000 to July 1, 2003.* Retrieved Janmuary 12, 2006, from http://www.census.gov/popest/estimates.php

5. Turner, C. F., Ku, L., Rogers, S. M., Lindberg, L. D., Pleck, J. H., & Sonenstein, F. L. (1998). Adolescent sexual behavior, drug use, and violence: Increased reporting with computer survey technology. *Science, 280,* 867–873.

6. Marsiglio, W. (2006). Young men and teen pregnancy: A review of sex, contraception, and fertility-related issues. In The National Campaign to Prevent Teen Pregnancy (Ed.), *It's a guy thing: Boys, young men, and teen pregnancy prevention* (pp. 9–100). Washington DC: The National Campaign to Prevent Teen Pregnancy. Retrieved September 17, 2007, from http://www.teenpregnancy.org/resources/reading/males.asp

7. Henshaw, S. K., & Feivelson, D. J. (2000). Teenage abortion and pregnancy statistics by state, 1996. *Family Planning Perspectives, 32*(6), 272–280; see also Ventura, S. J., Abma, J. C., Mosher, W. D., & Henshaw, S. (2004). Estimated pregnancy rates for the United States, 1990–2000: An Update. *National Vital Statistics Reports, 52*(23). Hyattsville, MD: National Center for Health Statistics.

8. Adoption.com. (2005). *Adoption statistics: Placing children.* Retrieved October 4, 2005, from http://www.adoption.com.

9. The National Campaign to Prevent Teen Pregnancy. (2004). *The relationship between teenage motherhood and marriage.* Retrieved January 12, 2006, from www.teenpregnancy.org/works/sciencesays.asp

10. Wikipedia. (2006). Sexual revolution. Retrieved October 27, 2006, from http://en.wikipedia.org/wiki/Sexual_revolution

11. Caron, S. L., & Moskey, E. G. (2002). Changes over time in teenage sexual relationships: Comparing the high school class of 1950, 1975 and 2000. *Adolescence, 37*(147), 515–526.

12. Roditti, M. (1997). Urban teen parents (p. 100). In N. K. Phillips & S. L. A. Straussner (Eds.), *Children in the urban environment: Linking social policy and clinical practice* (pp. 93–112). Springfield, IL: Charles C. Thomas.

13. Marsiglio, W. (2006). Young men and teen pregnancy: A review of sex, contraception, and fertility-related issues. In The National Campaign to Prevent Teen Pregnancy (Ed.), *It's a guy thing: Boys, young men, and teen pregnancy prevention* (pp. 9–100). Washington DC: The National Campaign to Prevent Teen Pregnancy. Retrieved September 17, 2007, from http://www.teenpregnancy.org/resources/reading/males.asp

14. Marcell, A. V., Raine, T., & Eyre, S. L. (2003). Where does reproductive health fit into the lives of adolescent males? (p.183). *Perspectives on Sexual and Reproductive Health, 35*(4), 180–186.

15. Ibid.

16. The National Campaign To Prevent Teen Pregnancy. (2003). *Science Says: The sexual attitudes and behavior of male teens* (p. 2). Retrieved January 12, 2006, from www.teenpregnancy.org/works/sciencesays.asp.

17. Marcell, A. V., Raine, T., & Eyre, S. L. (2003). Where does reproductive health fit into the lives of adolescent males? (p. 182). *Perspectives on Sexual and Reproductive Health, 35*(4), 180–186.

18. Tauber, M., Fields-Meyer, T., & Smith, K. (2005, January 31). Special Report: Young Teens and Sex. *People Magazine,* 86–96.

19. Ibid.

20. Marsiglio, W. (2006). Young men and teen pregnancy: A review of sex, contraception, and fertility-related issues. In The National Campaign to Prevent Teen Pregnancy (Ed.), *It's a guy thing: Boys, young men, and teen pregnancy prevention* (pp. 9–100). Washington DC: The National Campaign to Prevent Teen Pregnancy. Retrieved September 17, 2007, from http://www.teenpregnancy.org/resources/reading/males.asp

21. Brooks, G. R. (1995). The centerfold syndrome: How men can overcome objectification and achieved intimacy with women. San Francisco: Jossey-Bass.

22. Marsiglio, W. (2006). Young men and teen pregnancy: A review of sex, contraception, and fertility-related issues. In The National Campaign to Prevent Teen

Pregnancy (Ed.), *It's a guy thing: Boys, young men, and teen pregnancy prevention* (pp. 9–100). Washington DC: The National Campaign to Prevent Teen Pregnancy. Retrieved September 17, 2007, from http://www.teenpregnancy.org/resources/reading/males.asp

23. Answers.com. (2006). *Puberty* (par. 1). Retrieved October 27, 2006, from http://www.answers.com/topic/puberty

24. KidsHealth.com. (2000). *All about puberty.* Retrieved October 27, 2006, from http://kidshealth.org/kid/grow/body_stuff/puberty.html

25. Brooks-Gunn, J., & Paikoff, R. (1997). Sexuality and developmental transitions during adolescence. In J. Schulenberg, J. L. Magos & K. Hurrelmann (Eds.), *Health risks and developmental transitions during adolescence* (pp. 190–219). Cambridge: Cambridge University Press.

26. Freiden, J. (2001, February 7). *Early onset puberty worries some experts* (par. 4). Retrieved October 27, 2006, from www.mindfully.org/health/early-onset-puberty.htm

27. Herman-Giddens, M., Wang, L., & Koch, G. (2001). Secondary sexual characteristics in boys. *Archives of Pediatrics & Adolescent Medicine, 155,* 1022–1028.

28. Ibid.

29. Roberts, M. (2005, May 15). *Why puberty now begins at age seven.* Retrieved October 30, 2006, from http://news.bbc.co.uk/2/hi/health/4530743.stm

30. Herman-Giddens, M., Wang, L., & Koch, G. (2001). Secondary sexual characteristics in boys. *Archives of Pediatrics & Adolescent Medicine, 155,* 1022–1028.

31. Marcell, A. V., Raine, T., & Eyre, S. L. (2003). Where does reproductive health fit into the lives of adolescent males? (p. 183) *Perspectives on Sexual and Reproductive Health, 35*(4), 180–186.

32. Marsiglio, W. (2006). Young men and teen pregnancy: A review of sex, contraception, and fertility-related issues. In The National Campaign to Prevent Teen Pregnancy (Ed.), *It's a guy thing: Boys, young men, and teen pregnancy prevention* (pp. 9–100). Washington DC: The National Campaign to Prevent Teen Pregnancy. Retrieved September 17, 2007, from http://www.teenpregnancy.org/resources/reading/males.asp

33. Crosby, R. A. and Yarber, W. L. Perceived versus actual knowledge about correct condom use among U.S. adolescents: Results from a national study. *Journal of Adolescent Health, 2001, 128*(5), 415–420.

34. Miller, B. C., Benson, B., & Galbraith, K. A. (2001). Family relationships and adolescent pregnancy risk: A research synthesis. *Developmental Review, 21,* 1–38.

35. Tauber, M., Fields-Meyer, T., & Smith, K. (2005, January 31). Special Report: Young Teens and Sex. *People Magazine,* 86–96.

36. Hovell, M., Sipan, C., Blumberg, E., Atkins, C., Hofstetter, C. R., & Kreitner, S. (1994). Family influences on Latino and Anglo adolescents' sexual behavior. *Journal of Marriage and the Family, 56,* 973–986.

37. Marsiglio, W. (2006). Young men and teen pregnancy: A review of sex, contraception, and fertility-related issues. In The National Campaign to Prevent Teen Pregnancy (Ed.), *It's a guy thing: Boys, young men, and teen pregnancy prevention* (pp. 9–100). Washington DC: The National Campaign to Prevent Teen Pregnancy. Retrieved September 17, 2007, from http://www.teenpregnancy.org/resources/reading/males.asp

38. The National Campaign To Prevent Teen Pregnancy. (2003). *With one voice 2003: America's adults and teens sound off about teen pregnancy* (slide 4). Retrieved January 12, 2005, from http://www.teenpregnancy.org/resources/reading/workshops/default.asp

39. Tauber, M., Fields-Meyer, T., & Smith, K. (2005, January 31) Special Report: Young Teens and Sex. *People Magazine*, 86–96.

40. O'Donnell, L., O'Donnell, C. R., & Stueve, A. (2001). Early sexual initiation and subsequent sex-related risks among urban minority youth: The Reach for Health Study. *Family Planning Perspectives, 33*(6), 268–275.

41. Manlove, J., Terry, E., Gitelson, L., Papillo, A. R., & Russell, S. (2000). Explaining demographic trends in teenage fertility, 1980–1995. *Family Planning Perspectives, 32*(4), 166–175; see also Singh, S. & Darroch, J. E. (1999, September/October). Trends in sexual activity among adolescent American women: 1982–1995. *Family Planning Perspectives, 31*(5), 212–219.

42. Darroch, J. E., Singh, S., Frost, J. J., & the Study Team. (2001). Differences in teenage pregnancy rates among five developed countries: The roles of sexual activity and contraceptive use. *Family Planning Perspectives, 33*(6): 244–250, 281.

43. Bakken, R. J., & Winter, M. (2002). Family characteristics and sexual risk behaviors among Black men in the United States. *Perspectives on Sexual and Reproductive Health, 34*(5), 252–258.

44. Cohen, D. A., Farley, T. A., Taylor, S. N., Martin, D., & Shuster, M. (2002). When and where do youths have sex? The potential role of adult supervison. *Pediatrics, 110*(6). Retrieved January 26, 2006, from http://www.pediatrics.org/cgi/full/110/6/eff

45. Marcell, A. V., Raine, T., & Eyre, S. L. (2003). Where does reproductive health fit into the lives of adolescent males? (p. 183). *Perspectives on Sexual and Reproductive Health, 35*(4), 180–186.

46. Ibid.

47. Ibid.

48. Hollander, D. (2001, Sep/Oct). Update (p. 190). *Family Planning Perspectives, 33*(5), 190–191.

49. Roditti, M. (1997). Urban teen parents (p. 99). In N. K. Phillips & S. L. A. Straussner (Eds.), *Children in the urban environment: Linking social policy and clinical practice* (pp. 93–112). Springfield, IL: Charles C. Thomas.

50. Henshaw, S. K. (1998). Unintended pregnancy in the United States. *Family Planning Perspectives, 30*(1), 24–29 & 46.

51. Dash, L. (1989). *When children want children: An inside look at the crisis of teenage parenthood.* New York: Penguin Books.

52. Roditti, M. (1997). Urban teen parents (p. 102). In N. K. Phillips & S. L. A. Straussner (Eds.), *Children in the urban environment: Linking social policy and clinical practice* (pp. 93–112). Springfield, IL: Charles C. Thomas.

53. The National Campaign To Prevent Teen Pregnancy. (2003). *Science Says: The sexual attitudes and behavior of male teens* (p. 4). Retrieved January 12, 2006, from www.teenpregnancy.org/works/sciencesays.asp

54. Hernandez, R. (2002). *Fatherwork in the crossfire: Chicano teen fathers struggling to take care of business* (p. 7). (Report No. JSRI-WP-58). East Lansing, MI: Michigan State University, Julian Samora Research Institute. (ERIC Document Reproduction Services No. ED 471 926)

55. Dash, L. (1989). *When children want children: An inside look at the crisis of teenage parenthood.* New York: Penguin Books.

56. Kiselica, M. S. (1995). *Multicultural counseling with teenage fathers.* Thousand Oaks, CA: Sage.

57. Thomas, E. Jr. (1996, January 18). Is pregnancy a rational choice for poor teenagers? *The Wall Street Journal,* pp. BI, BII.

58. Kiselica, M. S. (1995). *Multicultural counseling with teenage fathers.* Thousand Oaks, CA: Sage.

59. South, S. J., & Baumer, E. P. (2000). Deciphering community and race effects on adolescent premarital childbearing (p. 400). *Social Forces, 78*(4), 1379–1408.

60. Garbarino, J. (1999). *Lost boys: Why our sons turn violent and how we can save them.* New York: Anchor Books.

61. Roditti, M. (1997). Urban teen parents (p. 94). In N. K. Phillips & S. L. A. Straussner (Eds.), *Children in the urban environment: Linking social policy and clinical practice* (pp. 93–112). Springfield, IL: Charles C. Thomas.

62. Roe v. Wade—What you need to know about Roe v. Wade. (undated). Retrieved January 24, 2006, from http://womensissues.about.com/od/abortionlaw/i/roevwade. htm

63. Henshaw, S. K., & Feivelson, D. J. (2000). Teenage abortion and pregnancy statistics by state, 1996. *Family Planning Perspectives, 32*(6), 272–280.

64. Henshaw, S. K. (1998). Unintended pregnancy in the United States. *Family Planning Perspectives, 30*(1), 24–29, 46.

65. Henshaw, S. K., & Feivelson, D. J. (2000). Teenage abortion and pregnancy statistics by state, 1996. *Family Planning Perspectives, 32*(6), 272–280.

66. Henshaw, S. K. (1998). Unintended pregnancy in the United States. *Family Planning Perspectives, 30* (1), 24–29, 46.

67. Boggess, S., & Bradner, C. (2000). Trends in adolescent males' abortion attitudes, 1988–1995: Differences by race and ethnicity. *Family Planning Perspectives, 32*(3), 118–123.

68. Henshaw, S. K. (1998). Unintended pregnancy in the United States. *Family Planning Perspectives, 30*(1), 24–29, 46.

69. Roditti, M. (1997). Urban teen parents. In N. K. Phillips & S. L. A. Straussner (Eds.), *Children in the urban environment: Linking social policy and clinical practice* (pp. 93–112). Springfield, IL: Charles C. Thomas.

70. Adoption.com. (2005). *Adoption statistics: Placing children.* Retrieved October 4, 2005, from http://www.adoption.com

71. National Adoption Information Clearinghouse. (2005). *Voluntary relinquishment for adoption: Numbers and trends.* Retrieved October 4, 2006, from http://naic.acf.hhs. gov/pubs/s_place.cfm

72. Ibid.

73. The National Campaign To Prevent Teen Pregnancy. (undated). *Fact sheet: Teen pregnancy rates in the United States, 1972–2000.* Retrieved August 1, 2006, from http://www.teenpregnancy.org/resources/reading/fact_sheets/default.asp

74. Centers for Disease Control and Prevention. (2002). Youth Risk Behavior Surveillance—United States, 2001. *Morbidity and Mortality Weekly Report, 51* (SS-4).

75. Cohen, D. A., Farley, T. A., Taylor, S. N., Martin, D., & Shuster, M. (2002). When and where do youths have sex? The potential role of adult supervison. *Pediatrics,*

110(6). Retrieved January 26, 2006, from http://pediatrics.aappublications.org/cgi/content/full/110/6/e66; see also The National Campaign To Prevent Teen Pregnancy. (2003). *Where and when teens have first sex.* Retrieved January 26, 2006, from http://www.teenpregnancy.org/works/sciencesays.asp

76. Centers for Disease Control and Prevention. (2004, May). Surveillance Summaries. MMWR 2004:53(No.SS-2); see also Hollander, D. (1998). Some teenagers just say no. *Family Planning Perspectives, 30*(6), 255.

77. Crosby, R. A., & Yarber, W. L. (2001). Perceived versus actual knowledge about correct condom use among U.S. adolescents: Results from a national study. *Journal of Adolescent Health, 2001, 128,* 415–420; see also Santelli, J. S., Lindberg, L. D., Abma, J., McNeeley, C. S., & Resnick, M. Adolescent sexual behavior: Estimates and trends from four nationally representative surveys. *Family Planning Perspectives, 2000, 32*(4): 156–165, 194; see also The National Campaign To Prevent Teen Pregnancy. (2004, Feburary). *Fact sheet: Recent trends in teen pregnancy, sexual activity, and contraceptive use.* Retrieved January 12, 2005, from http://www.teenpregnancy.org/resources/reading/fact_sheets/default.asp

78. The National Campaign To Prevent Teen Pregnancy. (2003, September). *The sexual behavior of young adolescents* (p. 1). Retrieved January 12, 2006, from www.teenpregnancy.org/works/sciencesays.asp

79. O'Donnell, L., O'Donnell, C. R., & Stueve, A. (2001). Early sexual initiation and subsequent sex-related risks among urban minority youth: The Reach for Health Study. *Family Planning Perspectives, 33*(6): 268–275.

80. Ibid.

81. Kaestle, C. E., Halpern, C. T., Miller, W. C., & Ford, C. A. (2005). Young age at first intercourse and sexually transmitted infection in adolescents and young adults. *American Journal of Epidemiology, 161,* 774–780; see also O'Donnell, L., O'Donnell, C. R., & Stueve, A. (2001). Early sexual initiation and subsequent sex-related risks among urban minority youth: The Reach for Health Study. *Family Planning Perspectives, 33,* 268–275; The National Campaign To Prevent Teen Pregnancy. (2003, September). *The sexual behavior of young adolescents.* Retrieved January 12, 2006, from www.teenpregnancy.org/works/sciencesays.asp

82. The National Campaign To Prevent Teen Pregnancy. (2003, September). *The sexual behavior of young adolescents.* RetrievedJanuary 12, 2006,from www.teenpregnancy.org/works/sciencesays.asp

83. Kelly, S. S., Borawski, E. A., Flocke, S. A., & Keen, K. J. (2003). The role of sequential and concurrent sexual relationships in the risk of sexually transmitted diseases among adolescents. *Journal of Adolescent Health, 2003, 32,* 296–305.

84. O'Donnell, L., O'Donnell, C. R., & Stueve, A. (2001). Early sexual initiation and subsequent sex-related risks among urban minority youth: The Reach for Health Study. *Family Planning Perspectives, 33*(6): 268–275.

85. Kelly, S. S., Borawski, E. A., Flocke, S. A., & Keen, K. J. (2003). The role of sequential and concurrent sexual relationships in the risk of sexually transmitted diseases among adolescents. *Journal of Adolescent Health, 2003, 32,* 296–305.

86. Turner, C. F., Ku, L., Rogers, S. M., Lindberg, L. D., Pleck, J. H., & Sonenstein, F. L. (1998). Adolescent sexual behavior, drug use, and violence: Increased reporting with computer survey technology. *Science, 280,* 867–873.

87. Henshaw, S. K. (1998). Unintended pregnancy in the United States. *Family Planning Perspectives, 30* (1), 24–29, 46.

88. The National Campaign To Prevent Teen Pregnancy. (undated). *Fact sheet: Teen pregnancy rates in the United States, 1972–2000.* Retrieved August 1, 2006, from http://www.teenpregnancy.org/resources/reading/fact_sheets/default.asp

89. Ibid.

90. National Center for Health Statistics. (2004). *NCHS data on teenage pregnancy.* Retrieved September 4, 2007, from http://www.cdc.gov/nchs; see also Ventura, S. J., Abma, J. C., Mosher, W. D., & Henshaw, S. (2004). Estimated pregnancy rates for the United States, 1990–2000: An Update. *National Vital Statistics Reports, 52,*(23). Hyattsville, MD: National Center for Health Statistics.

91. The National Campaign to Prevent Teen Pregnancy. (2004). *The relationship between teenage motherhood and marriage.* Retrieved January 12, 2006, from www.teenpregnancy.org/works/sciencesays.asp

92. Darroch, J. E., Singh, S., Frost, J. J., & the Study Team. (2001). Differences in teenage pregnancy rates among five developed countries: The roles of sexual activity and contraceptive use. *Family Planning Perspectives, 33*(6): 244–250, 281.

93. Panchaud, C., Singh, S., Feivelson, D. & Darroch, J. E. (2000). Sexually transmitted diseases among adolescents in developed countries. *Family Planning Perspectives, 33*(6), 251–258, 289.

94. William T. Grant Foundation. (2002). *Adolescent nonmarital childbearing and welfare.* Retrieved January 26, 2006, from http://www.cyfc.umn.edu/adolescents/research/IF1018.html

95. Ibid.

CHAPTER 3   PARENTING BEHAVIORS OF ADOLESCENT FATHERS

1. Mincy, R., Garfinkel, I., & Nepomnyaschy, L. (2005). In-hospital paternity establishment and father involvement in fragile families. *Journal of Marriage and Family, 67,* 611–626.

2. Phipps, M. G., Rosengard, C., Weitzen, S., & Boardman, L. A. (2005). Rates of voluntary paternity establishment for infants born to unmarried adolescents. *Journal of Reproductive Medicine, 50,* 764–770; see also Nock, S. L. (1998). The consequences of premarital fatherhood. *American Sociological Review, 63,* 250–263.

3. Conklin, R., & Crowe, D. (2000, March). Colorado teen pregnancy/pregnancy prevention. *PPFY Network Newsletter.* Retrieved March 6, 2006, from http://www.wested.org/ppfy/mooco.htm

4. Roberts, P. (2004, March). No minor matter: Developing a coherent policy on paternity establishment for children born to underage parents. *Clasp Policy Brief, Childbearing and Reproductive Health Series, Brief No. 2.* Washington DC: Center for Law and Social Policy. Retrieved September 18, 2007, from http://www.clasp.org/process_search.php?skip=0

5. Landry, D. J., & Forest, J. D. (1995). How old are U.S. fathers? *Family Planning Perspectives, 27,* 159–161.

6. Males, M., & Chew, K. S. (1996). The ages of fathers in California adolescent births. *American Journal of Public Health, 86*(4), 565–568.

7. Taylor, D. J., Chavez, G. F., Adams, E. J., Chabra, A., & Shah, G. S. (1999). Demographic characteristics in adult paternity for first births to adolescents under 15 years of age. *Journal of Adolescent Health, 24*(4), 251–258.

8. Zavodny, M. (2001). The effect of partner's characteristics on teenage pregnancy and its resolution. *Family Planning Perspectives, 33*(5), 192–199, 205.

9. Darroch, J. E., Landry, D. J., & Oslak, S. (1999). Age differences between sexual partners in the United States. *Family Planning Perspectives, 31,* 160–167.

10. Zavodny, M. (2001). The effect of partner's characteristics on teenage pregnancy and its resolution. *Family Planning Perspectives, 33*(5), 192–199, 205.

11. Darroch, J. E., Landry, D. J., & Oslak, S. (1999). Age differences between sexual partners in the United States (p. 166). *Family Planning Perspectives, 31,* 160–167.

12. Ibid., 167.

13. Nichols, S. L., & Good, T. L. (2004). *America's teenagers—myths and realities: Media images, schooling, and the costs of careless indifference* (p. 96). Mahwah, NJ: Erlbaum.

14. Males, M., & Chew, K. S. (1996). The ages of fathers in California adolescent births (p. 567). *American Journal of Public Health, 86* (4), 565–568.

15. Ibid.

16. Ibid.

17. Ibid.

18. Abma, J., Driscoll, A., & Moore, K. (1998). Young women's degree of control over first intercourse: An exploratory analysis. *Family Planning Perspectives, 30*(1): 12–18.

19. Cutrona, C., Hessling, R. M., Bacon, P. L., & Russell, D. W. (1998). Predictors and correlates of continuing involvement with the baby's father among adolescent mothers. *Journal of Family Psychology, 12*(3), 369–387.

20. Russell, S. T., Lee, F. C. H., & The Latina/o Teen Pregnancy Prevention Workgroup. (2004). Practitioner's perspectives on effective practices for Hispanic teenage pregnancy prevention. *Perspectives on Sexual and Reproductive Health, 36*(4), 142–149.

21. Hernandez, R. (2002). *Fatherwork in the crossfire: Chicano teen fathers struggling to take care of business.* (Report No. JSRI-WP-58). East Lansing, MI: Michigan State University, Julian Samora Research Institute. (ERIC Document Reproduction Services No. ED 471 926)

22. Robinson, B. (1988). *Teenage fathers* (p. 22). Lexington, MA: Lexington Books.

23. Ibid.

24. Romo, C., Bellamy, J., & Coleman, M. T. (2004). *TFF final evaluation report.* Austin, TX: Texas Fragile Families Initiative.

25. Rhein, L. H., Ginsburg, K. R., Schwarz, D. F., Pinto-Martin, J. A., Zhao, H., Morgan, A. P., & Slap, G. B. (1997). Teen father participation in child rearing: Family perspectives. *Journal of Adolescent Health, 21,* 244–252.

26. Benson, P. L., Scales, P. C., Leffert, N., & Roehlkepartain, E. C. (1999). *A fragile foundation: The state of developmental assets among American youth.* Minneapolis: Search Foundation.

27. Ibid.

28. Pears, K. C., Pierce, S. L., Kim, H. K., Capaldi, D. M. & Owen, L. D. (2005). The timing of entry into fatherhood in young, at-risk men (p. 443). *Journal of Marriage and Family, 67,* 429–447; see also Spingarn, M. D., & DuRant, R. H. (1996). Male adolescents involved in pregnancy: Associated health risk and problem behaviors (p. 262). *Pediatrics, 98*(2), 262–268; Thornberry, T. P., Wei, E. H., Stouthamer-Loeber,

M., & Van Dyke, J. (2000, January). Teenage fatherhood and delinquent behavior. *Juvenile Justice Bulletin.* Retrieved January 13, 2006, from http://www.ncjrs.org/html/ojjdp/jjbul2000_1/contents.html

29. Evans, G. W. (2004). The environment of childhood poverty (p. 77). *American Psychologist, 59*(2), 77–92.

30. Thornberry, T. P., Wei, E. H., Stouthamer-Loeber, M., & Van Dyke, J. (2000, January). Teenage fatherhood and delinquent behavior. *Juvenile Justice Bulletin.* Retrieved January 13, 2006, from http://www.ncjrs.org/html/ojjdp/jjbul2000_1/contents.html; see also Lerman, R. (1993). A national profile of young unwed fathers. In R. Lerman & T. Ooms (Eds.), *Young unwed fathers: Changing roles and emerging policies* (pp. 27–51). Philadelphia: Temple University Press; Smith, R., & Joe, T. (1994). *World without work: Causes and consequences of Black male joblessness.* Washington DC: Center for the Study of Social Policy.

31. Pirog-Good, M. A. (1995). The family background and attitudes of teen fathers. *Youth & Society, 26*(3), 351–376.

32. Kirby, D., Coyle, K., & Gould, J. B. (2001). Manifestations of poverty and birthrates among young teenagers in California zip code areas. *Family Planning Perspectives, 33*(2), 63–69.

33. Thornberry, T. P., Wei, E. H., Stouthamer-Loeber, M., & Van Dyke, J. (2000, January). Teenage fatherhood and delinquent behavior. *Juvenile Justice Bulletin.* Retrieved January 13, 2006, from http://www.ncjrs.org/html/ojjdp/jjbul2000_1/contents.html

34. DeNavas-Walt, C., Proctor, B. D., & Lee, C. H. (2005). Income, poverty, and health insurance coverage in the United States: 2004. *Current Population Reports,* P60–229. Washington DC: U.S. Census Bureau. Retrieved September 24, 2007, from www.census.gov/prod/2005pubs/p60–229.pdf

35. Ibid.

36. The National Campaign to Prevent Teen Pregnancy. (2006, October). *Teen sexual activity, pregnancy and childbearing among Black teens.* Retrieved September 17, 2007, from http://www.teenpregnancy.org/resources/reading/fact_sheets/default.asp; see also The National Campaign to Prevent Teen Pregnancy. (2006, October). *Teen sexual activity, pregnancy and childbearing among Latinos in the United States.* Retrieved September 17, 2007, from http://www.teenpregnancy.org/resources/reading/fact_sheets/default.asp; The National Campaign to Prevent Teen Pregnancy. (2006, October). *Teen sexual activity, pregnancy and childbearing among non-Hispanic White teens.* Retrieved September 17, 2007, from http://www.teenpregnancy.org/resources/reading/fact_sheets/default.asp

37. The National Campaign to Prevent Teen Pregnancy. (2006, October). *Teen sexual activity, pregnancy and childbearing among Black teens.* Retrieved September 17, 2007, from http://www.teenpregnancy.org/resources/reading/fact_sheets/default.asp; see also The National Campaign to Prevent Teen Pregnancy. (2006, October). *Teen sexual activity, pregnancy and childbearing among Latinos in the United States.* Retrieved September 17, 2007, from http://www.teenpregnancy.org/resources/reading/fact_sheets/default.asp; The National Campaign to Prevent Teen Pregnancy. (2006, October). *Teen sexual activity, pregnancy and childbearing among non-Hispanic White teens.* Retrieved September 17, 2007, from http://www.teenpregnancy.org/resources/reading/fact_sheets/default.asp

38. The National Campaign to Prevent Teen Pregnancy. (2006, October). *Teen sexual activity, pregnancy and childbearing among Black teens.* Retrieved September 17, 2007, from http://www.teenpregnancy.org/resources/reading/fact_sheets/default. asp; see also TheNational Campaign to Prevent Teen Pregnancy. (2006, October). *Teen sexual activity, pregnancy and childbearing among Latinos in the United States.* Retrieved September 17, 2007, from http://www.teenpregnancy.org/resources/reading/fact_sheets/default.asp; The National Campaign to Prevent Teen Pregnancy. (2006, October). *Teen sexual activity, pregnancy and childbearing among non-Hispanic White teens.* Retrieved September 17, 2007, from http://www.teen pregnancy.org/resources/reading/fact_sheets/default.asp

39. Hernandez, R. (2002). *Fatherwork in the crossfire: Chicano teen fathers struggling to take care of business.* (Report No. JSRI-WP-58). East Lansing, MI: Michigan State University, Julian Samora Research Institute. (ERIC Document Reproduction Services No. ED 471 926); see also McAdoo, J. L. (1999). Understanding African American fathers. In P. E. Leone (Ed.), *Understanding troubled and troubling youth* (pp. 229–245). Thousand Oaks, CA: Sage; Smith, L. A. (1988). Black adolescent fathers: Issues for service provision. *Social Work, 33*(3), 269–271.

40. Marsiglio, William. (1987). Adolescent fathers in the United States: Their initial living arrangements, marital experience and educational outcomes. *Family Planning Perspectives, 19,* 240–251; see also Moore, D. R., & Florsheim, P. (2001). Interpersonal processes and psychopathology among expectant and nonexpectant adolescent couples. *Journal of Consulting and Clinical Psychology, 69*(1), 101–113; Xie, H., Cairns, B. D., & Cairns, R. B. (2001). Predicting teen motherhood and teen fatherhood: Individual characteristics and peer affiliations. *Social Development, 10*(4), 488–511.

41. Pirog-Good, M. A. (1996). The educational and labor market outcomes of adolescent fathers. *Youth & Society, 28*(2), 236–262.

42. Nock, S. L. (1998). The consequences of premarital fatherhood. *American Sociological Review, 63,* 250–263.

43. Pirog-Good, M. A. (1996). The educational and labor market outcomes of adolescent fathers. *Youth & Society, 28*(2), 236–262.

44. Fagot, B. I., Pears, K. C., Capaldi, D. M., Crosby, L., & Leve, C. S. (1998). Becoming an adolescent father: Precursors and parenting. *Developmental Psychology, 34*(6), 1209–1219.

45. Kost, K. A. (1997). The effects of support on the economic well-being of young fathers. *Families in Society, 78,* 370–382.

46. Wilkinson, Z. G. (2000). *The crisis of the young African American male in the inner cities.* Vol. 1: Topic papers submitted to the Commission. Washington DC: United States Commission on Civil Rights.

47. Achatz, M., & MacAllum, C. A. (1994). *Young unwed fathers: Report from the field.* Philadelphia: Public/Private Ventures.

48. Brown, S. (1990). *If the shoes fit: Final report and program implementation guide of the Maine Young Fathers Project.* Portland, ME: Human Services Development Institute, University of Southern Maine.

49. Brindis, Claire (1993). *Keynote address.* Annual meeting of the Indiana Council on Adolescent Pregnancy, Indianapolis, IN.

50. Miller, A., Kiselica, M. S., Rotzien, A., & Gridley, B. (1998, August). *The development and validation of The Attitudes about Teen Parents Scale.* Paper presented at the Annual Convention of the American Psychological Association, San Francisco; see also Robinson, B. (1988). *Teenage fathers* (p. 22). Lexington, MA: Lexington Books.

51. Fagot, B. I., Pears, K. C., Capaldi, D. M., Crosby, L., & Leve, C. S. (1998). Becoming an adolescent father: Precursors and parenting. *Developmental Psychology, 34*(6), 1209–1219.

52. McLauglin, C. R., Reiner, S. M., Reams, P. N., & Joost, T. F. (1999). Factors associated with parenting among incarcerated juvenile offenders. *Adolescence, 34*(136), 665–670.

53. Sonenstein, F. L., Stewart, K., Lindberg, L. D., Pernas, M., & Williams, S. (1997). *Involving males in preventing teen pregnancy: A guide for program planners.* Washington DC: Urban Institute.

54. Stouthamer-Loeber, M., & Wei, E. H. (1998). The precursors of young fatherhood and its effect on delinquency of teenage males. *Journal of Adolescent Health, 22,* 56–65.

55. Pirog-Good, M. (1985). Teenage paternity, child support, and crime. *Social Science Quarterly, 69,* 527–546; see also Florsheim, P., Moore, D., Zollinger, L., MacDonald, J., & Sumida, E. (1999). The transition to parenthood among adolescent fathers and their partners: Does antisocial behavior predict problems in parenting? *Applied Developmental Science, 3*(3),178–191.

56. Kessler, R. C., Berglund, P. A., Foster, C. L., Saunders, W. B., Stang, P. E., & Walters, E. E. (1997). Social consequences of psychiatric disorders II: Teenage parenthood. *American Journal of Psychiatry, 154*(10), 1405–1411.

57. Moore, D. R., & Florsheim, P. (2001). Interpersonal processes and psychopathology among expectant and nonexpectant adolescent couples. *Journal of Consulting and Clinical Psychology, 69*(1), 101–113.

58. Whitaker, D. J., Miller, K. S., & Clark, L. F. (2000). Reconceptualizing adolescent sexual behavior: Beyond did they or didn't they? *Family Planning Perspectives, 32*(3), 111–117.

59. Spingarn, M. D., & DuRant, R. H. (1996). Male adolescents involved in pregnancy: Associated health risk and problem behaviors (p. 262). *Pediatrics, 98*(2), 262–268.

60. Pierre, N., Shrier, L. A., Emans, S. J., & DuRant, R. H. (1998). Adolescent males involved in pregnancy: Associations of forced sexual contact and risk behaviors. *Journal of Adolescent Health, 23*(6), 364–369.

61. Garbarino, J. (1999). *Lost boys: Why our sons turn violent and how we can save them.* New York: The Free Press.

62. Herrenkohl, E. C., Herrenkohl, R. C., Egolf, B. P., & Russo, M. J. (1998). The relationship between early maltreatment and teenage parenthood. *Journal of Adolescence, 21,* 291–303.

63. Pierre, N., Shrier, L. A., Emans, S. J., & DuRant, R. H. (1998). Adolescent males involved in pregnancy: Associations of forced sexual contact and risk behaviors (p. 364). *Journal of Adolescent Health, 23*(6), 364–369.

64. Shrier, L. A., Pierce, J. D., Emans, S. J., & DuRant, R. H. (1998). Gender differences in risk behaviors associated with reported forced sex. *Archives of Pediatrics and Adolescent Medicine, 152,* 57–63.

65. Saewyc, E. M., Magee, L. L., & Pettingell, S. E. (2004). Teenage pregnancy and associated risk behaviors among sexually abused adolescents. *Perspectives on Sexual and Reproductive Health, 36*(3), 98–105.

66. Ibid.

67. Ibid., 103.

68. Ibid.

69. Robinson, B. (1988). *Teenage fathers* (p. 22). Lexington, MA: Lexington Books.

70. Ibid.

71. Pirog-Good, M. A. (1995). The family background and attitudes of teen fathers. *Youth & Society, 26*(3), 351–376.

72. Ibid.

73. Robinson, R. B., & Frank, D. I. (1994). The relation between self-esteem, sexual activity, and pregnancy. *Adolescence, 29*(113), 27–35.

74. Ibid.

75. Hanson, S. L., Morrison, D. R., & Ginsburg, A. L. (1989). The antecedents of teenage fatherhood. *Demography, 26*(4), 579–596; see also Hendricks, L. E. (1981). Black unwed adolescent fathers. In L. E. Gary (Ed.), *Black men* (pp. 131–138). Beverly Hills, CA: Sage; Hendricks, L. E., Montgomery, T., & Fullilove, R. E. (1984). Educational achievement and locus of control among Black adolescent fathers. *Journal of Negro Education, 53,* 182–188; McCoy, J. E., & Tyler, F. B. (1985). Selected psychosocial characteristics of black, unwed fathers. *Journal of Adolescent Health Care, 6,* 12–16; Pirog-Good, M. A. (1995). The family background and attitudes of teen fathers. *Youth & Society, 26*(3), 351–376; Robinson, B. E., Barret, R. L., & Skeen, P. (1983). Locus of control of unwed adolescent fathers versus adolescent nonfathers. *Perceptual and Motor Skills, 56,* 397–398.

76. Thompson, S., Osteen, S. R., & Youngker, L. (2001). Who fares better? Postnatal adjustment of adolescent fathers and mothers. *Marriage and Family Review, 33*(4), 31–46.

77. Moses, A. (1995). *Teenage pregnancy prevention in California: 1995 policy roundtable series report.* Retrieved March 9, 2006, from www.library.ca.gov/CAFIS/reports/95-01/95-01.pdf

78. Bempechat, J. (1989). *Teenage pregnancy and drug abuse: Sources of problem behaviors.* (ERIC/CUE Digest No. 58). Retrieved March 9, 2006, from www.ericdigests.org

79. Kessler, R. C., Berglund, P. A., Foster, C. L., Saunders, W. B., Stang, P.E., & Walters, E. E. (1997). Social consequences of psychiatric disorders II: Teenage parenthood. *American Journal of Psychiatry, 154*(10), 1405–1411.

80. Ibid., 1409.

81. Ibid., 1409.

82. Ibid.

83. Markham, C. M., Tortolero, S. R., Escobar-Chaves, S. L., Parcel, G. S., Harrist, R., & Addy, R. C. (2003). Family connectedness and sexual risk-taking among urban youth attending alternative highs schools. *Perspectives on Sexual and Reproductive Health, 35*(4), 174–179.

84. Pears, K. C., Pierce, S. L., Kim, H. K., Capaldi, D. M. & Owen, L. D. (2005). The timing of entry into fatherhood in young, at-risk men. *Journal of Marriage and Family, 67,* 429–447; see also Thornberry, T. P., Smith, C. A., & Howard, G. J. (1997). Risk factors

for teenage fatherhood. *Journal of Marriage and the Family, 59*, 505–522; Thornberry, T. P., Wei, E. H., Stouthamer-Loeber, M., & Van Dyke, J. (2000, January). Teenage fatherhood and delinquent behavior. *Juvenile Justice Bulletin.* Retrieved January 13, 2006, from http://www.ncjrs.org/html/ojjdp/jjbul2000_1/contents.html

85. Thornberry, T. P., Wei, E. H., Stouthamer-Loeber, M., & Van Dyke, J. (2000, January). Teenage fatherhood and delinquent behavior. *Juvenile Justice Bulletin* (p. 3). Retrieved January 13, 2006, from http://www.ncjrs.org/html/ojjdp/jjbul2000_1/contents.html

86. Pears, K. C., Pierce, S. L., Kim, H. K., Capaldi, D. M. & Owen, L. D. (2005). The timing of entry into fatherhood in young, at-risk men (p. 443). *Journal of Marriage and Family, 67*, 429–447.

87. Dallas, C. M., & Chen, S. C. (1998). Experiences of African American adolescent fathers (p. 217). *Western Journal of Nursing Research, 20*(2), 210–222.

88. de Lissovoy, V. (1973). Child care by adolescent parents. *Children Today, 4*, 22–25; see also Fagot, B. I., Pears, K. C., Capaldi, D. M., Crosby, L., & Leve, C. S. (1998). Becoming an adolescent father: Precursors and parenting. *Developmental Psychology, 34*(6), 1209–1219.

89. Children's Defense Fund. (1986). *Adolescent pregnancy: What the states are saying.* Washington DC: Author; see also Coren, E., Barlow, J., & Stewart-Brown, S. (2003). The effectiveness of individual and group-based parenting programmes in improving outcomes for teenage mothers and their children: A systematic review. *Journal of Adolescence, 26*, 79–103; Kiselica, M. S. (1992, August). *Are we giving teenage fathers a mixed message?* In L. Silverstein (Chair), *Transforming fatherhood in a patriarchical society.* Symposium conducted at the Annual Convention of the American Psychological Association, Washington DC; Kiselica, M. S. (1998, March). *School-based services for teenage parents: Results of a state survey.* Paper presented at the World Conference of the American Counseling Association, Indianapolis, IN; Kiselica, M. S., & Sturmer, P. (1993). Is society giving teenage fathers a mixed message? *Youth and Society, 24*, 487–501; Kiselica, M. S., & Sturmer, P. (1995, August). *Outreach services for teenage parents: Has gender equity been realized?* Paper presented at the Annual Convention of the American Psychological Association, New York; Sample, J. (1997). *Engendering fatherhood: Provision of services and professional attitudes toward young fathers.* Unpublished master's thesis, Oklahoma State University, Stillwater, OK; Smollar, J., & Ooms, T. (1987). *Young unwed fathers: Research review, policy dilemmas, and options: Summary report.* Washington DC: Department of Health and Human Services; U.S. Congress. (1986). *Teen pregnancy: What is being done? A report of the select committee on children, youth, and families.* (December, 1985). Washington DC: U.S. Government Printing Office.

90. Fagot, B. I., Pears, K. C., Capaldi, D. M., Crosby, L., & Leve, C. S. (1998). Becoming an adolescent father: Precursors and parenting. *Developmental Psychology, 34*(6), 1209–1219.

91. Garbarino, J. (1999). *Lost boys: Why our sons turn violent and how we can save them.* New York: The Free Press.

92. Florsheim, P., Moore, D., Zollinger, L., MacDonald, J. & Sumida, E. (1999). The transition to parenthood among adolescent fathers and their partners: Does antisocial behavior predict problems in parenting? *Applied Developmental Science, 3*(3),178–191.

93. Ibid., 189.

94. Manlove, J., Terry, E., Gitelson, L., Papillo, A. R., & Russell, S. (2000). Explaining demographic trends in teenage fertility, 1980–1995. *Family Planning Perspectives, 32*(4), 166–175.

95. Pears, K. C., Pierce, S. L., Kim, H. K., Capaldi, D. M. & Owen, L. D. (2005). The timing of entry into fatherhood in young, at-risk men (p. 443). *Journal of Marriage and Family, 67*, 429–447.

96. Gee, C. B., & Rhodes, J. E. (2003). Adolescent mothers' relationship with their children's biological fathers: Social support, social strain, and relationship continuity (p. 372). *Journal of Family Psychology, 17*(3), 370–383.

97. Gee, C. B., & Rhodes, J. E. (2003). Adolescent mothers' relationship with their children's biological fathers: Social support, social strain, and relationship continuity. *Journal of Family Psychology, 17*(3), 370–383.

98. Krishnakumar, A., & Black, M. M. (2003). Family processes within three generation households and adolescent mothers' satisfaction with father involvement. *Journal of Family Psychology, 17*(4), 488–498.

99. Marsiglio, W. (1987). Adolescent fathers in the United States: Their initial living arrangements, marital experience and educational outcomes. *Family Planning Perspectives, 19*, 240–251.

100. Furstenberg, F. F., Brooks-Gunn, J., & Morgan, S. P. (1987). *Adolescent mothers in later life.* New York: Cambridge University Press; see also Hardy, J. B., & Zabin, L. S. (1991). *Adolescent pregnancy in an urban environment: Issues, programs and evaluation.* Washington DC: Urban Institute Press.

101. Kiselica, M. S. (1995). *Multicultural counseling with teenage fathers: A practical guide.* Thousand Oaks, CA: Sage.

102. Marcell, A. V., Raine, T., & Eyre, S. L. (2003). Where does reproductive health fit into the lives of adolescent males? (p. 182). *Perspectives on Sexual and Reproductive Health, 35*(4), 180–186.

103. Ibid.

104. Panzarine, S., & Elster, A. B. (1983). Coping in a group of expectant adolescent fathers: An exploratory study. *Journal of Adolescent Health Care, 4*, 117–120; see also Sullivan, M. L. (1985). *Teen fathers in the inner city: An exploratory ethnographic study.* (Report No. UD 024 536). New York: Vera Institute of Justice. (ERIC Document Reproduction Service No. ED 264 316); Vaz, R., Smolen, P., & Miller, C. (1983). Adolescent pregnancy: Involvement of the male partner. *Journal of Adolescent Health Care, 4*, 246–250.

105. Panzarine, S., & Elster, A. B. (1983). Coping in a group of expectant adolescent fathers: An exploratory study. *Journal of Adolescent Health Care, 4*, 117–120; see also Rivara, F. P., Sweeney, P. J., & Henderson, B. F. (1986). Black teenage fathers: What happens after the child is born? *Pediatrics, 78*, 151–158.

106. Allen, W. D., & Doherty, W. J. (1996). The responsibilities of fatherhood as perceived by African American teenage fathers (p. 148). *Families in Society: The Journal of Contemporary Human Services, 77*(2), 142–155.

107. Achatz, M., & MacAllum, C. A. (1994). *Young unwed fathers: Report from the field.* Philadelphia: Public/Private Ventures; see also Allen, W. D., & Doherty, W. J. (1996). The responsibilities of fatherhood as perceived by African American teenage fathers. *Families in Society: The Journal of Contemporary Human Services, 77*(2),

142–155; Vaz, R., Smolen, P., & Miller, C. (1983). Adolescent pregnancy: Involvement of the male partner. *Journal of Adolescent Health Care, 4,* 246–250.

108. Allen, W. D., & Doherty, W. J. (1996). The responsibilities of fatherhood as perceived by African American teenage fathers. *Families in Society: The Journal of Contemporary Human Services, 77*(2), 142–155; see also Dallas, C. M., & Chen, S. C. (1998). Experiences of African American adolescent fathers. *Western Journal of Nursing Research, 20*(2), 210–222; Rhein, L., H., Ginsburg, K. R., Schwarz, D. F., Pinto-Martin, J. A., Zhao, H., Morgan, A. P., & Slap, G. B. (1997). Teen father participation in child rearing: Family perspectives. *Journal of Adolescent Health, 21,* 244–252; Stack, C. (1974). *All our kin: Strategies for survival in a Black community.* New York: Harper & Row; Sullivan, M. L. (1985). *Teen fathers in the inner city: An exploratory ethnographic study.* (Report No. UD 024 536). New York: Vera Institute of Justice. (ERIC Document Reproduction Service No. ED 264 316)

109. Allen, W. D., & Doherty, W. J. (1996). The responsibilities of fatherhood as perceived by African American teenage fathers. *Families in Society: The Journal of Contemporary Human Services, 77*(2), 142–155; see also Gee, C. B., & Rhodes, J. E. (2003). Adolescent mothers' relationship with their children's biological fathers: Social support, social strain, and relationship continuity. *Journal of Family Psychology, 17,*(3), 370–383; Hendricks, L. E. (1980). Unwed adolescent fathers: Problems they face and their sources of social support. *Adolescence, 15,* 861–869.

110. Allen, W. D., & Doherty, W. J. (1996). The responsibilities of fatherhood as perceived by African American teenage fathers. *Families in Society: The Journal of Contemporary Human Services, 77*(2), 142–155.

111. Hernandez, R. (2002). *Fatherwork in the crossfire: Chicano teen fathers struggling to take care of business.* (Report No. JSRI-WP-58). East Lansing, MI: Michigan State University, Julian Samora Research Institute. (ERIC Document Reproduction Services No. ED 471 926)

112. Allen, W. D., & Doherty, W. J. (1996). The responsibilities of fatherhood as perceived by African American teenage fathers. *Families in Society: The Journal of Contemporary Human Services, 77*(2), 142–155.

113. Ibid., 148.

114. Hernandez, R. (2002). *Fatherwork in the crossfire: Chicano teen fathers struggling to take care of business* (p. 19). (Report No. JSRI-WP-58). East Lansing, MI: Michigan State University, Julian Samora Research Institute. (ERIC Document Reproduction Services No. ED 471 926)

115. Ibid., 17.

116. Gee, C. B., & Rhodes, J. E. (2003). Adolescent mothers' relationship with their children's biological fathers: Social support, social strain, and relationship continuity. *Journal of Family Psychology, 17*(3), 370–383; see also Roye, C. F., & Balk, S. J. (1996). The relationship of partner support to outcomes for teenage mothers and their children: A review. *Journal of Adolescent Health, 19,* 86–93.

117. Kowaleski-Jones, L., & Mott, F. L. (1998, July/August). Sex, contraception and childbearing among high-risk youth: Do different factors influence males and females? *Family Planning Perspectives, 30*(4), 163–169.

118. Allen, W. D., & Doherty, W. J. (1996). The responsibilities of fatherhood as perceived by African American teenage fathers (p. 152). *Families in Society: The Journal of Contemporary Human Services, 77*(2), 142–155.

119. Ibid., 150.

120. Heath, D. T., McKenry, P. C., & Leigh, G. K. (1995). The consequences of adolescent parenthood on men's depression, parental satisfaction, and fertility in adulthood (p. 145). *Journal of Social Service Research, 20,* 127–148.

121. Heath, D. T., McKenry, P. C., & Leigh, G. K. (1995). The consequences of adolescent parenthood on men's depression, parental satisfaction, and fertility in adulthood. *Journal of Social Service Research, 20,* 127–148.

122. Hernandez, R. (2002). *Fatherwork in the crossfire: Chicano teen fathers struggling to take care of business* (p. 23). (Report No. JSRI-WP-58). East Lansing, MI: Michigan State University, Julian Samora Research Institute. (ERIC Document Reproduction Services No. ED 471 926)

123. Kiselica, M. S. (1995). *Multicultural counseling with teenage fathers: A practical guide.* Thousand Oaks, CA: Sage.

124. Gee, C. B., & Rhodes, J. E. (2003). Adolescent mothers' relationship with their children's biological fathers: Social support, social strain, and relationship continuity. *Journal of Family Psychology, 17*(3), 370–383; see also Roye, C. F., & Balk, S. J. (1996). The relationship of partner support to outcomes for teenage mothers and their children: A review. *Journal of Adolescent Health, 19,* 86–93.

125. Gee, C. B., & Rhodes, J. E. (2003). Adolescent mothers' relationship with their children's biological fathers: Social support, social strain, and relationship continuity (p. 372). *Journal of Family Psychology, 17*(3), 370–383.

126. Gee, C. B., & Rhodes, J. E. (2003). Adolescent mothers' relationship with their children's biological fathers: Social support, social strain, and relationship continuity. *Journal of Family Psychology, 17*(3), 370–383.

CHAPTER 4   SERVICE NEEDS OF ADOLESCENT FATHERS

1. The National Campaign To Prevent Teen Pregnancy. (2003). *Science says: The sexual attitudes and behavior of male teens.* Retrieved January 12, 2006, from www.teenpregnancy.org/works/sciencesays.asp

2. Dallas, C. M., & Chen, S. C. (1998). Experiences of African American adolescent fathers (p. 215). *Western Journal of Nursing Research, 20*(2), 210–222.

3. Marcell, A. V., Raine, T., & Eyre, S. L. (2003). Where does reproductive health fit into the lives of adolescent males? *Perspectives on Sexual and Reproductive Health, 35,* 180–186.

4. Ibid., 183.

5. Ibid., 186.

6. Allen, W. D., & Doherty, W. J. (1996). The responsibilities of fatherhood as perceived by African American teenage fathers (p. 149). *Families in Society: The Journal of Contemporary Human Services, 77*(2), 142–155.

7. Heath, D. T., McKenry, P. C., & Leigh, G. K. (1995). The consequences of adolescent parenthood on men's depression, parental satisfaction, and fertility in adulthood. *Journal of Social Service Research, 20,* 127–148; see also, Kowaleski-Jones, L., & Mott, F. L. (1988, July/August). Sex, contraception and childbearing among high-risk youth: Do different factors influence males and females? *Family Planning Perspectives, 30*(4), 163–169; Robinson, B. E., & Barret, R. L. (1987). Self-concept and anxiety of adolescent and adult fathers. *Adolescence, 22,* 611–616.

8. Thompson, S. D., & Crase, S. J. (2004). Fathers of infants born to adolescent mothers: A comparison with non-parenting male peers and adolescent mothers. *Children and Youth Services Review, 26,* 489–505.

9. Robinson, R. B., & Frank, D. I. (1994). The relation between self-esteem, sexual activity, and pregnancy. *Adolescence, 29*(113), 27–35; see also Moses, A. (1995). *Teenage pregnancy prevention in California: 1995 policy roundtable series report.* Retrieved March 9, 2006, from www.library.ca.gov/CAFIS/reports/95–01/95–01.pdf; Thompson, S., Osteen, S. R., & Youngker, L. (2001). Who fares better? Postnatal adjustment of adolescent fathers and mothers. *Marriage and Family Review, 33*(4), 31–46.

10. Buchanan, M., & Robbins, C. (1990). Early adult psychological consequences for males of adolescent pregnancy and its resolution. *Journal of Youth and Adolescence, 19,* 413–424; see also Florsheim, P., Moore, D., Zollinger, L., MacDonald, J. & Sumida, E. (1999). The transition to parenthood among adolescent fathers and their partners: Does antisocial behavior predict problems in parenting? *Applied Developmental Science, 3*(3), 178–191; Heath, D. T., McKenry, P. C., & Leigh, G. K. (1995). The consequences of adolescent parenthood on men's depression, parental satisfaction, and fertility in adulthood. *Journal of Social Service Research, 20,* 127–148.

11. Weinman, M., Buzi, R. S., & Smith, P. B. (2005). Addressing risk behaviors, service needs, and mental health issues in programs for young fathers. *Families in Society: The Journal of Contemporary Social Services, 86*(2), 261–266.

12. Hendricks, L. E. (1988). Outreach with teenage fathers: A preliminary report on three ethnic groups. *Adolescence, 23*(91), 711–720.

13. Rhein, L. H., Ginsburg, K. R., Schwarz, D. F., Pinto-Martin, J. A., Zhao, H., Morgan, A. P., & Slap, G. B. (1997). Teen father participation in child rearing: Family perspectives. *Journal of Adolescent Health, 21,* 244–252; see also Weinman, M., Buzi, R. S., & Smith, P. B. (2005). Addressing risk behaviors, service needs, and mental health issues in programs for young fathers. *Families in Society: The Journal of Contemporary Social Services, 86*(2), 261–266.

14. Lehr, R., & MacMillan, P. (2001). The psychological and emotional impact of divorce: The noncustodial father's perspective. *Families in Society: The Journal of Contemporary Human Services, 82*(4), 373–382.

15. Rhein, L. H., Ginsburg, K. R., Schwarz, D. F., Pinto-Martin, J. A., Zhao, H., Morgan, A. P., & Slap, G. B. (1997). Teen father participation in child rearing: Family perspectives. *Journal of Adolescent Health, 21,* 244–252.

16. Allen, W. D., & Doherty, W. J. (1996). The responsibilities of fatherhood as perceived by African American teenage fathers. *Families in Society: The Journal of Contemporary Human Services, 77*(2), 142–155.

17. Rhein, L. H., Ginsburg, K. R., Schwarz, D. F., Pinto-Martin, J. A., Zhao, H., Morgan, A. P., & Slap, G. B. (1997). Teen father participation in child rearing: Family perspectives. *Journal of Adolescent Health, 21,* 244–252.

18. Pirog-Good, M. A. (1996). The education and labor market outcomes of adolescent fathers. *Youth & Society, 28*(2), 236–262.

19. Ibid.

20. U.S. Bureau of Labor Statistics. (2005). *Work activity of high school students: Data from the National Longitudinal Survey of Youth (USDL 05–732).* Washington DC: U.S. Department of Labor. Retrieved February 17, 2006, from http://www.bls.gov/nls/#news

21. Kost, K. A. (1997). The effects of support on the economic well-being of young fathers. *Families in Society, 78,* 370–382.

22. Klerman, J. A., & Karoly, L. A. (1994). Young men and the transition to stable employment (p. 46). *Monthly Labor Review, 117,* 31–48.

23. U.S. Bureau of Labor Statistics. (2006, January). *Labor force statistics from the current population survey.* Retrieved February 17, 2006, from http://data.bls.gov/cgi-bin/surveymost?

24. U.S. Bureau of Labor Statistics. (2006). *Number of unemployment spells experienced by individuals from age 18–38 in 1978–2002 by educational attainment, sex, race and Hispanic or Latino ethnicity.* Washington DC: U.S. Department of Labor. Retrieved February 17, 2006, from http://www.bls.gov/nls/#news

25. Fagot, B. I., Pears, K. C., Capaldi, D. M., Crosby, L., & Leve, C. S. (1998). Becoming an adolescent father: Precursors and parenting. *Developmental Psychology, 34*(6), 1209–1219.

26. Achatz, M., & MacAllum, C. A. (1994). *Young unwed fathers: Report from the field* (p. 23). Philadelphia: Public/Private Ventures.

27. Pirog-Good, M. A. (1996). The education and labor market outcomes of adolescent fathers (p. 252). *Youth & Society, 28*(2), 236–262.

28. Kost, K. A. (1997). The effects of support on the economic well-being of young fathers. *Families in Society, 78,* 370–382.

29. Hernandez, R. (2002). *Fatherwork in the crossfire: Chicano teen fathers struggling to take care of business* (p. 20). (Report No. JSRI-WP-58). East Lansing, MI: Michigan State University, Julian Samora Research Institute. (ERIC Document Reproduction Services No. ED 471 926)

30. Ibid., 7.

31. Ibid., 9.

32. Brown, S. (1990). *If the shoes fit: Final report and program implementation guide of the Maine Young Fathers Project.* Portland, ME: Human Services Development Institute, University of Southern Maine.

33. Hernandez, R. (2002). *Fatherwork in the crossfire: Chicano teen fathers struggling to take care of business.* (Report No. JSRI-WP-58). East Lansing, MI: Michigan State University, Julian Samora Research Institute. (ERIC Document Reproduction Services No. ED 471 926)

34. Gee, C. B., & Rhodes, J. E. (2003). Adolescent mothers' relationship with their children's biological fathers: Social support, social strain, and relationship continuity. *Journal of Family Psychology, 17*(3), 370–383.

35. Fagot, B. I., Pears, K. C., Capaldi, D. M., Crosby, L., & Leve, C. S. (1998). Becoming an adolescent father: Precursors and parenting. *Developmental Psychology, 34*(6), 1209–1219.

36. Hernandez, R. (2002). *Fatherwork in the crossfire: Chicano teen fathers struggling to take care of business* (p. 10). (Report No. JSRI-WP-58). East Lansing, MI: Michigan State University, Julian Samora Research Institute. (ERIC Document Reproduction Services No. ED 471 926)

37. Achatz, M., & MacAllum, C. A. (1994). *Young unwed fathers: Report from the field* (p. 14). Philadelphia: Public/Private Ventures.

38. Hernandez, R. (2002). *Fatherwork in the crossfire: Chicano teen fathers struggling to take care of business* (p. 19). (Report No. JSRI-WP-58). East Lansing, MI: Michigan

State University, Julian Samora Research Institute. (ERIC Document Reproduction Services No. ED 471 926)

39. Ibid., 18.

40. Rhein, L. H., Ginsburg, K. R., Schwarz, D. F., Pinto-Martin, J. A., Zhao, H., Morgan, A. P., & Slap, G. B. (1997). Teen father participation in child rearing: Family perspectives. *Journal of Adolescent Health, 21,* 244–252.

41. Ibid., 250.

42. Pirog-Good, M. A. (1996). The education and labor market outcomes of adolescent fathers. *Youth & Society, 28*(2), 236–262.

43. Ibid.

44. Miller, D. B. (1994). Influences on parental involvement of African American adolescent fathers. *Child and Adolescent Social Work Journal, 11*(5), 363–378.

45. Pirog-Good, M. A. (1996). The education and labor market outcomes of adolescent fathers. *Youth & Society, 28*(2), 236–262.

46. Kiselica, M. S. (1995). *Multicultural counseling with teenage fathers: A practical guide.* Thousand Oaks, CA: Sage.

47. Pirog-Good, M. A. (1996). The education and labor market outcomes of adolescent fathers. *Youth & Society, 28*(2), 236–262.

48. Nock, S. L. (1998). The consequences of premarital fatherhood. *American Sociological Review, 63,* 250–263.

49. Achatz, M., & MacAllum, C. A. (1994). *Young unwed fathers: Report from the field.* Philadelphia: Public/Private Ventures; see also Bartfeld, J., & Meyer, D. R. (1993). *Are there really deadbeat dads? The relationship between ability to pay, enforcement, and compliance in non-marital child support cases.* Madison, WI: Institute for Research on Poverty; Bolton, F. G. (1987). The father in the adolescent pregnancy at risk for child maltreatment. I. Helpmate or hindrance? *Journal of Family Violence, 2,* 67–80; Furstenberg, F. F. (1976). *Unplanned parenthood: The social consequences of teenage childbearing.* New York: The Free Press; Hardy, J. B., & Zabin, L. S. (1991). *Adolescent pregnancy in an urban environment: Issues, programs and evaluation.* Washington DC: Urban Institute Press; Sander, J. H., & Rosen, J. L. (1987). Teenage fathers: Working with the neglected partner in adolescent childbearing. *Family Planning Perspectives, 19,* 107–110.

50. Stack, C. (1974). *All our kin: Strategies for survival in a Black community.* New York: Harper & Row; see also Sullivan, M. L. (1985). *Teen fathers in the inner city: An exploratory ethnographic study.* (Report No. UD 024 536). New York: Vera Institute of Justice. (ERIC Document Reproduction Service No. ED 264 316)

51. Achatz, M., & MacAllum, C. A. (1994). *Young unwed fathers: Report from the field.* Philadelphia: Public/Private Ventures; see also Hendricks, L. E. (1980). Unwed adolescent fathers: Problems they face and their sources of social support. *Adolescence, 15,* 861–869; Klerman, L. V., & Jekel, J. F. (1973). *School-age mothers: Problems, programs, and policy.* Hamden, CT: Shoe String Press; Vaz, R., Smolen, P., & Miller, C. (1983). Adolescent pregnancy: Involvement of the male partner. *Journal of Adolescent Health Care, 4,* 246–250.

52. Hendricks, L. E. (1980). Unwed adolescent fathers: Problems they face and their sources of social support. *Adolescence, 15,* 861–869; see also Vaz, R., Smolen, P., & Miller, C. (1983). Adolescent pregnancy: Involvement of the male partner. *Journal of Adolescent Health Care, 4,* 246–250.

53. Achatz, M., & MacAllum, C. A. (1994). *Young unwed fathers: Report from the field* (p. 77). Philadelphia: Public/Private Ventures.

54. Sullivan, M. L. (1985). *Teen fathers in the inner city: An exploratory ethnographic study.* (Report No. UD 024 536). New York: Vera Institute of Justice. (ERIC Document Reproduction Service No. ED 264 316)

55. Furstenberg, F. F. (1976). Unplanned parenthood: The social consequences of teenage childbearing. New York: The Free Press; see also Hardy, J. B., & Zabin, L. S. (1991). *Adolescent pregnancy in an urban environment: Issues, programs and evaluation.* Washington DC: Urban Institute Press.

56. Elster, A. B., & Panzarine, S. (1983). Teenage fathers: Stresses during gestation and early parenthood. *Clinical Pediatrics, 22,* 700–703; see also Hendricks, L. E. (1980). Unwed adolescent fathers: Problems they face and their sources of social support. *Adolescence, 15,* 861–869.

57. Furstenberg, F. F. (1976). *Unplanned parenthood: The social consequences of teenage childbearing.* New York: The Free Press.

58. O'Connell, M., & Moore, M. (1980). The legitimacy status of first births to women aged 15–24, 1939–1978. *Family Planning Perspectives, 12,* 16–25.

59. Bachu, A. (1999). Trends in premarital childbearing: 1930–1994. *Current Population Reports,* Series P-23, No. 197.

60. Nakashima, I. I., & Camp, B. W. (1984). Fathers of infants born to adolescent mothers. *American Journal of Diseases of Children, 138,* 452–454; see also de Lissovoy, V. (1973). High school marriages: A longitudinal study. *Journal of Marriage and the Family, 35,* 245–255.

61. Associated Press. (2001, May 25). Teen brides have short marriages. *Bucks County Courier Times,* p. 5A.

62. Furstenberg, F. F., Brooks-Gunn, J., & Morgan, S. P. (1987). *Adolescent mothers in later life.* New York: Cambridge University Press.

63. Hardy, J. B., & Zabin, L. S. (1991). *Adolescent pregnancy in an urban environment: Issues, programs and evaluation.* Washington DC: Urban Institute Press.

64. Nakashima, I. I., & Camp, B. W. (1984). Fathers of infants born to adolescent mothers. *American Journal of Diseases of Children, 138,* 452–454.

65. Chilman, C. S. (1988). Never-married, single, adolescent parents. In C. S. Chilman, E. W. Nunnally, & F. M. Cox (Eds.), *Variant family forms* (pp. 17–38). Newbury Park, CA: Sage.

66. Ibid.

67. Furstenberg, F. F. (1976). *Unplanned parenthood: The social consequences of teenage childbearing.* New York: The Free Press.

68. Marsiglio, W. (1987). Adolescent fathers in the United States: Their initial living arrangements, marital experience and educational outcomes. *Family Planning Perspectives, 19,* 240–251.

69. Chilman, C. S. (1988). Never-married, single, adolescent parents. In C. S. Chilman, E. W. Nunnally, & F. M. Cox (Eds.), *Variant family forms* (pp. 17–38). Newbury Park, CA: Sage; see also Kost, K. A. (1997). The effects of support on the economic well-being of young fathers. *Families in Society, 78,* 370–382.

70. Moore, D. R., & Florsheim, P. (2001). Interpersonal processes and psychopathology among expectant and nonexpectant adolescent couples. *Journal of Consulting and Clinical Psychology, 69*(1), 101–113.

71. Ibid., 109.

72. Ibid., 111.

73. Ibid.

74. Gee, C. B., & Rhodes, J. E. (2003). Adolescent mothers' relationship with their children's biological fathers: Social support, social strain, and relationship continuity (p. 371). *Journal of Family Psychology, 17*,(3), 370–383.

75. Allen, W. D., & Doherty, W. J. (1996). The responsibilities of fatherhood as perceived by African American teenage fathers. *Families in Society: The Journal of Contemporary Human Services, 77*(2), 142–155; see also Lehr, R., & MacMillan, P. (2001). The psychological and emotional impact of divorce: The noncustodial father's perspective. *Families in Society: The Journal of Contemporary Human Services, 82*(4), 373–382; Rhein, L. H., Ginsburg, K. R., Schwarz, D. F., Pinto-Martin, J. A., Zhao, H., Morgan, A. P., & Slap, G. B. (1997). Teen father participation in child rearing: Family perspectives. *Journal of Adolescent Health, 21*, 244–252.

76. Cutrona, C., Hessling, R. M., Bacon, P. L., & Russell, D. W. (1998). Predictors and correlates of continuing involvement with the baby's father among adolescent mothers. *Journal of Family Psychology, 12*(3), 369–387.

77. Allen, W. D., & Doherty, W. J. (1996). The responsibilities of fatherhood as perceived by African American teenage fathers. *Families in Society: The Journal of Contemporary Human Services, 77*(2), 142–155; see also Davies, S. L., Dix, E. S., Rhodes, S. D., Harrington, K. F., Frison, S., & Willis, L. (2004). Attitudes of young African American fathers toward early childbearing. *American Journal of Health Behavior, 28*(5), 418–425; Hendricks, L. E. (1988). Outreach with teenage fathers: A preliminary report on three ethnic groups. *Adolescence, 23*(91), 711–720; Lehr, R., & MacMillan, P. (2001). The psychological and emotional impact of divorce: The noncustodial father's perspective. *Families in Society: The Journal of Contemporary Human Services, 82*(4), 373–382.

78. Davies, S. L., Dix, E. S., Rhodes, S. D., Harrington, K. F., Frison, S., & Willis, L. (2004). Attitudes of young African American fathers toward early childbearing (p. 421). *American Journal of Health Behavior, 28*(5), 418–425.

79. Allen, W. D., & Doherty, W. J. (1996). The responsibilities of fatherhood as perceived by African American teenage fathers (p. 150). *Families in Society: The Journal of Contemporary Human Services, 77*(2), 142–155.

80. Ibid.

81. Gee, C. B., & Rhodes, J. E. (2003). Adolescent mothers' relationship with their children's biological fathers: Social support, social strain, and relationship continuity. *Journal of Family Psychology, 17*,(3), 370–383.

82. Dallas, C. M., & Chen, S. C. (1998). Experiences of African American adolescent fathers (p. 219). *Western Journal of Nursing Research, 20*(2), 210–222.

83. Krishnakumar, A., & Black, M. M. (2003). Family processes within three generation households and adolescent mothers' satisfaction with father involvement. *Journal of Family Psychology, 17*(4), 488–498.

84. Dallas, C. M., & Chen, S. C. (1998). Experiences of African American adolescent fathers (p. 219). *Western Journal of Nursing Research, 20*(2), 210–222; see also Krishnakumar, A., & Black, M. M. (2003). Family processes within three generation households and adolescent mothers' satisfaction with father involvement. *Journal of Family Psychology, 17*(4), 488–498; Sullivan, M. L. (1985). *Teen fathers in the inner*

city: An exploratory ethnographic study. (Report No. UD 024 536). New York: Vera Institute of Justice. (ERIC Document Reproduction Service No. ED 264 316)

85. Hernandez, R. (2002). *Fatherwork in the crossfire: Chicano teen fathers struggling to take care of business.* (Report No. JSRI-WP-58). East Lansing, MI: Michigan State University, Julian Samora Research Institute. (ERIC Document Reproduction Services No. ED 471 926); see also Sullivan, M. L. (1985). *Teen fathers in the inner city: An exploratory ethnographic study.* (Report No. UD 024 536). New York: Vera Institute of Justice. (ERIC Document Reproduction Service No. ED 264 316)

86. Lehr, R., & MacMillan, P. (2001). The psychological and emotional impact of divorce: The noncustodial father's perspective. *Families in Society: The Journal of Contemporary Human Services, 82*(4), 373–382.

87. Kiselica, M. S. (1995). *Multicultural counseling with teenage fathers: A practical guide.* Newbury Park, CA: Sage.

88. Gardner, R. A. (1998). *The parental alienation syndrome: A guide for mental health and legal professionals* (2nd ed.). Cresskill, NJ: Creative Therapeutics.

89. Dunne, J. & Hedrick, M. (1994). The parental alienation syndrome: An analysis of sixteen selected cases. *Journal of Divorce and Remarriage, 21*(3–4), 21–38.

90. Lehr, R., & MacMillan, P. (2001). The psychological and emotional impact of divorce: The noncustodial father's perspective (pp. 376–377). *Families in Society: The Journal of Contemporary Human Services, 82*(4), 373–382.

91. Kiselica, M. S. (1995). *Multicultural counseling with teenage fathers: A practical guide* (p. 150). Newbury Park, CA: Sage.

92. Lehr, R., & MacMillan, P. (2001). The psychological and emotional impact of divorce: The noncustodial father's perspective (p. 380). *Families in Society: The Journal of Contemporary Human Services, 82*(4), 373–382.

93. Hernandez, R. (2002). *Fatherwork in the crossfire: Chicano teen fathers struggling to take care of business.* (Report No. JSRI-WP-58). East Lansing, MI: Michigan State University, Julian Samora Research Institute. (ERIC Document Reproduction Services No. ED 471 926)

94. Thornberry, T. P., Wei, E. H., Stouthamer-Loeber, M., & Van Dyke, J. (2000, January). Teenage fatherhood and delinquent behavior. *Juvenile Justice Bulletin.* Retrieved January 29, 2007, from http://www.ncjrs.org/html/ojjdp/jjbul2000_1/contents.html

95. Landry, D. J., & Forest, J. D. (1995). How old are U.S. fathers? *Family Planning Perspectives, 27*, 159–161.

96. Phipps, M. G., Blume, J. D., & DeMonner, S. M. (2002). Young maternal age associated with increased risk of neonatal death. *Obstetrics & Gynecology, 100*(3), 481–486.

97. Fagot, B. I., Pears, K. C., Capaldi, D. M., Crosby, L., & Leve, C. S. (1998). Becoming an adolescent father: Precursors and parenting. *Developmental Psychology, 34*(6), 1209–1219.

98. Green, L. (2000). *Breaking the cycle: Longitudinal study finds success factors for Baltimore inner-city youths: Grant results.* Princeton, NJ: Robert Wood Johnson Foundation. Retrieved February 21, 2006, from http://www.rwjf.org/reports/grr/028276s.htm

99. Massat, C. R. (1995). Is older better? Adolescent parenthood and maltreatment. *Child Welfare, 74*(2), 325–336.

100. Ibid.

101. Green, M. (1976). *Fathering.* New York: McGraw-Hill.

102. Rhein, L. H., Ginsburg, K. R., Schwarz, D. F., Pinto-Martin, J. A., Zhao, H., Morgan, A. P., & Slap, G. B. (1997). Teen father participation in child rearing: Family perspectives. *Journal of Adolescent Health, 21,* 244–252.

103. Stengel, R. (1985, December). The missing-father myth. *Time,* p. 90.

104. Hendricks, L. E. (1981). Black unwed adolescent fathers. In L. E. Gary (Ed.), *Black men* (pp. 131–138). Beverly Hills, CA: Sage.

105. Hendricks, L. E. (1988). Outreach with teenage fathers: A preliminary report on three ethnic groups. *Adolescence, 23*(91), 711–720.

106. Hardy, J. B., & Zabin, L. S. (1991). *Adolescent pregnancy in an urban environment: Issues, programs and evaluation.* Washington DC: Urban Institute Press.

107. Sullivan, M. L. (1985). *Teen fathers in the inner city: An exploratory ethnographic study.* (Report No. UD 024 536). New York: Vera Institute of Justice. (ERIC Document Reproduction Service No. ED 264 316)

108. Allen, W. D., & Doherty, W. J. (1998). "Being There": The perception of fatherhood among a group of African-American adolescent fathers (p. 233). In H. I. McCubbin, E. A. Thompson, A. I. Thompson, & J. E. Fromer (Eds.), *Resiliency in African-American families* (pp. 207–244). Thousand Oaks, CA: Sage.

109. Hernandez, R. (2002). *Fatherwork in the crossfire: Chicano teen fathers struggling to take care of business.* (Report No. JSRI-WP-58). East Lansing, MI: Michigan State University, Julian Samora Research Institute. (ERIC Document Reproduction Services No. ED 471 926)

110. Horie, M., & Horie, H. (1988). *Whatever became of fathering?* Downers Grove, IL: InterVarsity Press.

111. Green, M. (1976). *Fathering.* New York: McGraw-Hill.

112. Ibid.

113. Stengel, R. (1985, December). The missing-father myth. *Time,* p. 90.

114. National Institute of Child Health and Human Development. (1998, October). Improving children's well-being: Understanding nurturing fatherhood (p. 1). *Research on Today's Issues, 9,* 1–2.

115. Hendricks, L. E. (1988). Outreach with teenage fathers: A preliminary report on three ethnic groups. *Adolescence, 23*(91), 711–720; see also Sullivan, M. L. (1985). *Teen fathers in the inner city: An exploratory ethnographic study.* (Report No. UD 024 536). New York: Vera Institute of Justice. (ERIC Document Reproduction Service No. ED 264 316)

116. Dash, L. (1989). *When children want children: An inside look at the crisis of teenage parenthood.* New York: Penguin; see also Sullivan, M. L. (1985). *Teen fathers in the inner city: An exploratory ethnographic study.* (Report No. UD 024 536). New York: Vera Institute of Justice. (ERIC Document Reproduction Service No. ED 264 316)

117. Allen, W. D., & Doherty, W. J. (1998). "Being There": The perception of fatherhood among a group of African-American adolescent fathers. In H. I. McCubbin, E. A. Thompson, A. I. Thompson, & J. E. Fromer (Eds.), *Resiliency in African-American families* (pp. 207–244). Thousand Oaks, CA: Sage; see also Hernandez, R. (2002). *Fatherwork in the crossfire: Chicano teen fathers struggling to take care of business.* (Report No. JSRI-WP-58). East Lansing, MI: Michigan State University, Julian

Samora Research Institute. (ERIC Document Reproduction Services No. ED 471 926)

118. Davies, S. L., Dix, E. S., Rhodes, S. D., Harrington, K. F., Frison, S., & Willis, L. (2004). Attitudes of young African American fathers toward early childbearing (p. 423). *American Journal of Health Behavior, 28,* 418–425.

119. Fagot, B. I., Pears, K. C., Capaldi, D. M., Crosby, L., & Leve, C. S. (1998). Becoming an adolescent father: Precursors and parenting. *Developmental Psychology, 34*(6), 1209–1219.

120. Bunting, L., & McAuley, C. (2004). Research review: Teenage pregnancy and parenthood: The role of fathers. *Child and Family Social Work, 9,* 295–303.

121. Hernandez, R. (2002). *Fatherwork in the crossfire: Chicano teen fathers struggling to take care of business.* (Report No. JSRI-WP-58). East Lansing, MI: Michigan State University, Julian Samora Research Institute. (ERIC Document Reproduction Services No. ED 471 926); see also Sullivan, M. L. (1985). *Teen fathers in the inner city: An exploratory ethnographic study.* (Report No. UD 024 536). New York: Vera Institute of Justice. (ERIC Document Reproduction Service No. ED 264 316)

122. Hendricks, L. E. (1988). Outreach with teenage fathers: A preliminary report on three ethnic groups. *Adolescence, 23*(91), 711–720; see also Miller, D. B. (1994). Influences on parental involvement of African American adolescent fathers. *Child and Adolescent Social Work Journal, 11*(5), 363–378; Rhein, L. H., Ginsburg, K. R., Schwarz, D. F., Pinto-Martin, J. A., Zhao, H., Morgan, A. P., & Slap, G. B. (1997). Teen father participation in child rearing: Family perspectives. *Journal of Adolescent Health, 21,* 244–252.

123. Elster, A. B., & Hendricks, L. (1986). Stresses and coping strategies of adolescent fathers. In A. B. Elster & M. E. Lamb (Eds.), *Adolescent fatherhood* (pp. 55–66). Hillsdale, NJ: Erlbaum.

124. Robinson, B. (1988). *Teenage fathers* (p. 59). Lexington, MA: Lexington Books.

125. Elster, A. B., & Hendricks, L. (1986). Stresses and coping strategies of adolescent fathers. In A. B. Elster & M. E. Lamb (Eds.), *Adolescent fatherhood* (pp. 55–66). Hillsdale, NJ: Erlbaum.

126. Fry, P. S., & Trifiletti, R. J. (1983). Teenage fathers: An exploration of their developmental needs and anxieties and the implications for clinical-social intervention services. *Journal of Psychiatric Treatment and Evaluation, 5,* 219–227.

127. Dallas, C. M., & Chen, S. C. (1998). Experiences of African American adolescent fathers (p. 214). *Western Journal of Nursing Research, 20*(2), 210–222.

128. Elster, A. B., & Hendricks, L. (1986). Stresses and coping strategies of adolescent fathers. In A. B. Elster & M. E. Lamb (Eds.), *Adolescent fatherhood* (pp. 55–66). Hillsdale, NJ: Erlbaum.

129. Hendricks, L. E. (1988). Outreach with teenage fathers: A preliminary report on three ethnic groups. *Adolescence, 23*(91), 711–720; see also Kost, K. A. (1997). The effects of support on the economic well-being of young fathers. *Families in Society, 78,* 370–382.

130. Rhein, L. H., Ginsburg, K. R., Schwarz, D. F., Pinto-Martin, J. A., Zhao, H., Morgan, A. P., & Slap, G. B. (1997). Teen father participation in child rearing: Family perspectives. *Journal of Adolescent Health, 21,* 244–252; see also Weinman, M., Buzi, R. S., & Smith, P. B. (2005). Addressing risk behaviors, service needs, and mental health

issues in programs for young fathers. *Families in Society: The Journal of Contemporary Social Services, 86*(2), 261–266.

131. Romo, C., Bellamy, J., & Coleman, M. T. (2004). *TFF final evaluation report.* Austin, TX: Texas Fragile Families Initiative.

132. Weinman, M., Buzi, R. S., & Smith, P. B. (2005). Addressing risk behaviors, service needs, and mental health issues in programs for young fathers (p. 264). *Families in Society: The Journal of Contemporary Social Services, 86*(2), 261–266.

133. Kost, K. A. (1997). The effects of support on the economic well-being of young fathers. *Families in Society: The Journal of Contemporary Human Services, 78,* 370–382.

134. Ibid.; see also Pirog-Good, M. A. (1996). The education and labor market outcomes of adolescent fathers. *Youth & Society, 28*(2), 236–262.

135. Herr, E. L. (1999). *Counseling in a dynamic society: Context and practices for the 21st century* (2nd ed.). Alexandria, VA: American Counseling Association.

136. Weinman, M., Buzi, R. S., & Smith, P. B. (2005). Addressing risk behaviors, service needs, and mental health issues in programs for young fathers (p. 264). *Families in Society: The Journal of Contemporary Social Services, 86*(2), 261–266.

137. Children's Defense Fund. (1986). *Adolescent pregnancy: What the states are saying.* Washington DC: Author; see also Coren, E., Barlow, J., & Stewart-Brown, S. (2003). The effectiveness of individual and group-based parenting programmes in improving outcomes for teenage mothers and their children: A systematic review. *Journal of Adolescence, 26,* 79–103; Kiselica, M. S. (1992, August). *Are we giving teenage fathers a mixed message?* In L. Silverstein (Chair), *Transforming fatherhood in a patriarchical society.* Symposium conducted at the Annual Convention of the American Psychological Association, Washington DC; Kiselica, M. S. (1998, March). *School-based services for teenage parents: Results of a state survey.* Paper presented at the World Conference of the American Counseling Association, Indianapolis, IN; Kiselica, M. S., & Sturmer, P. (1993). Is society giving teenage fathers a mixed message? *Youth and Society, 24,* 487–501; Kiselica, M. S., & Sturmer, P. (1995, August). *Outreach services for teenage parents: Has gender equity been realized?* Paper presented at the Annual Convention of the American Psychological Association, New York; Sample, J. (1997). *Engendering fatherhood: Provision of services and professional attitudes toward young fathers.* Unpublished master's thesis, Oklahoma State University, Stillwater, OK; Smollar, J., & Ooms, T. (1987). *Young unwed fathers: Research review, policy dilemmas, and options: Summary report.* Washington DC: Department of Health and Human Services; U.S. Congress (1986). *Teen pregnancy: What is being done? A report of the select committee on children, youth, and families.* (December, 1985). Washington DC: U.S. Government Printing Office.

138. Kiselica, M. S., Gorczynski, J., & Capps, S. (1998). Teen mothers and fathers: School counselor perceptions of service needs. *Professional School Counseling, 2,* 146–152.

139. Softas-Nall, B., Baldo, T. D., & Williams, S. C. (1997). Counselor trainee perceptions of Hispanic, Black, and White teenage expectant mothers and fathers. *Journal of Multicultural Counseling & Development, 25,* 234–243.

140. Kiselica, M. S., & Sturmer, P. (1993). Is society giving teenage fathers a mixed message? (p. 488–489). *Youth and Society, 24,* 487–501.

141. Robinson, B. (1988). *Teenage fathers.* Lexington, MA: Lexington Books.

142. Cutrona, C., Hessling, R. M., Bacon, P. L., & Russell, D. W. (1998). Predictors and correlates of continuing involvement with the baby's father among adolescent mothers (p. 369). *Journal of Family Psychology, 12*(3), 369–387.

143. Davies, S. L., Dix, E. S., Rhodes, S. D., Harrington, K. F., Frison, S., & Willis, L. (2004). Attitudes of young African American fathers toward early childbearing. *American Journal of Health Behavior, 28*(5), 418–425.

144. Lehr, R., & MacMillan, P. (2001). The psychological and emotional impact of divorce: The noncustodial father's perspective. *Families in Society: The Journal of Contemporary Human Services, 82*(4), 373–382.

145. Miller, D. B. (1994). Influences on parental involvement of African American adolescent fathers (p. 375). *Child and Adolescent Social Work Journal, 11*(5), 363–378.

146. Robinson, B. (1988). *Teenage fathers* (p. 59). Lexington, MA: Lexington Books.

147. Kiselica, M. S. (1995). *Multicultural counseling with teenage fathers: A practical guide.* Newbury Park, CA: Sage.

148. Lehr, R., & MacMillan, P. (2001). The psychological and emotional impact of divorce: The noncustodial father's perspective (p. 379). *Families in Society: The Journal of Contemporary Human Services, 82*(4), 373–382.

149. Allen, W. D., & Doherty, W. J. (1996). The responsibilities of fatherhood as perceived by African American teenage fathers (p. 150). *Families in Society: The Journal of Contemporary Human Services, 77*(2), 142–155.

150. Crawford, L. (2000). *A place for pregnant teenagers.* Retrieved September 21, 2007, from http://www.gothamgazette.com/socialservices/aug.00.shtml

151. Kalmuss, D., Davidson, A., Cohall, A., Laraque, D., & Cassell, C. (2003). Preventing sexual risk behaviors among teenagers: Linking research and programs. *Perspectives on Sexual and Reproductive Health, 35,* 87–93.

152. Kost, K. A. (1997). The effects of support on the economic well-being of young fathers (p. 380). *Families in Society, 78,* 370–382.

153. Russell, S. T., Lee, F. C. H., & The Latina/o Teen Pregnancy Prevention Workgroup. (2004). Practitioner's perspectives on effective practices for Hispanic teenage pregnancy prevention (p. 146). *Perspectives on Sexual and Reproductive Health, 36*(4), 142–149.

154. Hendricks, L. E. (1988). Outreach with teenage fathers: A preliminary report on three ethnic groups. *Adolescence, 23*(91), 711–720.

155. Kiselica, M. S. (1995). *Multicultural counseling with teenage fathers: A practical guide.* Newbury Park, CA: Sage; see also Kiselica, M. S. (1999). Counseling teen fathers. In A. M. Horne & M. S. Kiselica (Eds.), *Handbook of counseling boys and adolescent males: A practitioner's guide* (pp. 179–198). Thousand Oaks, CA: Sage; Kiselica, M. S. (2001). A male-friendly therapeutic process with school-age boys. In G. R. Brooks & G. Good (Eds.), *The handbook of counseling and psychotherapy with men: A guide to settings and approaches.* (Vol. I, pp. 43–58). San Francisco: Jossey-Bass; Kiselica, M. S. (2003, Autumn). Male-sensitive counseling with boys. *Counselling in Education,* 16–19; Kiselica, M. S. (2003). Transforming psychotherapy in order to succeed with boys: Male-friendly practices. *Journal of Clinical Psychology: In Session, 59,* 1225–1236; Kiselica, M. S. (2006). Helping a boy become a parent: Male-sensitive psychotherapy with a teenage father. In M. Englar-Carlson & M. Stevens (Eds.), *In the room with men: A casebook of therapeutic change* (pp. 225–240). Washington DC: American Psychological Association.

156. Pennsylvania Consolidated Statutes. (undated).

157. SexLaws.org. (2006). *What is statutory rape?* Retrieved January 24, 2006, from http://www.sexlaws.org/statrape.html

158. Russell, S. T., Lee, F. C. H., & The Latina/o Teen Pregnancy Prevention Workgroup. (2004). Practitioner's perspectives on effective practices for Hispanic teenage pregnancy prevention (p. 146). *Perspectives on Sexual and Reproductive Health, 36*(4), 142–149.

159. Ibid.

160. *Not Me.* (1990). [Documentary]. Production People, Ltd.

161. Kiselica, M. S. (1995). *Multicultural counseling with teenage fathers: A practical guide* (p. 35). Newbury Park, CA: Sage.

162. Levant, R. F. (1992). Toward a reconstruction of masculinity. *Journal of Family Psychology, 5,* 379–402.

163. Marcell, A. V., Raine, T., & Eyre, S. L. (2003). Where does reproductive health fit into the lives of adolescent males? (p. 184). *Perspectives on Sexual and Reproductive Health, 35*(4), 180–186.

164. Addis, M. E., & Mahalik, J. R. (2003). Men, masculinity, and the contexts of help seeking. *American Psychologist, 58*(1), 5–14.

165. Ibid.

166. Ibid., 12.

167. Kiselica, M. S. (1995). *Multicultural counseling with teenage fathers: A practical guide.* Newbury Park, CA: Sage; see also Kiselica, M. S. (1999). Counseling teen fathers. In A. M. Horne & M. S. Kiselica (Eds.), *Handbook of counseling boys and adolescent males: A practitioner's guide* (pp. 179–198). Thousand Oaks, CA: Sage; Kiselica, M. S. (2001). A male-friendly therapeutic process with school-age boys. In G. R. Brooks & G. Good (Eds.), *The handbook of counseling and psychotherapy with men: A guide to settings and approaches.* (Vol. I, pp. 43–58). San Francisco: Jossey-Bass; Kiselica, M. S. (2003, Autumn). Male-sensitive counseling with boys. *Counselling in Education,* 16–19; Kiselica, M. S. (2003). Transforming psychotherapy in order to succeed with boys: Male-friendly practices. *Journal of Clinical Psychology: In Session, 59,* 1225–1236.

168. Kiselica, M. S. (1995). *Multicultural counseling with teenage fathers: A practical guide.* Newbury Park, CA: Sage.

169. Kost, K. A. (1997). The effects of support on the economic well-being of young fathers. *Families in Society, 78,* 370–382.

CHAPTER 5   HELPING TEENAGE FATHERS

1. Klinman, D. G., & Sander, J. H. (1985). *The teen parent collaboration: Reaching and serving the teenage father.* New York: Bank Street College of Education; see also Sander, J. H., & Rosen, J. L. (1987). Teenage fathers: Working with the neglected partner in adolescent childbearing. *Family Planning Perspectives, 19,* 107–110.

2. Sander, J. H., & Rosen, J. L. (1987). Teenage fathers: Working with the neglected partner in adolescent childbearing. *Family Planning Perspectives, 19,* 107–110.

3. Ibid.

4. Marcell, A. V., Raine, T., & Eyre, S. L. (2003). Where does reproductive health fit into the lives of adolescent males? (p. 186). *Perspectives on Sexual and Reproductive Health, 35*(4), 180–186.

5. Marcell, A. V., Raine, T., & Eyre, S. L. (2003). Where does reproductive health fit into the lives of adolescent males? *Perspectives on Sexual and Reproductive Health, 35*(4), 180–186.

6. Hendricks, L. E. (1988). Outreach with teenage fathers: A preliminary report on three ethnic groups. *Adolescence, 23,* 711–720.

7. Allen, W. D., & Doherty, W. J. (1996). The responsibilities of fatherhood as perceived by African American teenage fathers. *Families in Society: The Journal of Contemporary Human Services, 77*(2), 142–155; see also Barth, R. P., Claycomb, M., & Loomis, A. (1988). Services to adolescent fathers. *Health and Social Work, 13,* 277–287; Brindis, C., Barth, R. P., & Loomis, A. B. (1987). Continuous counseling: Case management with teenage parents. *Social Casework: The Journal of Contemporary Social Work, 68,* 164–172.

8. Klinman, D. G., & Sander, J. H. (1985). *The teen parent collaboration: Reaching and serving the teenage father.* New York: Bank Street College of Education; see also Sander, J. H., & Rosen, J. L. (1987). Teenage fathers: Working with the neglected partner in adolescent childbearing. *Family Planning Perspectives, 19,* 107–110; Weinman, M., Buzi, R. S., & Smith, P. B. (2005). Addressing risk behaviors, service needs, and mental health issues in programs for young fathers. *Families in Society: The Journal of Contemporary Social Services, 86,* 261–266.

9. Lehr, R., & MacMillan, P. (2001). The psychological and emotional impact of divorce: The noncustodial father's perspective. *Families in Society: The Journal of Contemporary Human Services, 82*(4), 373–382.

10. Barth, R. P., Claycomb, M., & Loomis, A. (1988). Services to adolescent fathers. *Health and Social Work, 13,* 277–287; see also Brown, S. (1990). *If the shoes fit: Final report and program implementation guide of the Maine Young Fathers Project.* Portland, ME: Office of Sponsored Research, University of Southern Maine; Sander, J. H., & Rosen, J. L. (1987). Teenage fathers: Working with the neglected partner in adolescent childbearing. *Family Planning Perspectives, 19,* 107–110.

11. Robinson, B. E. (1988). *Teenage fathers.* Lexington, MA: Lexington Books.

12. Huey, W. C. (1987). Counseling teenage fathers: The "Maximizing a Life Experience" (MALE) group. *School Counselor, 35,* 40–47; see also Kiselica, M. S., & Pfaller, J. (1993). Helping teenage parents: The independent and collaborative roles of school counselors and counselor educators. *Journal of Counseling and Development, 72,* 42–48; Kiselica, M. S., Stroud, J. C., Stroud, J. E., & Rotzien, A. (1992). Counseling the forgotten client: The teen father. *Journal of Mental Health Counseling, 14,* 338–350; Sander, J. H., & Rosen, J. L. (1987). Teenage fathers: Working with the neglected partner in adolescent childbearing. *Family Planning Perspectives, 19,* 107–110.

13. Barth, R. P., Claycomb, M., & Loomis, A. (1988). Services to adolescent fathers. *Health and Social Work, 13,* 277–287; see also Huey, W. C. (1987). Counseling teenage fathers: The "Maximizing a Life Experience" (MALE) group. *School Counselor, 35,* 40–47.

14. Dallas, C. M., & Chen, S. C. (1998). Experiences of African American adolescent fathers (pp. 220–221). *Western Journal of Nursing Research, 20*(2), 210–222.

15. Robinson, B. E. (1988). *Teenage fathers.* Lexington, MA: Lexington Books.

16. Rosenbaum, S. (1985). *Providing effective prenatal care programs for teenagers.* Washington DC: Children's Defense Fund.

17. Beymer, L. (1995). *Meeting the guidance and counseling needs of boys* (p. 26). Alexandria, VA: American Counseling Association.

18. Marcell, A. V., Raine, T., & Eyre, S. L. (2003). Where does reproductive health fit into the lives of adolescent males? *Perspectives on Sexual and Reproductive Health, 35,* 180–186.

19. Ibid., 184.

20. Robinson, B. E. (1988). *Teenage fathers.* Lexington, MA: Lexington Books.

21. Kiselica, M. S. (1995). *Multicultural counseling with teenage fathers: A practical guide.* Newbury Park, CA: Sage.

22. Weinman, M., Buzi, R. S., & Smith, P. B. (2005). Addressing risk behaviors, service needs, and mental health issues in programs for young fathers (p. 265). *Families in Society: The Journal of Contemporary Social Services, 86,* 261–266.

23. Allen-Meares, P. (1984). Adolescent pregnancy and parenting: The forgotten adolescent father and his parents. *Journal of Social Work and Human Sexuality, 3,* 27–38.

24. Hendricks, L. E. (1988). Outreach with teenage fathers: A preliminary report on three ethnic groups. *Adolescence, 23,* 711–720.

25. Kiselica, M. S. (2006). Helping a boy become a parent: Male-sensitive psychotherapy with a teenage father. In M. Englar-Carlson & M. Stevens (Eds.), *In the room with men: A casebook of therapeutic change* (pp. 225–240). Washington DC: American Psychological Association.

26. Kiselica, M. S., Stroud, J. C., Stroud, J. E., & Rotzien, A. (1992). Counseling the forgotten client: The teen father. *Journal of Mental Health Counseling, 14,* 338–350.

27. Hendricks, L. E. (1988). Outreach with teenage fathers: A preliminary report on three ethnic groups. *Adolescence, 23,* 711–720.

28. Kiselica, M. S. (2001). A male-friendly therapeutic process with school-age boys. In G. R. Brooks and G. Good (Eds.), *The handbook of counseling and psychotherapy with men: A guide to settings and approaches.* (Vol. I, pp. 43–58). San Francisco: Jossey-Bass; see also Kiselica, M. S. (2003, Autumn). Male-sensitive counseling with boys. *Counselling in Education,* 16–19; Kiselica, M. S. (2003). Transforming psychotherapy in order to succeed with boys: Male-friendly practices. *Journal of Clinical Psychology: In Session, 59,* 1225–1236; Kiselica, M. S. (2006). Helping a boy become a parent: Male-sensitive psychotherapy with a teenage father. In M. Englar-Carlson & M. Stevens (Eds.), *In the room with men: A casebook of therapeutic change* (pp. 225–240). Washington DC: American Psychological Association.

29. Hendricks, L. E. (1988). Outreach with teenage fathers: A preliminary report on three ethnic groups. *Adolescence, 23,* 711–720.

30. Kiselica, M. S. (1993, March). *Male involvement in teenage pregnancy and parenthood.* Symposium conducted at the Annual Conference of the Indiana Council on Adolescent Pregnancy, Indianapolis, IN; see also Kiselica, M. S. (2006). Helping a boy become a parent: Male-sensitive psychotherapy with a teenage father. In M. Englar-Carlson & M. Stevens (Eds.), *In the room with men: A casebook of therapeutic change* (pp. 225–240). Washington DC: American Psychological Association.

31. Robinson, B. E. (1988). *Teenage fathers.* Lexington, MA: Lexington Books.

32. Kiselica, M. S. (1995). *Multicultural counseling with teenage fathers: A practical guide.* Newbury Park, CA: Sage.

33. Weinman, M., Buzi, R. S., & Smith, P. B. (2005). Addressing risk behaviors, service needs, and mental health issues in programs for young fathers. *Families in Society: The Journal of Contemporary Social Services, 86,* 261–266; see also Kiselica, M. S. (1996). Parenting skills training with teenage fathers. In M. P. Andronico (Ed.), *Men in groups: Insights, interventions, and psychoeducational work* (pp. 283–300). Washington DC: American Psychological Association; Kiselica, M. S., Rotzien, A., & Doms, J. (1994). Preparing teenage fathers for parenthood: A group psychoeducational approach. *Journal for Specialists in Group Work, 19,* 83–94; Kiselica, M. S., & Scheckel, S. (1995). The couvade syndrome (sympathetic pregnancy) and teenage fathers: A primer for school counselors. *The School Counselor, 43,* 42–51.

34. Hendricks, L. E. (1988). Outreach with teenage fathers: A preliminary report on three ethnic groups. *Adolescence, 23,* 711–720.

35. Kiselica, M. S. (2003). Transforming psychotherapy in order to succeed with boys: Male-friendly practices. *Journal of Clinical Psychology: In Session, 59,* 1225–1236; see also Kiselica, M. S. (2006). Helping a boy become a parent: Male-sensitive psychotherapy with a teenage father. In M. Englar-Carlson & M. Stevens (Eds.), *In the room with men: A casebook of therapeutic change* (pp. 225–240). Washington DC: American Psychological Association.

36. Brown, S. (1990). *If the shoes fit: Final report and program implementation guide of the Maine Young Fathers Project* (p. 36). Portland, ME: Office of Sponsored Research, University of Southern Maine.

37. Brown, S. (1990). *If the shoes fit: Final report and program implementation guide of the Maine Young Fathers Project.* Portland, ME: Office of Sponsored Research, University of Southern Maine.

38. Kost, K. A. (1997). The effects of support on the economic well-being of young fathers. *Families in Society, 78,* 370–382.

39. Brindis, C., Barth, R. P., & Loomis, A. B. (1987). Continuous counseling: Case management with teenage parents. *Social Casework: The Journal of Contemporary Social Work, 68,* 164–172.

40. Ammen, S. A. (2000). A play-based teen parenting program to facilitate parent-child attachment. In H. G. Kadusen & C. E. Schaefer (Eds.), *Short-term play therapy for children* (pp. 345–369). New York: Guilford.

41. Hernandez, R. (2002). *Fatherwork in the crossfire: Chicano teen fathers struggling to take care of business* (p. 14). (Report No. JSRI-WP-58). East Lansing, MI: Michigan State University, Julian Samora Research Institute. (ERIC Document Reproduction Services No. ED 471 926)

42. Kiselica, M. S. (2006). Helping a boy become a parent: Male-sensitive psychotherapy with a teenage father. In M. Englar-Carlson & M. Stevens (Eds.), *In the room with men: A casebook of therapeutic change* (pp. 225–240). Washington DC: American Psychological Association.

43. Smith, L. A. (1988). Black adolescent fathers: Issues for service provision. *Social Work, 33,* 269–271.

44. Achatz, M., & MacAllum, C. A. (1994). *Young unwed fathers: Report from the field* (pp. 23–24). Philadelphia: Public/Private Ventures.

45. Kiselica, M. S. (1995). *Multicultural counseling with teenage fathers: A practical guide.* Newbury Park, CA: Sage.

46. Ibid.

47. Russell, S. T., Lee, F. C. H., & The Latina/o Teen Pregnancy Prevention Workgroup. (2004). Practitioner's perspectives on effective practices for Hispanic teenage pregnancy prevention. *Perspectives on Sexual and Reproductive Health, 36*(4), 142–149; see also Kiselica, M. S. (1995). *Multicultural counseling with teenage fathers: A practical guide.* Newbury Park, CA: Sage.

48. Brown, S. (1990). *If the shoes fit: Final report and program implementation guide of the Maine Young Fathers Project.* Portland, ME: Office of Sponsored Research, University of Southern Maine.

49. Kiselica, M. S. (1995). *Multicultural counseling with teenage fathers: A practical guide.* Newbury Park, CA: Sage.

50. Ibid., 184.

51. Achatz, M., & MacAllum, C. A. (1994). *Young unwed fathers: Report from the field* (p. 37). Philadelphia: Public/Private Ventures.

52. Associated Press. (1993, January 26). Girl, 17, delivers baby, concocts story. *Muncie Star,* p. D2.

53. Courtroom Television Network. (1998). *Grossberg to serve two-and-half years; Peterson receives two-year sentence.* Retrieved March 20, 2006, from http://www.courttv. com/archive/trials/grossberg/070998.html

54. Kiselica, M. S. (1995). *Multicultural counseling with teenage fathers: A practical guide.* Newbury Park, CA: Sage.

55. Ibid.; see also Lindsay, J. W. (1997). Crisis counseling with pregnant teens. In T. N. Fairchild (Ed.), *Crisis intervention strategies for school-based helpers* (pp. 370–398). Springfield, IL: Charles C. Thomas.

56. Kiselica, M. S. (1995). *Multicultural counseling with teenage fathers: A practical guide.* Newbury Park, CA: Sage.

57. Kiselica, M. S., & Pfaller, J. (1993). Helping teenage parents: The independent and collaborative roles of school counselors and counselor educators. *Journal of Counseling and Development, 72,* 42–48.

58. Kiselica, M. S. (1999). Counseling teen fathers. In A. M. Horne & M. S. Kiselica (Eds.), *Handbook of counseling boys and adolescent males: A practitioner's guide* (pp. 179–198). Thousand Oaks, CA: Sage.

59. Lindsay, J. W. (1997). Crisis counseling with pregnant teens. In T. N. Fairchild (Ed.), *Crisis intervention strategies for school-based helpers* (pp. 370–398). Springfield, IL: Charles C. Thomas.

60. Kiselica, M. S. (1999). Counseling teen fathers. In A. M. Horne & M. S. Kiselica (Eds.), *Handbook of counseling boys and adolescent males: A practitioner's guide* (pp. 179–198). Thousand Oaks, CA: Sage.

61. Lindsay, J. W. (1997). Crisis counseling with pregnant teens. In T. N. Fairchild (Ed.), *Crisis intervention strategies for school-based helpers* (pp. 370–398). Springfield, IL: Charles C. Thomas.

62. Ibid.

63. Kiselica, M. S. (1999). Counseling teen fathers (p. 184). In A. M. Horne & M. S. Kiselica (Eds.), *Handbook of counseling boys and adolescent males: A practitioner's guide* (pp. 179–198). Thousand Oaks, CA: Sage.

64. Kiselica, M. S. (1995). *Multicultural counseling with teenage fathers: A practical guide.* Newbury Park, CA: Sage.

65. Achatz, M., & MacAllum, C. A. (1994). *Young unwed fathers: Report from the field* (p. 94). Philadelphia: Public/Private Ventures.

66. Kiselica, M. S., & Murphy, D. K. (1994). Developmental career counseling with teenage parents. *Career Development Quarterly, 42,* 238–244.

67. Kost, K. A. (1997). The effects of support on the economic well-being of young fathers. *Families in Society: The Journal of Contemporary Human Services, 78,* 370–382.

68. Kiselica, M. S., & Murphy, D. K. (1994). Developmental career counseling with teenage parents. *Career Development Quarterly, 42,* 238–244.

69. Achatz, M., & MacAllum, C. A. (1994). *Young unwed fathers: Report from the field* (pp. 63–64). Philadelphia: Public/Private Ventures.

70. Achatz, M., & MacAllum, C. A. (1994). *Young unwed fathers: Report from the field.* Philadelphia: Public/Private Ventures; see also Hendricks, L. E. (1988). Outreach with teenage fathers: A preliminary report on three ethnic groups. *Adolescence, 23,* 711–720.

71. Kiselica, M. S., Rotzien, A., & Doms, J. (1994). Preparing teenage fathers for parenthood: A group psychoeducational approach. *Journal for Specialists in Group Work, 19,* 83–94; see also Kiselica, M. S. (1996). Parenting skills training with teenage fathers. In M. P. Andronico (Ed.), *Men in groups: Insights, interventions, and psychoeducational work* (pp. 283–300). Washington DC: American Psychological Association.

72. Achatz, M., & MacAllum, C. A. (1994). *Young unwed fathers: Report from the field* (p. 55). Philadelphia: Public/Private Ventures.

73. Kiselica, M. S., Rotzien, A., & Doms, J. (1994). Preparing teenage fathers for parenthood: A group psychoeducational approach. *Journal for Specialists in Group Work, 19,* 83–94; see also Kiselica, M. S. (1996). Parenting skills training with teenage fathers. In M. P. Andronico (Ed.), *Men in groups: Insights, interventions, and psychoeducational work* (pp. 283–300). Washington DC: American Psychological Association.

74. Achatz, M., & MacAllum, C. A. (1994). *Young unwed fathers: Report from the field.* Philadelphia: Public/Private Ventures.

75. Kiselica, M. S., & Scheckel, S. (1995). The couvade syndrome (sympathetic pregnancy) and teenage fathers: A primer for school counselors. *The School Counselor, 43,* 42–51.

76. Bogren, L. Y., (1986). The couvade syndrome. *International Journal of Family Psychiatry, 7,* 123–136.

77. Barnhill, L., Rubenstein, G., & Rocklin, N. (1979). From generation to generation: Father-to-be in transition. *The Family Coordinator, 28,* 229–235.

78. Kiselica, M. S., & Scheckel, S. (1995). The couvade syndrome (sympathetic pregnancy) and teenage fathers: A primer for school counselors. *The School Counselor, 43,* 42–51.

79. Ibid.

80. Kiselica, M. S., Rotzien, A., & Doms, J. (1994). Preparing teenage fathers for parenthood: A group psychoeducational approach. *Journal for Specialists in Group Work, 19,* 83–94; see also Kiselica, M. S. (1996). Parenting skills training with teenage fathers. In M. P. Andronico (Ed.), *Men in groups: Insights, interventions, and psychoeducational work* (pp. 283–300). Washington DC: American Psychological Association.

81. Kiselica, M. S. (1999). Counseling teen fathers (p. 187). In A. M. Horne & M. S. Kiselica (Eds.), *Handbook of counseling boys and adolescent males: A practitioner's guide* (pp. 179–198). Thousand Oaks, CA: Sage.

82. Fagot, B. I., Pears, K. C., Capaldi, D. M., Crosby, L., & Leve, C. S. (1998). Becoming an adolescent father: Precursors and parenting (p. 1217). *Developmental Psychology, 34*(6), 1209–1219.

83. Krishnakumar, A., & Black, M. M. (2003). Family processes within three-generation households and adolescent mothers' satisfaction with father involvement (p. 496). *Journal of Family Psychology, 17*(4), 488–498.

84. Krishnakumar, A., & Black, M. M. (2003). Family processes within three-generation households and adolescent mothers' satisfaction with father involvement. *Journal of Family Psychology, 17*(4), 488–498.

85. National Fatherhood Initiative. (undated). *24/7 dad.* Gaithersburg, MD: National Fatherhood Initiative.

86. Hayes, E., & Sherwood, K. (2000). *The responsible fatherhood curriculum.* New York: Manpower Demonstration Research Corporation. Available online at http://www.mdrc.org/publications/40/abstract.html

87. National Family Preservation Network. (undated). *Basic fatherhood training curriculum.* Buhl, ID: National Family Preservation Network.

88. SmithBattle, L. (1996). Intergenerational ethics of caring for adolescent mothers and their children (p. 62). *Family Relations, 45,* 56–64.

89. Smith, L. (1983). A conceptual model of families incorporating adolescent mother and child. *Advances in Nursing Science, 6*(1), 45–60.

90. Ibid.

91. SmithBattle, L. (1996). Intergenerational ethics of caring for adolescent mothers and their children. *Family Relations, 45,* 56–64.

92. Ibid. 63.

93. Dellmann-Jenkins, M., Sattler, S. H., & Richardson, R. A. (1993). Adolescent parenting: A positive, intergenerational approach (p. 600). *Families in Society: The Journal of Contemporary Human Services, 74*(10), 590–601.

94. Levine, J. A., & Pitt, E. W. (1995). *New expectations: Community strategies for responsible fatherhood.* New York: Family and Work Institute.

95. Achatz, M., & MacAllum, C. A. (1994). *Young unwed fathers: Report from the field* (p. 55). Philadelphia: Public/Private Ventures.

96. Clemmens, D. A. (2002). Adolescent mothers' depression after the birth of their babies: Weathering the storm. *Adolescence, 37,* 551–565.

97. Lehr, R, & MacMillan, P. (2001). The psychological and emotional impact of divorce: The noncustodial father's perspective (pp. 379–380). *Families in Society: The Journal of Contemporary Human Services, 82,* 373–382.

98. Ammen, S. A. (2000). A play-based teen parenting program to facilitate parent-child attachment (pp. 359–360). In H. G. Kadusen & C. E. Schaefer (Eds.), *Short-term play therapy for children* (pp. 345–369). New York: Guilford.

99. Ibid., 366.

100. Allen, W. D., & Doherty, W. J. (1996). The responsibilities of fatherhood as perceived by African American teenage fathers. *Families in Society: The Journal of Contemporary Human Services, 77*(2), 142–155; see also Hernandez, R. (2002). *Fatherwork*

in the crossfire: Chicano teen fathers struggling to take care of business. (Report No. JSRI-WP-58). East Lansing, MI: Michigan State University, Julian Samora Research Institute. (ERIC Document Reproduction Services No. ED 471 926)

101. Allen-Meares, P. (1984). Adolescent pregnancy and parenting: The forgotten adolescent father and his parents. *Journal of Social Work and Human Sexuality, 3,* 27–38; see also Hernandez, R. (2002). *Fatherwork in the crossfire: Chicano teen fathers struggling to take care of business.* (Report No. JSRI-WP-58). East Lansing, MI: Michigan State University, Julian Samora Research Institute. (ERIC Document Reproduction Services No. ED 471 926); Sullivan, M. L. (1985). *Teen fathers in the inner city: An exploratory ethnographic study.* (Report No. UD 024 536). New York: Vera Institute of Justice. (ERIC Document Reproduction Service No. ED 264 316)

102. Allen-Meares, P. (1984). Adolescent pregnancy and parenting: The forgotten adolescent father and his parents. *Journal of Social Work and Human Sexuality, 3,* 27–38; see also Dallas, C. M., & Chen, S. C. (1998). Experiences of African American adolescent fathers. *Western Journal of Nursing Research, 20*(2), 210–222; Davies, S. L., Dix, E. S., Rhodes, S. D., Harrington, K. F., Frison, S., & Willis, L. (2004). Attitudes of young African fathers toward early childbearing. *American Journal of Health Behavior, 28*(5), 418–425; Sullivan, M. L. (1985). *Teen fathers in the inner city: An exploratory ethnographic study.* (Report No. UD 024 536). New York: Vera Institute of Justice. (ERIC Document Reproduction Service No. ED 264 316)

103. Furstenberg, F. F., & Crawford, A. G. (1989). Family support: Helping teenage mothers to cope. In N. Cervera & L.Videka-Sherman (Eds.), *Working with pregnant and parenting teenage clients* (pp.108–133). Milwaukee: Family Service America; see also Sullivan, M. L. (1985). *Teen fathers in the inner city: An exploratory ethnographic study.* (Report No. UD 024 536). New York: Vera Institute of Justice. (ERIC Document Reproduction Service No. ED 264 316)

104. Davies, S. L., Dix, E. S., Rhodes, S. D., Harrington, K. F., Frison, S., & Willis, L. (2004). Attitudes of young African fathers toward early childbearing. *American Journal of Health Behavior, 28*(5), 418–425.

105. Miller, B. C., Benson, B., & Galbraith, K. A. (2001). Family relationships and adolescent pregnancy risk: A research synthesis. *Developmental Review, 21,* 1–38.

106. Ibid.

107. Kiselica, M. S. (1995). *Multicultural counseling with teenage fathers: A practical guide.* Newbury Park, CA: Sage.

108. Christmon, K. (1990). The unwed adolescent father's perceptions of his family and of himself as a father. *Child and Adolescent Social Work Journal, 7,* 275–283; see also Hendricks, L. E. (1980). Unwed adolescent fathers: Problems they face and their sources of social support. *Adolescence, 15,* 861–869.

109. Kiselica, M. S. (1995). *Multicultural counseling with teenage fathers: A practical guide.* Newbury Park, CA: Sage.

110. Ibid.

111. Bunting, L., & McAuley, C. (2004). Research review: Teenage pregnancy and parenthood: The role of fathers. *Child and Family Social Work, 9,* 295–303.

112. Cutrona, C., Hessling, R. M., Bacon, P. L., & Russell, D. W. (1998). Predictors and correlates of continuing involvement with the baby's father among adolescent mothers. *Journal of Family Psychology, 12*(3), 369–387.

113. Krishnakumar, A., & Black, M. M. (2003). Family processes within three-genera-
     tion households and adolescent mothers' satisfaction with father involvement.
     Journal of Family Psychology, 17(4), 488–498.

114. Roye, C. F., & Balk, S. J. (1996). The relationship of partner support to outcomes for
     teenage mothers and their children: A review (p. 91). *Journal of Adolescent Health,
     19,* 86–93.

115. Kiselica, M. S. (1995). *Multicultural counseling with teenage fathers: A practical guide.*
     Newbury Park, CA: Sage.

116. Lindsay, J. W. (1990). *School-age parents: The challenge of three-generation living.*
     Buena Park, CA: Morning Glory Press.

117. Sullivan, M. L. (1985). *Teen fathers in the inner city: An exploratory ethnographic study.*
     (Report No. UD 024 536). New York: Vera Institute of Justice. (ERIC Document
     Reproduction Service No. ED 264 316)

118. Furstenberg, F. F. (1979). Burdens and benefits: The impact of early childbearing
     on the family. In T. Ooms (Ed.), *Teenage pregnancy and family impact: New perspec-
     tives on policy. Family impact seminar.* (pp. 21–22). Washington DC: George Washing-
     ton University's Institute for Edcuation Leadership; see also Lindsay, J. W. (1990).
     School-age parents: The challenge of three-generation living. Buena Park, CA: Morning
     Glory Press.

119. Scherman, A., Korkames-Rowe, D., & Howard, S. (1990). An examination of the liv-
     ing arrangements and needs expressed by teenage mothers. *The School Counselor,
     38,* 133–142.

120. Lindsay, J. W. (1990). *School-age parents: The challenge of three-generation living.*
     Buena Park, CA: Morning Glory Press.

121. Sullivan, M. L. (1985). *Teen fathers in the inner city: An exploratory ethnographic study.*
     (Report No. UD 024 536). New York: Vera Institute of Justice. (ERIC Document
     Reproduction Service No. ED 264 316)

122. Allen, W. D., & Doherty, W. J. (1996). The responsibilities of fatherhood as per-
     ceived by African American teenage fathers (p. 149). *Families in Society: The Journal
     of Contemporary Human Services, 77*(2), 142–155.

123. Hernandez, R. (2002). *Fatherwork in the crossfire: Chicano teen fathers struggling to
     take care of business* (p. 16). (Report No. JSRI-WP-58). East Lansing, MI: Michigan
     State University, Julian Samora Research Institute. (ERIC Document Reproduction
     Services No. ED 471 926)

124. Kiselica, M. S. (1995). *Multicultural counseling with teenage fathers: A practical guide.*
     Newbury Park, CA: Sage; see also Kiselica, M. S. (1995, Spring). Healing the father-
     son wounds of teenage fathers. *The Psychotherapy Bulletin, 30*(1), 66–69.

125. Moore, D. R., & Florsheim, P. (2001). Interpersonal processes and psychopathology
     among expectant and nonexpectant adolescent couples (p. 110). *Journal of Consult-
     ing and Clinical Psychology, 69*(1), 101–113.

126. Ibid.

127. Ibid.

128. Gee, C. B., & Rhodes, J. E. (2003). Adolescent mothers' relationship with their
     children's biological fathers: Social support, social strain, and relationship conti-
     nuity. *Journal of Family Psychology, 17*(3), 370–383.

129. Krishnakumar, A., & Black, M. M. (2003). Family processes within three-generation households and adolescent mothers' satisfaction with father involvement (p. 496). *Journal of Family Psychology, 17*(4), 488–498.

130. Lehr, R, & MacMillan, P. (2001). The psychological and emotional impact of divorce: The noncustodial father's perspective (p. 381). *Families in Society: The Journal of Contemporary Human Services, 82,* 373–382.

131. Lehr, R, & MacMillan, P. (2001). The psychological and emotional impact of divorce: The noncustodial father's perspective. *Families in Society: The Journal of Contemporary Human Services, 82,* 373–382.

132. Kiselica, M. S. (1995). *Multicultural counseling with teenage fathers: A practical guide.* Newbury Park, CA: Sage.

133. Fagot, B. I., Pears, K. C., Capaldi, D. M., Crosby, L., & Leve, C. S. (1998). Becoming an adolescent father: Precursors and parenting (p. 1214). *Developmental Psychology, 34*(6), 1209–1219.

134. Achatz, M., & MacAllum, C. A. (1994). *Young unwed fathers: Report from the field.* Philadelphia: Public/Private Ventures.

135. Thornberry, T. P., Smith, C. A., & Howard, G. J. (1997). Risk factors for teenage fatherhood. *Journal of Marriage and the Family, 59,* 505–522; see also Xie, H., Cairns, B. D., & Cairns, R. B. (2001). Predicting teen motherhood and teen fatherhood: Individual characteristics and peer affiliations. *Social Development, 10*(4), 488–511.

136. Kiselica, M. S., Rotzien, A., & Doms, J. (1994). Preparing teenage fathers for parenthood: A group psychoeducational approach. *Journal for Specialists in Group Work, 19,* 83–94.

137. Miller, K. S., Levin, M. L., Whitaker, D. J., & Xu, X. (1999, October). Patterns of condom use among adolescents: The impact of mother-daughter communication. *American Journal of Public Health, 88*(10), 1542–1544.

138. Hovell, M., Sipan, C., Blumberg, E., Atkins, C., Hofstetter, C. R., & Kreitner, S. (1994). Family influences on Latino and Anglo adolescents' sexual behavior (p. 984). *Journal of Marriage and the Family, 56,* 973–986.

139. Miller, K. S., & Whitaker, D. J. (2001). Predictors of mother-adolescent discussions about condoms: Implications for providers who serve youth. *Pediatrics, 108* (2), 5. Available online at http://www.pediatrics.org/cgi/content/full/108/2/e28

140. Ibid.

141. Bakken, R. J., & Winter, M. (2002). Family characteristics and sexual risk behaviors among Black men in the United States. *Perspectives on Sexual and Reproductive Health, 34,* 252–258.

142. Carrera, M. A. (1992). Involving adolescent males in pregnancy and STD prevention programs. *Adolescent Medicine: State of the Art Reviews, 3,* 1–13.

143. Allen, W. D., & Doherty, W. J. (1996). The responsibilities of fatherhood as perceived by African American teenage fathers. *Families in Society: The Journal of Contemporary Human Services, 77*(2), 142–155.

144. Kiselica, M. S. (1995). *Multicultural counseling with teenage fathers: A practical guide.* Newbury Park, CA: Sage.

145. Brown, S. (1990). *If the shoes fit: Final report and program implementation guide of the Maine Young Fathers Project.* Portland, ME: Office of Sponsored Research, University

of Southern Maine; see also Hendricks, L. E. (1988). Outreach with teenage fathers: A preliminary report on three ethnic groups. *Adolescence, 23*, 711–720.

146. Brown, S. (1990). *If the shoes fit: Final report and program implementation guide of the Maine Young Fathers Project.* Portland, ME: Office of Sponsored Research, University of Southern Maine.

147. Kiselica, M. S. (1995). *Multicultural counseling with teenage fathers: A practical guide.* Newbury Park, CA: Sage.

148. Kiselica, M. S., & Murphy, D. K. (1994). Developmental career counseling with teenage parents. *Career Development Quarterly, 42*, 238–244.

149. Allen-Meares, P. (1989). An in-school program for adolescent parents: Implications for social work practice and multi-disciplinary teaming. In N. Cervera & L. Videka-Sherman (Eds.), *Working with pregnant and parenting teenage clients* (pp. 190–200). Milwaukee, WI: Family Service America.

150. Brown, S. (1990). *If the shoes fit: Final report and program implementation guide of the Maine Young Fathers Project.* Portland, ME: Office of Sponsored Research, University of Southern Maine.

151. Carrera, M. A. (1992). Involving adolescent males in pregnancy and STD prevention programs. *Adolescent Medicine: State of the Art Reviews, 3*, 1–13.

152. Pierre, N., Shrier, L. A., Emans, S. J., & DuRant, R. H. (1998). Adolescent males involved in pregnancy: Associations of forced sexual contact and risk behaviors. *Journal of Adolescent Health, 23*(6), 364–369; see also Saewyc, E. M., Magee, L. L., & Pettingell, S. E. (2004). Teenage pregnancy and associated risk behaviors among sexually abused adolescents. *Perspectives on Sexual and Reproductive Health, 36*(3), 98–105; Shrier, L. A., Pierce, J. D., Emans, S. J., & DuRant, R. H. (1998). Gender differences in risk behaviors associated with reported forced sex. *Archives of Pediatric Medicine, 152*, 57–63.

153. Herrenkohl, E. C., Herrenkohl, R. C., Egolf, B. P., & Russo, M. J. (1998). The relationship between early maltreatment and teenage parenthood. *Journal of Adolescence, 21*, 291–303.

154. Kiselica, M. S., & Novack, G. (2008). Promoting strength and recovery: Counseling boys who have been sexually abused. In M. S. Kiselica, M. Englar-Carlson, & A. M. Horne (Eds.), *Counseling troubled boys: A guidebook for professionals* (pp. 97–123). New York: Routledge.

155. Saewyc, E. M., Magee, L. L., & Pettingell, S. E. (2004). Teenage pregnancy and associated risk behaviors among sexually abused adolescents (p. 103). *Perspectives on Sexual and Reproductive Health, 36*(3), 98–105.

156. Ibid.

157. Kessler, R. C., Berglund, P. A., Foster, C. L., Saunders, W. B., Stang, P.E., & Walters, E. E. (1997). Social consequences of psychiatric disorders II: Teenage parenthood. *American Journal of Psychiatry, 154*(10), 1405–1411; see also Moore, D. R., & Florsheim, P. (2001). Interpersonal processes and psychopathology among expectant and nonexpectant adolescent couples. *Journal of Consulting and Clinical Psychology, 69*(1), 101–113.

158. Moore, D. R., & Florsheim, P. (2001). Interpersonal processes and psychopathology among expectant and nonexpectant adolescent couples (p. 110). *Journal of Consulting and Clinical Psychology, 69*(1), 101–113.

159. Carr, A. (2006). *The handbook of child and adolescent clinical psychology*. New York: Routledge; see also, Steiner, H. (Ed.). (2004). *Handbook of mental health interventions in children and adolescents: An integrated developmental approach*. San Francisco: Jossey-Bass.

160. Lebow, J. L. (Ed.). (2005). *Handbook of clinical family therapy*. Hoboken, NJ: John Wiley & Sons.

161. Gilberg, C., Harrington, R. & Steinhausen, H. (Eds). (2006). *A clinician's handbook of child and adolescent psychiatry*. New York: Cambridge University Press.

162. Kiselica, M. S., Englar-Carlson, M., & Horne, A. M. (Eds.). (2008). *Counseling troubled boys: A guidebook for professionals*. New York: Routledge.

163. Kiselica, M. S. (1995). *Multicultural counseling with teenage fathers: A practical guide* (p. 35). Newbury Park, CA: Sage.

164. Practitioners are referred to the following resources about the process of counseling antisocial youth and their families: Horne, A., & Sager, T. (1990). *Understanding and treating conduct oppositional defiant disorders in children*. Boston: Allyn & Bacon; Kazdin, A. E. (2005). Parent management training: Treatment for oppositional, aggressive, and antisocial behavior in children and adolescents. New York: Oxford University Press.

165. Smith, P., Buzi, R. S., & Weinman, M. L. (2002). Programs for young fathers: Essential components and evaluation issues. *North American Journal of Psychology, 4*(1), 81–92.

166. Wolf, W. C., & Leiderman, S. (2001). *Investing in "young families": Some thoughts on advantages, disadvantages and possible next steps*. Trenton, NJ: Center for Assessment and Policy Development. Available online at http://www.capd.org/pubfiles/pub-2001–03–02.pdf

167. Weinman, M, Buzi, R. S., & Smith, P. B. (2005). Addressing risk behaviors, service needs, and mental health issues in programs for young fathers. *Families in Society: The Journal of Contemporary Social Services, 86,* 261–266.

168. Nesmith, J. D, Klerman, L. V., Oh, M. K., & Feinstein, R. A. (1997). Procreative experiences and orientations toward paternity held by incarcerated adolescent males. *Journal of Adolescent Health, 20,* 198–203.

169. Weinman, M., Buzi, R. S., & Smith, P. B. (2005). Addressing risk behaviors, service needs, and mental health issues in programs for young fathers (p. 265). *Families in Society: The Journal of Contemporary Social Services, 86,* 261–266.

170. Smith, P., Buzi, R. S., & Weinman, M. L. (2002). Programs for young fathers: Essential components and evaluation issues. *North American Journal of Psychology, 4*(1), 81–92.

171. Stevens-Simon, C., & Nelligan, D. (1998). Strategies for identifying and treating adolescents at risk for maltreating their children. *Aggression and Violent Behavior, 3,* 197–217.

172. Fagot, B. I., Pears, K. C., Capaldi, D. M., Crosby, L., & Leve, C. S. (1998). Becoming an adolescent father: Precursors and parenting. *Developmental Psychology, 34*(6), 1209–1219.

173. Stevens-Simon, C., & Nelligan, D. (1998). Strategies for identifying and treating adolescents at risk for maltreating their children (p. 209). *Aggression and Violent Behavior, 3,* 197–217.

174. Ibid.

175. Florsheim, P., Moore, D., Zollinger, L., MacDonald, J. & Sumida, E. (1999). The transition to parenthood among adolescent fathers and their partners: Does anti-social behavior predict problems in parenting? *Applied Developmental Science, 3*(3), 178–191.

176. Nesmith, J. D, Klerman, L. V., Oh, M. K., & Feinstein, R. A. (1997). Procreative experiences and orientations toward paternity held by incarcerated adolescent males. *Journal of Adolescent Health, 20,* 198–203.

CHAPTER 6   MODEL PROGRAMS AND USEFUL RESOURCES

1. Klinman, D. G., Sander, J. H., Rosen, J. L., Longo, K. R., Martinez, L. P. (1985). *The teen parent collaboration: Reaching and serving the teenage father.* New York: Bank Street College of Education.

2. Brindis, C. D. (1991). *Adolescent pregnancy prevention: A guidebook for communities.* Palo Alto, CA: Health Promotion Resource Center.

3. Kiselica, M. S. (1995). *Multicultural counseling with teenage fathers: A practical guide.* Thousand Oaks, CA: Sage.

4. Sander, J. H., & Rosen, J. L. (1987). Teenage fathers: Working with the neglected partner in adolescent childbearing. *Family Planning Perspectives, 19,* 107–110.

5. Lindsay, J. W., & Rodine, S. (1989). *Teenage pregnancy challenge. Book two: Programs for kids* (p. 77). Buena Park, CA: Morning Glory Press.

6. Kiselica, M. S. (1995). *Multicultural counseling with teenage fathers: A practical guide.* Thousand Oaks, CA: Sage.

7. Kegler, M. C., & Wyatt, V. H. (2003). A multiple case study of neighborhood partnerships for positive youth development. *American Journal of Health Behavior, 27,* 159–169.

8. Brindis, C. D. (1991). *Adolescent pregnancy prevention: A guidebook for communities.* Palo Alto, CA: Health Promotion Resource Center.

9. Duggan, A. K., DeAngelis, C., & Hardy, J. B. (1991). Comprehensive versus traditional services for pregnant and parenting adolescents: A comparative analysis. In J. B. Hardy & L. S. Zabin (Eds.), *Adolescent pregnancy in an urban environment: Issues, programs and evaluation* (pp. 255–278). Washington DC: The Urban Institute Press.

10. Brown, S. (1990). *If the shoes fit: Final report and program implementation guide of the Maine Young Fathers Project.* Portland, ME: Human Services Development Institute, University of Southern Maine.

11. Ibid.

12. Klinman, D. G., Sander, J. H., Rosen, J. L., Longo, K. R., Martinez, L. P. (1985). *The teen parent collaboration: Reaching and serving the teenage father* (p. 87). New York: Bank Street College of Education.

13. Brindis, C. D. (1991). *Adolescent pregnancy prevention: A guidebook for communities.* Palo Alto, CA: Health Promotion Resource Center; see also Kiselica, M. S. (1995). *Multicultural counseling with teenage fathers: A practical guide.* Thousand Oaks, CA: Sage.

14. Romo, C., Bellamy, J., & Coleman, M. T. (2004). *TFF final evaluation report.* Austin, TX: Texas Fragile Families Initiative.

15. Brown, S. (1990). *If the shoes fit: Final report and program implementation guide of the Maine Young Fathers Project* (p. 10). Portland, ME: Human Services Development Institute, University of Southern Maine.

16. Brindis, C. D. (1991). *Adolescent pregnancy prevention: A guidebook for communities* (pp. 214–215). Palo Alto, CA: Health Promotion Resource Center.

17. Brown, S. (1990). *If the shoes fit: Final report and program implementation guide of the Maine Young Fathers Project.* Portland, ME: Human Services Development Institute, University of Southern Maine.

18. Romo, C., Bellamy, J., & Coleman, M. T. (2004). *TFF final evaluation report.* Austin, TX: Texas Fragile Families Initiative.

19. Ibid., 117.

20. Smith, P., Buzi, R. S., & Weinman, M. L. (2002). Programs for young fathers: Essential components and evaluation issues. *North American Journal of Psychology, 4,* 81–92.

21. Baker, S. B. (1992). *School counseling for the twenty-first century.* New York: Merrill.

22. Smith, P., Buzi, R. S., & Weinman, M. L. (2002). Programs for young fathers: Essential components and evaluation issues. *North American Journal of Psychology, 4,* 81–92.

23. Card, J. J., Reagan, R. T., & Ritter, P. E. (1988). *Sourcebook of comparison data for evaluating adolescent pregnancy and parenting programs.* Los Altos, CA: Sociometrics Corp.

24. NationalNet. (1990). *A basic bibliography on adolescent sexuality, pregnancy prevention and care programs and program evaluation.* Los Altos, CA: Social Research Applications.

25. Klinman, D. G., Sander, J. H., Rosen, J. L., Longo, K. R., Martinez, L. P. (1985). *The teen parent collaboration: Reaching and serving the teenage father* (p. 87). New York: Bank Street College of Education.

26. Brown, S. (1990). *If the shoes fit: Final report and program implementation guide of the Maine Young Fathers Project.* Portland, ME: Human Services Development Institute, University of Southern Maine.

27. Achatz, M., & MacAllum, C. A. (1994). *Young unwed fathers: Report from the field.* Philadelphia: Public/Private Ventures.

28. Romo, C., Bellamy, J., & Coleman, M. T. (2004). *TFF final evaluation report.* Austin, TX: Texas Fragile Families Initiative.

29. William T. Grant Foundation. (2002). *Adolescent nonmarital childbearing and welfare* (par. 4). Retrieved January 26, 2006, from http://www.cyfc.umn.edu/adolescents/research/IF1018.html; see also Romo, C., Bellamy, J., & Coleman, M. T. (2004). *TFF final evaluation report.* Austin, TX: Texas Fragile Families Initiative.

30. Klinman, D. G., Sander, J. H., Rosen, J. L., Longo, K. R., Martinez, L. P. (1985). *The teen parent collaboration: Reaching and serving the teenage father* (p. 87). New York: Bank Street College of Education.

31. Romo, C., Bellamy, J., & Coleman, M. T. (2004). *TFF final evaluation report* (p. 67). Austin, TX: Texas Fragile Families Initiative.

32. Klinman, D. G., Sander, J. H., Rosen, J. L., Longo, K. R., Martinez, L. P. (1985). *The teen parent collaboration: Reaching and serving the teenage father* (p. 87). New York: Bank Street College of Education; see also Brown, S. (1990). *If the shoes fit: Final*

report and program implementation guide of the Maine Young Fathers Project. Portland, ME: Human Services Development Institute, University of Southern Maine; Achatz, M., & MacAllum, C. A. (1994). *Young unwed fathers: Report from the field.* Philadelphia: Public/Private Ventures; Romo, C., Bellamy, J., & Coleman, M. T. (2004). *TFF final evaluation report.* Austin, TX: Texas Fragile Families Initiative.

33. Klinman, D. G., Sander, J. H., Rosen, J. L., Longo, K. R., Martinez, L. P. (1985). *The teen parent collaboration: Reaching and serving the teenage father* (p. 87). New York: Bank Street College of Education; see also Brown, S. (1990). *If the shoes fit: Final report and program implementation guide of the Maine Young Fathers Project.* Portland, ME: Human Services Development Institute, University of Southern Maine; Achatz, M., & MacAllum, C. A. (1994). *Young unwed fathers: Report from the field.* Philadelphia: Public/Private Ventures; Romo, C., Bellamy, J., & Coleman, M. T. (2004). *TFF final evaluation report.* Austin, TX: Texas Fragile Families Initiative.

34. Roditti, M. (1997). Urban teen parents (p. 103). In N. K. Phillips & S. L.A. Straussner (Eds.), *Children in the urban environment: Linking social policy and clinical practice* (pp. 93–112). Springfield, IL: Charles C. Thomas.

35. Kiselica, M. S. (1995). *Multicultural counseling with teenage fathers: A practical guide.* Thousand Oaks, CA: Sage.

36. Roditti, M. (1997). Urban teen parents (p. 104). In N. K. Phillips & S. L.A. Straussner (Eds.), *Children in the urban environment: Linking social policy and clinical practice* (pp. 93–112). Springfield, IL: Charles C. Thomas.

37. Roditti, M. (1997). Urban teen parents. In N. K. Phillips & S. L.A. Straussner (Eds.), *Children in the urban environment: Linking social policy and clinical practice* (pp. 93–112). Springfield, IL: Charles C. Thomas.

38. Kiselica, M. S. (1995). *Multicultural counseling with teenage fathers: A practical guide.* Thousand Oaks, CA: Sage.

39. Romo, C., Bellamy, J., & Coleman, M. T. (2004). *TFF final evaluation report.* Austin, TX: Texas Fragile Families Initiative.

40. Miller, B. C., Benson, B., & Galbraith, K. A. (2001). Family relationships and adolescent pregnancy risk: A research synthesis. *Developmental Review, 21,* 1–38.

41. Achatz, M., & MacAllum, C. A. (1994). *Young unwed fathers: Report from the field.* Philadelphia: Public/Private Ventures.

42. Ibid., 95.

43. Bakken, R. J., & Winter, M. (2002). Family characteristics and sexual risk behaviors among Black men in the United States. *Perspectives on Sexual and Reproductive Health, 34,* 252–258.

44. Hendricks, L. E. (1988). Outreach with teenage fathers: A preliminary report on three ethnic groups. *Adolescence, 23,* 711–720. Brown, S. (1990). *If the shoes fit: Final report and program implementation guide of the Maine Young Fathers Project.* Portland, ME: Human Services Development Institute, University of Southern Maine.

45. Brown, S. (1990). *If the shoes fit: Final report and program implementation guide of the Maine Young Fathers Project.* Portland, ME: Human Services Development Institute, University of Southern Maine.

46. Ibid., 34.

47. Romo, C., Bellamy, J., & Coleman, M. T. (2004). *TFF final evaluation report.* Austin, TX: Texas Fragile Families Initiative.

48. Lesser, J., Verdugo, R. L., Koniak-Griffin, D., Tello, J., Kappos, B., & Cumberland, W. G. (2005). Respective and protecting relationships: A community research HIV prevention program for teen fathers and mothers. *AIDS Education and Prevention, 17*, 347–360.

49. Ibid.

50. The National Campaign to Prevent Teen Pregnancy. (2004). *Fact sheet: Teen sexual activity, pregnancy, and childbearing among non-Hispanic white teens.* Washington DC: Author.

51. Kiselica, M. S. (1995). *Multicultural counseling with teenage fathers: A practical guide.* Thousand Oaks, CA: Sage.

52. Kunjufu, J. (1986). *Countering the conspiracy to destroy black boys* (Vol. 2). Chicago: African American images; see also Johnson, L. B., & Staples, R. E. (1979, October). Family planning and the young minority male: A pilot project. *The Family Coordinator, 535–543.*

53. Kiselica, M. S. (1995). *Multicultural counseling with teenage fathers: A practical guide.* Thousand Oaks, CA: Sage.

54. Sander, J. H., & Rosen, J. L. (1987). Teenage fathers: Working with the neglected partner in adolescent childbearing. *Family Planning Perspectives, 19*, 107–110.

55. Ibid.

56. Ibid.

57. Klinman, D. G., Sander, J. H., Rosen, J. L., Longo, K. R., Martinez, L. P. (1985). *The teen parent collaboration: Reaching and serving the teenage father.* New York: Bank Street College of Education.

58. Huey, W. C. (1987). Counseling teenage fathers: The "Maximizing a Life Experience" (MALE) group. *School Counselor, 35*, 40–47.

59. Ibid.

60. Ibid.

61. Ibid.

62. Brown, S. (1990). *If the shoes fit: Final report and program implementation guide of the Maine Young Fathers Project.* Portland, ME: Human Services Development Institute, University of Southern Maine.

63. Ibid.

64. Achatz, M., & MacAllum, C. A. (1994). *Young unwed fathers: Report from the field.* Philadelphia: Public/Private Ventures.

65. Ibid.

66. Mazza, C. (2002). Young dads: The effects of a parenting program on urban African-American adolescent fathers. *Adolescence, 37*(148), 681–693.

67. Ibid., 685.

68. Ibid.

69. Kost, K. A. (1997). The effects of support on the economic well-being of young fathers. *Families in Society, 78*, 370–382.

70. Romo, C., Bellamy, J., & Coleman, M. T. (2004). *TFF final evaluation report.* Austin, TX: Texas Fragile Families Initiative.

71. Ibid.

72. Center for Public Policy Priorities. (2004). News release: *Study sheds new light on the needs of low income fathers*. Austin, TX: Texas Fragile Families Initiative.

73. Ammen, S. A. (2000). A play-based teen parenting program to facilitate parent-child attachment. In H. G. Kadusen & C. E. Schaefer (Eds.), *Short-term play therapy for children* (pp. 345–369). New York: Guilford.

74. Pennsylvania Department of Education. (2005). *Teen parent program* (par. 1). Retrieved May 15, 2006, from http://www.pde.state.pa.us/svcs_students/cwp/view.asp?a=175&Q=48401&svcs_studentsNav=%7C

75. Pennsylvania Department of Education. (2005). *Teen parent program* (par. 2). Retrieved May 15, 2006, from http://www.pde.state.pa.us/svcs_students/cwp/view.asp?a=175&Q=48401&svcs_studentsNav=%7C

76. Philliber, S., Brooks, L., Lehrer, M. O., & Waggoner, S. (2003). Outcomes of teen parenting programs in New Mexico. *Adolescence, 38*(151), 535–553.

77. Ibid.

78. Lesser, J., Verdugo, R. L., Koniak-Griffin, D., Tello, J., Kappos, B., & Cumberland, W. G. (2005). Respective and protecting relationships: A community research HIV prevention program for teen fathers and mothers. *AIDS Education and Prevention, 17*, 347–360.

79. Ibid.

80. Quality Improvement Center on Non-Resident Fathers and the Child Welfare System (2007). *Review of initiatives for QIC-NRF curriculum development*. Englewood, CO: American Humane.

81. Families and Work Institute. (undated). *The Fatherhood Project* (par. 1). Retrieved May 26, 2006, from http://www.familiesandwork.org/index.html

82. National Fatherhood Initiative. (2006). *NFI history* (par. 3). Retrieved May 16, 2006, from http://www.fatherhood.org/history.asp

83. National Fatherhood Initiative. (2006). *NFI mission & accomplishments* (par. 1). Retrieved May 16, 2006, from http://www.fatherhood.org/mission.asp

84. National Latino Fatherhood and Family Institute. (undated). *National Latino Fatherhood and Family Institute home page* (par. 2). Retrieved May 15, 2006, from http://www.nlffi.org/index.htm

85. National Urban League. (2005). *Education and youth* (par. 3). Retrieved May 26, 2006, from http://www.nul.org/educationandyouth.html

86. National Practitioners Network for Fathers and Families. (2003). *National Practitioners Network for Fathers and Families, Inc.* (par. 1). Retrieved May 15, 2006, from http://www.npnff.org

87. Trapani, M. (1999). *Reality check: Teenage fathers speak out* (Rev. ed.). New York: Rosen Publishing Group.

88. Lindsay, J. W. (1993). *Teen dads: Rights, responsibilities, and joys*. Buena Park, CA: Morning Glory Press.

89. Gravelle, K., & Peterson, L. (1992). *Teenage fathers*. Lincoln, NE: iUniverse, Inc.

CHAPTER 7   POLICY CONSIDERATIONS

1. Achatz, M., & MacAllum, C. A. (1994). *Young unwed fathers: Report from the field* (p. 14). Philadelphia: Public/Private Ventures; see also Glikman, H. (2004). Low-income

young fathers: Contexts, connections, and self. *Social Work, 49*, 195–206; Lehr, R., & MacMillan, P. (2001). The psychological and emotional impact of divorce: The noncustodial father's perspective. *Families in Society: The Journal of Contemporary Human Services, 82*(4), 373–382.

2. Achatz, M., & MacAllum, C. A. (1994). *Young unwed fathers: Report from the field* (p. 14). Philadelphia: Public/Private Ventures; see also Glikman, H. (2004). Low-income young fathers: Contexts, connections, and self. *Social Work, 49,* 195–206; Kost, K. A. (1997). The effects of support on the economic well-being of young fathers. *Families in Society, 78,* 370–382.

3. Jaffe, E. D. (1983). Fathers and child welfare services: The forgotten clients. In M. E. Lamb & A. Sagi (Eds.), *Fatherhood and social policy* (pp. 129–137). Hillsdale, NJ: Erlbaum.

4. Ibid.

5. Klinman, D. G., Sander, J. H., Rosen, J. L., Longo, K. R., Martinez, L. P. (1985). *The teen parent collaboration: Reaching and serving the teenage father.* New York: Bank Street College of Education.

6. Achatz, M., & MacAllum, C. A. (1994). *Young unwed fathers: Report from the field.* Philadelphia: Public/Private Ventures.

7. Romo, C., Bellamy, J., & Coleman, M. T. (2004). *TFF final evaluation report.* Austin, TX: Texas Fragile Families Initiative.

8. Ibid., 72.

9. Ibid.

10. Jaffe, E. D. (1983). Fathers and child welfare services: The forgotten clients (p. 135). In M. E. Lamb & A. Sagi (Eds.), *Fatherhood and social policy* (pp. 129–137). Hillsdale, NJ: Erlbaum.

11. Romo, C., Bellamy, J., & Coleman, M. T. (2004). *TFF final evaluation report.* Austin, TX: Texas Fragile Families Initiative.

12. Klinman, D. G., Sander, J. H., Rosen, J. L., Longo, K. R., Martinez, L. P. (1985). *The teen parent collaboration: Reaching and serving the teenage father.* New York: Bank Street College of Education; see also Romo, C., Bellamy, J., & Coleman, M. T. (2004). *TFF final evaluation report.* Austin, TX: Texas Fragile Families Initiative.

13. Hendricks, L. E. (1988). Outreach with teenage fathers: A preliminary report on three ethnic groups. *Adolescence, 23,* 711–720; see also Brown, S. (1990). *If the shoes fit: Final report and program implementation guide of the Maine Young Fathers Project.* Portland, ME: Human Services Development Institute, University of Southern Maine.

14. Romo, C., Bellamy, J., & Coleman, M. T. (2004). *TFF final evaluation report.* Austin, TX: Texas Fragile Families Initiative; see also Brown, S. (1990). *If the shoes fit: Final report and program implementation guide of the Maine Young Fathers Project.* Portland, ME: Human Services Development Institute, University of Southern Maine.

15. Kiselica, M. S. (1995). *Multicultural counseling with teenage fathers: A practical guide.* Newbury Park, CA: Sage.

16. Lamb, M. E. (1983). Fatherhood and social policy in international perspective: An introduction. In M. E. Lamb & A. Sagi (Eds.), *Fatherhood and social policy* (pp. 1–11). Hillsdale, NJ: Erlbaum.

17. Achatz, M., & MacAllum, C. A. (1994). *Young unwed fathers: Report from the field* (p. 38). Philadelphia: Public/Private Ventures.

18. National Academy of Sciences. (1994). *America's fathers and public policy: Introduction.* Retrieved May 4, 2007, from http://books.nap.edu/html/amerfath/chapter1.html

19. Kogan, M. (2006). *Major dads.* Retrieved May 4, 2007, from http://www.govexec.com/features/0498s4.htm

20. U.S. Department of Health and Human Services. (1996). *Fatherhood initiative* (par. 5). Retrieved May 4, 2007, from http://www.acf.hhs.gov/programs/cse/pubs/1996/news/dadfacts

21. U.S. Government. (2001). *A Blueprint for new beginnings: A responsible budget for America's priorities* (p. 75). Retrieved April 30, 2007, from http://www.whitehouse.gov/news/usbudget/blueprint/blueprint.pdf-806.2K

22. Ibid.

23. Ibid.

24. U.S. Department of Health and Human Services. (2007). *Promoting responsible fatherhood: Home page.* Retrieved May 4, 2007, from http://fatherhood.hhs.gov/index.shtml

25. The National Campaign to Prevent Teen Pregnancy. (2004). *The relationship between teenage motherhood and marriage.* Retrieved January 12, 2006, from www.teenpregnancy.org/works/sciencesays.asp

26. Pirog-Good, M. A., & Good, D. H. (1994). *Child support enforcement for teenage fathers: Problems and prospects.* Discussion Paper no. 1029–94, Institute for Research on Poverty, University of Wisconsin, Madison, WI. Retrieved April 30, 2007, from http://ideas.repec.org/p/wop/wispod/1029-94.html

27. Mincy, R., Garfinkel, I., & Nepomnyaschy, L. (2005). In-hospital paternity establishment and father involvement in fragile families. *Journal of Marriage and Family, 67,* 611–626.

28. State of Alaska. (undated). *Frequently asked questions about paternity establishment* (par. 1). Retrieved May 22, 2007, from http://www.csed.state.ak.us/FAQ/FAQ_Paternity.asp

29. Ibid., (par. 2).

30. Public Policy Institute of California. (1999). *Child support and low-income families: Deadbeat dads or policy mismatch?* Research Brief, Issue # 26. Retrieved May 24, 2007, from http://www.ppic.org/main/publication.asp?i=176

31. Achatz, M., & MacAllum, C. A. (1994). *Young unwed fathers: Report from the field.* Philadelphia: Public/Private Ventures.

32. Public Policy Institute of California. (1999). *Child support and low-income families: Deadbeat dads or policy mismatch?* Research Brief, Issue # 26. Retrieved May 24, 2007, from http://www.ppic.org/main/publication.asp?i=176

33. Pirog-Good, M. A., & Good, D. H. (1994). *Child support enforcement for teenage fathers: Problems and prospects* (p. 4). Discussion Paper no. 1029–94, Institute for Research on Poverty, University of Wisconsin, Madison, WI. Retrieved April 30, 2007, from http://ideas.repec.org/p/wop/wispod/1029-94.html

34. Ibid., 7.

35. Ibid., 6.

36. Ibid., 22.

37. Romo, C., Bellamy, J., & Coleman, M. T. (2004). *TFF final evaluation report* (p. 16). Austin, TX: Texas Fragile Families Initiative.

38. Ibid.

39. Miller, C., & Knox, V. (2001). *The challenge of helping low-income fathers support their children: Final lessons from Parents' Fair Share* (p. 7). New York: Manpower Research Development.

40. Ibid.

41. Krishnakumar, A., & Black, M. M. (2003). Family processes within three-generation households and adolescent mothers' satisfaction with father involvement. *Journal of Family Psychology, 17*(4), 488–498.

42. Ibid., 496.

43. Pirog-Good, M. A., & Good, D. H. (1994). *Child support enforcement for teenage fathers: Problems and prospects* (p. 25). Discussion Paper no. 1029–94, Institute for Research on Poverty, University of Wisconsin, Madison, WI. Retrieved April 30, 2007, from http://ideas.repec.org/p/wop/wispod/1029–94.html

44. Miller, C., & Knox, V. (2001). *The challenge of helping low-income fathers support their children: Final lessons from Parents' Fair Share* (p. 7). New York: Manpower Research Development.

45. Miller, C., & Knox, V. (2001). *The challenge of helping low-income fathers support their children: Final lessons from Parents' Fair Share.* New York: Manpower Research Development.

46. Romo, C., Bellamy, J., & Coleman, M. T. (2004). *TFF final evaluation report* (p. 16). Austin, TX: Texas Fragile Families Initiative.

47. Pirog-Good, M. A., & Good, D. H. (1994). *Child support enforcement for teenage fathers: Problems and prospects* (p. 25). Discussion Paper no. 1029–94, Institute for Research on Poverty, University of Wisconsin, Madison, WI. Retrieved April 30, 2007, from http://ideas.repec.org/p/wop/wispod/1029–94.html

48. Ibid.

49. Miller, C., & Knox, V. (2001). *The challenge of helping low-income fathers support their children: Final lessons from Parents' Fair Share.* New York: Manpower Research Development.

50. Romo, C., Bellamy, J., & Coleman, M. T. (2004). *TFF final evaluation report* (p. 16). Austin, TX: Texas Fragile Families Initiative.

51. Public Policy Institute of California. (1999). *Child support and low-income families: Deadbeat dads or policy mismatch?* Research Brief, Issue # 26. Retrieved May 24, 2007, from http://www.ppic.org/main/publication.asp?i=176

52. Smith, P., Buzi, R. S., & Weinman, M. L. (2002). Programs for young fathers: Essential components and evaluation issues (p. 88). *North American Journal of Psychology, 4,* 81–92.

53. Wolf, W. C., & Leiderman, S. (2001). *Investing in "young families": Some thoughts on advantages, disadvantages and possible next steps.* Trenton, NJ: Center for Assessment and Policy Development. Retrieved May 23, 2007, from http://www.capd.org/pubfiles/pub-2001–03–02.pdf

54. Smith, P., Buzi, R. S., & Weinman, M. L. (2002). Programs for young fathers: Essential components and evaluation issues. *North American Journal of Psychology, 4*(1), 81–92.

55. Unruh, D., Bullis, M., & Yovanoff, P. (2003). Community reintegration outcomes of formerly incarcerated adolescent fathers and nonfathers (p. 154). *Journal of Emotional and Behavioral Disorders, 11,* 144–156.

56. Unruh, D., Bullis, M., & Yovanoff, P. (2003). Community reintegration outcomes of formerly incarcerated adolescent fathers and nonfathers. *Journal of Emotional and Behavioral Disorders, 11,* 144–156.

57. Hernandez, R. (2002). *Fatherwork in the crossfire: Chicano teen fathers struggling to take care of business.* (Report No. JSRI-WP-58). East Lansing, MI: Michigan State University, Julian Samora Research Institute. (ERIC Document Reproduction Services No. ED 471 926); see also Sullivan, M. L. (1985). *Teen fathers in the inner city: An exploratory ethnographic study.* (Report No. UD 024 536). New York: Vera Institute of Justice. (ERIC Document Reproduction Service No. ED 264 316)

58. Kiselica, M. S. (1995). *Multicultural counseling with teenage fathers: A practical guide.* Thousand Oaks, CA: Sage.

59. Pirog-Good, M. A., & Good, D. H. (1994). *Child support enforcement for teenage fathers: Problems and prospects* (p. 25). Discussion Paper no. 1029–94, Institute for Research on Poverty, University of Wisconsin, Madison, WI. Retrieved April 30, 2007, from http://ideas.repec.org/p/wop/wispod/1029–94.html; see also National Center for Youth Law. (2007). *Incorporating teens into traditional legal services programs.* Retrieved May 23, 2007, from http://www.youthlaw.org/publications/yln/2005/october_december_2005/incorporating_teens_into_traditional_legal_services_programs

60. Pirog-Good, M. A., & Good, D. H. (1994). *Child support enforcement for teenage fathers: Problems and prospects* (p. 5). Discussion Paper no. 1029–94, Institute for Research on Poverty, University of Wisconsin, Madison, WI. Retrieved April 30, 2007, from http://ideas.repec.org/p/wop/wispod/1029–94.html

61. Pirog-Good, M. A., & Good, D. H. (1994). *Child support enforcement for teenage fathers: Problems and prospects* (p. 24). Discussion Paper no. 1029–94, Institute for Research on Poverty, University of Wisconsin, Madison, WI. Retrieved April 30, 2007, from http://ideas.repec.org/p/wop/wispod/1029–94.html

62. Pirog-Good, M. A., & Good, D. H. (1994). *Child support enforcement for teenage fathers: Problems and prospects.* Discussion Paper no. 1029–94, Institute for Research on Poverty, University of Wisconsin, Madison, WI. Retrieved April 30, 2007, from http://ideas.repec.org/p/wop/wispod/1029–94.html

63. Lamb, M. E. (1983). Fatherhood and social policy in international perspective: An introduction (p. 2). In M. E. Lamb & A. Sagi (Eds.), *Fatherhood and social policy* (pp. 1–11). Hillsdale, NJ: Erlbaum.

64. Jaffe, E. D. (1983). Fathers and child welfare services: The forgotten clients. In M. E. Lamb & A. Sagi (Eds.), *Fatherhood and social policy* (pp. 129–137). Hillsdale, NJ: Erlbaum.

65. Lamb, M. E. (1983). Fatherhood and social policy in international perspective: An introduction (p. 2). In M. E. Lamb & A. Sagi (Eds.), *Fatherhood and social policy* (pp. 1–11). Hillsdale, NJ: Erlbaum.

66. Bolton, F. G. (1987). The father in the adolescent pregnancy at risk for child maltreatment. I. Helpmate or hindrance? *Journal of Family Violence, 2,* 67–80; see also Furstenberg, F. F., & Crawford, A. G. (1989). Family support: Helping teenage mothers to cope. In N. Cervera & L.Videka-Sherman (Eds.), *Working with pregnant and parenting teenage clients* (pp.108–133). Milwaukee: Family Service America; Hardy, J. B., & Zabin, L. S. (1991). *Adolescent pregnancy in an urban environment: Issues, programs and evaluation.* Washington DC: Urban Institute Press.

67. Romo, C., Bellamy, J., & Coleman, M. T. (2004). *TFF final evaluation report.* Austin, TX: Texas Fragile Families Initiative.

68. Thompson, R. A. (1983). The father's case in child custody disputes: The contributions of psychological research (p. 91). In M. E. Lamb & A. Sagi (Eds.), *Fatherhood and social policy* (pp. 53–100). Hillsdale, NJ: Erlbaum.

69. Ibid., 92.

70. Ibid., 92.

71. Ibid., 94.

72. Lamb, M. E. (1983). Fatherhood and social policy in international perspective: An introduction (p. 2). In M. E. Lamb & A. Sagi (Eds.), *Fatherhood and social policy* (pp. 1–11). Hillsdale, NJ: Erlbaum.

73. Coley, R. L., & Chase-Lansdale, P. L. (1998). Adolescent pregnancy and parenthood: Recent evidence and future directions. *American Psychologist, 53,* 152–166.

74. Ibid.

75. Wikipedia. (2007). *The Personal Responsibility and Work Opportunity Reconciliation Act of 1996.* Retrieved April 30, 2007, from http://en.wikipedia.org/wiki/Personal_Responsibility_and_Work_Opportunity_Act

76. U.S. Department of Health and Human Services, Administration for Children & Families. (1996). *Fact sheet: The Personal Responsibility and Work Opportunity Reconciliation Act of 1996.* Retrieved April 30, 2007, from http://www.acf.dhhs.gov/programs/ofa/prwora96.htm

77. U.S. Department of Health and Human Services. (2006). *Promoting responsible fatherhood.* Retrieved December 17, 2006, from http://fatherhood.hhs.gov

78. Coley, R. L., & Chase-Lansdale, P. L. (1998). Adolescent pregnancy and parenthood: Recent evidence and future directions. *American Psychologist, 53,* 152–166.

79. Collins, M. E. (2000). Impact of welfare reform on teenage parent recipients: An analysis of two cohorts. *American Journal of Orthopsychiatry, 70,* 135–140.

80. U.S. Department of Health and Human Services. (2007). *The next phase of reform: Implementing The Deficit Reduction Act of 2005* (par. 3). Retrieved April 30, 2007, from http://www.hhs.gov/news/press/2002pres/welfare.html

81. Boushey, H. (2007). *Viewpoints: The effects of the Personal Responsibility and Work Opportunity Reconciliation Act on working families.* Washington DC: Economic Policy Institute. Retrieved May 1, 2007, from http://www.epinet.org/content.cfm/webfeatures_viewpoints_tanf_testimony

82. Center for Media & Democracy. (2004). *The Personal Responsibility and Work Opportunity Reconciliation Act of 1996.* Retrieved April 30, 2007, from http://www.sourcewatch.org/index.php?title=1996_Personal_Responsibility_and_Work_Opportunity_Reconciliation_Act; see also Wikipedia. (2007). *The Personal Responsibility and Work Opportunity Reconciliation Act of 1996.* Retrieved April 30, 2007, from http://en.wikipedia.org/wiki/Personal_Responsibility_and_Work_Opportunity_Act

83. Collins, M. E. (2000). Impact of welfare reform on teenage parent recipients: An analysis of two cohorts. *American Journal of Orthopsychiatry, 70,* 135–140.

84. Boushey, H. (2007). *Viewpoints: The effects of the Personal Responsibility and Work Opportunity Reconciliation Act on working families* (par. 3). Washington DC: Economic Policy Institute. Retrieved May 1, 2007, from http://www.epinet.org/content.cfm/webfeatures_viewpoints_tanf_testimony

85. Ibid.

86. Boushey, H. (2007). *Viewpoints: The effects of the Personal Responsibility and Work Opportunity Reconciliation Act on working families.* Washington DC: Economic Policy Institute. Retrieved May 1, 2007, from http://www.epinet.org/content. cfm/webfeatures_viewpoints_tanf_testimony

87. Coley, R. L., & Chase-Lansdale, P. L. (1998). Adolescent pregnancy and parenthood: Recent evidence and future directions (p. 163). *American Psychologist, 53,* 152–166.

88. Lewin, T. (2001, July 31). Surprising result in welfare-to-work studies. *The New York Times,* p. A16.

89. Coley, R. L., & Chase-Lansdale, P. L. (1998). Adolescent pregnancy and parenthood: Recent evidence and future directions. *American Psychologist, 53,* 152–166.

90. Gee, C. B., & Rhodes, J. E. (2003). Adolescent mothers' relationship with their children's biological fathers: Social support, social strain, and relationship continuity. *Journal of Family Psychology, 17*(3), 370–383; see also Public Policy Institute of California. (1999). *Child support and low-income families: Deadbeat dads or policy mismatch?* Research Brief, Issue # 26. Retrieved May 24, 2007, from http://www. ppic.org/main/publication.asp?i=176

91. Coley, R. L., & Chase-Lansdale, P. L. (1998). Adolescent pregnancy and parenthood: Recent evidence and future directions (p. 163). *American Psychologist, 53,* 152–166.

92. Boushey, H. (2007). *Viewpoints: The effects of the Personal Responsibility and Work Opportunity Reconciliation Act on working families.* Washington DC: Economic Policy Institute. Retrieved May 1, 2007, from http://www.epinet.org/content. cfm/webfeatures_viewpoints_tanf_testimony

93. Romo, C., Bellamy, J., & Coleman, M. T. (2004). *TFF final evaluation report* (pp. 21–22). Austin, TX: Texas Fragile Families Initiative.

94. Public Policy Institute of California. (1999). *Child support and low-income families: Deadbeat dads or policy mismatch?* Research Brief, Issue # 26 (p. 2). Retrieved May 24, 2007, from http://www.ppic.org/main/publication.asp?i=176

95. Coley, R. L., & Chase-Lansdale, P. L. (1998). Adolescent pregnancy and parenthood: Recent evidence and future directions (p. 163). *American Psychologist, 53,* 152–166.

96. Wikipedia. (2007). *Statutory rape.* Retrieved May 27, 2007, from http://en.wikipedia. org/wiki/Statutory_rape

97. Ibid., (par. 9).

98. Males, M., & Chew, K.S. (1996). The ages of fathers in California adolescent births. *American Journal of Public Health, 86*(4), 565–568.

99. Russell, S. T., Lee, F. C. H., & The Latina/o Teen Pregnancy Prevention Workgroup. (2004). Practitioner's perspectives on effective practices for Hispanic teenage pregnancy prevention. *Perspectives on Sexual and Reproductive Health, 36*(4), 142–149.

100. Ibid.

101. Wikipedia. (2007). *Statutory rape.* Retrieved May 27, 2007, from http://en.wikipedia. org/wiki/Statutory_rape

102. Ibid., (par. 7).

103. U.S. Department of Education. (1999). *School-based and school-linked programs for pregnant and parenting teens and their children* (p. 18). Jessup, MD: Education

Publications Center, U.S. Department of Education, P.O. Box 1398, Jessup, MD 20794–1398.

104. Ibid.

105. America's Promise Alliance. (undated). *Every child, every promise: Main report* (p. 4). Retrieved May 27, 2007, from http://www.americaspromise.org/APAPage. aspx?id=6584

106. Ibid., 1.

107. Howell, E. M., Pettit, K. L. S., & Kingsley, G. T. (2005). Trends in maternal and infant health in poor urban neighborhoods: Good news from the 1990s, but challenges remain. *Public Health Reports, 120,* 409–417.

108. Cubbin, C., Santelli, J., Brindis, C. D., & Braverman, P. (2005). Neighborhood context and sexual behaviors among adolescents: Findings from the national longitudinal study of adolescent health (p. 131). *Perspectives on Sexual and Reproductive Health, 37,* 125–134.

109. Hoffman, S. D. (1998). Teenage childbearing is not so bad after all . . . or is it? A review of the literature. (p. 243). *Family Planning Perspectives, 30,* 236–239, 243.

110. Achatz, M., & MacAllum, C. A. (1994). *Young unwed fathers: Report from the field* (pp. 13–14). Philadelphia: Public/Private Ventures.

111. Singh, S., Darroch, J. E., Frost, J. J., & the Study Team. (2001). Socioeconomic disadvantage and adolescent women's sexual and reproductive behavior: The case of five developed countries. *Family Planning Perspectives, 33,* 251–258, 289.

112. Cubbin, C., Santelli, J., Brindis, C. D., & Braverman, P. (2005). Neighborhood context and sexual behaviors among adolescents: Findings from the national longitudinal study of adolescent health (p. 131). *Perspectives on Sexual and Reproductive Health, 37,* 125–134.

113. Whitaker, D. J., Miller, K. S, & Clark, L. F. (2000). Reconceptualizing adolescent sexual behavior beyond did they or didn't they? (p. 116). *Family Planning Perspectives, 32,* 111–117.

114. Whitaker, D. J., Miller, K. S, & Clark, L. F. (2000). Reconceptualizing adolescent sexual behavior beyond did they or didn't they? *Family Planning Perspectives, 32,* 111–117.

115. Marcell, A. V., Raine, T., & Eyre, S. L. (2003). Where does reproductive health fit into the lives of adolescent males? *Perspectives on Sexual and Reproductive Health, 35,* 180–186.

116. Achatz, M., & MacAllum, C. A. (1994). *Young unwed fathers: Report from the field* (p. 14). Philadelphia: Public/Private Ventures.

117. Thornberry, T. P., Smith, C. A., & Howard, G. J. (1997). Risk factors for teenage fatherhood. *Journal of Marriage and the Family, 59,* 505–522.

118. Romo, C., Bellamy, J., & Coleman, M. T. (2004). *TFF final evaluation report.* Austin, TX: Texas Fragile Families Initiative.

119. Thornberry, T. P., Wei, E. H., Stouthamer-Loeber, M., & Van Dyke, J. (2000, January). Teenage fatherhood and delinquent behavior. *Juvenile Justice Bulletin.* Available online at http://www.ncjrs.org/html/ojjdp/jjbul2000_1/contents.html

120. Gillman, J. E., Reivich, K, & Shatt, A. (2002). Positive youth development, prevention, and positive psychology: Commentary on "Positive Youth Development in the United States." *Prevention & Treatment, 5,* item 18.

121. Kegler, M. C., & Harris, V. H. (2003). A multiple case study of neighborhood part-nerships for positive youth development. *American Journal of Health Behavior, 27,* 159–169.

122. Paine-Andrews, A., Harris, K. J., Fisher, J. L., Lewis, R. K., Williams, E. L., Fawcett, S. B., & Vincent, M. L. (1999). Effects of a replication of a multicomponent model for preventing adolescent pregnancy in three Kansas communities. *Family Planning Perspectives, 31,* 182–189.

123. Philliber, S., Kaye, J. W., Herrling, S., & West, E. (2002). Preventing pregnancy and improving health care access among teenagers: An evaluation of the Children's Aid Society-Carrera Program. *Perspectives on Sexual and Reproductive Health, 34,* 244–251.

124. Mazza, C. (2002). Young dads: The effects of a parenting program on urban Afri-can-American adolescent fathers. *Adolescence, 37,* 681–693.

125. Darroch, J. E., Singh, S., Frost, J. J., & the Study Team. (2001). Differences in teen-age pregnancy rates among five developed countries: The roles of sexual activity and contraceptive use. *Family Planning Perspectives, 33*(6), 244–250, 281; see also Panchaud, C., Singh, S., Feivelson, D., & Darroch, J. E. (2000). Sexually transmitted diseases among adolescents in developed countries. *Family Planning Perspectives, 33*(6), 251–258, 289.

126. Hock-Long, L., Herceg-Baron, R., Cassidy, A. M., & Whittaker, P. G. (2003). Access to adolescent reproductive health services: Financial and structural barriers to care. *Perspectives on Sexual and Reproductive Health, 35,* 144–147; see also Darroch, J. E., Singh, S., Frost, J. J., & the Study Team. (2001). Differences in teenage preg-nancy rates among five developed countries: The roles of sexual activity and contraceptive use. *Family Planning Perspectives, 33*(6): 244–250, 281; Panchaud, C., Singh, S., Feivelson, D., & Darroch, J. E. (2000). Sexually transmitted diseases among adolescents in developed countries. *Family Planning Perspectives, 33*(6), 251–258, 289.

127. Hock-Long, L., Herceg-Baron, R., Cassidy, A. M., & Whittaker, P. G. (2003). Access to adolescent reproductive health services: Financial and structural barriers to care. *Perspectives on Sexual and Reproductive Health, 35,* 144–147; see also Roditti, M. (1997). Urban teen parents. In N. K. Phillips & S. L. A. Straussner (Eds.), *Children in the urban environment: Linking social policy and clinical practice* (pp. 93–112). Spring-field, IL: Charles C. Thomas.

128. Bakken, R. J., & Winter, M. (2002). Family characteristics and sexual risk behav-iors among Black men in the United States. *Perspectives on Sexual and Reproductive Health, 34,* 252–258.

129. Whitaker, D. J., Miller, K. S., & Clark, L. F. (2000). Reconceptualizing adolescent sexual behavior beyond did they or didn't they? *Family Planning Perspectives, 32,* 111–117.

130. Ibid.

131. Ibid., 116.

132. Kirby, D. (2002). *Do abstinence-only programs delay the initiation of sex among young people and reduce teen pregnancy?* (p. 6). Washington DC: National Campaign to Prevent Teen Pregnancy. Retrieved May 30, 2007, from http://www.teenpregnancy. org/resources/data/report_summaries/default.asp

133. Advocates for Youth. (2006). *Science and success: Supplement I. Additional sex education and other programs that work to prevent teen pregnancy, HIV and sexually transmitted infections.* Retrieved May 29, 2007, from http://www.advocatesforyouth. org/publications/sciencesuccess_supplement.htm

134. Hock-Long, L., Herceg-Baron, R., Cassidy, A. M., & Whittaker, P. G. (2003). Access to adolescent reproductive health services: Financial and structural barriers to care (p. 146). *Perspectives on Sexual and Reproductive Health, 35,* 144–147.

135. Donovan, P. (1999). The 'illegitimacy bonus' and state efforts to reduce out-of-wedlock births (p. 96). *Family Planning Perspectives, 31,* 94–97.

136. Advocates for Youth. (2003). *Science and success: Sex education and other programs that work to prevent teen pregnancy, HIV and sexually transmitted infections.* Retrieved May 29, 2007, from http://www.advocatesforyouth.org/programsthatwork/intro .htm

137. Donovan, P. (1998). School-based sexuality in education: The issues and challenges. *Family Planning Perspectives, 30,* 188–193.

138. Landry, D. J., Kaeser, L., & Richards, C. L. (1999). Abstinence promotion and the provision of information about contraception in public school district sexuality education policies (p. 280). *Family Planning Perspectives, 31,* 280–286.

139. East, P., & Adams, J. (2002). Sexual assertiveness and adolescents' sexual rights. *Perspectives on Sexual and Reproductive Health, 34,* 212–213.

140. Donovan, P. (1998). School-based sexuality in education: The issues and challenges. *Family Planning Perspectives, 30,* 188–193.

141. Guttmacher, S., Lieberman, L., Ward, D., Freudenberg, N., Radosh, A., & Des Jarlais, D. (1997). Condom availability in New York City public schools: Relationships to condom use and sexual behavior. *American Journal of Public Health, 87,* 1427–1433; see also Blake, S. M., Ledsky, R., Goodenow, C., Sawyer, R., Lohrmann, D., & Windsor, R. (2003). Condom availability programs in Massachusetts high schools: Relationships with condom use and sexual behavior. *American Journal of Public Health, 93,* 955–962; Hock-Long, L., Herceg-Baron, R., Cassidy, A. M., & Whittaker, P. G. (2003). Access to adolescent reproductive health services: Financial and structural barriers to care. *Perspectives on Sexual and Reproductive Health, 35,* 144–147.

142. Kirby, D. (2002). *Do abstinence-only programs delay the initiation of sex among young people and reduce teen pregnancy?* (p. 6). Washington DC: National Campaign to Prevent Teen Pregnancy. Retrieved May 30, 2007, from http://www.teenpregnancy. org/resources/data/report_summaries/default.asp

143. Rector, R. E. (2004). *Facts about abstinence education.* Retrieved May 30, 2007, from at http://www.heritage.org/Research/Abstinence/wm461.cfm

144. Wodarski, J. S. (2007). Confronting the deadly HIV/AIDS virus among our nation's youth (par. 8). [Review of book, *Teenagers, HIV, and AIDS: Insights from youths living with the virus.*] *PsycCRITIQUES,* April 4, 2007, vol. 52(14), article 15. Online journal article retrieved April 9, 2007, from http://psycinfo.apa. org/psyccritiques/display/?artid=psq_2006_4230_1_1

145. Crano, W. D. (2007). A titanic surrender to the implausible. [Review of *America's War on Sex: The Attack on Law, Lust, and Liberty* by Marty Klein]. *PsycCRITIQUES,* April 4, 2007, vol. 52(14), article 14. Online journal article retrieved April 9, 2007, from http://psycinfo.apa.org/psyccritiques/display/?artid=psq_2006_4108_1_1

146. East, P., & Adams, J. (2002). Sexual assertiveness and adolescents' sexual rights. *Perspectives on Sexual and Reproductive Health, 34,* 212–213.

147. All of the guidelines recommended in this section are drawn from pages 88–91 of Kalmuss, D., Davidson, A., Cohall, A., Laraque, D., & Cassell, C. (2003). Preventing sexual risk behaviors and pregnancy among teenagers: Linking research and programs. *Perspectives on Sexual and Reproductive Health, 35,* 87–93.

148. Sonenstein, F. L., Pleck, J. H., & Ku, L. C. (1993). Paternity risk among adolescent males. In R. I. Lerman & T.J. Ooms (Eds.), *Young unwed fathers: Changing roles and emerging policies* (pp. 99–116). Philadelphia: Temple University Press.

149. Finer, L. B., Darroch, J. E, & Frost, J. J. (2003). Services for men at publicly funded family planning agencies: 1998–1999. *Perspectives on Sexual and Reproductive Health, 35,* 87–93.

150. Ibid., 207.

151. Raine, T., Marcell, A. V., Rocca, C. H., & Harper, C. C. (2003). The other half of the equation: Serving young men in a young women's reproductive health clinic (p. 209). *Perspectives on Sexual and Reproductive Health, 35,* 208–214.

152. Ibid., 210.

153. Ibid., 208.

154. Office of Population Affairs Clearinghouse. (undated). *Publications access area.* Retrieved May 30, 2007, from http://opa.osophs.dhhs.gov/pubs/publications.html

155. Hovell, M., Sipan, C., Blumberg, E., Atkins, C., Hofstetter, C. R., & Kreitner, S. (1994). Family influences on Latino and Anglo adolescents' sexual behavior. *Journal of Marriage and the Family, 56,* 973–986.

156. Jones, R. K., & Boonstra, H. (2004). Confidential reproductive health services for minors: The potential impact of mandated parental involvement for contraception. *Perspectives on Sexual and Reproductive Health, 36,* 182–191.

157. Guttmacher Institute. (2007). *State policies in brief: An overview of abortion laws.* Retrieved May 24, 2007, from http://www.guttmacher.org/statecenter/spibs/index.html

158. American Civil Liberties Union of New Jersey. (2002). *Minors' rights to confidential reproductive health care in New Jersey.* Retrieve May 25, 2007, from http://www.aclu-nj.org/issues/reproductivefreedom

159. Jones, R. K., & Boonstra, H. (2004). Confidential reproductive health services for minors: The potential impact of mandated parental involvement for contraception (p. 182). *Perspectives on Sexual and Reproductive Health, 36,* 182–191.

160. United States Conference of Catholic Bishops. (undated). *Parental notification needed in Title X program* (par. 10). Retrieved May 24, 2007, from http://www.usccb.org/prolife/issues/abortion/factistook-2.shtml

161. Green, T. L. (2002). *Planned parenthood-funded study says girls 'impeded' from use of sexual health services* (par. 16). Retrieved May 25, 2007, from http://www.cwfa.org/articles/1556/CWA/life/index.htm

162. Federal Legislative Office of the National Right to Life Committee. (1999). *Why we need the Child Custody Prevention Act.* Retrieved May 25, 2007, from http://www.nrlc.org/federal/CCPA/why_we_need_CCPA.htm

163. Kiselica, M. S. (1995). *Multicultural counseling with teenage fathers: A practical guide.* Thousand Oaks, CA: Sage.

164. Federal Legislative Office of the National Right to Life Committee. (1999). *Why we need the Child Custody Prevention Act.* Retrieved May 25, 2007, from http://www.nrlc. org/federal/CCPA/why_we_need_CCPA.htm

165. Ibid.

166. Ibid.

167. Jones, R. K., & Boonstra, H. (2004). Confidential reproductive health services for minors: The potential impact of mandated parental involvement for contraception (p. 182). *Perspectives on Sexual and Reproductive Health, 36,* 182–191.

168. Guttmacher, S., Lieberman, L., Ward, D., Freudenberg, N., Radosh, A., & Des Jarlais, D. (1997). Condom availability in New York City public schools: Relationships to condom use and sexual behavior. *American Journal of Public Health, 87,* 1427–1433.

169. Blake, S. M., Ledsky, R., Goodenow, C., Sawyer, R., Lohrmann, D., & Windsor, R. (2003). Condom availability programs in Massachusetts high schools: Relationships with condom use and sexual behavior. *American Journal of Public Health, 93,* 955–962.

170. Hock-Long, L., Herceg-Baron, R., Cassidy, A. M., & Whittaker, P. G. (2003). Access to adolescent reproductive health services: Financial and structural barriers to care. *Perspectives on Sexual and Reproductive Health, 35,* 144–147.

171. Jones, R. K., & Boonstra, H. (2004). Confidential reproductive health services for minors: The potential impact of mandated parental involvement for contraception (p. 182). *Perspectives on Sexual and Reproductive Health, 36,* 182–191.

172. Ibid.

173. Borgmann, C., & Weiss, C. (2003). Beyond moral apocalypse and apology: A moral defense of abortion. *Perspectives on Sexual and Reproductive Health, 35,* 40–43.

174. Wikipedia. (2007). *Minors and abortion.* Retrieved May 25, 2007, from http:// en.wikipedia.org/wiki/Minors_and_abortion#Arguments_in_support_of_parental_ notification

175. Ibid.

176. Ford, C. A., Millstein, S. G., Halpern-Felsher, B. L., & Irwin, C. E. (1997). Influence of physician confidentiality assurance on adolescents' willingness to disclose information and seek future health care: A randomized controlled trial. *Journal of the American Medical Association, 278,* 1029–1034; see also Akinbami, L. J., Gandhi, H, & Cheng, T. L. (2003). Availability of adolescent health services and confidentiality in primary care practices. *Pediatrics, 111,* 394–401.

177. Jones, R. K., & Boonstra, H. (2004). Confidential reproductive health services for minors: The potential impact of mandated parental involvement for contraception (p. 182). *Perspectives on Sexual and Reproductive Health, 36,* 182–191.

178. Franzini, L., Marks, E., Cromwell, P. F., Risser, J., McGill, L., Markham, C., Selwyn, B., & Shapiro, C. (2004). Projected economic costs due to health consequences of teenagers' loss of confidentiality in obtaining reproductive health care services in Texas. *Archives of Pediatrics and Adolescent Medicine, 158,* 1140–1146.

179. Hendricks, L. E. (1988). Outreach with teenage fathers: A preliminary report on three ethnic groups. *Adolescence, 23,* 711–720.

180. Achatz, M., & MacAllum, C. A. (1994). *Young unwed fathers: Report from the field.* Philadelphia: Public/Private Ventures.

181. Jones, R. K., & Boonstra, H. (2004). Confidential reproductive health services for minors: The potential impact of mandated parental involvement for contraception (p. 183). *Perspectives on Sexual and Reproductive Health, 36,* 182–191.

182. Ibid.

183. Eisenberg, M. E., Bearinger, L. H., Sieving, R. E., Swain, C., & Resnick, M. D. (2004). Parents' beliefs about condoms and oral contraceptives: Are they medically accurate? *Perspectives on Sexual and Reproductive Health, 36,* 50–57.

184. Jones, R. K., & Boonstra, H. (2004). Confidential reproductive health services for minors: The potential impact of mandated parental involvement for contraception (p. 183). *Perspectives on Sexual and Reproductive Health, 36,* 182–191.

185. Romo, C., Bellamy, J., & Coleman, M. T. (2004). *TFF final evaluation report.* Austin, TX: Texas Fragile Families Initiative.

186. Klinman, D. G., Sander, J. H., Rosen, J. L., Longo, K. R., Martinez, L. P. (1985). *The teen parent collaboration: Reaching and serving the teenage father.* New York: Bank Street College of Education.

187. Brown, S. (1990). *If the shoes fit: Final report and program implementation guide of the Maine Young Fathers Project.* Portland, ME: Human Services Development Institute, University of Southern Maine.

188. Achatz, M., & MacAllum, C. A. (1994). *Young unwed fathers: Report from the field.* Philadelphia: Public/Private Ventures.

189. Romo, C., Bellamy, J., & Coleman, M. T. (2004). *TFF final evaluation report.* Austin, TX: Texas Fragile Families Initiative.

190. Ibid.

191. Achatz, M., & MacAllum, C. A. (1994). *Young unwed fathers: Report from the field.* Philadelphia: Public/Private Ventures.

192. Romo, C., Bellamy, J., & Coleman, M. T. (2004). *TFF final evaluation report.* Austin, TX: Texas Fragile Families Initiative; see also Achatz, M., & MacAllum, C. A. (1994). *Young unwed fathers: Report from the field.* Philadelphia: Public/Private Ventures.

193. Achatz, M., & MacAllum, C. A. (1994). *Young unwed fathers: Report from the field* (p. 60). Philadelphia: Public/Private Ventures.

194. U.S. Department of Education. (1991). *Teenage pregnancy and parenthood issues under Title IX of the Education Amendments of 1972.* Washington DC: U.S. Department of Education.

195. Romo, C., Bellamy, J., & Coleman, M. T. (2004). *TFF final evaluation report.* Austin, TX: Texas Fragile Families Initiative; see also Kiselica, M. S., & Sturmer, P. (1993). Is society giving teenage fathers a mixed message? *Youth and Society, 24,* 487–501; Kiselica, M. S., & Sturmer, P. (1995, August). *Outreach services for teenage parents: Has gender equity been realized?* Paper presented at the Annual Convention of the American Psychological Association, New York; Kiselica, M. S. (1998, March). *School-based services for teenage parents: Results of a state survey.* Paper presented at the World Conference of the American Counseling Association, Indianapolis, IN.

196. Kiselica, M. S., Gorczynski, J., & Capps, S. (1998). Teen mothers and fathers: School counselor perceptions of service needs. *Professional School Counseling, 2,* 146–152.

197. Heath, D. T., & McKenry, P. C. (1993). Adult family life of men who fathered as adolescents. *Families in Society: The Journal of Contemporary Human Services, 74,* 36–45.

198. All five of the rationales are drawn from page 106 of Romo, C., Bellamy, J., & Coleman, M. T. (2004). *TFF final evaluation report.* Austin, TX: Texas Fragile Families Initiative.

199. All five recommendations are drawn from pages 31–32 of Romo, C., Bellamy, J., & Coleman, M. T. (2004). *TFF final evaluation report.* Austin, TX: Texas Fragile Families Initiative.

200. Mazza, C. (2002). Young dads: The effects of a parenting program on urban African-American adolescent fathers (p. 691). *Adolescence, 37,* 681–693.

INDEX

ABOUT THE AUTHOR

MARK S. KISELICA is a professor of counselor education at The College of New Jersey and a licensed psychologist, licensed professional counselor, and a national certified counselor. He is the author, coauthor, or coeditor of over a hundred professional publications, most of which are focused on counseling boys and men, especially teenage fathers, and on the process of confronting racism. He is a fellow and former president of the Society for the Psychological Study of Men and Masculinity, a former consulting scholar for the Country Boys Community Engagement Outreach Campaign, and a member of the American Psychological Association Working Group to Develop Guidelines for Psychological Practice with Boys and Men. He is also a member of the National Advisory Board for the Quality Improvement Center on Non-Resident Fathers and the Child Welfare System. He has served on the board of directors for the Indiana Council on Adolescent Pregnancy and the Teen Pregnancy Task Force of Bucks County Pennsylvania. He has won several national awards for his books, *Multicultural Counseling with Teenage Fathers* (1995), *Confronting Prejudice and Racism during Multicultural Training* (1999), *Handbook of Counseling Boys and Adolescent Males* (1999), and *Counseling Troubled Boys: A Guidebook for Professionals* (2008). Dr. Kiselica is the editor of the *Routledge Series on Counseling and Psychotherapy with Boys and Men.*

When boys become parents :
adolescent fatherhood in America /
Mark S. Kiselica.

DATE DUE

Demco, Inc. 38-293